STRANGE
TELESCOPES

By the same author

LOST COSMONAUT

STRANGE TELESCOPES

FOLLOWING THE APOCALYPSE
FROM MOSCOW TO SIBERIA

DANIEL KALDER

THE OVERLOOK PRESS
NEW YORK

This edition first published in the United States in 2009 by

The Overlook Press, Peter Mayer Publishers, Inc.
141 Wooster Street
New York, NY 10012
www.overlookpress.com

Cataloging-in-Publication Data is available from the Library of Congress

Printed in the United States of America
FIRST EDITION
1 3 5 7 9 8 6 4 2
ISBN 978-1-59020-226-5

To Nancy

The Secret of This Book

The publishers have asked me to provide a prologue, as they feel the reader needs 'some kind of psychic compass to guide him through the madness'. Having reflected, I think there are in fact four possible ways in, from which you, the reader, are free to choose.

(1) This book should be read as an inspirational 'self-help' manual, on the theme of pursuing your dream. In essence my message is: if you want something badly enough, reach out and take it. The universe is benign and speaks the language of the heart. It will never turn you down if your desire is pure.

(2) This book should be read as an epic, semi-mythical quest, in which the hero travels to the underworld, does battle with demons, scales a mountain in pursuit of enlightenment and finally attains the object of his desire in a mysterious tower inhabited by a magus-like figure amid windswept icy wastes.

(3) This book should be read as a profound investigation into the tenebrous depths of the human soul, the power of the imagination, and the stark options faced by those who cannot compromise but are compelled, as if by demons, to obey the demands of their own restless creativity.

(4) This book should be read as all of the above, none of the above, some of the above, or perhaps something else entirely.

I think that's cleared that up. Except I would like to add one last thing: I know I've told the truth. As for the other people whose words are recorded here – well, that's a different matter.

Скучно на зтом свете, господа!
It's dull in this world, gentlemen!

Nikolai Gogol

MEMOIR FOUND IN A SEWER

I

Descent of the Eloi

1

In 1997, not long after I had first arrived in Moscow, my friend Sergei told me about the Diggers. They were a group of sensitive, educated people who had turned their backs on modern life and retreated to the network of tunnels and secret bunkers beneath the city. There they had formed a new society that was fairer and more just than the surface one. It was dark, beautiful, surreal – precisely the kind of world I wanted to live in.

I was reminded of a documentary on the homeless of Manhattan I had seen a few years earlier. According to that film, a number of the city's dispossessed had retreated underground, where they had formed their own shadow settlement. It was like something out of a 1970s science-fiction apocalypse movie: a parallel civilisation developing in darkness beneath the golden monuments to avarice and ambition above.

With Moscow being the size it was, why, there had to be *someone* living down there. But what I really liked about Sergei's story was this: these 'Diggers' had *chosen* to go underground. They had not been driven there by homelessness or indigence or madness. They were intellectuals and artists, carving out something new, by choice.

I wanted to know more. But the more I pushed, the more the details began to recede from me. Sergei had seen them on TV; they existed; they had a leader. That was all he could say. The programme hadn't lasted very long, and he'd only seen it by chance, anyway. He'd switched it on hoping for *Dorozhny Patrol*, the show that detailed all the deaths and fires in the city that day. It was an interesting programme, after all: it showed lots of pictures of mangled corpses, and always ended with a scorecard listing the number of homicides.

2

A year later I left Moscow. But all the time I was away I thought about getting back. And I had a plan. Once I returned, I'd make contact with the Diggers. I wouldn't join, that would be going too far; but I'd befriend them, and thus gain access to their secret world. I might spend about six months down there, studying their rites and rituals, then write about my experiences.

But even before I returned to Moscow, the practicalities were troubling me. I couldn't be sure the Diggers would accept me; and even if they did, well, my Russian wasn't great. How would I be able to record their rites and stories in any detail? I tried to picture myself down there but all I could imagine was wandering up and down sewers all day. What would I actually *do*? How would I eat? What if I caught some lethal virus? What if I was attacked by giant radioactive rats?

Still, I didn't give up. When I met Sergei again I reminded him of the topic. 'Do you know how I could get in touch with the Diggers?'

'With who?'

'The Diggers.'

'Who?'

'The people living under Moscow.'

'Oh no, they don't live there,'

'Eh?'

'They live on the surface, in flats, like everybody else.' There was a smile on his face that said, *How naïve of you.*

'But I thought . . .'

'No, it's just a hobby. Well, maybe there are one or two who live underground all the time, but I doubt it . . .'

So that was that. For two years I'd nurtured my belief in these subterranean dwellers, in the contralogical poetry of their existence. They'd given me hope that it was possible to step outside society, the world of work, of leisure, of money and to live according to your own rules without starving to death. Who wants to sit in an office, eat food, watch TV every day? Not me. It was hard to give that hope up.

And so I didn't. Moscow was vast, cruel, phantasmagorical. It held so many mysteries, so many secrets – there had to be *someone* living down there.

II

First Contact

1

Five years later I was sitting in my kitchen flicking through an expat magazine dedicated to Moscow's real estate racket. I don't make a habit of reading that sort of crap, but I need somewhere to put my eyes while I eat, and there was nothing else in the local supermarket's free newspaper rack that day.

The magazine, which we shall call *Residential Property Shit* as it is very close to its real name, consisted of pages and pages of ads for flats in the centre of Moscow that were leased by cowboys in suits to Western snobs at hilarious prices: $14,000 a month for one room, unfurnished, near the Kremlin, 24-hour security, device for extracting the blood of young virgins included, that sort of thing.

Just as I was reaching the point where I was ready to plant bombs to hasten the revolution, I stumbled upon an article at the back that had nothing to do with the magazine's usual rubbish. In fact, its position there made so little sense it looked like a surreal prank.

It was called 'Notes from Underground. Touring Moscow's Catacombs: Skeletons, Ancient Treasures and Stalin Bunkers'. Instantly I realised that *this* was what Sergei had been talking about: the 'Diggers of the Underground Planet'. The journalist had spent a day with Vadim Mikhailov, the leader of the Diggers, following him underground, collecting legends.

I started reading.

2 Legends of the underworld

Legend #1: The Moscow metro has a dark double, the M2, the secret metro for government officials and the state security services.

Allegedly it links the Kremlin to the KGB headquarters at Lubyanka and ultimately to a vast nuclear bunker in the west of the city. Mikhailov didn't say much; just that it existed.*

Legend #2: Ivan the Terrible's lost library. Beating his daughter until she had a miscarriage, accidentally murdering his own son and hunting an archbishop stitched into a bearskin with dogs have overshadowed Tsar Ivan's reputation as one of the most learned scholars in his country, acclaimed by some as the greatest prose stylist of his day. Legend has it that he had in his possession some arcane manuscripts that had escaped the fire at the great library at Alexandria, but that these rare papers vanished soon after his death. Mikhailov didn't say much; just that the manuscripts did indeed exist, and they were probably in a secret chamber under the Kremlin.

Other Legends: The Digger spun tales of subterranean vampires and dwarves, of bands of maniacs and tribes of cannibals, and claimed he had seen rats that were one and a half metres in length. Not only that, but he was a new type of human, a genetically altered mutant with telepathic powers. He was going to run for the Russian parliament; and once elected would attend parties in a coat made of rat fur.

3

In the photos the Digger was wearing an orange jumpsuit and a white helmet. He was tall and athletic, with a strong jaw, hair pulled back tight in a ponytail and an expression of fierce determination on his face. The images of his subterranean kingdom, on the other hand, were less impressive. It was a world of abandoned gas masks and rotting space junk, of strange machines going bad in broken-down bunkers.

The most interesting image was a plan drawn up by Mikhailov himself of the whole clandestine world below central Moscow. There was an ancient river rushing through a stone tunnel, a three-storey bunker containing a huge sculpture of Stalin wreathed in cobwebs, a train rushing through a secret tunnel and, most outrageously of all, at the deepest level, huge roads, along which trucks and cars and tanks were speeding: the secret city built by the Soviet elite, to which they would retreat in the event of a nuclear war . . .

* Sergei had told me about this too, and even taken me on a train ride to Kievskaya station where, he claimed, you could see the beginning of one of the secret tunnels. As the wall and wires rushed past I saw nothing, of course.

The magazine had printed the Digger's phone number at the end of the interview. There was a note for journalists that a tour with the Digger cost $100.

4

I had just sold my first book, *Lost Cosmonaut*. It had taken the best part of two years to complete, and so I didn't want to jump into another big project immediately. I thought it would be better to write a few articles on stories that interested me, things I could tie up in a couple of thousand words, without too much pressure. The Diggers and their legends seemed ideal.

I approached a magazine that specialised in stories of murder and psychosis. Some of the Digger's more outrageous claims would fit nicely, I thought. My plan was to put meat on the bones of the legends I had read in *Residential Property Shit*, to set foot on the secret metro, to enter Stalin's lost bunker, to open this lost world.

I wasn't doing it for the magazine's fee, though. I was doing it because this story had fascinated me for so long. I loved Moscow and knew the surface of the city well. I had spent years exploring not only its black heart but also the outlying labyrinth of industrial zones and sleeper districts. I could be dumped in almost any neighbourhood and still make my way home on foot.

Yet I knew nothing of the vastness that lay beneath: only the façades of the metro stations. This gap in my knowledge haunted me.

The magazine accepted the proposal. I was on my way.

5

'Hello, is that Vadim Mikhalkov?'

'No, it's Vadim *Mikhailov*.'

That was a good start. I introduced myself, saying what I wanted.

'Absolutely impossible.' The voice was gruff, brusque.

'Why?'

'The police won't let me take foreigners underground right now. It would be dangerous. For me and for you. Maybe in the spring.'

It was October 2004. Spring was at least six months away. But that was OK; I didn't believe him. I thought he was playing hardball, for reasons of his own.

'I can't wait that long,' I said. 'I need to do it now.' There was silence on the other end of the phone. He gave me a number. 'That's my assistant, Tatiana. Call her. She deals with all enquiries.' He hung up.

His assistant? I called the number. The voice on the other end of the telephone was soft, almost a whisper.

'Mr Kalder,' she said, 'Vadim cannot take anyone underground at the moment. Because of the current terrorist situation in our country . . . the police don't like people going places where they shouldn't.'

'OK but –'

'Foreigners,' she repeated, 'are not welcome underground. It is getting more difficult even for the Diggers themselves. Vadim is willing to give an interview, but under no circumstances will he take you underground.'

The offer didn't interest me at all. 'An interview is not enough,' I said.

'I will ask him, but I fear it is impossible.'

6

Later that evening Tatiana called back.

'Vadim says a tour is possible. It will cost four hundred dollars.'

'*What?*'

'Two hundred for the meeting, and two hundred for the tour.'

'I'm not a tourist,' I said. 'I've lived in Moscow for a long time. I know how much things cost.'

'You must understand, it is dangerous for Vadim to take you down there. He will have to pay bribes to at least two different sets of police . . .'

'Four hundred dollars is too much.'

There was silence. Tatiana sighed. 'OK. I'll talk to him again. But he isn't usually very flexible.'

Fifteen minutes later Tatiana phoned back. 'Vadim would like you to come to his flat, to discuss things.'

'Discuss what?'

'He didn't say.'

I thought about it for a moment. Why not? I'd go over there, look him in the eye, listen to what he had to say. That in itself would be an experience. There was always the off chance that he'd bury an axe in my head, cut me up and lick my bits, but what the fuck: I decided to take the risk.

7 Approaching Digger HQ

The scene: Late October; winter was coming and with it, the long nights, the omnipresent cold and the sense of a life lived underground.

Digger HQ: The yellow building next door to the peppermint green Belarus station. It is in the Stalinist neo-classical style, covered with plasterwork depicting sheaves of wheat, sickles, every symbol of agricultural plenitude, with little turrets at the top. Somewhere in there, the Lord of the Diggers himself is waiting.

The Tunnel: A haven for stray dogs and homeless alcoholics. Hawkers sit in cramped glass kiosks selling pies, pirate CDs, little gold Buddhas and porcelain dogs.

The chemical toilet: A bored woman stands guard, collecting crumpled paper in exchange for deposits of urine and faecal matter.

The Land Rover: At the arc leading into the courtyard, next to a hot dog stand, this vehicle is decorated with orange and yellow emergency stripes, *Diggerspas* (Diggersave) written on the bonnet and the doors. Its tyres are flat, its frame rotting. This Land Rover hasn't saved anyone for a long time.

8

I had brought my friend Semyon with me, to help translate. I knew that talking to the Digger would not be easy, and so I wanted to make sure I could understand everything precisely. Semyon punched Vadim's number into the door code. It rang out. Eventually, at the other end a hand picked up a phone and held it close to a mouth.

'Who is it?' It was a woman's voice, old, with a slight tremble: probably the Digger's mother, I thought.

Semyon explained who we were.

'I know nothing about this,' said the voice.

'Is Vadim in?'

'I can't let you in.'

'But –'

'Call back later.'

'When?'

'I don't know. In an hour.'

'But we organised . . .'

'Go away.'

9

9

We hopped cafés for a while, eventually going back through the underpasses to a swanky place across the road. We took seats by the window looking out at the Digger's building, looming in the darkness behind the streaming lights of Leningradsky Prospekt. There it was, a grimy yellow fortress containing secrets, secrets that I wanted.

I was dealing with the Digger, with the Underground Man. I couldn't expect order, normality or even manners. Those who do, have no business crossing through to parallel dimensions. For in truth, that is what I was about to do: enter another reality.

After an hour we called again. This time the voice was less panicked.

'He is waiting for you.'

III

Lord of the Underground

1 Digger HQ, interior

(1) The entrance: A middle-aged woman stands framed in an open door, surrounded by mustard yellow walls. Her eyes: weary, watery. Her hair dyed black so many times you could grab some in your fingers and snap it off. Also,

(2) a dark, cluttered, hall leading to –

(3) the Digger's room, which is tiny. Inside:

(i) Dominating the room: an enormous piece of exercise equipment. A white helmet with a golden visor hangs from one of the metal bars.

(ii) In front of the exercise machine: some bits of wood and a chunk of old stone with carvings in Old Church Slavonic on it.

(iii) Leaning against the wardrobe: a replica AK47.

(iv) Something living, albeit only just: a cat with protruding ribs mewling for food.

(v) Piled up by the head of the bed: technical manuals on tunnels and stacks of old books; among the authors, Lenin's favourite – Jack London.

(vi) At the other end of the sofa bed: a combined TV and video, small and blue, shining with pride at its own newness. There is a shelf of video cassettes along the wall, among them *Mousehunt*,* starring the mystifyingly successful Lee Evans.

(vii) Along one side: a cabinet, decorated with photos. The photos are mainly of Mikhailov himself, although there is one of Steven Seagal. There is a slight resemblance; the slicked-back ponytail Mikhailov shares with his idol suggests an element of intentionality,

---

* 'Utter shit', the *Beano*, 18 May 1997.

though not on Seagal's part, of course.

(viii) Also on the cabinet: coloured pencil sketches of machines I do not recognise, fantastical tanks, for a war on Mars.

(ix) Finally, hanging on a wall: A colour pencil sketch of Arnold Schwarzenegger as Conan the Destroyer, standing there in his helmet, wielding his sword, muscles rippling, signed *Vadim Mikhailov*.

2

The Digger strode into the room. He was tall, and differed from the photograph in *Residential Property Shit* only in that his skin had a strange, greyish tinge, and was pockmarked, with one or two facial warts, like those you see on poor pensioners rifling through dead folks' clothes in charity shops. Spending his days underground wasn't doing his complexion any good.

Vadim sat down in an old Soviet-era armchair, under the drawing of Conan. He turned to me, his face severe.

'What do you want?'

I explained.

'Yes, but what information do you want?'

I wasn't sure how to begin. I thought it was clear what I wanted; I had said it on the phone often enough. *He* was the one who had invited *me* to this discussion. 'I'm a collector of stories . . .' I said. I wanted it to sound mystical; it sounded shit.

'Stories? Get to the point.'

'For example, I've heard that there's a secret metro, the M2 –'

3

'Crap!' he roared. 'It's not the M2, it's called the D6! And there isn't one secret metro, there are two! The D6 connects the Kremlin to the KGB headquarters and some other strategic sites, but there's also the D-R: it services a huge underground bunker in Ramenki, in the west of the city.' He glared at me contemptuously. 'So what else do you know? What do you know about *the diggers of the underground planet*?'

My mind raced: what else did I know? I thought he might toss me out if I disgraced myself, if I proved myself unworthy of receiving his pearls. 'Well,' I said, 'I've heard that sometimes you work with Mayor Luzhkov and the Moscow city authorities . . .'

'Lies!' Vadim stood up and stared down at me, fire in his eyes. Clearly this was a still worse error. 'I despise Luzhkov! I work with the federal government only! I work directly with Putin, do you understand? With Putin!' He pointed at a black radio crackling away on the shelf. It was one of those security radios that you see police and the military using around disaster areas or public protests, muttering quietly to their distant masters through the mouthpiece. 'That connects me directly to the Ministry of Emergency Situations!'

Suddenly Vadim's voice dropped. 'Listen, what is this?' He pointed at me. 'Have you come here to find out classified information? To get me to talk about *NORD OST*? Is that what this is?' There was a real, quiet, forceful anger in his voice. 'I've had enough of this. I refuse to talk to you any longer, through your interpreter. I will only use *my* interpreter.'

He turned and strode out of the room.

4 The siege of *Nord Ost*

Vadim was referring to the theatre siege that had taken place almost exactly two years earlier, on 23 October 2002. It was a wet Wednesday evening and 800 people were sitting in the Dubrovka Theatre a few kilometres south of the Kremlin watching *Nord Ost*, a musical tale of love and polar exploration. Their proximity to the seat of power was no guarantee of security, however: at just after 9 p.m. a masked man ran onstage, firing a gun into the air and demanding an end to the war in Chechnya. The show's staging was extravagant – at the end an aeroplane 'landed' on stage, and allegedly some members of the audience thought this was part of the show. They rapidly realised their mistake as forty-one masked gunmen and women swarmed into the theatre. The women, swathed in black cloth and with bombs strapped to their waists, positioned themselves by the pillars holding up the building's roof. The audience sat in terror as more bombs, not attached to living organisms, were set in place around the theatre. Moscow had experienced suicide attacks before but nothing as grotesque as this. Yet it was no nightmare, but something terrifyingly real that was happening in central Moscow, at that moment, to them.

The hostages pleaded to be released, but only some children and a handful of Muslims were set free. The terrorists made no demands and did not reveal who they were, except for their leader, Movsar Barayev, the 25-year-old nephew of Arbi Barayev, a Chechen warlord and Islamic radical who had been killed by Russian forces in 2001. Barayev Sr claimed to have personally killed 170 people. Barayev Jr appeared to be no less ruthless, warning the Russian state not to intervene – for every one of his men killed they would kill ten hostages.

Thus passed the night of the 23rd, bleeding into the morning of the 24th. Barayev demanded that the Russian army had to withdraw from Chechnya by the end of the week. If not, everyone in the theatre would die. He had nothing to fear: he and his fellow martyrs would go to paradise. Hostage negotiators, among them doctors, journalists, politicians and even a Soviet-era crooner called Iosif Kobzon, managed to secure the release of some more hostages, but the majority remained inside. Several executions were carried out: one man was shot as a supposed FSB* agent, and one woman was shot after breaking *in*. Others were shot trying to escape. The Kremlin offered Barayev and his gang safe passage to a third country if they would set the hostages free; the offer was turned down. And all the while the situation for the captives in the theatre worsened: they became dehydrated and started to run out of food. Forbidden to go to the toilet in case they attempt an escape, they were forced to piss and shit in the orchestra pit. The air in the auditorium became putrid.

And so it went on: promises were made that all foreigners would be released; they weren't. Promises were made that all Muslims would be released. Some were; others weren't. On 25 October all children under twelve were finally set free but the majority of captives remained inside, awaiting the end. One negotiator emerged stating that they were preparing to die.

At this point, reality becomes blurred. The truth about the end of the siege is difficult to pin down. The Russian authorities claim that on the night of 25 October they intercepted a phone call from the terrorists to their 'foreign masters'. The slaughter of the hostages would begin the next morning. What is definitely true is that on 26 October at 5:30 a.m. Ekho Moskvi radio station received a panicked phone call from one of their journalists who was being held hostage inside the theatre: she could smell gas, and feared the actions of her government. Soon afterwards shots were heard coming from within the theatre, and Russian Spetsnaz Special Forces immediately stormed the building, breaking inside at 6:30. The gas was so potent that the terrorists in the hall had

---

* Federal Security Service, the Russian successor organisation to the Soviet KGB.

passed out before they could detonate their explosives; they were executed where they slept. Those in the foyer, conscious but groggy, were mowed down in a gun battle. The terrorists were routed. No Spetsnaz operatives lost their lives. The mission was a success except . . .

The toxic gas had affected the hostages too. Body after body was pulled out of the theatre as anxious relatives stood at the police cordon; but there were too few ambulances outside to take the survivors to hospital, and those who did arrive could not receive the correct treatment. The Spetsnaz were refusing to disclose what gas they had used: doctors didn't know which antidote to administer.

The final death toll of hostages at the *Nord Ost* siege was set at 129, all of them from the gas. This number has been disputed from the start. Some organisations claim the number of victims was as high as 174. Officials, of course, deny this.

5

Residential Property Shit had reported that Mikhailov had 'helped' the secret services in some undefined way during the crisis, and quoted a Moscow city government spokeswoman as admitting that the authorities sometimes used his expertise when the emergency services needed to penetrate the tunnels and bunkers beneath Moscow.

But exactly how was Mikhailov involved? Perhaps the poison gas, I thought. Who would know the tunnels under the theatre better than the Digger? Was it he who had led the Spetsnaz to the vents through which they had pumped the toxic mist that killed all the terrorists and so many of the hostages also?

Maybe, maybe not. Actually, it was no business of mine, and I wasn't a journalist looking for a scoop to advance my career. But he was the one who had mentioned it. Something had happened there that still meant a lot to him.

6

About twenty minutes later the mysterious Tatiana arrived. Vadim's 'assistant' was somewhere in her thirties, very thin, with close-cropped blonde hair. Her skull ballooned outwards from the nape of her neck, curving over to terminate sharply at the extreme point of her nose, giving her the air of an intensely curious bird. She sat down beside me on the sofa bed. It collapsed, and we slid backwards to the wall.

Vadim resumed his position in the ancient armchair. He mumbled something, staring at the empty frame of the doorway. Tatiana interpreted. The situation was as follows:

(1) It was only a month since a gang of terrorists had seized school no. 1 in Beslan in North Ossetia, a republic in the Russian Caucasus. That siege had come to an even worse end than *Nord Ost*: 331 people had died, most of them children. Consequently the police in Moscow were extremely paranoid. They were everywhere: on the street, in metro stations, prowling around with dogs and metal detectors, checking documents, bags, pockets. And it wasn't the usual game of shaking down anyone they could for bribes. Right now, they weren't taking pay-offs, or at least they were taking much bigger ones than usual, and so Vadim couldn't take foreigners underground. He didn't want to take any risks. Going underground what was gave him fulfilment, it was his reason for living. It was illegal for him too, but he was tolerated. And yet he had enemies among the powers that be who were looking for a chance to shut him down. If he was caught with a foreigner . . .

(2) However, he *was* willing to be interviewed and to grant me access to his vast archive. He was the world's leading expert on the secrets of subterranean Moscow and had worked with many TV companies, magazines, and newspapers. The fee was non-negotiable: $200. He had no profession other than Lord of the Diggers, no source of income other than what he earned from giving interviews. 'That's what I sell: information,' he said.

Vadim then began listing all the famous organisations he had rejected. At the top of the list came National Geographic: I can't remember why, but I think they hadn't offered enough cash. Then there was the British production company who had wanted to make a film about him. They had offered $5,000; he demanded $10,000. The project fell through.

Tatiana cut in: 'I said to him, "Vadim, what are you doing? You have nothing, you live like an animal, you don't even have bread to eat, please, take the five thousand dollars."'

'It wasn't just the money,' said Vadim.

'Yes,' said Tatiana. 'He had complaints about the editorial content of the film . . .'

Vadim muttered something, his lip curled in disgust. I caught it immediately, but Tatiana translated anyway.

'The director was a woman. Vadim didn't want to work with a woman.'

Tatiana indicated Vadim's flat. 'You can see how he lives. He is not greedy. This is his passion. If he is not comfortable, he will not compromise.'

The thing was, I already understood Vadim. I knew that his innards were aflame, permanently burning with the mad black energy that forced him to do the things he did, to make his way through the world in this peculiar way. I knew that he was full of stories and that it was a physical *necessity* for him to tell them. He was driven by a passion nobody else understood: his life was extraordinary, but so isolating. He needed to break out of that isolation, and share his extraordinary tales. We all do, but how much more urgent was it for a man like him, whose stories were all the more extraordinary?

I knew that if I just waited he would tell me more than I needed for the article, and no cash would need to change hands. But of course, I wasn't going to exploit him like that. And then, sure enough, the words started streaming out of him. He just had to unburden himself, even to a total stranger, because it was too heavy a task to carry his own world around with him, to keep it inside all the time. Men aren't built for that degree of isolation. They need to share their beliefs. And so he had to get his world out there; he wanted it to be seen and heard, and inhabited, and not just by him. People, somehow, had to join him on it. If they didn't, then how was he to know that he wasn't just imagining his life? That it wasn't simply psychosis?

He needed the relief.

7 Tales of Diggerdom

I *A dark tale*

It was a few years ago: some depraved child killers had escaped from prison. They were dangerous, the police knew they could kill again. Still worse, the prison authorities couldn't figure out how they'd done it, and that meant the prison was wide open: more criminals could escape if they knew the route. Vadim was called in. He spent days investigating the pipes and sewage tunnels under the prison, until he had unravelled the mystery. He showed the cops the secret exit the cons had dug over a period of weeks, or maybe even months. The prison authorities were able to block it, and later the killers were found. Vadim showed me a diagram he had drawn of the route the criminals had taken, complete with little figures moving through cells and tunnels. It looked like something you might play on with counters and dice in the *Escaping Paedophiles Annual 1979*.

II *Biographical fragments*

Vadim entered a prestigious medical academy to train as a doctor, but dropped out. Then he entered a prestigious art academy to train as a painter, but dropped out. Then he entered a prestigious dramatic academy to become an actor, but dropped out. Each time he applied himself to something, he succeeded. He had started so many lives. He was so talented he could have done anything. But if there was one thing he couldn't stand, it was people telling him what to do. What did they know that he didn't? And so he had dropped all of these possible destinies, to return underground, to follow his true path . . .

III *The mayor*

Yuri Luzhkov, the mayor of Moscow had the city in the palm of his hand. The proof of his power and skill: he had been Putin's rival for the post of prime minister of Russia in the late 1990s, and so when Putin later became president with the power of political life and death over all his subjects, everyone had considered Luzhkov a carcass waiting to be buried or burnt. But he had survived, and even consolidated his grip on the city. He had no rivals, no opponents. Moscow could not run without him.

Vadim was friends with Luzhkov at first. The split came when they sparred over the resurrection of the Church of Christ the Saviour on the banks of the Moskva river.

IV *The church*

The Church of Christ the Saviour was built to celebrate Russia's victory over Napoleon in 1812. It took forty years to build, but only seconds to destroy when Stalin had it blown up in 1933, fifty years after it opened. The communist government planned to erect an enormous skyscraper, The Palace of Soviets, on the site. The tallest building in the world was to be topped by a 100-metre-tall statue of Lenin that would have been lost in the clouds most days, invisible to the

Muscovites below except for his shoes and ankles maybe . . . However, the ground was too unstable, so Khrushchev gave orders for an open-air swimming pool to be constructed instead. You might have thought that someone would realise that a heated open-air pool would create a lot of steam when the temperature dropped to minus 25 in the winter, and that that was not really a good thing when the Pushkin Museum, containing numerous priceless works of art, was located just across the road. But evidently not. And so the pool occupied the site until the early nineties, exhaling vapour, slowly corrupting the canvases by Van Gogh, Gaugin, Matisse, Picasso.

V *The split*

Before construction on the new cathedral began, Luzhkov asked Vadim to explore the area beneath the foundation pit. Vadim went down and found something, or something that looked like it might be something, in an old tunnel. He returned to the surface and told Luzhkov to stop construction: he needed more time to probe, there might be archaeological treasures awaiting discovery! Luzhkov promptly gave the order to pour the concrete, closing the door on that mystery for ever. Since then Luzhkov had been his sworn enemy:* Vadim complained to me that the mayor was now trying to pass 'anti-digger laws'.

VI *Brutal reality*

Vadim worked and worked and worked, but he was never recognised, never paid, never thanked for his efforts. His phone number was listed, and if called, he'd go and investigate buildings, looking for structural flaws. He never asked for money. It wasn't about money. But even so, the city never thanked him for this work. When he had wanted to start a business, taking people on guided tours of the underworld, he was denied permission. *Nord Ost?* He gave no details, only that he had 'helped' but had received no award, and yet the members of the city's *duma* had all been given medals. And yet what had they done? When the bodies were being pulled out of the theatre, there weren't enough ambulances waiting, and as a consequence, too many

---

* Vadim is not the only Muscovite to dislike the Mayor. Luzhkov's wife, Yelena Baturina, became Russia's first female billionaire in 2004. That she made her money in construction in Moscow, a field in which her husband has some influence over who receives which contracts, has led to accusations of corruption in City Hall. Can't imagine why.

people had died. That was the city for you. Then he had wanted to open a museum of beautiful military vehicles. The Russian army had lots of them, and they were just sitting around, rotting in warehouses, but they wouldn't give him one! They demanded money, hundreds of thousands of dollars! The greedy bastards!

8

Vadim now showed me his albums of photographs. I saw:

> Vadim, thumbs up, standing beside a bearded man dressed in black leather, the leader of the 'Night Wolves', a notorious pack of Russian Hell's Angels.
> Vadim, in happier days, inspecting a hole in the ground with Luzhkov and some other city officials . . .
> . . . and then the very moment of the beginning of their acrimonious split: Vadim turning away from the master of the city, his lip curled in disgust.
> Vadim emerging from a tunnel . . .
> . . . then disappearing into one.
> Vadim and some young guys carrying flaming torches through what looks like a sewer.
> Six young men kneeling before Vadim, the master. He touches one acolyte on the shoulder with a sword, as if knighting him. They are being inaugurated into the society of the diggers. 'This is the culmination of the ceremony . . . First they must create fire, and then pledge to live healthy lives, take no drugs, to love their motherland, to bring light into darkness . . .'
> Vadim in a small, dark, dirty underground room. He is with a puffy-faced man in filthy clothes who is clearly experiencing multiple forms of agony simultaneously.

'What's that?' I asked.
'It's a *bomzh*.'
'What's he doing underground?'
'He lives there, of course.'

9

Bomzh (*Bez Opredelyonnogo Mesta Zhitelstva*): tramp, homeless person. *Lit.* 'without definite place of living'.

Bereft of the romantic associations connected with the English word 'tramp', a *bomzh* is a homeless alcoholic who spends his days drifting from bin to bin, scavenging for leftovers, like a human rat. The streets of Moscow are full of them, but at the same time they are unseen. They cling to shadows, and even when they step out of the shadows and into the sunlight few people see or hear them. The *bomzh* will never beg or draw attention to himself for fear of a beating from the police. In a thunderstorm, they will stay in the rain rather than come and stand in a bus shelter with integrated humans. They are filthy, diseased, covered in scabs, permanently being devoured by the parasites that feed on human flesh.

Note: Female *bomzhi* are rare. A life of constant drinking and eating the rotting remains of other people's kebabs destroys women faster than it does men.

10

Homeless people underground? It was grotesque, hideous. And, consequently fascinating. My mind started to fill with the possibilities . . .

But suddenly Vadim's radio crackled into life. 'It's the Ministry!' he cried. He jumped out of his chair, grabbed it and disappeared into the hall.

While he was gone I flicked through the photos, thinking. I forgot about underground cities, secret metros, Stalin's lost bunker. This was real, this was now, a dark, dark world of truth. Suddenly all of Vadim's demands seemed reasonable to me. Of course he wasn't just after money. He was doing good work, and yet no one was funding him. His poverty depressed me. His life was so hard.

Then something even stranger: when he returned I'd forgotten even that this had all started from my own very personal desire to go underground, to clutch at a mystery that had eluded me for years.

No: that was lost too. It had slipped out of my grasp at some point while I sat there, listening to him. Now I was simply writing an article about this strange, gifted man with a difficult life. I thought I could help him, and I thought I could use his material without going underground. I said I'd talk to the editor.

INTERLUDE: FROM THE DIGGER ARCHIVE

The film opens in Arbatskaya metro station, a vast pagan temple under the very heart of the city, with impossibly heavy chandeliers hanging from the ceiling, chandeliers that illuminate a deep, deep cavern connected to the surface by long escalators. It is winter, and so everybody on the crowded platform is wearing the classic Russian uniform: fur coats for the women, fur hats for the men.

Cut to the interior of a train: the benches are heaving with people. Their faces are grey and grim.

The filmmaker explains he spent a few months in Moscow in the early nineties, making a documentary about the metro. Cut to images of the stations: the stained-glass windows of Novoslobodskaya, the grim-faced bronze sculptures of Ploschad Revolutsii, the bright mosaics of Ukrainian farm life of Kievskaya, the tall white marble columns of Kropotkinskaya, fossilised trees on the dead ocean bed of an alien planet . . . and then, amid all this wonder, more shots of Russians in fur hats and big coats, cold, grim, depressed. The iconography is Cold War. The New Russia of mafia glamour is yet to emerge.

And the narrator is still talking about this marvellous underground world, these palaces beneath the grey dystopia above, the worker's paradise, the proletarian cathedrals, this glittering Hades . . .

But then suddenly the film changes tack. 'And then one day I heard of a man creating a new world under the city.'

And there is Vadim, holding a flaming torch. Turning his back on civilisation, creating his own world, just like Sergei told me. Vadim knights new members of the Diggers, trembling on their knees before their leader and guide, their spiritual father . . .

Next we see Vadim, running in fear down some vast wet tunnel. He has spotted something terrible, something dangerous lurking round the corner. The camera shakes as the narrator flees. His voice: 'I stayed months, enraptured by this . . .'

Cut to Vadim, frozen, hand outstretched: 'Can you hear that?' A strange, groaning noise, in the distance, coming from the end of the tunnel. But then it passes. 'It's OK, we can go on . . .'

Cut to Vadim: 'People! Look out!' And fleeing again –

Cut to Vadim, approaching a door. 'It's inhabited.'

He kicks it open; Vadim is, after all, a master of the martial arts. There is darkness, the camera isn't focused yet, a sound of scrabbling, like rats, but much bigger. Vadim knows what it is.

'Don't worry, we're Diggers. Good people. We're friends.'

The scrabbling stops. The camera focuses. The torchlight picks out the form of a *bomzh*, sodden, filthy with a scum-encrusted beard, trembling in the corner of this abandoned store room. He is alone.

'Who are you?' asks Vadim.

'It's not important.'

'How long have you been here?'

'It's not important'

'How did you get here?'

The tramp looks at Vadim, shrugs.

'Fate.'

IV

Profound Mysteries of the Russian Soul Explained

1

The next day, I thought a lot about my naïveté. It staggered me. Of course going underground was dangerous. What if the cops had got me? I would have had to bribe my way out of a nasty situation, and it wouldn't have been a small bribe. There could have been serious troubles for my visa, perhaps a beating too. And what if they had got Vadim? What would have happened to him? Would he have been barred from going underground? Russia's terrorism situation was far worse than anything faced by Western Europe. The police were entirely right to make the subterranean parts of the city off limits.

2

I felt foolish, too, when I thought about my original ideas. Of course he didn't live underground. How could you do that, with no light, and nowhere to grow food? With rats, damp, cold, darkness everywhere? No: the Lord of the Diggers lived with his mother. He had no girlfriend. No wife. He didn't work. He had his passion, his obsession and that was all. And he was 40. Soon he would be old, and it would be harder to clamber through the tunnels. And what then? Did he think about that?

I had wanted to believe it was possible to leave society and enter another reality, and live there in a world of your own creation. That even if I couldn't do it, others could. But life wasn't like that. It came and got you. You had to struggle against it, if you were going to force it to do your will. And it was a struggle, quite literally, to the death.

Vadim's life was one such struggle. He was possessed by his vision; he couldn't do anything other than follow it. It fulfilled him and tormented him at the same time. He was like some weird Martin Luther, but nailing his ninety-five theses to his own flesh instead of the door of a church in Wittenberg in 1517. More excruciating still, these theses were written in a private language no one else could understand. 'Here I stand, I can do no other.' That was all I could make out. Beyond that, it just seemed as though he was crucifying himself, slowly.

But this, of course, only made me more sympathetic.

3

I contacted the magazine and explained the situation. The editor not only agreed to pay for the interview and access to the archive, but added an extra $100 as a contribution to Vadim's work.

So now everything was set up. I would do an interview, and consult his archive, and that was all. But the desire for mysteries would not let me go. Vadim had said it was impossible to go beneath, and I knew now that he really meant it, that he wasn't just trying to raise the price on me. Even so, I still found myself thinking that maybe, if I wrote a really good article on Vadim, he'd be so impressed he'd invite me to join the Diggers, to become an honorary digger . . . I'd still be able to go underground, to see the wonders that were down there, beneath the city . . .

4

A week later I returned to Digger HQ with Semyon, although I didn't anticipate he would be doing any translating. I just thought he would be interested to see how the story played out.

Vadim's mum was there, but Vadim wasn't. There was another Digger in the kitchen, though, tall as a basketball player, with limbs that filled the room. It couldn't have been easy for him, clambering around in those tunnels, like a giraffe trapped in a sewer. I noted a look of profound boredom in his dark eyes. He had clearly been waiting for his leader for a long, long time. We grunted at each other. I passed through the tiny corridor to Vadim's room.

It hadn't changed. It was still crammed with relics, although there were more replica guns this time. But it was disturbing to be in the room a second time. The novelty was gone: now I was looking at the naked reality of a life lived in poverty.

The cat was still hungry. Semyon petted it for a while, then it walked out, in search of food.

5

After half an hour or so the Digger from the kitchen appeared in the doorway. He sat down in Vadim's chair and started interrogating me. I gazed at him blankly; he was talking too fast. So he switched to English, and it was bizarre: his English was fantastic, fluid and fluent and spoken without a trace of a Russian accent. In fact he sounded rather plummy, as if he might be a minor member of the royal family. His name was Edward. He wasn't a Digger at all but rather a music producer and documentary filmmaker. I told him I was a journalist, working on a story about Vadim.

'Well, in that case you might be interested in me. I'm making a documentary on exorcisms and I myself sometimes assist an exorcist based in the Moscow region in the casting out of demons.'

He stared at me, blinking, waiting for a response.

'Really?' I said.

'Yes.'

'That's interesting.'

I couldn't think of anything else to say. We exchanged phone numbers, as I thought it might be interesting to get into exorcisms once my adventures with the Digger were over.

6

Edward started talking about the unfathomable mysteries of the Russian soul, as Russians frequently do with people they've just met. We discussed it for several minutes, and Edward was getting quite excited at our insights, but then Vadim entered the room, interrupting the flow of profundity.

Vadim shook Edward's hand, grunted at me, and then sat in his usual chair, looking away. He never looked at me. When he talked he stared into space, or at the person doing the interpreting, but never at me. Was it the language gap? But Vadim had had a lot of experience dealing with foreigners . . .

Tatiana hadn't arrived yet, and once more Vadim refused to talk without her. He sat in silence, glaring at the empty doorway. Then his mum came in and gave him a cup of tea. Vadim sat there, face like granite, sipping on his tea. Edward, Semyon and I eyed his cup thirstily.

Edward tried to rekindle our analysis of the Russian soul. What about the Russian state's tendency to sacrifice large numbers of its population for the sake of grandiose, fantastical projects? He decided that this was just part of Russia's attitude to all its resources – too much oil, too much gas, too much land, too many people, so none of it was valued, vast amounts were wasted, because there was always more.

We might have got even deeper, but then Tatiana arrived. We briefly discussed business, money changed hands. Now Vadim was ready to talk.

V

Fragments of the 'Diggeriad'

1

'My father was a metro driver. When I was a child he would take me into the driver's cabin with him and lead me through those dark tunnels, and together we would watch the play of light and dark on the tunnel walls. As we travelled through the underworld, my father explained to me what lay above us, and that the place beneath the surface was full of buried secrets, that here lay the history of civilisation . . .

'Then when I was twelve, my father died. On my birthday that year I gathered together a group of my friends and together we started to explore the underworld. Digging had officially begun.

'We broke into basements and climbed into manholes. One day I got into the warehouse of the Academy of Oceanography. I wandered through a labyrinth of dark, empty tunnels, with dripping ceilings. Then suddenly I came upon a huge room full of dead things in jars. Pickled squids, eels, other sea creatures, all pale and lifeless. And I knew then that the underground was mysterious and full of secrets. But suddenly the whole room rumbled, and we realised that a metro tunnel passed close by. I tried to find a way from this basement into the tunnel. I didn't succeed, but from that day I became obsessed with what lay beneath the surface.

'This was in the seventies. It was difficult then, because the KGB didn't want young kids exploring down there. Sometimes we were caught, and questioned. One time we exited a drain that led us right into the backyard of the KGB building. They interrogated me for hours. But once Gorbachev came to power, things relaxed and it became easier to go underground . . .

'Later of course I understood that this devotion to the underground was a mania, an illness. It was not common. Only selected people have it. My grandparents were also connected to the underground. My great-grandfather was a manager of mines. Mine is a close connection, a spiritual bond to the world below. It is difficult for me to live without going underground. The longer I am separated the more I feel a compulsion to return beneath. It is something genetic . . . I try to go underground as often as possible. It is a madness, a *hunger* for this underground world!'

2

Vadim was sitting up in his chair now, declaiming, arms waving. The longer he recounted his origin story, the more animated he became: he was the Homer to his own Odysseus, hero and narrator of the same heroic quest, composer and transmitter of this endlessly evolving oral narrative, that had been passed on many times . . .

But still he wouldn't meet my eye. He never met my eye. He'd look at Ed, Tatiana, the cat . . . anyone except me.

3

'Once I had pneumonia. For one whole week I didn't go underground. I felt then that I had lost my connection to that world, my special closeness. It's my second home. Wherever I travel, I always go underground. In Paris, in New York, I have been underground. I need it to feel the atmosphere, to feel my own sense of self-worth. I don't need to go underground for a long period, not every day. To restore my spirit, it is enough to find a place in the suburbs of Moscow, perhaps to descend fifteen metres into a well or tunnel, then walk for a while, and that will restore my spiritual harmony. But once a week, at least, for some time . . .'

And then a sudden shift:

'For it was I who created the philosophy of underground spaces created by man. I developed it from my father. It is based around the idea of light entering darkness – and by that I don't just mean physical light, for me it's a principle – that light *must* enter the darkness . . . For me every tunnel, every cavern sublimates historical energy. I receive information from these places. I don't need to read books: I can feel it, in the air and in the stones.'

4

And then suddenly another shift, away from the tales of what Vadim had seen and done, towards a lecture on the history and philosophy of the Diggers. He began by explaining that he had taken the name from a progressive Christian group founded by Gerrard Winstanley in England in 1649. According to Vadim they had promoted social reform and democracy. And then he was in full flight, mixing together Easter Island, Atlantis, the Dogon Tribe of Africa, Thor Heyerdahl, and the famous Soviet explorer Yuri Senkevich, who had operated on himself on top of a mountain, removing his own appendix with a pair of scissors and a rusty tin opener, or something like that . . . And Vadim tied all these digressions together into a theory that civilisation had begun under the earth.

'The only reason nobody has ever found proof of this underground civilisation is that nobody has ever looked, I mean it exists, it just has to exist. What about all the motifs and figures recurring in the mythologies of ancient societies on different sides of the globe, hm? How do you explain that? Well of course: there is a network of tunnels connecting the continents, and the secret ancient ancestors of modern humanity would pass back and forth, spreading these stories! What else could it be?'

5

And so on.

6

My eyes glazed over. I stopped taking notes. Tatiana stopped translating.

Meanwhile I wondered about various things: how many other Diggers there were, for example. Most of the photos I had seen showed Vadim on his own, and he only ever spoke in the first person singular: 'I' this or 'I' that, I, I, I, I . . . never 'we'. Tatiana had admitted that he found it hard to keep his acolytes close at hand. I wondered if he was actually the only Digger, that the others had all gone, and the idea of a society was a fiction he maintained for his own personal, psychological purposes. But Tatiana reassured me that there was a small team of long-term Diggers although she was evasive as to how small that hardcore was. Boys, much younger than Vadim, would pass through, but would give it up as their upper lips sprouted cheesy moustaches and they realised that splashing about in shitty tunnels was not the best way to attract girls.

Then I wondered about Tatiana, sitting at my side. Ever since Vadim had mentioned his assistant I had wondered who she was, how she had come to be involved with this strange, strange man. The first time I had asked she looked away, changing the subject to Edward Limonov, a Russian author we both admired. This evasiveness, of course, led me to suspect that in the long, distant past, there had been some kind of romance between her and Vadim.

Some time later I asked her again. This time she was a little more forthcoming:

'Well you see, I am an economist. My job requires me to sit in an office all day, in front of a computer screen, working with numbers. It is extremely boring . . . But helping Vadim gives me an opportunity to enter another world. Because of him I have been underground. I have met lots of interesting and unusual people. He is very difficult to work with of course . . . but he has no one else to translate for him. And so when he asks me to help, I always come back.'

7

Edward interrupted Vadim's flow:

'Daniel, have you heard about the monster that Vadim saw under the city?'

'No,' I said.

Edward looked over at Vadim. 'Well?'

'I never said I saw a monster,' said Vadim defensively. 'I just said I saw *something* that might have been *something* . . . but it was very fast . . .'

'It was like a cheetah, but underground.'

'I only glimpsed it –'

'Well, what about the underground ocean and *that* monster?'

Vadim was still ruminating on his lost underground civilisation. He didn't like being disturbed. He told me the story very quickly.

'In 1983 we went down under a construction site, where the Marriott hotel stands today. There was a crack in the earth; we went through it and found a cave, which led in turn to some tunnels. The tunnels were filled with poisonous gas, so we required respiration equipment to breathe. It was dangerous and unpleasant. But gradually, as we followed the tunnels, the air started to change, becoming cleaner. We rushed forward in order to find the place where we could breathe freely. Suddenly the tunnel opened out onto a huge space, and below us was a vast underground sea.

'There was no horizon: space is curved underground. There was something in the water, but I couldn't be sure what. Perhaps it was a whale, perhaps a submarine, perhaps a cloud of plankton, or maybe just bacteria, producing light. Was it a big creature or millions of small ones? I can't say. It was frightening: I was afraid it might eat me. So we left. It was a very long journey to get there, but even longer back.'

8

Vadim returned to the theme of an ancient subterranean civilisation. There wasn't much air in his room and I started to feel as though he were jumping on my brains. So I tried again to get him back onto less – how shall I put it? – *speculative* material.

'What about Ivan the Terrible's library?' I asked. Actually I didn't give a shit about this particular legend, but it was all I could think of at that moment.

'It's a pile of books from Byzantium. Some of the manuscripts date back to the pharaohs. It's probably under the Kremlin somewhere.'

'What about bunkers? Secret bunkers?'

'In the 1980s I discovered that the city has many subterranean levels. At some points there are six, but at others twelve. We found lots of stuff then, including a secret bunker for Stalin. It was easy to break in. There was nobody guarding it. But the KGB walled the bunkers up as soon as we found them. They're inaccessible now.' He stopped.

'I read an article where you talked about cannibals underground . . .'

'The *bomzhi* believe a tribe of cannibals roams around in the deeper levels of the city, that if you stray too far from the crowd they catch you and devour you. I've never seen one of these cannibals, though. I think the *bomzhi* just get lost and starve to death.'

'What about you? Have you seen a corpse?'

'I've seen dead *bomzhi*. They crawl down a ventilation shaft to stay warm, then fall asleep. While they're sleeping the heat dehydrates them and they die. Then sometimes you find bodies that have been shot or stabbed: gangland killings.'

'What do you do?'

'Well, first I take a scalpel, then I make an incision in the chest and reach down into the cavity to –' He looked at me as though I were stupid. 'I call the police of course. Once I found a chamber and there was the naked body of a baby girl in it, lying on a table. The corpse was fresh. The heart had been cut out, and eaten. There were pentagrams, and other strange markings on the walls. I told the police and they asked me to keep an eye on the place. They were certain the people who had done it would return to the site of their black mass. But I refused. No way I was going to wait for a group of murdering Satanists.'

Then I remembered the legendary secret city under Moscow, that subterranean Xanadu, built for the elite in the event of a nuclear war, with its freeways, apartments, theatres . . . Mikhailov had included it in his diagram for *Residential Property Shit*, and I'd even read instructions how to enter in a guidebook once.* I asked Vadim about it.

'It exists,' he said. 'It was stocked with supplies to keep the country's leaders alive for twenty years. Since then, however, *bomzhi* have eaten all the food and it isn't maintained any more. It's big enough to house six million people, and requires one and a half-million people to keep it functioning.'

'One and a half million?'

'*Yeah.*'

He didn't even blink, but rather stared at me with an intense conviction that these entirely absurd figures, which he had obviously just snatched from the ether, were completely accurate.

9

And then suddenly we were talking about *Nord Ost*. This was what had happened: Vadim had been sitting at home, listening to the Ministry of Emergency Situations on his special radio, when he realised that something was going on at the Dubrovka Theatre. He didn't know what, but he knew it was big. He decided to get there immediately.

When he arrived, the barriers were already up around the theatre, and cops were everywhere, keeping people away. Vadim approached them in full digger gear, and explained that he had an appointment

* Via a drain behind the Karl Marx monument facing the Bolshoi Theatre, if you're interested.

with the head of the FSB. It was a bluff of course, but the cops didn't dismiss it. In fact, within minutes the head of the FSB had agreed to talk to him, to see what help the Digger could offer.

And suddenly I was listening. Because this story was completely different from the others. This was no guff about lost civilisations, or some rumour lifted from the fringes of the Russian internet . . . no, not at all. The tone was different. The details were different. In place of wild generalities were specifics. There were dates, times, names. This was a real story, animated by its precision.

Then he fumbled it. Perhaps he realised he was telling me too much. The denouement was a fog of vagueness: suddenly Vadim was underground, with the Special Forces . . . just showing them some vents, some closed entrances, some ways in, but in the end . . . well, nothing really.

His mum ran in.

'Don't talk about this horrible subject!'

Vadim laughed. 'Mum, I'm not going to –'

'Don't talk about it! Look!'

'What?'

'The windows are open!'

'So?'

'People might be listening'.

'Mum, the FSB aren't at the window.'

She started slapping him around the head.

'Don't talk about it! Don't talk about it!'

She grabbed a box of videotapes and started rifling through them. 'Let's watch a film,' she said. 'We don't need to talk about this subject. It's not safe.'

She grabbed a tape and fed it to the video. Little wheels began squeaking and the screen flickered into life. She turned the volume up. 'Yes, this is an interesting one.'

INTERLUDE: FROM THE DIGGER ARCHIVE

It was a documentary Vadim had made with a Russian TV channel. He was leading a camera crew through metro tunnels. At one point a train rushed past; he claimed it was running on the secret metro line. But of course, who could tell? A tunnel is a tunnel is a tunnel. But then he showed something that was real, that was indisputably scandalous, and it reminded me why he wasn't just dismissed as an eccentric. He descended a few levels, down rusting iron ladders, and then ran through a series of narrow, damp, dark corridors. This time there were other Diggers with him, about four or five of them. They came to a halt and then Vadim pointed out that the rubber insulation around the electricity cables for the metro was rotting, and that the tunnel walls were dripping with water. With a gloved hand he picked at the cables and bits of rubber flaked off. Worse, he had proven by his example how easy it was to get underground. The territory beneath Moscow was completely unguarded: terrorists could strike at any time.

Vadim turned away from the screen and told me that he had met people beneath the city. They were men in uniforms, in gas masks, carrying halogen lamps, but they weren't cops, or soldiers. In fact, he didn't know who they were. He told the authorities, but they didn't listen to him. Were they terrorists? He didn't know.

'Actually, maybe this film is one of the reasons why Luzhkov hates me,' he said. 'He looked very bad after it was screened.'

VI

The Diggers of Moscow State University

1

It had been a rather bad experience, a ritual stripping away of stories, of myths, of illusions, all of them mine. It was the subterranean city that did it. Six million people?

It was ridiculous. But not the amusing or interesting kind of ridiculous. It was just ridiculous.

Then there was the drama over the photographs. I needed some for the magazine. I asked for the shot of the Hell's Angel: he wouldn't give it to me. I asked for a shot of the *bomzh*.

'I don't have one.'

'Yes you do.'

'No I don't!'

'You do. I saw it –'

'I don't! I would never, never have such an image in this house. It's bad luck!'

'Vadim, I saw the picture –'

'It's impossible! What you're saying is impossible!'

I let it go. The pictures I did get were mainly of Vadim underground, on his own, gurning for the camera. Tunnels and water, tunnels and water. How dismal, how mundane his underground kingdom looked!

2

Over the next couple of days I reflected on the glories of the Underground Planet.

There weren't any.

Even, for example, if there was some truth to these rumours and legends, well, what could that truth be? The secret metro: a train, in a tunnel, with some Russian politicians on it. Stalin's bunker: an empty room under the ground that was never actually used.

Worse though was the connection Vadim himself had made between the death of his father and the birth of Digging. His dad was an underground man; he, meanwhile, idolised his dad. His father's premature death had been traumatic. And so now he travelled underground to keep alive some emotional connection with him. Well, not exactly, there was more to it than that, but you get my drift.

Don't get me wrong here – that Vadim lost his dad at an early age was a tragedy. And by the sounds of things he was a remarkable man. He wasn't only a metro train driver, but also a journalist for the Soviet press and a member of the Moscow city parliament.

But for me, there was something terribly flattening about being able to explain Vadim's digging so easily, through something as banal as human psychology. I had started with so much more, with a revolutionary act of bizarre existential defiance, something grand and preposterous that made no sense.

There was a moral in there, I knew. But ultimately, I decided to ignore it.

3

Because as I was putting the piece together I began to doubt my doubt. I thought my fascination with Moscow's depths was dead, that I'd finally faced the inevitable, dreary truth: there was no wonder down there, that it was just sewers and tunnels and cables . . .

But that was just the logical, reasoning surface of my mind talking. And how could it hope to win against the strange poetry of the mythical Underground Planet? Because then a friend told me there was another group of Diggers, connected to Moscow State University, who were really devout in their pursuit of the mysteries of the depths. They took risks, embraced death, sought the apocalypse beneath the earth, believing and acting as though they were living in a weird Eastern European science-fiction film. In fact, Vadim had mentioned them in passing as a group who had fragmented off from him, who had learned at his feet and then formed their own parallel clan of malicious and destructive Diggers. Whereas he sought to preserve the history beneath the earth, they wanted to destroy it. They didn't care about the underworld as he did. They were vandals, pure and simple – evil, destructive people!

4

For Vadim is far from being the only Digger in the world. Although he styles himself as the father of Digging, he has rivals, and not only in Moscow. Others exist: in Samara, in Sevastopol, in St Petersburg. I once met a Digger in the ancient city of Novgorod, for example. He was lean and wild-eyed. He liked to eat magic mushrooms and watch the sun set. Later he became a professor of philosophy at the university there.

I recall what he told me: that there were tunnels that reached from under the Kremlin into the city. Some of them passed below water. He stressed that these were ancient tunnels, centuries old . . . and then he looked at me with his eyes wide open and his arms raised and said: 'And how is that possible?' As if something strange was afoot, as if it was beyond the abilities of mediaeval engineers to dig under a river. He wasn't suggesting aliens; if anything he was only hinting, hinting at lost knowledge, arcane devices, secret treaties . . . not masons, but something deeper than masons, deeper than alchemists, deeper than Diggers, even – something lost and dark and ancient, that preferred the depths to the surface.

And meanwhile, across the former Soviet Union, other teams of dissenters, of idealists, of utopianists, of shamen, of ufologists, alchemists, lycanthropes, oneirocritics, pataphysicians, heresiarchs, rhabdomancers and parorexians were lifting manhole covers and descending into the realm of phantasmagoria, of shadows, of pure imagination, heading down, not up, for their glimpse of the transcendent.

5

I went out on the net and located the website of these alternative Diggers. It was minimal, without names or faces. I took this as a good sign. Unlike Vadim, they were not interested in garnering fame or recognition.

On the other hand, the name of their group was crap. 'Diggers of the Underground Planet' has 'Diggers of Moscow State University' beat hands down. And the more I read, the more I realised they were basically students, pratting around, enjoying an unusual hobby. They could just as easily have been rock climbers. In fact, the more I thought about it, the healthier it sounded.

I didn't like that one bit. What was the point of going underground *just for fun*? Surely it had to be some kind of act of madness, an enacting of the strange and troubling wars and fantasies of your own psyche. Vadim was on a quest for dragons, for myths, for the ghost of his father.

There was, in fact, nothing under Moscow you couldn't find in any other big city: just tunnels and water. So if you didn't populate the underworld with your own fantasies, what was there to see? Maybe just the thrill of trespassing . . . and that too would be enough to explain their anonymity. It wasn't a semi-mystical belief in the denial of the self. It was just practical: if they put their names up, they'd be prosecuted. These were nice, sensible, career-minded boys who enjoyed the urban version of potholing. They'd grow out of it in a couple of years and become good computer programmers or economists.

Meanwhile, over on Vadim's homepage he was declaring himself poet, singer, living legend, founder of world Diggerism, author, novelist, actor, founder of the culture of the true underground, founder of underground bodybuilding, philosopher, one-man orchestra, master of 'deep magic', ESP-ist, artist and sculptor, president of the non-profit centre for underground research, founder of Diggerspas, and also that he was looking for mulatto, black or Asian babes with supple bodies, nice asses, big tits and sensual lips interested in nature, sport, and especially sex. He had left his phone number and the coordinates of his favourite table in the McDonald's on Tverskaya Street, where he sat every Monday–Wednesday 1430–1600 and other days 1530–1830.

I wrote to the students anyway. They never replied to my letter.

6

I returned to Vadim's flat with his precious albums. The photos were unusable: taken on a simple point-and-shoot camera, they showed only Vadim in various poses, without any other Diggers, and the mysterious Underground Planet was simply a backdrop, and not a very interesting one at that – long, dark tunnels, a rusty ladder and the occasional bit of water. And if there were no pictures, there was no story. So in the end I'd persuaded the magazine to spend cash on three thousand words they couldn't print. I had created a fiasco, walked into it, and embroiled other people, all out of my compulsion to believe in the Underground Planet. It was embarrassing. Now I just wanted it to end, to extract myself from this tangle of the public world and someone else's private reality.

I was hoping I'd be able to take the stairs to the first landing, leave the books with Vadim's mum and vanish. But it was Vadim himself who answered the doorphone. He buzzed me in, and one last time I took the steps up to Digger HQ. The door was hanging open. I realised now that it was always open, and suspected that this was not so much a friendly gesture towards the neighbours, but rather an act of hope: hope that *something* would arrive, whether it was a man from the government with a medal for Vadim, the permission to open a museum of old military vehicles, or just a foreigner with a bag sagging with gold coins . . .

He was standing in the kitchen, in a leather jacket and a clean pair of jeans, about to go out. He wanted to look good for someone: maybe that beautiful Asian babe with big tits he was looking for.

But this time he was different: friendly, open. He wanted to know if the pictures were good enough, if the editors had liked my article. I lied, of course, and said *yes*, everything was great. He smiled. He was happy. He even looked me in the eye. We walked out together. Then he hit me with it.

'Yep,' he said, 'I'm thinking it's about time for another expedition.'

'An expedition?'

'Yes, it's time to venture below the earth.'

'When will that be?'

'Not for two weeks, I think. Maybe three.'

'Interesting,' I said, sniffing around, trying to discern whether he was inviting me without embarrassing myself.

'Give me a call nearer the time.'

'Is it possible?'

'Oh yeah. It's possible.'

'But I thought –'

'Don't worry about it. Just a few more weeks and we'll be able to go under.'

Vadim smiled. We were standing next to his decaying Land Rover, in a fog of rotting kebabs. Suddenly his radio crackled.

'Excuse me, this is important.'

7

I decided to vanish while Vadim was still well disposed towards me. An expedition . . . and just like that my weariness, my doubt evaporated. My scepticism was gone. I was a believer again. The Underground Planet was opening at last . . .

In the end though, Vadim returned to demanding $200. There were more protracted negotiations, but the magazine needed photos, so they agreed to pay. And that was that. All it had ever required was for me to surrender.

Maybe I should have done it at the start. It would have been a lot less tiring.

INTERLUDE: FROM THE KALDER ARCHIVE

It was in the summer of 1998 that the depths began eating the city. The process started slowly at first – a small section in the suburbs gave way and swallowed a man as he was walking home with his dog one night. That's how it happened – one minute he was walking along the surface and next he wasn't, he was below, boiling to death in an upsurge of water, his dog's yelps mixing with his screams as they both became broth.

The papers blamed it on hot water running free of cracked pipes. That weakened the pavements. That in turn was blamed on Luzhkov: the people thought he wasn't doing his job. He was letting the city run to ruin while he enriched himself. As the graffiti outside my building read: Luzhkov: Mayor of Babylon.

But death was everywhere in those days. Businessmen were shot in the head so often it never made the newspapers, and the life expectancy of the Russian male had plunged to 57, less than it was before the Revolution. The inhabitants of the world's former second superpower were drinking themselves to death, finding that preferable to living in poverty and humiliation, in a society where it was impossible to find honest work, or to feed your family, or yourself. The Grim Reaper rode out, laughing, and nobody could do anything. They just tried to keep their heads down, to avoid his scythe, and went to work, if they had work to go to . . . where they weren't paid, of course.

So when the city started swallowing humans, nobody batted an eyelid, even though it happened again and again that summer. And then Vadim popped up in the press, claiming that he had a list of a hundred, or maybe it was a thousand, areas in the city in danger of imminent collapse. The whole of Moscow was about to be devoured by the underworld, he said. A spokesman for the administration dismissed the Digger's claims . . .

Finally, a whole stretch of street in the centre of town collapsed. Prior to that all the people and property that had vanished had been in poor areas, so the city didn't really give a fuck, or at least, not that much of a fuck. People were dying every day, in enormous quantities, what were a few more here and there? The whole country was collapsing in on itself; a few streets in the suburbs of Moscow meant nothing. But this time the depths had swallowed a street only a hundred metres from the Kremlin itself, a street containing two theatres, shops, boutiques and the *stolovaya* I frequented in the days when there were still Soviet-style canteens in central Moscow. A Mercedes was swallowed whole. For six months, maybe longer, the pit lay open and passers-by could peer into the guts of the ravenous underworld.

Then it was filled in. New tarmac was laid. The whole area was jazzed up and my Soviet café was replaced with a boutique selling rich man's shit.

For the moment, the underworld was sated. It ate no more.

VII

Pleasures of the Stairwell

1

I met the photographer on the platform at Belorusskaya, a metro station decorated with black floor tiles, plaster sheaves of wheat and rare pink marble from Birobidzhan, capital of the Jewish Autonomous Region Stalin established in Russia's far east. Dmitri was a big guy with a beard and a long ponytail, who had covered the wars in Tadjikistan and Chechnya. We took the escalator to the surface and then I guided him through the tunnels beneath Leningradsky Prospekt to Digger HQ. I had never met a war photographer before and was keen to hear some stories. Unfortunately he insisted on talking to me in impenetrable English, and he told me some wild story about commandeering a Russian army helicopter so he could take a shit in a nice toilet on an airbase. 'I was tired of shitting in forests,' he said. Or at least that's what I think he said, but I could be wrong. The story, I will admit, makes no sense whatsoever.

Vadim opened the door.

'Vadim Mikhailov, hero of *Nord Ost*,' he said, extending his hand to Dmitri.

'Dmitri. I was there too.'

Vadim continued. 'I mean *Nord Ost*, man, I went there and helped and nobody thanked me or anything, damn Luzhkov –'

'I know. I was there too.'

Vadim halted, startled. 'Doing what?'

'I was the only photographer to enter the building when the Special Forces raided it.'

Vadim stood there, just nodding. After all, Dmitri's claim was no less bold than his, his claim to bravery even greater.

44

'Well, I wasn't the only photographer. My best friend got in too. But I got out. He didn't.'

2

Vadim warmed to Dmitri immediately. He invited him in, and showed him a piece of tank that was sitting in the hall, praising its many fine qualities. Dmitri nodded. Then Vadim turned to me.

'We'll have to wait until it gets fully dark. As dark as possible.'

It was four o'clock.

Vadim excused himself. Some guy was sitting in the kitchen, hunched over a radio, listening to a crackling signal. Digger business, no doubt.

'I've got stuff to do. Just hang out on the landing for a while.'

3

We hung out.

4

'This is typical,' I said to Dmitri, half-apologising. 'Vadim's not easy to work with. He's a little strange.'

Dmitri laughed. He was mixing Russian words in with his English now and was a lot easier to understand. 'Strange? Maybe crazy!' But then his face grew thoughtful. 'Actually,' he said, 'he isn't crazy at all. You know, I have many friends in my country's security services. Now, few people know this, but in the waters around the Kremlin, there is a crack squad of frogmen. Do you know what a frogman is?'

'Yes,' I said.

'These are underwater security guards, keeping an eye on the River Moskva and all the underground passages beneath the Kremlin. I heard that one day Vadim went too far on one of his expeditions and he ran into them. You understand that these are very serious men; you do not mess around with them. Our Digger was *very* frightened. He never even went near that place again. So you see, he knows his limits, and he never goes beyond them. A truly crazy man, on the other hand cannot make these judgements.'

Yes, I thought. As much as Vadim raged against Mayor Luzhkov, and as much as most people considered him utterly cracked, still *he*

45

knew his limits. Dmitri was onto something here. I'd need to think about it. But suddenly Dmitri changed the subject:

'Did you hear about the suicide bombing at Rizhskaya Ploschad two days ago?'

I had. One woman's head had been blown clean off her body; the other had been ripped in half at the gut. I can't remember now, but I think she might have gone on living for a while after her bomb exploded – in excruciating agony, of course.

'I live there. I was the first photographer on the scene. Before that I'd been in London for two years. It was my first day back in Moscow.'

He raised his eyebrows, as if to say *pretty convenient*.

5

Dmitri's stories were very interesting. But after three hours we were still hanging out on the landing and I was growing more and more frustrated. It was then that I remembered: the first time I had spoken to Vadim he had suggested going underground at around two in the morning, to make sure we weren't seen.

6

Shit.

7

I hadn't eaten. My feet were sore. I was very bored. Vadim's mum arrived, climbing up the stairs, huffing and puffing. She said hello, then bustled into the kitchen, where she removed a jar of pills from her bag, swallowed one, then filled a cup of water and passed another to Vadim, who necked it. Suddenly Dmitri was right in there, photographing the curious mother/son relationship. He got a good picture of Vadim's mum placing a loving hand on her son's cheek as she encouraged him to take his medicine. Miraculously, neither of them seemed to notice that this six-foot-plus bearded giant was zipping around them, snapping the intimate scene. It was a remarkable talent of his, this ability to somehow vanish, as he stood right in front of you sticking a camera lens up your nose. And indeed, Vadim's mum ignored him and turned to me.

'Have you been out yet?'

'No,' I said. 'We're still waiting.'

'Vadim!'

'We can't go yet, Mum,' he replied. 'We have to wait until after dark.'

She took her coat off and set about making a cup of tea. Dmitri and I went back out onto the landing.

'That was perfect,' he said. 'I got some really good shots. And did you see what she gave him?'

'No,' I replied.

'Those were nerve pills. To calm you down. I know. My mum takes them.'

There was a gleam in Dmitri's eye. He wasn't bothered by the delay. On the contrary, he was clearly getting into the chaos, and was happily surfing the sluggish waves of absurdity and boredom. The photographic agency had chosen well. He was definitely the man for this job.

8

At last Vadim opened a closet in the hall and started pulling out olive green suits. 'These are anti-radiation suits' he said, 'so you won't be affected by any of the deadly toxins below the city.'

He had been given them years earlier, for free, when the authorities were more kindly disposed towards him. Now they were old and dirty. He would need new suits soon. Even so, we were lucky: these were officers' anti-radiation suits, which had both a top part and a bottom part. Ordinary soldiers didn't get the trousers, just a big green poncho. Their legs went unprotected.

Vadim sorted through the suits, filling them up with air and pressing down on them. If they didn't deflate with a hiss, it meant the trousers were without leaks.

He found three pairs. It didn't mean we were ready, though. It just meant we got to wait on the landing some more, next to our anti-radiation suits and boots.

9

We had been there four and a half hours when Vadim finally emerged from the flat.

'OK,' he said, turning to me. 'I'm ready. Do you have a car?'

I looked at him. 'No.'

'Hm. That's a problem. My jeep doesn't work any more. And we can hardly go on the metro with all this equipment . . . We need a car.'

'I don't have a car.'

'Hm. That's a problem. It's a long walk to Tverskoi Bulvar. Over an hour . . .'

'We could get a taxi,' said Dmitri.

10

It was now night, and thousands of cars were hurtling past. But there was real beauty out there: Leningradsky Prospekt was dazzling, a rushing river of light and sound, as the black tarmac at our feet reflected headlights and neon in the icy rain, the miserable stars in the sky so dim in comparison to this man-made wonder . . .

Vadim strode right into the middle of the highway as if he was the Emperor of Moscow, and it was the business of the cars to avoid *him*. Then he extended his arm, ready to flag down any car willing to take us for a fee we would negotiate when it stopped.*

But no luck: car after car zoomed past, without slowing down to inspect the possible fare. Why? Well, maybe because Vadim was already in his helmet and radiation suit and had an enormous steel crowbar in his hands. So we just stood there in the rain for a few minutes, as Mercedes and Ladas alike ignored us, until Dmitri took over. He managed to get an Audi to stop, but as soon as the driver saw Vadim, he shook his head, slammed the door shut and got the fuck away as fast as his wheels could propel him.

11

This happened again and again. Then, after about ten minutes had passed, Dmitri had a cunning plan. He walked to another part of the road where it split off, and where no one could see Vadim. *Et voilà!* The next car agreed to take us. Vadim rushed forward from the darkness and was already half-inside before the driver realised what was going on.

* Although real taxis exist in Moscow, they are rather expensive and few eople can be bothered to use them. It is far more common to use gypsy cabs – usually beaten-up Ladas driven by ex-professors of theoretical physics, immigrants from the Caucasus region or people working jobs where the pay is so bad that the only way they can get by is to pick up strangers and shuttle them around for a few roubles.

'Hey! What's this? That guy is clean, isn't he?'

'Yes, yes,' Dmitri assured him.

'What's that weird suit he wearing?'

'Don't worry,' said Dmitri. 'It's safe.'

'Why's he got that crowbar?'

'Don't worry. He's not a robber.'

The driver wasn't happy, but it was too late: we were all in the car now, Dmitri in the front, Vadim and me in the back. As we drove, Vadim grew more and more excited. He started talking about guns, comparing Russian automatics to American ones, discussing their different capacities, how many bullets a minute they could fire etc. etc.

'Who the fuck are you guys?' asked the driver.

'I am the Lord of the Diggers,' said Vadim. 'Pleased to meet you.'

12

The driver dropped us off at an intersection of two roads near the Old Circus, at the start of a stretch of the boulevard that followed the route of the old city walls. This particular stretch resembled the scene of a particularly awful terrorist atrocity: the earth had been ripped open, and massive pipes and lengths of cable lay around us in the dirt. Of course, it was just that this was a very prestigious neighbourhood and the city was working on making the infrastructure better for the nice rich people who lived nearby.

But there was no time to take in the beauty of it all: Vadim was moving fast, and we had to follow. He led us to a bench, between blue builders' Portakabins, beyond which lay heaps of mud, filth, and bricks. Vadim dumped his bag on the bench.

'Get into your anti-radiation suits! I'm going down to reconnoitre the area!'

Vadim ran onto the road, and as car after car after car hurtled past, barely missing him, he heaved off the cover of a manhole with his crowbar.

Meanwhile, Dmitri and I clambered into our suits. There was a technique involved and it took me a few minutes. Finally the top part was over my head, and I looked up and saw a man watching us from the other side of the road. Something told me he had been watching the whole time, from the moment of our arrival. He had watched as Vadim went underground, and then turned his gaze upon us, just watching, not speaking, not trying to hail us, or to find out what we were doing. He made me nervous. I was doing something illegal, after all. It was better to get down now, before the police arrived. But Vadim was taking a long, long time.

'What did he say he was looking for?' I asked.

'I don't know,' said Dmitri. 'Monsters, I think.'

VIII

A Drain of Skeletons

1

There were things in the drain I had never seen before. They looked like a combination of shit and slug, shit-slugs, clinging to the walls, as if the turds in the stream had acquired some form of intelligence from all the poisons and chemicals in the sewer and were making a slow break for the surface. Soon they would slime forth, and cover the city in their repugnant shit trails. The exteriors of blocks of flats would turn black as the shit-slugs climbed towards the heavens they hoped to conquer, where they planned to smear the wings of angels with their excrescence; and women and children would wake from sleep to find shit-slugs in their beds, in their hair, slowly moving over the surface of their skin. All Moscow would belong to the shit-slugs. And yet that was only the beginning . . .

I caught myself. It was important to stay focused. I didn't want to drown in a stream of Moscow's turds and urine. One foot, then two, then three, so slowly I descended the iron ladder until at last the water was right beneath me, rushing past, hurtling past, with only a faint smell of treated sewage reaching up to tickle my nostrils.

Looking down I saw a circle of light: a final word from the world above, from the stars in space and the sodium lamps on earth, before I entered the Underground Planet once and for all: *beyond this circle of light, there is only the uttermost darkness.*

2

Dmitri was an experienced caver and had brought his own headlamp with him. I waded through the rushing river, following that weak light, careful, careful, making sure I always planted my feet squarely on something solid, that I didn't step on anything that slid or shifted about underfoot. I didn't want a mouthful of sewer.

The riverbed was full of sudden dips: I would plunge in up to my waist, and then with the next step find myself standing in a part so shallow it barely reached above my knees. At last I reached the ledge where Dmitri was sitting and scrutinising his camera equipment. I sat there for a minute, letting my eyes adjust as best as they could to the dark, trying to orient myself. I looked over at the disc of light from above: it was meagre, and yet it was enough to illuminate the walls.

We were in a large concrete tunnel. The water was turbid, muddy, grey, bleak. This was the Neglinka, an ancient river that had for many centuries been a muddy smear on the surface of the city. But two hundred years ago Catherine the Great had encased it in stone and buried it underground. Since then it had followed its subterranean course.

It was the Neglinka, yes, but it was something else besides. It was the portal to the Underground Planet.

I had arrived at last.

3 Ritual of entry

Vadim stood in the middle of the Neglinka, the water up to his waist. Suddenly he extended his arms and in a booming voice began declaiming:

'Oh, Spirits of the Underground, receive the Underground Man . . .'

I zoned out. I was still adjusting to the fact that I was in a sewer. But I had read about this in *Residential Property Shit*, so I knew that it was part of his ritual: a respectful address to the subterranean planet itself before venturing into its depths.

But then he did something they hadn't mentioned in the magazine: he burst into song. Completely unaccompanied, Vadim started belting his way through some twelve-bar blues. He had a good, strong voice, but there was a lot of echo in the tunnel, and of course, the river was very loud, so all I could make out was the end of the chorus: *Diggerski Blues.*

The song was long. I counted five verses, interspersed with choruses. After that he sang again, and then again – Russian pop tunes, currently on the radio, but with new lyrics, added by him, about life as a Digger in the world below. As he sang, he grew larger and larger, until he was filling the whole tunnel with his voice, his life. Then the excitement got to be too much for him. Obviously he couldn't hold it in any longer: he stuck out a thumb, put it in his mouth and . . . blasted out a solo on the air saxophone.

I had to give it to him: he was pretty good on the air sax. He'd clearly had a lot of practice. The solo lasted a whole minute. When it was finished he took his thumb out of his mouth and pointed south: 'That way leads directly to the Kremlin.' He grinned. 'But we're not going there, of course.'

4

The next twenty minutes were spent on a photo shoot. Vadim quickly struck up the poses he preferred, just like an old pro: Vadim striding forward manfully, face set in intense concentration, kicking up shitty water as he goes, drenching the lens of Dmitri's camera; or Vadim climbing up and then back down a small cave to make it appear as though he is descending upside down deep into the Underground Planet; or Vadim holding his chin and looking thoughtful; or Vadim striding forward, flattened palm raised at a right angle to his eyes, as if he is hunting something – a monster perhaps?

Meanwhile I stood there in the streaming sewage, watching, waiting, entirely in darkness.

It was boring.

5 The tour, part 1

There was a much smaller tunnel branching off from the large concrete one, so we trudged through the water for about three metres until we reached it. These walls, made of old stone, dated from Catherine the Great's time. Vadim paused at the entrance and announced that old graveyards periodically emptied their contents into the river, that sometimes corpses could be found floating down these waters; that the tunnel was full of human bones. 'The Neglinka,' he declared, eyes wide, 'is a drain of skeletons!'

He took a step forward, and then froze. I heard a strange, low, weary groan coming from the darkness. Vadim stuck his hand out, signalling for us to stop: 'Did you hear that? What was it? What was that unearthly sound?? Is it some unnatural beast???'

We stood there for half a minute, waiting. The water rushed by, the smell of treated sewage filled my nostrils. No monster emerged from the darkness to devour us. 'Ach, we're all right. It's probably just wind in the tunnel. It's safe. We can continue.'

6 The tour, part 2

Now there was a new smell, methane, and it was getting stronger, overpowering the aroma of treated sewage. Vadim sloshed forward for about twenty meters, then stopped so Dmitri could take more photos. He went to a sluice, dropped to his knees, and started splashing himself in the face, laughing like a kid playing in the bath. He had his visor down, but even so, there was something alarming about the image of a grown man splashing himself with effluent. Dmitri liked it, however, and so we spent about ten minutes taking variations of this picture, then walked further, following the light from Vadim's helmet. The tunnel was deep, then shallow. At one stage I slipped and plunged in up to my chest, but managed to correct my balance before I drowned in shit.

Ahead of us a huge pipe intersected with the tunnel, blocking off our path. Under it there was a small island of sand. I looked down. The sand was dotted with crisp bags, bits of cup, a beer bottle or two, and fragments of polystyrene. Vadim dropped to his knees.

'And here . . .' he said, 'we find that the underground is full of treasure.'

He picked up the handle of a cup, dropped it. Then he picked up a fragment of blue porcelain. 'Why, this is . . . fourteenth century . . . no, fifteenth century . . . I think it's Byzantine. And this –' He picked up a piece of discoloured rock. 'Is it gold? No, no – I don't think it is.'

7

Vadim continued at some length, but Dmitri wasn't taking any pictures now. Eventually he stopped. 'OK,' he said. 'Well we can't go any further because of this big pipe. So we'll have to return to the surface. Let's go.'

We trooped back to the large concrete tunnel. In a few minutes we found ourselves standing under the open manhole cover, looking up through that perfect circle at the luminous night sky. Probably we had walked about twenty metres in all.

The great expedition was over.

IX

Notes on an Apocalypse that Will Soon Be Forgotten

1

Back on the boulevard, Dmitri and I took our anti-radiation suits off. Vadim kept his on.

'Well,' he said, 'that was good. Yes, I enjoyed that. Did you get what you need?'

'Not really,' I said. 'For two hundred dollars I expected more than a sewer.'

Vadim was visibly ill at ease. 'OK,' he said. 'What else do you need?'

'Bunkers, for example. Maybe a locked room with a few stores for a nuclear apocalypse, some gas masks lying around.'

'There really aren't many of those left. They're all locked, or the gas masks are gone.'

'OK,' I said. 'Forget the gas masks. But I want tramps. I want to see the underground city of *bomzhi*.'

'What?'

I thought of the photo in Vadim's album, of the documentary I had seen on Manhattan so long ago, and the opposite of these images: Sergei's mythical permanent underground settlement of intellectuals and artists. 'They exist, don't they? And it's winter. We should be able to find some.'

Vadim stared into the distance. 'Well?' I said. 'The magazine needs a picture.'

'OK,' said Vadim. 'There's a place on Tverskaya where they hang out. We can ask them the way to their underground base. But you'll need to bring an offering.'

'*What?*'

'You'll need to bring a gift.'

'What kind of gift?'

'Vodka, of course.'

2

There was a 24-hour kiosk nearby that sold nothing but drink, chocolate bars and cold cabbage pies. The window faced directly onto the manhole we had emerged from. The woman behind the counter was staring at Vadim, still dripping wet in his radiation suit. She stared at me too. I realised she had been watching all along, as I crawled out of that hole, all the way up to the entrance to her shop, through the door and then inside, where I looked around once, and then said in a foreign accent:

'Give me your cheapest vodka.'

3

I returned with the vodka. Vadim wasn't happy. I didn't care. It had taken almost two months to get this far: two months of phone calls, demands, denials, rejections, sudden changes and generally difficult behaviour. Of course, that was what happened when you dealt with the Digger, and I had walked right into it, so I had no right to complain . . .

But whether I had the right or not, at that moment it meant nothing to me. I was worn out on bullshit. Maybe if I'd met him just the once it would have been fine. But this repeated exposure to his world, this repeated necessity of entering into his reality and playing along . . . I couldn't take it any more. It was time to assert my own will, and to infiltrate his fantasies with mine. All the other stuff, the mysteries, the history, the diplomacy fell away. And at that moment, all I had were the *bomzhi*, and the photograph I had seen in Vadim's house the very first night we had met. Out of nowhere, it returned, and it gripped me, just like that. The original myth of the subterranean colony of intellectuals and artists was gone; in its place only this dismal, twisted parody remained. But I had to go. I had to find them. I could not leave Vadim until I had done so.

Don't ask me why.

4

Vadim said nothing for a while. Then he started discussing something with Dmitri. Meanwhile, across the street from us, a man with a long straggly beard was attempting to unwrap a loaf without falling off his crutches into the mud. I watched as slowly and painstakingly he got the plastic off, dropped it, then lowered his head to take a bite. It was a complicated procedure. And it was freezing too. He didn't have a hat, his hands were gloveless. But he really tore into that bread. He was starving.

But no one was looking at him. No: it was Vadim who was getting all the attention, standing there in his suit, crowbar over his shoulder. Two girls walked past: 'Are you making a movie? Take our picture!' Dmitri pointed his camera, pretended to shoot. They giggled and walked away.

'So what are we doing now?' Vadim asked innocently.

'The *bomzhi*,' I said. 'We need *bomzhi*.'

5

We wandered about for a long time, skirting Moscow's centre, crawling about in backstreets. We walked on, and on. Vadim mustered some high spirits and improvised a song about his crowbar: *Moi Droog Lom*.* Some old ladies looked at him strangely. He greeted them on behalf of the Underground Planet. Some boys looked at him with curiosity. He invited them to join the Diggers.

I meanwhile had the vodka in my hand, and was concentrating on staying on the ice. It was past ten now, and I hadn't eaten in hours. I was cold, I was tired. Suddenly Vadim turned away from the centre and started leading us through another web of back alleys, lined with old crumbling houses, mansions, offices, all looming in the darkness above us, black silhouettes with blackened window panes. Nobody was home. 'There's a secret entrance not far from here,' Vadim said. 'It's in the basement of one of these buildings. There's a door in an old bomb shelter that leads below the surface to where the *bomzhi* often congregate.'

'Good,' I said. 'Good . . .'

Two girls walked by. 'Good evening, ladies,' said Vadim. 'Do you have a kiss for the Lord of the Underworld?'

'No, we don't,' they said, stepping up the pace to get away as fast as possible.

* 'My Friend the Crowbar'.

6

Finally, we reached a square courtyard lined with tall apartment buildings. Underfoot it was sand, then mud, then ice, then slush, then mud again. Just ahead of us there was a wire fence, beyond which lay a vast foundation pit.

'Bollocks,' said Vadim.

'What?'

'This is the entrance to the *bomzh* zone!'

'This hole?'

'Yes. But last time I was here it was a building. Now Luzhkov has torn it down.' He laughed.

'What?'

'He's torn it down to make offices! Nobody lives here any more. The *bomzhi* have moved on. They can't get in through the rubble.'

'I see,' I said.

'Pity,' said Vadim.

'So what now?' I said.

Vadim shrugged. 'There's another place . . . near Proletarskaya . . .'

I looked at my watch. It was past 10:30; Proletarskaya was an hour away. I imagined following Vadim out there, wandering around in some more backstreets, only to find that that zone had also vanished . . .

I couldn't take it any more. 'Let's do it tomorrow,' I said.

'Yes, tomorrow. That's a good idea.'

'I can't do it tomorrow,' said Dmitri.

'Then how about the day after?'

'OK, we'll do it the day after.'

'We'll go to Proletarskaya.'

'Yes, Proletarskaya.'

'Because I need to see *bomzhi*.'

'Yes.'

7

We walked the rest of the way back to the Digger's flat. It was a long journey, along black ice, following a noisy road that was lined with boutiques. Above the boutiques were apartments: the Soviet elite had lived there. Now it was all lawyers, pop stars, actors.

Vadim didn't say much; he was walking ahead of Dmitri and me all the time now. But then, just as we were passing Mayakovskaya metro station he stopped suddenly and turned to us:

'You know,' he said, 'what you can see of Mayakovskaya is only half the station. There's another part that extends backwards, towards the Peking hotel. But it's closed off to the public. Stalin used it as a bunker in World War II. It has a really interesting design. Maybe I could show you . . .'

'Uh-huh,' I said.

'We couldn't go now, of course. I'd have to talk to a man I know who works for the metro, to get permission from him. It would take about two weeks. But maybe that would be interesting for you . . .'

'Uh-huh,' I said, and kept on walking. Dmitri stopped me. 'Daniel, didn't you hear what he said? That would be amazing.'

8

I had always been fascinated by the idea of the secret metro. Just the thought of that network of rails carrying the ubersadists and super-butchers of Soviet history thrilled me. And how were the stations designed, I wondered? With what mosaics, sculptures? And what were their names? I had once worked in a building that contained an archive of plans for lines and stations that were never built, and I had studied them obsessively. I had even made a special trip to the Moscow residence of Leonid Brezhnev, just so I could step into a room that a man whom I knew to be a liar had told me was a former entrance vestibule to the M2, the D1 or the D6, whatever it was called. Whether it was or not I couldn't say, because by the time I got there this alleged vestibule had become a showroom for hi-end home-cinema equipment. But the liar had told me that also, so all along I had known what I was going to find.

And I loved the other Moscow metro, the visible, non-mythic one that I rode every day. And I loved Mayakovskaya in particular. I liked the fact that it was named after Vladimir Mayakovsky, the poet who in despair shot himself when he saw the way Stalin's USSR was going, instead of waiting to become sausages as so many of his contemporaries did. I also liked a line from one of his poems that had been written on the wall of the Futurist cafeteria on Myasnitskaya Street in 1913: *I like watching children die.*

Then there is the station itself, which is simply stunning, with its elegant arced titanium pillars, and bright, optimistic mosaics of Soviet progress on the ceiling: views from the ground of sportsmen, airships, aeroplanes, parachutists sailing through the sky. And yet for all this imagery of liberation through flight, its main designer, Alexei Dushkin, actually drew inspiration from the masters who constructed the underground labyrinths of the Egyptian tombs. His wife played Bach and Prokofiev while he transformed ancient tombs into futuristic shrines to rapid movement.

Sometimes I would get off at the station just to walk around this majestic work of art, as if I were in a museum or a gallery. Mayakovskaya won an award for Dushkin, from the capitalist United States at the New York World's Fair in 1939. And not only that, but it had a unique and fascinating history. During the war, the Anti-Aircraft Defence Forces moved its HQ there; it also served as an air-raid shelter.* In 1941 the celebrations for the twenty-fourth anniversary of the October Revolution were held on the platform. Stalin, it is claimed, had a secret office built beneath it. Certainly, he arrived on numerous occasions to give speeches, and I had read that this was the origin of the legends of the secret metro – after all, Stalin would not ride to Mayakovskaya on any normal metro carriage, nor could so godlike a figure be expected to use a common set of rails. I recall photographs of the Generalissimo, the master butcher with the cockroach moustache, huddling over maps with his marshals, beneath the mosaics, between the stainless-steel pillars. But did I actually see them, or did I imagine them? Does it make a difference?

Suddenly, though, my interest had been killed. Vadim had rendered it completely inert. After months of preparation, of listening to myths, of feeding dreams, it had all culminated in a trip to a sewer. I had made a fatal mistake, of course. I should have left it all in the realm of rumour and legend. A secret metro was never going to be more than a train in a tunnel with bureaucrats on it, anyway, so why give a fuck? I

---

* The metro during wartime is a fascinating story. Construction continued on new stations as many existing ones were put to alternative use. Mosaics were flown in from besieged Leningrad to decorate the ceiling of Novokuznetskaya, just south of the Moscow river. Perhaps over one million people died during the siege; some resorted to cannibalism; but still the commitment to resist the invader saw such extraordinary feats of resilience. Other stations have wartime stories too: Kurskaya, in the east of the city, became a library. Arbatskaya, in the centre, was a bomb shelter. Subterranean classical concerts were held. A whole shadow life went on beneath the city during the war.

Visiting a replica of Mayakovskaya metro station at the New York World's Fair, 1939

didn't believe that this secret Mayakovskaya existed, and more importantly, and what was new this time, I didn't *care* that I didn't believe. I was driven only by an overwhelming determination to put an end to my time spent in Vadim's reality. It was exhausting me. And so we walked on, the cars hammering past us, the icy wind stripping the skin from our faces, all the way to the Digger's flat.

9

Once we arrived Vadim disappeared into the kitchen with his mum. Dmitri and I went through to his room, and sat among the toy Kalashnikovs. An hour went by. Our stomachs rumbled. Outside a train trundled past, ferrying passengers to the earthly paradise of Belarus. It was now well past midnight. 'What's he doing?' I asked. Dmitri shrugged.

We went through to press for the *bomzhi*, though I already knew the time for that had passed. Vadim was sitting on a stool, leaning forward, his head pressed against the kitchen counter. His mum was standing by his side.

'Vadim,' said Dmitri, 'what about the pictures . . . ?'

Vadim exploded.

10

He railed against my perverted demands, against the world, against us, who were paid for our work – but who paid him? Of course, the magazine had, and it had paid him well. But that was hardly the point now.

The Digger was much bigger than me; and though Dmitri looked like he knew how to handle himself, this was not his fight. Nor was it mine. Nor was it anybody's. In fact, exactly what was going on, what I was doing, or why, I no longer understood. That being the case I decided it was time to vanish, before the rising madness left someone bleeding.

I understood Vadim's anger: I was forcing him to back up his outrageous claims. I was asking him to prove everything he had told me, though of course, both of us knew this was impossible. We were in the end zone of the game: I was now invading and challenging his reality. Naturally, he didn't like that. Maybe I should have just left it. I was leaving it now.

I stepped out onto the landing, through Vadim's open door, and half ran down the steps, Dmitri following behind me. The night air was freezing, but fresh, and it felt good to be in it. I left the vodka next to a bin, for the first *bomzh* that came along to find. It wouldn't be there long.

I felt exhausted, but free. And with that sense of my own liberation, I knew that the entrance to the Underground Planet had closed on me for ever. My last image of that strange world was this: Vadim resting his head against his mother's apron. She was nodding to us, as if to say, *just go*. But I didn't see anger in her eyes, or accusation –only sadness. Sadness and suffering and a bottomless but tormented love.

MY SATANIC EDUCATION

I

The Phone Call

1

Christmas and New Year came and went, and slowly I began to
recover from my dealings with the Digger. It wasn't so much the
stroll in the sewer that had been exhausting as everything that had
led up to that golden hour of shimmering happiness. Never in the
field of human endeavour had so much effort been exerted for so
anti-climactic a finale; at least not any human endeavour I'd been
involved in.

Well, never mind: I had my idea for a second book now and had
applied for another full year multi-entry Russian visa to give me maximum flexibility for the considerable research it would involve, both in
and outside the country. The day after flying back from Scotland I
went to the inviting agency (coincidentally only ten minutes' walk
from the Digger's flat) to drop off my passport for registration with
the police. I was on my way back to the metro when suddenly I heard
the unpleasant sound of my mobile ringing. I had resisted owning one
for years and used it sparingly. I didn't give the number out to many
people, and I didn't have caller ID, so I looked at the unfamiliar string
of digits with suspicion. *Should I answer? Probably not. If I wanted to
talk to this person then I'd know the number.* At the last minute, however, some impulse took over and I punched the key with the little
green telephone symbol on it and held it up to my ear:

'Hello?'

'Daniel!'

The voice, English and posh, sounded familiar – but I couldn't place
it. The speaker, however, definitely knew me.

'Who is this?'

'It's Edward!'

'Who?'

'Edward, from Vadim's flat! Remember?'

For a moment I was lost. Then I remembered: the exorcist. In the Digger's kitchen.

2

'So how *are* you?' Edward sounded exuberant, as though we were long-lost school friends, finally reunited after a long separation.

'Fine,' I said. A car hammered past, splashing me with slush.

'I called you in December but you didn't answer the phone.' There was a pause. He was waiting for an explanation.

'I was away,' I said.

'Ha-ha! Now I see. Well, I was wondering if you'd like to meet. I have some – er – *interesting material* I'd like to show you!'

'Very good,' I said. I couldn't think of much else to say: I was too startled by his sudden irruption into my life.

'*Very* interesting material. So when can I give it to you? How about this evening?'

He talked as though we were best friends, and it was normal for me to drop everything so I could meet him. It was a bit overwhelming, especially as I couldn't actually remember what he looked like.

'How about the weekend?' I said.

'Saturday?'

'Sunday afternoon.'

'Where?'

'Let's meet on the Arbat, in the Shokoladnitsa café. Three o'clock.'

'Magnificent!' said Edward. 'See you then.'

He hung up.

3

Immediately, three questions entered my head:

1. Why had Edward appeared now, when he'd had three months to call?

2. What was this 'interesting material' he was talking about?

And, most crucially –

3. What did he want from me?

I had three days to meditate on these questions and prepare myself. I was still burnt out after indulging the whims and fantasies of Mikhailov for so long, and was wary of allowing myself to be taken for a ride again, especially if that ride was going to terminate in another lake of human faeces, or the exorcist equivalent thereof. Meanwhile I was busy with research for the projected second book, which was very politico-historical and so this had absolutely nothing to do with my theme. If anything, it was a dangerous diversion that threatened to use up both energy and resources. I contemplated staying at home and switching the mobile off for a couple of hours.

But at the same time, it isn't every day a part-time exorcist, music producer and documentary maker calls you up and invites you to step into his world. And don't we all dream of that one, miraculous phone call that will transform our dreary, everyday lives? I know I do. This almost certainly wasn't it, but all the same, I couldn't turn him away. The lure of derangement was too hard to resist. I had to see where this would lead. Which led to two more questions:

4. What if Edward really was deeply embroiled in the world of exorcisms?
5. What if he had some really good stuff to show me?

I thought about both, but could come to no satisfactory answers. I supposed I could flog an interview with a bearded priest talking about demons to a magazine somewhere. But I didn't want to. I would have had to satisfy the editor's assumptions about the story before my own, probably removing everything that made the story interesting to me in the first place. It had happened before. But I didn't want to do that. I like to do things my way.

Anyway, who cared about all that? It was enough that it might prove to be an interesting encounter. I agreed to meet him.

4

The café I had mentioned was only three minutes from my front door, but even so I arrived ten minutes late, as my inner voice told me that Edward was not the kind of guy to be on time. My inner voice was correct, but he was even later than I had anticipated. I wound up sitting alone at a table, sipping on a lukewarm hot chocolate, listening to the shrieking and gibbering of Moscow's Golden Youth, a gaggle of pretty boygirls and babywomen in designer jeans, a single pair of which cost twice my monthly rent.

I was starting to think that maybe I should have chosen McDonald's. It was further to walk, but the clientele were less irritating. There wasn't anything I could do to filter out their chirruping, and to make matters worse, I had decided not to bring my mobile phone, a self-defeating and ultimately pointless act of rebellion against . . . I'm not sure what, exactly, but there it was, and so I couldn't call to find out what had happened to Edward. So I had no choice but to sit amid them, surrounded by smoke and blabber, waiting, waiting, waiting . . .

While I was there I realised that I liked this generation less than the previous one. At least their fathers had made a bit of effort when they nicked everything in the country: some of them even got shot in the head for their troubles. But these pasty-faced wankers, what use were they?

5

Half an hour passed. He wasn't coming. I paid the bill and left.

Later Edward called, very apologetic. He had been caught in one of Moscow's epic traffic jams, and was keen to reschedule our meeting, as though he feared I might lose interest in exorcism if he gave me long enough to think about it. I thought of the perpetual reorganising and eternally fluctuating demands of the Digger: I didn't want to get involved in that kind of nonsense again. I said I could only meet the next day. Edward agreed.

II

Demons

1

He was taller than I remembered: about six foot six, but he wasn't the sort of giant embarrassed by his own height, who stoops to avoid attention. No; he strode like a colossus, consuming all the space that was available, and when he sat down, his legs filled most of the café, like overturned lamp-posts. His English was almost flawless and there was that startling, plummy private school accent again, as if he were a cousin of the Queen. If he'd stuck a monocle over one eye, it wouldn't have looked out of place. At the same time, though, there was none of the balding inbred about him, as you might expect from a British royal. In fact he was built like a bull, an extremely big bull, and though friendly and enthusiastic there was knowledge of darkness in his black eyes.

I sat there, waiting for his opening conversational gambit. This meeting was his idea after all. But instead of talking about exorcisms or 'the material', he started grilling me about my life in Moscow. What did I do? How long had I been living there? At the time I wasn't doing much except thinking about my second book, so I wasn't sure about the answers myself. I fobbed him off with some vague responses. Edward nodded, listening, trying to penetrate the ink I was squirting at him, like a shark chasing an octopus. Perhaps I was disappointing him: about the only thing I did make clear was that I had no secret access to the BBC or Channel 4. He had an inexplicably high opinion of British TV, and thought that maybe a film like his would be more suited to that market, which was more 'serious'. I told him that TV in the UK was as crap as TV anywhere else. In fact, I said, I preferred Russian TV, which, in addition to the usual reality-show fodder, also supplied the viewer with a steady, brain-debilitating feed of hallucinatory violence and stomach-twirling variety shows filmed in the

Kremlin. It, at least, was brutally direct in its rubbishness. Edward laughed: he thought I was joking.

I decided to nudge him towards discussing his film. I was wary of opening the conversation with a reference to demons so I asked about funding instead. Surely it was difficult to raise money for his documentary?

'That's why I'm late,' said Edward. 'I just came from a meeting at Alfa Bank. I was trying to negotiate a loan for my film – I'm sure you understand that it's very difficult to persuade a bank manager to give you thousands of dollars to make a documentary about demonic possession. Russia isn't like Britain. There isn't a market for non-fiction films, especially those with a strange and unsettling subject like mine. I explained that demonic possession is a very serious problem in our society and that the people must know about it, but he just wouldn't listen.'

'Maybe you should try another bank.'

Edward shrugged. 'I've been to all of them. I even approached a Ukrainian oligarch for funding.' He paused. He had put that one out there for me, as bait. I took it. 'How do you know him?'

'An exorcist I know arranged a meeting for us. He is a priest; the oligarch built a church for him. At first he was interested, but then his wife banned him from pursuing it any further. She didn't want him getting mixed up in a war with the occult.'

'Wives can be like that,' I said.

'Yes,' said Edward, sipping on his hot chocolate. 'They can.' A shadow of gloom passed across his features, as though a cloud had just moved in front of his own personal sun. 'But she is foolish, for she is at risk as surely as anyone else. After all, we know that demons exist, because in Matthew's gospel chapter eight, verses twenty-eight to thirty-four Christ exorcised the two demoniacs, and sent the evil spirits into the herd of swine, which charged over the hill.'

He paused, and looked at me, deep sincerity in his eyes. 'So if the founder of Christianity accepted the existence of the diabolic, then I think we must also, no?'

2 How Edward discovered infinite evil

Edward continued:

'Let me tell you, I used to live life my own way. I had no interest in these matters. But a few years ago, while I was staying at my dacha in northern Russia a friend invited me to attend an exorcism in the local church there. I was nominally Christian up until that point, but it was not a large part of my life. But I am interested in all forms of intellectual pursuit and it sounded interesting, and so I went along. During the service, I saw a man fall to the ground, and begin speaking in an inhuman voice. It was low and guttural, and he was saying terrible things, about the priest, about Christ. And then – his body began to produce smoke! Smoke, do you hear? How do you explain that? That is not hysteria. I am not stupid. I have a lawyer's education. I have an analytical cast of mind. But I could not deny what I had seen with my own eyes! And that's not all. Since then I have travelled all over Russia and I have seen other strange phenomena: levitation, for example.'

'Real levitation?'

'Close to it. This man, he started to quake and shudder and then rise up off the ground, but he did not hover in the air. Another time, in Siberia, however . . .' The sentence tailed off; Edward fixed me with a piercing stare, allowing me to fill in the blank. He was waiting for some response. 'That's . . . pretty extreme,' I said, immediately embarrassed by the feebleness of my adjective. I knew he was expecting better.

'Extreme? It is more than that – it's diabolical! And just last week in a church in the Moscow region I saw a young girl, about fourteen, snarling and thrashing and snapping her teeth like a wild beast. It took two men to hold her down for the priest to pray over her.'

The words streamed out of him, so many, and so quickly, that it was overwhelming. Listening to him was like being arm-wrestled to hand-crushing defeat in seconds again and again. The way Edward told it, all over Russia, and not just in the remote regional darkness but also in the neon-lit capital city, bearded priests were mumbling incantations over possessed children and adults, with the same frequency that plumbers patched up the pipes in the crumbling tower blocks of the former Soviet Union. Right now, perhaps, somewhere in the hopeless abyss, a filthy, evil presence was being cast out of the mortal shell of a young, trembling girl. There was one thing that puzzled me:

'How are you able to watch all these exorcisms?' I asked. In my mind I saw a locked room, the possessed tied to a chair, and a priest reading out Latin prayers and passages from the Bible, burning incense and splashing holy water around the place. But there was a problem with the image. I couldn't see Edward in it. He wasn't ordained, and more than that, he was too lanky. His long lamp-post limbs would be all over the place.

'Oh, I know lots of priests involved in the exorcism ministry all over the world. In America, in Germany. Even in Scotland. Have you heard of Father James MacManus?' Edward enunciated the sounds of the surname with pleasure, exaggerating its Scottishness, like Mel Gibson declaiming in *Braveheart*.

'No.'

'He is a Catholic exorcist who lives in Perth.'

'I'm not Catholic and I'm not from Perth.'

'Hm. It's interesting. There don't seem to be many Protestant exorcists. I wonder why that is . . .'

'I couldn't tell you.'

'I could put you in touch with him if you'd like. Do you live far from Perth?'

'About two hours by car.'

'Well, if you ever want to talk to him, let me know and I will give you the Father's telephone number.'

I thanked him. 'But that's not what I was asking. I meant – how are you able to get access to so many exorcisms?'

Edward laughed. 'It's easy. It's not always easy to film but it's simple to get access. Exorcisms in the Russian Orthodox Church are held in public.'

I was silent for a second: surely I had misunderstood. 'You mean anyone can walk in and watch?'

'Yes. Or be exorcised. There are special services for this purpose; not in every church of course, but there are at least two in the Moscow region where such services are held regularly.'

Russia: no matter how long I lived there, it was always possible to be startled afresh.

3

But there was something I didn't quite grasp.

I had met a lot of Orthodox Christians, but none of them had ever mentioned public exorcisms. Edward explained that this was because the 'deliverance ministry' was not in the mainstream of Russian Christianity and those priests who practised it often did so in the face of opposition from their bishops. The subject was taboo, even among the devout. This made life difficult for Edward, as many exorcists were scared of talking on film for fear of attracting unwanted attention. His large network of exorcist contacts had been painstakingly put together over a period of two years, entirely through word of mouth. First he had to earn the trust of one priest involved in 'deliverance', which *sometimes* led to contacts with others. But it was always a difficult, laborious process, and priests on his list could 'vanish', when their bishops found out what they were doing. Where exactly they vanished to, Edward never knew, but they dropped out of sight and he rarely found them again.

The attitude of the Church's hierarchy, he thought, was a major problem. As the existence of the demonic was ignored or even suppressed by the Church, ordinary people were more vulnerable to the lures and snares of evil spirits. His film, therefore, would function as a corrective. He envisaged it as a series of exorcisms and testimonies. He needed to catch extreme manifestations on camera to persuade both believers and non-believers alike of the reality of the phenomenon, and then interview priests and the formerly possessed to get across the effectiveness of exorcism as a defence. Right now he was travelling all over Russia and Ukraine gathering material.

'Exorcism needs to be brought out of the shadows and given its rightful place in religious life. Of course, it is not the solution to everything: people needed to live in accordance with the teachings of the gospel. Right now, though, the pressing issue is to get the subject above ground, so people will be aware of how omnipresent the demonic is, and thus be better prepared to fight it. For as long as the issue remains taboo, for as long as the Church shies away from discussing it, then the greater is the danger and the more souls will be lost!'

4

Suddenly though, and with no loss of passion, Edward switched to an exploration of the mysteries of the Holy Trinity, quoting biblical chapter and verse and the thoughts of various mediaeval theologians on the topic. Edward was trying to put the whole thing on a logical basis. He was, after all, a man of an analytical mind, with a lawyer's education. I didn't have much to contribute, so I muttered something about 'the mysteries of faith' in the hope that Edward might find inner peace and get back to discussing demons; I still had questions. He wasn't buying it, though, and soon we were embroiled in a wide-ranging discussion about Russian Orthodox rite. Or rather he was: I just sat there and nodded at appropriate moments. Edward thought the Church needed to focus more closely on the gospel and less on dogma accreted over two thousand years. But the Russian Orthodox Church is deeply conservative and its members are not supposed to query the decisions of the hierarchy or the traditions of old. My silence made him nervous: he interpreted it as disapproval.

'Ha!' he said. 'Do I shock you? Are you holding a dagger behind your back?'

'No. What you say makes sense; but I'm not a member of the Russian Church. I'm not in a position to make any judgements in front of someone who is.'

He wasn't satisfied with my explanation. As far as he was concerned the matter was too important *not* to have an opinion on it. And so he continued on for about two hours, until my dissolving brains were ready to come bubbling out of my ears and nostrils. I kept thinking about how to leave, but he had me in a psychological headlock and I couldn't find an opening. Then, suddenly, he looked at his watch and drew our meeting to a close himself. He reached into his bag and whipped out a video cassette.

'This,' he said, 'is the "material" I want to give you. There are a number of films on the tape, some of which I was involved in making,' he said. 'Watch the tape. If you are interested, then there is a church, not far from Moscow, where they hold exorcisms. I know the priest. I could take you there.'

5 Everything you need to know about the Russian Orthodox Church (for the purposes of this book, at least)

ORIGINS: The Russian Orthodox Church is a member of the family of Eastern Churches that became known as the Eastern Orthodox Church after the division of the Church in 1054 into the Western – Catholic – Church and the Eastern – Orthodox – Church. The cause of the division was the Bishop of Rome's claim to primacy over the whole Church. The Eastern Patriarchs were willing to acknowledge the Bishop of Rome as *primus inter pares* – first among equals – but they were not willing to accept the Bishop of Rome's claim to be the sole leader of the whole Church. Since then Russian Patriarchs have been autonomous (from Roman control at least, if not state), and the

Russian Church considers the whole area of the former Soviet Union as its spiritual property, at least as far as Christians are concerned; Roman Catholic attempts to proselytise on its territory are met with great hostility.

Since the fifteenth century, with fall of the Byzantine Empire, Moscow has been referred to as the Third Rome. The first Rome (in Italy) fell spiritually. Constantinople, the second Rome, fell to the Muslims. Moscow is now the Third Rome and the task of world evangelisation has now become the destiny of the Russian Orthodox Church.

In addition to saints shared with the other Eastern Orthodox churches and with the Catholic Church in the West, the Russian Orthodox Church has also large numbers of indigenous Russian saints, and holy places located on sacred soil. The Virgin Mary too is revered.

SOVIET PERIOD: According to Marx, the Church was meant to wither away in the face of the superior challenge of scientific materialism, but the communists were impatient and decided to spur the process along. Thousands of priests were shot, and churches were demolished or turned into workers' clubs, cinemas, grain warehouses – even public toilets. Membership of the Orthodox Church was not illegal, but nor was it good for one's career or educational opportunities.

RECENT DEVELOPMENTS: Since the collapse of communism and the Soviet Union the Church has grown in influence and has called on the government to take action against foreign 'sects' operating on Russian soil, many of which flooded into the country after 1991. These 'sects' include not only groups such as Jehovah's Witnesses and Mormons, but also the majority of Protestant churches, especially those of an evangelical bent, which are considered heretical.

In 1997 Boris Yeltsin signed off on a law promoted by the Orthodox Church requiring religious organisations in Russia to prove fifteen years of activity in the country to qualify for full rights, thus effectively discriminating against any church that hadn't been in the country before the 1917 revolution, as in 1982 the country was officially atheist. These 'new' groups would have to register with the authorities and face restrictions, especially regarding the ownership of buildings. In the Soviet period, however, the Pentecostals, Baptists and Evangelical Christian Brethren were forcibly unified as one denominational group so that they could be more easily controlled. These churches have also experienced difficulties and restrictions under the 1997 law.

The spirit of ecumenism then is alien to the Russian Orthodox Church. Outsiders are looked upon with suspicion. It is a measure of the strength of the Russian Orthodox Church that the Patriarch, Alexei II, was able to veto a visit to Moscow from Pope John Paul II, even when it was reportedly Vladimir Putin's personal wish that the visit should go ahead.

PRIESTS: Priests may marry and have children. Only monks are required to take a vow of celibacy. The Patriarch and the metropolitans and bishops are all celibate and are therefore drawn only from the ranks of the monks.

LEADERSHIP: The head of the Russian Orthodox Church is Patriarch Alexei II of Moscow and All Russia. Born in Estonia, he has been in the job since 1990, though he studied and started his priestly career under Stalin in the 1950s. In 1999 it was alleged that Alexei II had been a KGB agent. The Church strongly denies this claim.

LANGUAGE: The Bible and liturgy of the Russian Orthodox Church are written in a language separate from but related to Russian called Old Church Slavonic that was developed from a southern Slavonic dialect reduced to writing by the Byzantine missionaries Cyril and Methodius. Centuries later it is still the language of the Russian Orthodox Church liturgy and remains a distinct language that many, if not most, Russians do not understand – as if the Church of England insisted on holding its services in Chaucer's English.

THE AESTHETIC: Attending an Orthodox Church service is like travelling a thousand years backwards in time. Priests have beards and long hair and wear black robes. Churches have richly painted interiors, featuring frescoes of scenes of the Last Judgement, scenes from the Bible, and the lives of saints. Incense burns. Little old ladies with dried walnut faces in headscarves cross themselves. Mobsters give money to atone for their crimes. There are no chairs or pews because it is disrespectful to sit in the presence of God; a worshipper must stand or kneel or prostrate himself instead. The liturgy is sung/spoken by the priest and lasts about three hours.

MAJOR FESTIVALS: The Eastern Orthodox churches celebrate Christmas on 7 January, but the most important date on the religious calendar is Easter, which is preceded by a forty-day fast. Candle-lit services are held at midnight on Easter Sunday.
Atheist archbishops: *Nyet.*
Women bishops: *Nyet.*
Gay priests: *Shutish?**

6 Four films about deliverance

I

In the northern city of Pskov men and women dressed against the cold were standing inside a bleak barn of a church. These were the true poor, those who suffered every time Russia experienced social upheaval, the ones who never got near a whiff of the money or power. The priest, Father Miron, was swinging a censer, praying in a deep, commanding voice as women wept, cursed, howled, moaned, barked, collapsed all around him. As they cried out, little smoky puffs of winter vapour escaped their lips.

Outside, the women were calmer. They discussed how much better they felt after 'deliverance', though it seemed that multiple exorcisms on a regular basis were necessary to deal with demons effectively. One beefy woman dragged her husband in front of the camera. He stood there, like a scolded little boy, mumbling through his ragged beard about his alcoholism and how his wife had been on the verge of leaving him until he had agreed to let Father Miron cast out his demon: he no longer drank. Another woman had been afflicted not only with the torment of demons but cancer: Father Miron had cured her. Meanwhile, Father Miron himself was hanging around in the background, staring into the camera. He didn't speak, but he had a dangerous, unpredictable glint in his eye; there was something wily and peasant-like about him, as though he might clock you with his fist as soon as he'd bless you.

II

A sunny green zone somewhere in Ukraine. This Church looked much more inviting: it was painted a bright yellow and had shiny

* 'Are you joking?'

gold cupolas. But inside, it was the same scene: women and men wailing and trembling as a priest relieved them of their demons. This priest had a ginger beard and a dyspeptic look. He was articulate and combative, accustomed to defending himself against critics. Of course, he said, sometimes he was approached by the mentally ill. But those cases he referred to a psychologist. Only after he had ruled out all the other options would he accept the presence of the diabolical, and then he reserved the right to perform exorcisms.

Next came the dialectic compulsory to all TV documentaries on 'the supernatural': the materialist saying it was all mass hysteria, the priest's retort, and then in between the moderate theologian who believed in God but suspected that exorcism would not help those who believed themselves possessed, but rather make them worse.

III

Siberia. Edward was onscreen, sharing a taxi with some journalists he was guiding to the dark side. A grimy winter cityscape slid past the mud-spattered windows of the cab.

Edward took a flirty blonde reporter to a church in Novokuznetsk. A sad-eyed priest with a long grey beard was intoning over his congregation. Suddenly one of the women went wild, cursing and swearing so much she had to be held down by several deacons. The flirty blonde was so scared she began crossing herself furiously, as tears streamed down her cheeks.

IV

A Russian translation of a German documentary on Anneliese Michel, a young woman from Bavaria whose exorcism culminated in her death. A scientist in wire-framed spectacles pointed at a bearded man in paisley-pattern pyjamas who was wired up to a brain-monitoring device. The scientist said: 'This man is epileptic. He has spasms. The possessed also have spasms. Therefore all demonic possession is merely epilepsy.'

QED.

7 My satanic education

As winter dragged on, I met Edward several times, as he sought to further my education in matters demonic. Usually he had a book to give me, invariably written by a Catholic. I always read these volumes, but didn't learn too much: one priest revealed that there were six different types of demon and explained the various stages of exorcism, but later I read other accounts that contradicted his definitions, and even discovered that this priest, whom Edward considered the ultimate authority on the subject, was considered half-renegade by the Vatican. In other books I learned that there was such a thing as holy salt, and of the efficacy of St Benedict medals against evil spirits. Maybe the most interesting fact was that Pope John Paul II himself had tried to cast a demon out of a tormented woman, but had failed. This demon was too powerful for even the infallible head of one billion Catholics. It said something for the man's honesty that he went public with this failure.

But I was disappointed in the books. After a while they became repetitive, simply listing the phenomena (flying objects, bizarre voices, a drop in temperature, violence) and cure (prayer, incense, readings from the Bible) over and over again. I was hoping for something more mediaeval, with lists of demons identified by name, perhaps some gruesome methods of torture and extracting confessions; at the very least some profound metaphysical ramblings. Instead the writers dealt in things that were already familiar from movies and documentaries. None referred to the cold, wild practices I had seen in Edward's film. These were Western devils that were being cast out, in the Western style.

What I did like, though, was that Edward would always choose fast-food joints as a place to meet. There was something almost *avant-garde* about discussing demonic possession over a background of rancid Russian pop music while teenage romance blossomed in the booth next to ours, or a weary office drone gnawed on processed food beside us. We spoke in a language that was foreign to our neighbours in more ways than one; they had no idea of the darkness we were discussing. And I liked the jarring estrangement from the dreary world of slush and the struggle to survive that I got from juxtaposing burgers and demonology with Edward, although he saw nothing remarkable about discussing possession under the sign of the Golden Arches. Indeed, the world of demons was so pressing to Edward, so obvious and immediate, that sometimes he lost himself and forgot that others didn't live inside it with him: one time we were in the leather-upholstered MakKafe section of a McDonald's in the centre of town. He was repeating himself, so I started looking around. A girl was sitting across from us, dressed in cheap clothes, but nibbling on an expensive cake.

Suddenly Edward, growing especially passionate, started waving his finger at her: 'Do you see that girl? That one there, eating the cake! I was at a church and have a recording, it is sound only, but in it, a girl, just like her, is growling. And it took six men to hold her down. A girl, like that! Look at her!'

She was lost in some private world, a glacial expression on her face. She spooned another fragment of cake between her lips. But with all the noise Edward was making, I knew she would soon become aware of the six-foot-six man-mountain gesticulating wildly at her. It was a struggle to calm him down.

But the truth is: I enjoyed these outbursts. I felt as though I was taking part in a performance no one else knew was taking place, and I was entering that dark, surreal world again, the one Sergei had hinted at the first time he talked about the Digger: that strange, *other* place I wanted to live in . . .

8

However often I saw Edward, though, in many ways, he remained an enigma. Sometimes there was deep darkness visible behind his gaze, and it looked as though he was teetering on the brink of a steep precipice. It was hard then to get him to talk, and he would sit in his chair heavy and sullen and distracted while I did most of the work. At other times he was ebullient, endlessly cracking corny jokes. Personal details, however, were hard to prise out of him. I learned that he was 28 and the son of Soviet diplomats who had been based in London during the 1980s. He had gone to a plush English school for four years, hence his uncanny accent and excellent command of the language. This, though, had left him with a distorted view of the UK. He thought that most British people were highly cultured ladies and gents who liked to discuss Tchaikovsky and fine wines. When I suggested that they were as thick as everybody else and were more likely to watch reality TV, go out on the lash and then vomit on a stranger's rose bushes, he laughed, as if to say: *How absurd! Obviously you are joking.*

As a student he had developed an obsession with Russian Orthodox chant and had even produced a CD which he later licensed to be sold around the world. (This had led to encounters with expensively educated English enthusiasts for this kind of music, thus entrenching him in his belief that the UK was a land of incomparably sophisticated philosopher-kings). He appeared, therefore, to be a man of organisational skill and considerable entrepreneurial energy, able to make his enthusiasms a profitable reality. But no sooner had this career begun than he encountered the possessed man in the north, after which he had immediately started to make his film, casting all thoughts of CDs and royalties aside. He had now been filming it for two years. Like the Digger, he had no money and no job and no backers, but dedicated himself full time to his vision in the face of colossal indifference. He worked endlessly, travelling around Russia whenever he had the funds, and filming un-navigated areas of human suffering. He would occasionally lend his expertise to some TV company and get a little cash, but it came seldom, and he had to make it last a long time. He lived with his parents, but that is not unusual for unmarried Muscovites of Edward's age.

As for what Mum and Dad thought of his radical departure from a career in law, he didn't say. All I could get out of him was that they weren't especially religious. And as for women, or friends, although he seemed less radically alone than the Digger, he was so obsessed with his film and mission it was hard to understand how he could develop normal relationships. But then, what did relationships matter? In his own words:

'If there are demons, and they are trying to lure people from the path of salvation, then it is vital that I make this film, to alert people to their existence and the danger they pose to our souls.'

For Edward, his Christian duty to alert his society to this danger was everything. His personal life was secondary, if it even ranked that highly. His career didn't rank at all. For there was a ruthless clarity of vision with Edward, and he would not spare himself. His arguments and extrapolations were almost mathematical in their rigour, as long as you accepted his starting points: the truth of scripture and his own observed experience of the demonic. When he had seen the smoking man in that northern church, therefore, his world had changed completely. Knowing now that demons existed, everything else had become instantly trivial. He was faced with a question – *what is to be done?* The answer was obvious.

By the time spring arrived my theoretical education in matters demonic was complete, and he invited me to join him in filming the next instalment of his documentary, so I could witness the phenomenon in practice.

I didn't hesitate to accept.

III

The Catastrophe Artist

At 4:30 p.m. my mobile rang. It was Edward. We were supposed to be travelling to Pskov later that night, so I could see my first exorcism in Father Miron's church. Father Miron was the priest in the first film on the videotape Edward had given me, the one who had cast out the demon of alcoholism and cured cancer. Edward reassured me that his exorcisms were *very* dramatic. There was just one problem:
'What day is it today?' he asked.
'Friday.'
'Are you sure?'
'Yes.'
'Not Thursday?'
'No.'
We went back and forth on the subject until he decided to check the calendar on his watch. There was a moment's silence, then he came back on the phone, laughing: 'Right you are, Daniel, right you are! Except . . .'
'It's now too late to buy tickets for Pskov.'
'Yes.'
We discussed the possibilities: there was another church outside the city where a different priest performed exorcisms every Sunday. Pskov was a hotbed of occult activity. We could attend this other service.
But the train ride was more than twelve hours long. And I knew Edward, ever mindful of economic pressures, was going to insist on travelling in the dirt-cheap open *platskartny* section. I had travelled that way a few times, but always found it difficult to sleep due to the heat and stench of sixty-odd sweaty carcasses stewing in their own

juices. I knew some people who found these carriages quaint and picturesque, a pleasing piece of Russian exotica. I was not one of them.

'It's a long way to go for just one day,' I said.

'Well, we could stay until Monday and perhaps explore Pskov a little . . . they have a *krom*! Do you know what a *krom* is?'

'A kremlin. I've seen pictures. I'd like to, but I need to be back in Moscow on Monday.'

'So we have a problem.'

'Yes.'

'Hm.'

2

The next morning Edward called again with a different idea. A world expert on the occult in Russia was going to be present at VDNKh, an exhibition centre in the north of Moscow. Here was an excellent opportunity for me to broaden my knowledge of exorcism, to wade deeper into that world, and also establish a useful contact, should I wish to write a magazine article at some point.

After the collapse of the Pskov trip I had consoled myself by watching *Godzilla: Final Wars*, an update of Godzilla for the twenty-first century that mixed the traditional men in rubber monster suits with state-of-the-art computer graphics and *Matrix*-style acrobatics. Godzilla had destroyed all the other monsters in his universe in one eye-popping final showdown. I switched off the film at 3 a.m., drained by all the excitement. I wasn't feeling too fresh.

But I knew Edward felt guilty for messing up the Pskov dates and he was trying to substitute our trip with something else interesting. In the end I agreed. I had nothing else planned, and I had never met an expert on the occult before. I am a firm believer that when a strange door is lying open in front of you, it is always better to step through, even if you think it will probably lead to nowhere and nothingness.

3

I stood deep below the surface of the earth, listening to the screams of metal on metal until finally Edward appeared, stumbling out of a carriage at the far end of the metro platform. He was forty-five minutes late. He apologised, but didn't say what had kept him. Then, stepping onto the metro he pressed a thick tome on demons into my hands. 'It's in Russian,' he said, 'but I think you'll manage, yes?'

I looked at the book. It was a translation from German. I doubted I'd make it past the first three pages, but slipped it into my jacket pocket anyway. Then I looked up at Edward. He wasn't saying much, just standing there, hanging on to the railing. His dark eyes looked troubled; it was one of those days when he looked as though he was on the edge of a precipice.

The night before I had had a dream, my first dream about demons in all the time I had known him. I decided to tell him about it, to break the strange, heavy silence.

4

'I was in a cold and draughty church in Pskov,' I said, 'with a crowd that had gathered for an exorcism. Father Miron was there, and he started swinging his censer and chanting. He was exorcising a possessed woman, but she wasn't reacting. Suddenly though the man *next* to me fell to the ground, howling and barking. He started emitting smoke. And then I realised that I was breathing it in, and suddenly I wondered if the smoke *was* the demon, if indeed I was inhaling a demon. I'd only breathed in a little, but the panic was real. I started crossing myself furiously, over and over, in the hope that the holy sign would make it too uncomfortable for the demon. But while I was doing that I remembered reading in some of the books you gave me that the more powerful ones aren't affected by all that stuff . . . I was terrified, really terrified.'

Edward was listening closely. Once I was finished he nodded and asked: 'What did the smoke smell of?' He smiled a strange smile. 'Because it has a very, how shall we say, *pungent* odour.'

'It was odourless,' I replied.

'Oh.'

It was as if it wasn't a dream, and my answer proved that what I had seen was crap, not a real case of possession at all. He pulled out a copy of *Sport Express* and started reading.

'I see Arsenal are doing well,' he said.

5 A rich multi-confessional tapestry

VDNKh was the former All-Union Exhibition of Economic Achievements. The complex had a new name and new acronym now,

VVTs, but nobody I knew used it, and the nearby metro station still went by the Soviet-era name also. It was a huge park full of Stalinist neo-classical pavilions that had at one time housed displays on the agricultural and industrial might of the Soviet Union, from achievements in aeronautics to advanced beekeeping.

Nowadays though, the pavilions were put to other uses. Usually they were just warehouses flogging TVs, sewing machines and electronics, but I had also seen the complex host raves, an international arms fair and 'Sexpo 2000', a rather dismal display of skin magazines and live 'body art' (most of the exhibits had been compounded at customs). But holding an expo on religious life in Russia here: now that was a particularly leaden irony.

Edward led me to the pavilion dedicated to the former Soviet Republic of Georgia. The wine stands and the small art gallery that usually filled the halls were gone, and in their place stood a strange bazaar offering faiths for sale. Russian Orthodox Christians, Seventh Day Adventists, Evangelicals, Tatar Muslims and Jews had all staked out their little corners and were standing behind stalls in their respective religious uniforms, all of them pointedly not talking to each other.

Edward stopped a nun and asked if the expert on the occult had spoken yet, but she didn't know who he was talking about. I, meanwhile, wondered about the smell of meat that permeated the halls. I looked around for the source and saw stands for a halal butcher, a kosher deli and some other guy selling special Russian Orthodox sausages. I went up to have a look at the sausages, to find out what was so Orthodox about them. But there was no information, and I didn't care enough to ask the butcher in question, a big man in spotless white overalls.

Edward, meanwhile, was now standing by a Muslim stall studying something closely. I walked up to him and saw that it was a video on *djinns*, evil spirits of the Islamic tradition. 'Very interesting,' he said. 'Very interesting.' He was lost in reflection; he seemed to have forgotten about the expert on the occult.

With all this wonderful diversity on display I started walking around, looking for signs of conflict. But I have to admit, there wasn't much. Some Muslim children were doing a little play on why Mohammed was the best. Round the corner, Evangelicals were handing out free Gideon Bibles, but discreetly. Evangelicals are a much-persecuted group in Russia, and the young boy and girl, dressed in jeans and T-shirts were glancing about nervously, as though they expected to be harassed any second and told to pack up their leaflets on the sinfulness of pre-marital sex and move on.

Is this it? I thought. *Is no one willing to punch someone else on the nose in the name of Religious Truth? Are they all just going to sit here and . . . ignore each other?* But just then I heard the sound of raised voices coming from the next hall. I went through and saw a straggly bearded Russian Orthodox Christian with greasy hair and dirty specs haranguing some Jews in yarmulkes. Walking closer I listened and realised he was angry with them for crucifying Our Saviour. The subjects of his ire, however, listened patiently, even attempting to debate with him. He didn't really want that, though. He just kept repeating himself, ever louder, goading them, pushing them, and generally making a nuisance of himself. But it didn't work. No one laid a finger on him.

Later I saw him haranguing the Seventh Day Adventists for attempting to spread their pernicious sect on Holy Russian soil. The Seventh Day Adventists' stall was directly opposite a Muslim bookstand, staffed by big ladies wearing headscarves and long black dresses. Curiously, he left them alone. How strange. Maybe he was worried they would declare a *jihad* on his ass. And if they did that, then how would he be able to enjoy himself shouting at Jews?

Oh, and one other thing: Edward's expert on the occult hadn't turned up.

6

We went outside. Edward bought me a Pepsi from a drinks machine and then we wandered aimlessly for a few minutes, until we stopped to sit on a bench facing the Ostankino TV tower. Edward seemed exhausted, the darkness I sometimes saw behind his eyes suddenly darker. He was silent and sullen. He looked hounded.

I had seen him in low spirits before, but never as bad as this. He started talking about the difficulty of his mission, but he was expressing himself so vaguely it was hard to grasp with any precision what he meant – and yet I could easily imagine the enormous pressure he was under. He dedicated himself to the study of supernatural evil; he was at war with it; and he was alone. What he did took not only courage but an epic quantity of faith, much more than was available to most believers. Then he told me he had spent the previous day on the sofa, lying around, unable to motivate himself. Of course, it sounded like depression – he had no job, no wife and the future of his film, which was his entire reason for existing, was always in jeopardy. Continuing in the face of these grim facts required a monumental act of will that was hard to sustain, and it was only natural to collapse in exhaustion, to cave in, from time to time. Edward, however, did not even consider this explanation long enough to dismiss it. This lethargy, he hinted, was not purely human in origin. This evil knew that it was under study and didn't like the attention. It didn't like being exposed.

'When did it start?' I asked.

He sighed. 'Remember that audio file I gave you to listen to?'

'Which one?'

'The girl.'

I remembered. Edward had been present at this exorcism a few months earlier. The subject was just a teenager, a mere slip of a thing, he said, and yet this slow, gravelly growl had come scraping out of her throat. It was obscene. It sounded almost as if there was something living in her, some slithering eyeless thing, deep, deep in her gut. Close your eyes and you could almost see a black tentacle come worming out of the girl's pale throat. How could I forget it?

'I posted it on the internet,' said Edward. 'It got ten thousand hits in one week. I thought: this is great, my message is getting out there, you know? But then I started to receive emails. People were asking me if I had more "stuff like that". Now what do they mean by *stuff like that*? This isn't a game. And one of them even signed his email with a "Hail Satan!"'

I said nothing, just listened. This was a problem he was going to have to face, and I had thought so for a long time. As I saw it, the actual audience for Edward's film was not repentant sinners turning from the path of darkness so much as kids in black clothes and face paint, dripping with Gothic jewellery, dabbling with Ouija boards and satanic iconography. And among the casual devotees of the arcane arts seeking to piss off their parents, there would also be a smaller, hard-core group of genuine nut-jobs.

Edward continued: 'I wrote back, telling them not to play with these things, that this is a serious business. But since then, well . . . I've been under attack. Spiritually, I mean. I just find it hard to get motivated. And you know –' He paused. 'The Enemy enters through the spine.'

88

'The spine?'

'Yes. In the form of a miasma, a vapour. You hear it first, a hissing, and then, there's a cool sensation, as it enters –' Edward twisted round, indicating a spot on his back, right in between his shoulder blades.

'That's where the demon enters. Right there.' He paused. A long silence hung in the air. 'I want to be prayed over. But I can't ask any of the Orthodox priests I know. I can't do anything that might disturb them. It would be bad for my film. I must always be cheerful, solid . . . I can't show weakness.'

Then suddenly he switched to talking about the possibility of mass possession – that not merely individuals, but whole races or ideological groups might be controlled by evil powers. After all, if Christ had exorcised one man who contained many demons . . . why not consider the possibility of many people controlled by one vast, powerful evil force? 'What do you think?' he asked. 'Do you think the evil Russia witnessed under Stalin, with his persecution of the Church – can it be explained in merely human terms?'

Edward was picking himself up, switching himself back on. Slowly the darkness in his eyes receded, the slump in his posture lifted and as we walked back to the metro he was once again aflame with possibilities. He continued pursuing this idea of mass possession, not only of the leadership of a nation, but of entire transnational ideological groups. The question was purely hypothetical, of course. Edward, as he himself had told me, enjoyed all manner of intellectual speculation. But it was too much for me. I felt as though he had my brain in his fist, and he was slowly squeezing the juice out of it.

I didn't answer.

7

I had my own opinions about what Edward told me, of course. I just wasn't very interested in them. Neither will there be any discussion of the truth or falsity of his ideas in this book. I am not writing to persuade you for or against belief in the existence of 'the supernatural'. You will have your own conclusions about that; you don't need mine.

What I was very interested in, however, was the experience of living in a world where the reality of demons was already beyond dispute, and not just that, but one where they were the major enemy of humanity. That world is real, regardless of whether demons exist or not. Edward lived in it, and not just him, but many others.

I wanted to travel inside that world. And if I started challenging him every time he opened his mouth I wouldn't get very far. And what would have been the point anyway? Edward had seen the man producing smoke from his flesh in the northern church; he had seen a little girl so strong she had to be held down by several grown men; he had heard the rasping demonic voice, uttering blasphemies and curses, over and over again.

He knew that Satan was real.

8

Back on the metro Edward tried to resurrect our Pskov trip. He wanted to go to Leningradsky Vokzal, buy some train tickets and just take a chance. But I didn't feel like another failure, and I knew it would be a failure. We were on a roll, as far as fiascos were concerned. Besides, even if we pulled it off, I would need a lot of energy if I was to meet Father Miron or any other exorcist, and at that moment I was exhausted. I wanted to go home. Maybe I'd watch *Godzilla: Final Wars* again.

My instincts, it turned out, were correct. Later Edward found out that Father Miron had had a heart attack that very weekend; and as for the other priest he had suggested going to see, well he had been ordered to stop performing exorcisms by his bishop.

9

I was disturbed by the air of catastrophe around Edward. The deeper I entered his world, the more I saw how frequently he had to wrestle with obstacles and disappointment. Though his career as a music producer had been a sudden and surprising success, as far as the film was concerned, nothing ever worked out for him quite the way it should have. People vanished, leads fell through, old supporters backed away from him suddenly. Money he was promised was withheld. He saw this as proof of an opposition to his plans that was more than coincidental: *these matters I am investigating . . . they do not want to be investigated, if you understand my meaning.*

Maybe. As for me, I was reminded of the chaos and disorder that had surrounded my dealings with the Digger. It was easy to believe it was a natural consequence of living for your obsession, in the face of general indifference.

I could have walked away. But I didn't want to. My satanic education was not complete. I had read books, watched films, listened to discourses. But that wasn't enough: I wanted to see the smoking man Edward had told me about. I wanted to hear inhuman screams, devilish growls. I wanted to stand witness as a three-year-old was held down by a team of ten professional wrestlers. I still wanted to cross into that reality.

And so, in a strange way, the more things went wrong, the more people vanished or withdrew, the more reasons, in fact, that I was given to forget about Edward's world, the more I was lured forward, deeper into it.

I knew I was expending energy on what could well be a quixotic quest. I knew that maybe I would see nothing. But I kept going forward, regardless. In fact, I started to get involved in the actual organisation of Edward's film. And so I was already inside his reality, whether I had planned it or not.

There was no way I could step back from it now.

IV

Satan Takes a Trip

1 The Exorcism Song Contest

A couple of weeks later President Yuschenko of Ukraine announced that he was simplifying entry requirements for citizens of the EU: visas would no longer be necessary for tourists coming to the country for a short stay. My heart sank.

Allow me to explain: of course I know that all cultures are rich and fascinating and believe with all my heart that every nation on our beautiful planet is equally tremendous. But even so, there was a terrible, reactionary part of my soul that whispered to me that Ukraine was one of those places like Canada, New Zealand, or Belgium: not without a few modest pleasures, but otherwise trapped permanently in the shadow of a much more interesting country. The insidious voice whispered further that since Ukraine had been an appendage of Russia for the best part of a thousand years, it wouldn't be all that different from what I already knew, or at least not different enough to warrant the expense and bother of a trip there. After spending so long in Russia, Ukraine could only be a disappointment.

In a world without exorcisms this would not have been a problem. I just wouldn't have gone. In a world with exorcisms, however, the situation was a little different. Edward had been trying to persuade me to go there for months. He loved Ukraine and often waxed lyrical about how big the strawberries were and how black the soil was. I was unmoved by these poetic evocations of a rural arcadia, and knowing that the whisperings of my soul would sound too frivolous for a man as intense as Edward, I fobbed him off instead with stories of how difficult it was for British citizens to organise a visa for Ukraine. It was no more difficult than it was to organise a tourist visa for anywhere else, but it did the trick. Now, however, that excuse was gone.

I waited for my mobile to ring.

2

'Daniel! Have you heard the fantastic news?'

3

I met Edward in a café in the south of Moscow two days after Yuschenko had made his announcement. He got straight down to business.

'I have a plan,' he said, his eyes gleaming with an excitement that bordered on the visionary.

'Go on.'

'We'll go down to Odessa – I have good relations with many exorcists down there. We will attend some deliverance services, and you will see some very powerful phenomena. After that, we can relax on the beach. They have beautiful beaches in Odessa, you know, and even at this time of year, in April, the water will be warm . . .'

Odessa: the name, like Paris, or Alexandria, held magic. I'd actually thought about going there seven years before but had been too lazy. On the other hand, I wasn't very excited by the prospect of walking along the beach with Edward. Beaches bore me, unless they have things like dead whales or rotting nuclear submarines on them. But Edward wasn't finished.

'And that's not all . . . afterwards we'll take the train north to Kiev and attend . . . er . . . *Yevrovideniye*. Do you know what I mean?'

Yevrovideniye: Eurovision. Of course. Ukraine had won the Eurovision Song Contest the year before and so now it was Kiev's turn to host that most kitsch of entertainment extravaganzas. That was why Yuschenko had scrapped visa requirements for EU citizens: to make it as easy as possible for the maximum number of foreigners from the countries involved to attend. In Britain we may scoff, but in a country like Ukraine, Eurovision would be a Big Deal. Ukraine doesn't get to host many international events, not even the rubbish ones.

'Are you suggesting that we have an exorcism-musical-beach holiday?' I asked.

He nodded. 'Precisely. Let's fuse work and pleasure.'

Suddenly all doubts vanished. It was nothing short of brilliant – a stroke of genius, unprecedented in the annals of humanity. Now here was the beautiful car crash that would scramble my senses absolutely, shaking them up once and for all, leaving the world looking entirely different. More than that, Edward had suddenly introduced a startling lightness to the tone of this meeting that had never been present in any of our other ones. Until that moment, exorcism had always been an unremittingly dark topic, a 'very serious matter'. It still was, but now it was possible to mix in other concepts with it.

By the time I got home, however, the strength of Edward's vision of things was waning and I was starting to see things differently, doubting the whole plan. The whole of Ukraine's elite would be attending Eurovision. Tickets would be rarer than a gay-pride rally in the Middle East and pricier than a seat in the House of Lords, New Labour-style. We were doomed.

Except . . . maybe it didn't matter if we attended Eurovision or not. If I was serious about it, there were some interesting things about Ukraine.

4

Do you remember the Orange Revolution? It is forgivable if you don't, because by the time you read this the euphoria and excitement that surrounded those days in December and January of 2004 and 2005 will be for most people a distant half-memory of a few flickering phantoms on a TV screen: some tanks, a flower held out to an unsmiling soldier, the downfall of darkness, the triumph of light.

It wasn't the only revolution taking place in the former Soviet Union at that time either. There was one in Georgia just before it, and one in Kyrgyzstan just after it, though that one was met with less enthusiasm by the Western media. The Kyrgyz were just too far away to care, too difficult to describe, too poor and insignificant to bother with.

This is what happened in Ukraine: the scandal-tainted President Leonid Kuchma had reached the end of his second term and everything looked set for his prime minister, Viktor Yanukovych to assume control of the country in a tidy handover of power, just as Putin had taken over from Yeltsin in Russia four years earlier. Yanukovych was viewed as a pro-Russian supporter of the current oligarchic order. He proposed making Russian an official language, a move unpopular with nationalists in the Ukrainian-speaking west of the country. He also had a criminal record, having done time in Soviet jails for assault in his youth.

Yanukovych's only serious opponent was another former prime minister of Kuchma's, Viktor Yuschenko. Yuschenko presented himself as the pro-West Ukrainian nationalist candidate. He pledged to root out corruption, bring the country into NATO and to seek membership of the EU. He was especially popular where Yanukovych was hated: in western Ukraine. As the election drew nearer, however, Yuschenko fell ill and had to be flown to Austria for emergency treatment. Yuschenko's camp said he'd been poisoned. Anti-Yuschenko forces claimed he was a pansy who'd eaten some rotten food.

Yuschenko recovered, but was left badly disfigured, an effect not usually associated with dodgy kebabs. He looked as though he'd aged twenty years. He went on to fight the election and lose, but refused to concede defeat, citing fraud. With his supporters, who included not only his running mate Yulia Tymoshenko but also the head of the renegade Ukrainian Orthodox Church (which had broken away from the Moscow patriarchate) and Ukraine's Eurovision Song Contest champion Ruslana, he camped out on Independence Square, demanding a recount.

The world's media descended on Kiev. A sea of orange flags (the colour of Yuschenko's side) was broadcast around the globe every night. Eventually a recount was held: this time, Yuschenko and Tymoshenko won. There was great jubilation in Kiev, and around the world. Ukraine was coming in from the cold, freedom and democracy were spreading and the bluebird of happiness was trilling in every tree.

I myself was sceptical. Election fraud notwithstanding, practically no journalist or commentator paid any attention to the fact that Viktor Yuschenko and Yulia Tymoshenko were both former members of the preceding president's cabinet: that is to say, they had at one time been players in the very regime they had just overthrown, a regime in which they had grown rich and powerful. I didn't think it was possible to have operated at so high a level of a political system that was riddled with corruption without getting a bit of filth under your fingernails, not to mention in your hair, up your nostrils and in every other orifice besides. And so it was hard to believe that they wouldn't soon start fucking up. As the Russian saying goes: *A humpback will only be corrected in the grave.*

And if you've paid any attention to events in Ukraine since those glorious days you'll know things did go wrong, and quite swiftly. Within six months Yuschenko and Tymoshenko had fallen out and become political enemies. And in little over a year, Yuschenko, unable to form a government otherwise, was forced to invite Yanukovych, his arch nemesis, the one who had allegedly tried to steal the election, to be his prime minister. And that relationship also dissolved in acrimony, amassed crowds and face-offs on Independence Square; and who knows what new drama will have unfolded by the time this is published . . .

5

The collapse of the Orange Revolution, however, lay in the future. There was still euphoria abroad in Ukraine, and bitterness in Moscow towards the country's new leaders. I had never been to a country in the spring of revolution before. I was too young to visit the new democracies of Eastern Europe when the Berlin Wall collapsed and unborn when most of the Third World was cut loose from European control. Mixed with a dash of demon hunting, it could be excellent. I liked the juxtaposition of incongruous elements: probing the promise of a golden future on earth, while pursuing the invisible enemies of all mankind, dedicated to our eternal damnation.

I was beginning to think maybe I had been too hasty in writing off the potential delights of Ukraine. And anyway, as far as exorcism was concerned, Edward was in charge. If I was to get anywhere in my satanic education, I had to subjugate myself to his will. It was his reality, not mine. As soon as I stepped away from his orbit, it would disappear.

And Edward *was* hell-bent on Ukraine. Within a few days we had tickets for Odessa. The sun was shining the day we bought them, and, buoyed by the promise of new borders to be crossed, we went for a celebratory walk through Moscow. I had never seen Edward so relaxed or in such a good mood. But this was what he lived for: the thrill of the demon hunt, the opportunity to capture his dark vision of the world on film so that others would be forced to acknowledge what he knew but they ignored. We stopped for a coffee in front of Chistiye Prudy metro station and he sketched out a rough schedule of our week in Odessa: there were seven exorcists on that piece of paper. It was going to be tight; we were going to witness many exorcisms. Then he put it aside and started to talk about women.

Edward's original itinerary: seven exorcists in seven days. It didn't quite work out that way

6 Advice for the lonely of heart

He had just turned 29. He thought it was time to get married, but he had no idea how to find a girl who would understand his mission.

'I mean,' he said, 'I need someone who understands my work. I need a girl who isn't afraid of the subject of my film. And I need a girl who is my intellectual equal, and who doesn't complain when I spend large amounts of time lying on the sofa, doing nothing. Because I need to think in my work, and that requires me to lie on the sofa for very long periods.' He looked me straight in the eyes. 'Do you think it will be hard to find her?'

'A bit,' I said.

'But I am tired of waiting. I would like to have children . . .'

'I've got a suggestion,' I said.

'What?'

'When you meet a girl for the first time, don't talk about exorcism.'

Edward laughed. I had just said something ridiculous. 'But it's important!'

'I know, Edward . . . But it's not a good subject for romantic conversation. It scares girls off. On the first date, you shouldn't talk about it.'

'Come, come . . .'

'I'm serious. Tell her about the CD you made. Make out like that's your main interest. And on the second date, you shouldn't talk about demons either. Nor on the third. Or the fourth. Talk about your love for children and small animals instead. In fact, you should wait a couple of months before you reveal your interest in evil spirits, and even then you shouldn't make out that it's all that serious. Act like it's a hobby. You can tell her that you've dedicated your life to making a film about exorcisms only once you're married. By that point it'll be too late.'

Edward laughed. He thought I was joking.

7

In the days that followed I prepared for my trip south. My reluctance *vis-à-vis* Ukraine had vanished completely, but at the same time, I could never become completely excited: I could not completely lose myself in anticipation of the trip. There were two reasons for this:

(1) I wasn't sure how the various priests I was going to meet would take to me. They might be extremely hostile to an outsider sniffing around in an area considered taboo by the church.

(2) I was going to be witness to some profound human suffering. Regardless of whether or not it was caused by demonic possession, the pain on the faces of the women in Edward's videos was real and brutal; profoundly unexotic, deeply unmysterious. It was not something to be taken lightly. The habitual true/false approach to discussing something like exorcism disguises the reality of the phenomenon as it is experienced – namely, pure suffering. Nor does it affect only the possessed – I had seen traces of it on the faces of the exorcists themselves; I had seen it in Edward's eyes. Since I wasn't conducting an investigation into the disputed existence of the paranormal but rather an exploration of it as something accepted and tangible that is lived with I was going to be confronted with this directly.

So on the day of our departure for Odessa, I felt conflicted. There was something unresolved in my attitude towards this trip. Edward had a mission; I had curiosity. Thinking about it like that, I felt uneasy about what I was doing. Curiosity just didn't seem like enough.

I got to Kievsky station early and was at the platform standing in front of our train a good twenty minutes before it was scheduled to leave. Edward, of course, was nowhere to be seen. Then, two minutes before departure, as the ticket attendants were making the final call for passengers to board, I saw him running towards me, grinning from ear to ear and dragging a huge bag along behind him. It contained all his equipment: two cameras, notebooks, clothes, books.

Edward reached me and stopped, reaching into his jacket pocket for his ticket. It wasn't there. He searched another pocket, then another, then his bag. Then the train started, very slowly, to trundle out of the station.

Pskov had just been a warm-up, a hint at what he was capable of. Edward truly was a master practitioner of the art of catastrophe.

8 Odessa: The Devil rides out

I had always wondered how it would feel to stand on a platform and watch a train that I had a ticket for trundle away. Now I knew: strangely serene. It was pleasant that this train knew nothing of me, that its driver and passengers cared not a whit for my plans. They didn't know I wasn't on it, that I was missing my chance to hunt down demons. They were off to lead their lives without me . . . And that was somehow good.

Edward, however, had turned pale. Apologies and self-recriminations poured from his lips. 'I am an idiot, I have messed up your opportunity . . .'

'These things happen,' I said.

'But never to me! This has never happened to me before!'

I found that hard to believe. 'Maybe you left the ticket at home.'

'No, I had it. I checked in the taxi. It was in my hands!'

'Maybe it fell out of your pocket afterwards.'

'It couldn't have. It just isn't possible. No, there's something else going on here . . . Sometimes when you're investigating these matters, well, the matters that we are investigating, if you understand what I mean, do not want to be investigated. Yes,' he said. 'It's happened before, only not with tickets. But – keys disappear when I need them . . . Or sometimes I film a deliverance, only to discover that the camera has not recorded . . . It's our Enemy. He doesn't like it when people try to expose what he's doing.'

Was the Devil riding to Odessa right now, going there in our stead?

Could it be that Beelzebub himself, in top hat and tails, and terribly polite, was making his way to our seats even as we stood on the platform? *Excuse me . . .* he'd say, and the woman in the berth below him, with the big, red and white checked shuttle-trader bags, would start to feel ill as soon as she got off the train, and would waste away, and the doctors wouldn't be able to treat her, until, a mere pale skeleton, she expired. And then the tall gentleman would stroll through Odessa, wreaking havoc, causing plant pots to fall on people's heads, and others to tumble beneath the wheels of oncoming trams and be decapitated . . .

9

We ran into the station to get tickets for the next train, but there were none. Or rather there were, but the woman behind the counter was tired of selling them and slammed her metal blind down. It was past ten; she wanted to go home. Edward was devastated.

'Can you believe that?' he said. 'She has tickets, but she won't sell them . . . It's outrageous . . .'

My own feeling was that since we were surfing the catastrophe wave, the catastrophe tsunami in fact, it was probably better not to go. With Edward, when something went wrong, at least two or three other crises were likely to follow in rapid succession. It was still possible to recoup most of the cost of my ticket. In the end, when it was absolutely clear that there were no more trains that night heading even vaguely in the direction of Ukraine, I persuaded him to wait a week.

I left him, a slightly forlorn figure, standing in front of the grandiose entrance to Kievsky station, looking for a bus. I knew that this was just a temporary setback, however. In VDNKh he had started speculating on mass possession as a prelude to bouncing back. He was resilient that way – demonic forces could only slow him down; they could not stop him, no matter what they threw at him. And that was just as well, if he was going to make a film like the one he was working on, entirely on his own.

I entered the underpass leading to the metro, took the escalator deep below the earth and rode the train home.

10 World of the strange

Once inside my building, however, I experienced two strange phenomena that are worth commenting on. The first was this: I met my neighbour, the famous and well-respected Soviet actor Vasily Lanovoi, on the landing, clad only in silk Japanese pyjamas. He acknowledged me with a sonorous 'good evening' (he always spoke in his stage voice). This was surprising: as he was the recipient of many plaudits and awards, a grubby and obscure foreigner such as I could not hope to register on his plane of existence. He was too high; I was too low. Usually he didn't see me, not even if I was standing right under his aquiline nose. But that wasn't the only strange thing. Suddenly he manoeuvred himself towards the doorway, and tried to peer inside my flat. I had to close the door on him to frustrate his voyeuristic tendencies.

What happened next, however, was even more inexplicable. Just after I dropped my bags in the hall, the kettle switched itself on in the kitchen. There was a click, the little red light came on and the water started to heat up . . . to bubble . . . then it switched itself off. *Eh?* I thought. *Did I really see that?* Then it switched itself on again . . . the water heated up . . . and then off. And then on once more . . .

It was eerie. The hair at the back of my neck stood up. The kettle had never done this before. What was happening? How was this possible?

It was classical, like something from one of Edward's books: a prelude to a sudden drop in temperature and objects flying around the room. One author had cautioned the reader that the deeper he walked into the world of the diabolic, the more he would start to encounter problems – in both his private and professional life. Demons didn't like to be spied on, bothered, disrupted, he wrote. They wanted freedom to lead human souls to damnation, without undue attention. Attention made it harder for them to influence people, made their potential victims wise to their tricks. As Edward had said, *the matters that we are investigating, they do not want to be investigated.* Was this a warning?

But then I thought: *What kind of devil is this, switching kettles on and off? That's crap.*

After that the kettle behaved itself.

The very next day Edward bought more tickets, for Kiev this time. His contacts in Odessa were going to be out of town the next week, so we would go to the capital instead. Truth be told, I was a lot less interested in Kiev than Odessa. But I was teetering on the brink of a grand darkness now. It didn't matter where I found it.

V

Ukraine

1 Moskva–Kiev

We were travelling *platskartny*, in one of the open carriages that Edward favoured so much for their 'economical' prices. I wasn't suffering too much, however. Though it was hot and hard to breathe, and the guy in the bunk across from mine was torturing a Soviet rock song on a cardboard guitar, and I had no hope of sleeping, I had noticed at least one great benefit of this style of carriage: its very openness made it much easier to be unsociable. When I travelled in a closed carriage with three other passengers it always took a certain degree of psychological effort not to talk to them. We were too close together; silence was unnatural. In a big open carriage there was no such pressure, and it was very easy to ignore everyone.

Everyone except Edward, that is: all six foot six of his intimidating frame was bouncing up and down on his bunk with the enthusiasm of a ten-year-old boy on the way to the fairground. He showed me his press card, discussed previous trips, and talked admiringly about his mythical England, the one that was ruled by morally elevated enlightened rationalists. My inclination was to keep quiet; we were on a strange mission after all, and I didn't think it wise to draw attention to ourselves. Edward, on the other hand, was dying to show someone his press card and start talking about his film. He especially wanted to flash the card at the Ukrainian border guards, the very last people I would have shown it to. Edward would have made an excellent missionary: he was without a sense of embarrassment or awkwardness when it came to talking about his faith. He knew that what he believed in was startling to most people, but that was all to the good. That led to more questions, more opportunities to explain his worldview.

I myself was slightly nervous about two things:

(1) I had never spent more than five or six hours in Edward's company, but that was usually enough to leave me exhausted. I wasn't sure what state I'd be in by the end of the week, but expected to feel like a smear of greasy human pulp.

(2) The new visa regulations. I didn't think many EU citizens were entering Ukraine by train from Russia. Most would come by plane, or if they were entering by train they would do so from the west, passing through Slovakia. I wasn't confident the border guards would know the rules had changed. Neither was Edward.

At around 2 a.m. the Russian border guards entered the train. They were cold, unfriendly – the way border officials usually are. Following that we spent two hours trundling through darkness before the train stopped at the Ukrainian border. I would have liked to sleep, but couldn't. And so I knew I was not dreaming that great distance between the borders: but where had we been travelling all that time? Some other place, some non-country, some no-man's land?

The Ukrainian border guards put an end to my sense of nebulous mystery. They were chubby, friendly, and spoke Russian. In the east of Ukraine, most people do: better than they speak Ukrainian, even.

I handed over my passport. The guard seemed satisfied, but then suddenly exclaimed: 'Hey, wait a minute, doesn't he need a visa?'

Shit, I thought. *Here it comes.*

'Dunno,' said his colleague. 'Yeah. I think he does.'

'Got a visa?' he asked me.

'Wait, lads,' said Edward. 'He doesn't need one. Don't you remember? Your president changed the law.'

'Did he?'

'Yes. For citizens of the EU.'

'Is that right?' asked the one holding my passport.

'Could be,' said his colleague. 'Actually, yeah. I think he's right.'

'It's for Eurovision,' said Edward.

'Oh yeah.' The guard gave me my passport back, and smiled: 'Welcome to Ukraine!'

After that it was a simple matter of not sleeping for a further three hours, until the train pulled into the accumulation of buildings half-completed, abandoned and rotting, the industrial rubbish, and the rusting tanks of *benzin* that marked the entrance to Kiev.

2

It was a damp, chilly morning and the sky above was grey and dismal. God had clearly forgotten the people of Ukraine were living in the glorious spring of revolution.

We merged with the crowd shuffling towards the entrance vestibule of the metro when suddenly Edward realised he had forgotten to pay the ticket inspector for the tea we had drunk on the train the night before. He panicked: 'It is not good to start a journey in debt to someone else.'

'It's just a few pennies,' I said. 'Forget about it.'

Edward looked at me again, startled. Surely I was joking. His ethical system would not permit it: what I was suggesting was tantamount to stealing.

'Stay here,' he said. 'I am going to find him.'

He turned and pushed into the crowd, until eventually I lost sight of him. I studied my new surroundings. They contained many objects familiar from similar contexts in Russia:

Old ladies selling cabbage pies.
Crusty-bearded *bomzhi* rooting around in bins at six in the morning.
Pasty-faced wannabe gangsters with bad haircuts and leather jackets
from the provinces.
Cheap Chinese clothes.
A general air of sadness.

But then, just as I was losing hope of finding some new image to add to my store, I spotted something I hadn't seen before: a young man was sitting on a wooden chair by the entrance to the metro with a mobile phone tied to his wrist. The cardboard sign round his neck stated that in exchange for money you could borrow his mobile and make a call.

Presumably this was because the public phones were no longer working and many citizens of Ukraine were too poor to buy their own mobiles. I was impressed by his entrepreneurial spirit.

Eventually Edward returned. The ticket inspector hadn't remembered him. Not only that, he had refused to take any money for the tea. It was just pennies, after all.

3

We took the metro north, travelling through tunnels and subterranean stations that were eerily familiar, like parallel-universe versions of the ones in Moscow, albeit smaller, darker and slightly shabbier. It was strange too, considering the train was identical to those I rode every day in Moscow, to find Ukrainian-language signs everywhere, in the ads for glue, for mobile phones, and in the rules of the metro.

If people had been speaking Ukrainian it would have been easier to make the transition; but nobody was. The language spoken around us was Russian; the magazines and the cheap thrillers commuters were reading were in Russian. The government clearly wanted to change that. In fact, although Russian is spoken as a first language by around a third of the population and fluently by most of it, it does not have official status in Ukraine, and Yuschenko's government was busy forcing Russian-language schools, even in Russian majority areas like the Crimea, to switch to educating their pupils in Ukrainian.

I imagined returning to Scotland to find that everyone still spoke English but all the signs and billboards were now written in Gaelic because the Scottish parliament wanted to foster a sense of separateness from England. It wouldn't be so strange in some of the islands, but anywhere else such a policy would be absurd. So I couldn't help wondering what the attitude of all those seemingly dormant commuters was to the absence of signs in the language most of them spoke. But they all had their noses buried in Russian publications, so I couldn't study their responses.

4

Ours was the penultimate stop on the line. We followed the steps to the surface and found ourselves in one of the lunar settlements that exist on the outskirts of every city in the former Soviet Union. A vast alley lined with Soviet-era tower blocks stretched to the horizon, but because Kiev was the capital and thus had a bit of money, some futuristic buildings had been built for the new rich: semi-skyscrapers that stuck out amid the aging Soviet infrastructure like gold implants in a mouthful of rotting teeth.

Edward informed me that this was a famous neighbourhood, home to a popular type of beer. It was hammering down with rain though, so I wasn't able to fully absorb the beauty. We were going to see his Auntie Lyuda, who was providing us with accommodation for the duration of our stay. I hoped Auntie Lyuda lived in one of the new buildings: after all, Edward came from a well-connected diplomatic family. His address in Moscow was prestigious and I was curious to see what constituted luxury in Ukraine.

After twenty minutes of racing through the downpour and wading through small lakes in the sunken concrete, however, I realised that we had passed all the futuristic towers and were heading towards one of the classical Brezhnev constructions on Heroes of Stalingrad Street. (It also had a new, Ukrainian name, but out here, far beyond the centre, the old Soviet-era Russian street signs were still up, and not only Edward but also his relatives used the old name.)

We passed a dead restaurant, and then a lorry with British licence plates, a giant ad for Yorkie bars on its side. Auntie Lyuda's rotten tooth was standing right behind it.

5 Catastrophe surfing

The rest of the day was spent embroiled in various catastrophes. Edward called up a priest who had forgotten who Edward was; we went out to see him; the priest had vanished by the time we got there; no one knew when he would be back; certainly not for several days, anyway; and who did you say you were again?

Etc.

But I was accustomed to Edward's unique 'methodology' by now, and as I had been fully conscious for almost forty-eight hours I was even half-relieved. I would need a good night's sleep if I was going to sit in on an exorcism; that sort of thing shouldn't be done half-awake. More than that, I knew the priests would be suspicious of me, and if I wasn't able to think and analyse the situation clearly I could find myself in some very awkward situations.

I was drawing closer to dark knowledge, to the fulfilment of my satanic education, this I knew. It was becoming real, if it wasn't quite real yet.

In a shiny McDonald's decorated with abstract expressionist prints by Mark Rothko, Edward outlined a change of strategy. We were going to travel to Kremenchug instead, where he was on very good terms with a powerful priest.

'Where's Kremenchug?'

'It's in Poltava region, the legendary black soil country, the bread-basket of Ukraine, here they grow strawberries the size of your fist . . . and it's also the birthplace of Nikolai Gogol – do you know Gogol?

Have you read *Evenings on a Farm near Dikanka*? Or *Viy*, the story of the demon whose eyelids were so heavy he needed other demons to lift them open for him? Tomorrow, I promise, you will see something that will shock you to your core!'

A POSTCARD FROM UKRAINE

Eternal Venice
The minibus next to ours had Venetsiya written on it.
Venetsiya: Venice. The Ukrainian Venice, that is. And what
could that be? Gondolas drifting down canals of mud?
Crumbling factories in place of decaying palaces and man-
sions? I wanted to see this Ukrainain Venice. I wanted to see
the men and women wearing masks for the carnival, I wanted
to see their colourful costumes against the backdrop of
smokestacks and industrial decay. And somewhere in the
parade, between the fire-breathers and the stilt walkers, a real,
live rhino.

6 Black earth, fat bastard

The bus was state of the art: it had a TV, a DVD player and a surround-sound speaker system. I had not expected entertainment on the way to Kremenchug. Maybe it was just there to tease us, to torment us, like the TVs they used to put on the Edinburgh–London bus. I never saw one of those in use, much the same way I never felt the air conditioning operating during those long night odysseys spent in the company of backpackers, skag heads and weirdo forty-something loners venturing south on mysterious business. But no, the driver started the engine and slipped in a disc before we had even left the station. I felt curiously excited. What were we going to see?

It was a Russian film, produced by a major Russian studio. But the credits were in Ukrainian. My heart sank: had they dubbed it? Was I going to be subjected to something totally impenetrable? But as soon as the credits had finished rolling, the actors started speaking in Russian.

I knew that somewhere out there the tortured logic for putting Ukrainian credits on Russian-made films that were shown in the Russian language to people who spoke Russian fluently had been formalised and written down. I knew even that there was probably at least one government cubicle where I could meet the official authorised to enforce this law, and that he would justify it to me. He would be either a bureaucratic automaton, a petty nationalist or very, very cynical.

The film, a *Die Hard* knock-off, was a replay of the *Nord Ost* hostage crisis, except for two crucial differences: (1) here a circus and not theatre audience was being held captive by a squad of murderous Chechen terrorists, and (2) the film had a happy ending. A lone Russian special forces operative (with the help of a good Chechen*) saved all the hostages, and killed all the terrorists. He also managed to blow up an Osama Bin Laden lookalike hiding out in a Middle Eastern desert and save Rome from destruction, though I couldn't figure out how that last bit was connected.

Being a regular attendee at the Old Circus in Moscow I recognised many of the extras: there was the Armenian guy whose racially sensitive act consisted of dressing a monkey like a rabbi,† the Tin Man who juggled pointy hats, the two brothers who pretended they were statues, and the woman who cycled around with lots of poodles on a specially adapted bike. High art, I'm sure you'll agree.

But these were just performers I had seen from a seat in the auditorium. The actor playing the chief of the American newsroom reporting on the crisis I actually knew personally, and it was a real shock to see him on-screen. He was an obese, oleaginous guy with the face of a walrus; we had worked for the same company when I first arrived in Moscow. He never talked to anyone who wasn't young, pretty and equipped with a vagina, and he spent much of his time scouring Russian dating sites for potential brides while exhaling heavily through his nose. I also had an enduring memory of him leafing through a gossip magazine and repeating to himself in his nasally voice:

'Nicole Kidman: yum . . . yum . . . yum.'

His wife had left him to bring up their five-year-old daughter alone. Usually he brought her with him when he came to use the work computers to trawl the impoverished Russian provinces for a wife. I remember her, playing with her raggedy doll in the office, bored out of her skull as Daddy went sharking for a provincial piece of ass. Legend had it that he'd been abandoned by his first Russian wife, who had

* Yes, there is political correctness in Russia too.
† But not a lot.

somehow made it to the States, leaving him in Moscow with the kid: a startling reversal of the cosmic order. I hadn't thought about him in years, and now here he was, acting in a movie, on a TV in a bus I was riding en route to watching some exorcisms.

It was jarring, seeing him again like this. Something was wrong. A border had been crossed. He didn't belong in this reality. I felt confused, bewildered, almost offended. What was that fat bastard doing on my TV in Ukraine?

I turned to Edward: 'See that enormous sweaty guy up there on the screen? I know him.'

'Oh,' said Edward, not giving a fuck. This manifestation had no connection to the world of the demonic after all.

I needed a better reaction than that. But there was no one else to tell.

7

The bus stopped at the Kafe Sofia, a roadside shack with coffee and dry sandwiches for sale. The yard in front of the entrance was decorated with little plastic ducklings and a gnome holding a spanner; but this was just a small concrete and corrugated-iron oasis in what was a vast oceanic spread of green fields. Surrounded by so much of God's bounty, Edward started to wax lyrical.

'Do you see how high the crops grow? The soil here is of such high quality that you just need to drop a seed in it and the goodness will burst forth!'

And yet in the 1930s there had been a terrible famine here, orchestrated by Stalin. Family members ate each other; millions died. And today, though nobody was starving, this rich soil could not lift the people who lived on it out of poverty. I didn't talk about that, however. I had a simpler conundrum on my mind.

'Edward,' I asked, 'where are the men?'

'What do you mean?'

'Look at the fields: they're full of women.'

He looked around. It was true: there wasn't one man at work amid the crops; only hefty middle-aged women in headscarves wielding scythes and sickles.

'Hm. Interesting point. I don't know.'

There was a table in front of the Kafe Sofia, heaped high with food and wreaths, and women in headscarves were busying themselves with preparations. Edward explained that this was for a wake. Someone had died under the blue Poltavan sky; perhaps that body was already adding its nutrients to that astonishing soil, bringing forth yet more giant strawberries that farmers would harvest for pennies.

Unless they had burnt it, in which case it wouldn't be bringing forth anything at all.

A POSTCARD FROM UKRAINE

Kremenchug

Long alleys of low-rise blocks of flats; rows of trees; old women selling vegetables by the roadside; mobile-phone shops; old buses; dust; rain. There was nothing apocalyptic here, and nothing interesting either. In fact, my final impression was essentially just that: nothing. I moved through Kremenchug in a daze, which is how outsiders usually experience the town. It is a transit zone, a place people pass through en route to where they actually need to be. For us it was no different. Edward's priest did not live in Kremenchug, but rather in a village called Salivki, that was itself located outside Komsomolsk, a town twenty kilometres from Kremenchug.

And so only the locals would ever know what happened at the local Palace of Culture the following Saturday, when, according to a poster, a 'magic healer' was going to cure the citizenry's physical ailments and solve all their psychological problems, or so he claimed.

Call it a wild hunch, but something told me he'd have his work cut out for him.

8 Temple of death

The rain was so heavy it was hard to see through the windows of the taxi. The vibrant greens and blues of Edward's beloved Poltava were now a memory only, supplanted by a dismal mush of brown and grey.

I wiped the window with my sleeve and saw a grandiose Soviet industrial monster looming ahead of us. The complex was enormous; it just went on and on and on, a sprawl of ladders and vats and pipes and wire, rusting metal and spilt grease. Fat funnels spewed poisons up into the air; tuberous pipes shat poisons into the earth. At one point it reached over our heads with a metallic arm to claw at the mud flat across the road.

It was a Shrine of Decline, a vast Temple of Death. The green Poltavan fields had been OK, but this was more my sort of landscape, scarred and bleak and sinister as it was. There had to be some good stories here – some secret, terrible beauty. I wanted to get out and walk around, or take a few pictures at least – but I knew my request would have been incomprehensible to Edward.

And anyway, the factory was already behind us, receding into the past.

9

'Where are you guys from?' asked the driver.

'Moscow,' said Edward. 'I'm a journalist and filmmaker.'

I was stunned. We hadn't agreed a price at the beginning, which was foolish enough, but now Edward had notified the driver that we were rich bastards from the hated metropolis and it was his patriotic duty to fleece us. Clearly this had not occurred to Edward, who, sitting in the passenger seat, was excitedly chatting away to the driver. But then, he enjoyed provoking the curiosity of others: it gave him an opportunity to proselytise.

'What are you making a film about, then?'

'*Otchitka.*'

'What?'

Otchitka was the Russian word for exorcism. After picking it up from Edward I had used it myself in conversations with friends in Moscow. It drew a blank every time.

Edward explained: 'The casting out of demons.'

'Oh, right,' said the guy, uneasy. 'What are you making a film about that for, then?'

'It's important. People need to know of the dangerous occult forces surrounding them. I am interviewing a lot of priests and also people possessed by demons. There is a powerful exorcist in Salivki, Father Grigory, do you know him?'

'Er . . . no,' said the driver.

After that, there was no more talking, only the din of rain battering off the roof of the car. I listened to that for a minute or so. Then the driver switched on his radio. Russian pop filled the void where the silence had been.

'You don't mind if I play music, do you?'

10

At last the rain stopped, just as a settlement of little wooden hovels and a single enormous stone house with a satellite dish on its roof came into view. The stone house dominated the scene; behind it was an area of fields.

I wasn't happy. In a few minutes I was going to have to get out and interact with people. It wasn't that Father Grigory was an exorcist; I was ready for that now. He wasn't the first person with strange and unsettling beliefs I had spoken to, after all. No, it was the village. I don't like villages. Some people idealise that sort of life, spent close to the soil, rooted deep in traditional beliefs, believing it is somehow more 'authentic' than a life spent in the city. I don't. To me village life seems impoverished, backbreaking, boring and claustrophobic. I don't want to know my neighbour and I don't want to marry my cousin. I am happy to drink my milk from a carton and not from a cow's teat. I like the asphalt and glass and concrete and sharp edges of cities. I like anonymity. I like alienation. I like the dark alleyway full of shadows and garbage, stinking of piss, containing a serial killer and his victim. Villages, though, with all those cows and tractors and plants . . . villages make me nervous.

Edward felt differently. His eyes were gleaming again. We were deep in his world, deep in the territory he had mapped out, that only he fully understood. Although the driver had been down this road many times before, he had never been down *this* road. He did not know that we were tracing a route marked on an invisible map, one that existed only in Edward's head, linking together all the exorcists he knew across Russia and Ukraine and even abroad, in America and Britain. It was marked with little flags and monuments and arrows that only he saw, the significance of which only he understood. We were following a secret, magical route now, one that linked together demons and priests and salvation.

This was where he belonged.

11

Suddenly Edward turned to me. 'Have you seen *The Passion of the Christ?*'

'No.'

He was startled. 'You didn't watch it?'

'I already knew the ending.'

'Father Grigory really looks like Jim Caviezel, the actor who played Christ.'

'I see.'

'Just wait until you see him. By the way, did I mention that Father Grigory has fourteen children?'

'*Fourteen?*'

'Well, he may have fifteen by now. It's been a year since I last saw him.'

Immediately I knew a catastrophe was looming ahead, one perhaps greater than anything Edward had managed to embroil us in up to that point. Because if he didn't think that Father Grigory's fourteen children was a fact worth mentioning until the very last minute, if it only occurred to him as an afterthought just as we were about to step across the threshold of his house, well . . . what else had he missed out?

That was the problem: Edward was so deep inside his own world that he was constantly forgetting about the other, bigger one that existed outside his head. But a lot of people were moving around in it, and they had their own plans and ideas. And though I respected him for his dedication to the cause, sometimes I wished he'd pay just a bit more attention to everything else. It would have made life easier for him, never mind me.

12

We pulled up in front of the big stone house. 'This is where Father Grigory lives,' said Edward. I immediately thought of an anti-clerical painting in the Tretyakov Gallery in Moscow, where a bloated priest dripping in gold jewellery drank tea from a bone china cup as filthy peasants pleaded with him for prayers. The house was too big. It didn't look good. But then I remembered that Father Grigory had fourteen kids, and suddenly its size seemed quite reasonable.

A man dressed in black with long black hair and a thick greying beard was standing in some mud next to the front door.

Edward turned to the taxi driver. 'Wait here a minute.' Then he climbed out. 'Father Grigory!'

Father Grigory peered towards us.

'Remember me?'

Father Grigory looked Edward up and down very slowly. I could see his eyes – beady and cunning, narrowing as he took in the young man in front of him. Edward looked like a young lawyer from the big city. I heard him talking about his film. Then, slowly, Father Grigory started nodding. Yes, he remembered.

I didn't see any close resemblance between Father Grigory and Jim Caviezel. Instead he reminded me of another painting I'd seen in the Tretyakov, this one of Tolstoy during his prophet phase, when the world famous author of *War and Peace* had turned vegetarian pacifist and decided to live a life of self-denial close to the people and the land. In the picture the bearded writer had hitched himself to a plough and was dragging it through a field on his own.*

'Is that the exorcist?' asked the taxi driver.

I nodded. I didn't want him to hear my accent and raise the price on us still higher than he was already going to. We had a limited supply of hryvna and I was already worried.

As I sat there watching Edward talk to Father Grigory I realised the priest had not known we were coming. I couldn't believe it: Edward had just turned up on his doorstep. My presentiment was correct; a catastrophe was brewing. Suddenly Edward indicated me, sitting in the cab. I climbed out of the car and smiled sheepishly. 'And I've brought Daniel, my friend from Scotland. You do have a spare room or a guest house for us, don't you?'

Father Grigory looked shocked, bewildered at this sudden ambush. In fact there was no guest house, nor was there a spare room. With fourteen kids, space was at a premium. Edward looked alarmed. But Father Grigory knew we had come a long way, and there was nowhere else to stay in the village. He invited us in.

Edward went back to get his bags and pay the taxi driver, who duly raped us.

13

Father Grigory rushed through a dark hallway and led us into a spacious dining room. Two tables had been put together, forming a big T that was pushed up against the back wall. Father Grigory sat in the centre of the T, facing the doorway. Up close I saw that he was enormous, with massive fists, huge shoulders and thick black hair that

* And for readers of a less literary bent, I can tell you exactly who he looked like: Alan Moore, author of the graphic novel *Watchmen*.

sprouted from a solid skull. A great blunt nose hung over a sprawling wiry grey beard. Like Father Miron, the priest in Pskov I had seen in Edward's film, Father Grigory looked as though he could pound me into a fertiliser, and I suspected that, unlike some priests, he might just do so, given the right amount of provocation. Belying this impression of brute force, however, were his eyes, which were clever and nimble. They darted back and forth, alighting now on me, now on Edward. However startled he had been by our sudden arrival at his house, he was rapidly assessing the situation, analysing everything.

Edward planted himself next to him and started chatting away merrily. I sat off to the side, struggling to gather myself together. Father Grigory's obvious surprise at our sudden appearance in his world had left me feeling like a trespasser; worse than that – an exposed one.

'Did you get the video I sent you, Father?' asked Edward eagerly.

Father Grigory put his hand to his chin and nodded. Edward waited eagerly for more, but the priest said nothing. He was staring at me.

'Was it interesting?' Edward prompted.

Father Grigory nodded, and stared at me. I knew he hadn't watched the film at all, or that if he had, his recollection of it was vague. He wasn't very interested in it right now, anyway, because he was thinking about something else. I knew what it was. He was thinking:

Who the fuck is this foreigner and what is he doing in my house?

14

I wasn't sure myself. We had agreed in Moscow that for the purposes of this trip I was either Edward's 'assistant' or a 'researcher into Russian Orthodoxy', both of which were sufficiently lacking in precision to be true in this context, but Edward hadn't introduced me that way. In fact, he hadn't introduced me at all, except for the few brief words in the mud outside describing me as 'a friend'. Edward had said many times that exorcists preferred to operate undercover, that they shunned attention. That being the case, I doubted Father Grigory was keen on 'friends' of people he knew vaguely just turning up at his house to hang out. Edward might as well have said: *Hi this is Daniel, he's come to stare at you freaks.*

No, I needed a better cover story than that; we needed to phrase what I was doing very carefully so Father Grigory would relax and trust me. But it was too late now: the priest was confused and suspicious. At that moment I was the strangest phenomenon in his world, demons or no demons. Edward really hadn't planned this well. In fact, he hadn't planned it at all. Worse, as I listened in to their conversation I realised I couldn't understand anything Father Grigory said: he was speaking Russian with a strong accent.

I needed to become invisible, to melt into the background and observe proceedings in silence. But how? I decided to make a mental inventory of everything around me, as if by thinking about the furniture I would somehow be able to transform myself into something as banal as a chair in Father Grigory's eyes. *Yes,* I thought, *I will enter into a spirit of oneness with the wallpaper.* Unlikely, I know, but it was a start, at least.

There wasn't much in the room though, only:

(1) A large wooden wardrobe.
(2) A big, boxy TV.
(3) A page from an illuminated manuscript hanging on the wall behind Father Grigory. Decoding a few words, I realised it was the Lord's Prayer in Ukrainian.
(4) A black and white photograph of a beautiful yet mournful young woman.
(5) A long strip of dark brown flypaper, dangling over the centre of the table. It swung back and forth like a pendulum, heavy with the carcasses of bloated black flies. Hordes of still-living flies were buzzing around it, circling the corpses of their brothers and sisters.

It wasn't working. I still stuck out like a Thai ladyboy in a crowd of Ayatollahs, I still couldn't understand the priest, I still hadn't thought of a good reason for being in his house, and he was still staring at me. I heard Edward speaking: 'Father, we have a big problem with the occult in Moscow. The kids are getting more and more involved with satanic music and culture. We need people like you to speak out against it . . .'

'Uh-huh,' said Father Grigory, still staring at me. Edward could see Father Grigory wasn't paying any attention to him, but didn't know why.

'I mean, really, Father! What is to be done? What?'

Suddenly, a flash of understanding in Edward's eyes: he had realised the source of the exorcist's distractedness.

15 A priest impersonator

'Ha-ha!' he said. 'You are staring at my friend. I know why! Don't you think Daniel looks like an Orthodox priest, Father? He's often mistaken for one!'

Eh?

'Oh really?' He looked unimpressed.

I'm in the shit, now, I thought. It was true, but I had never been mistaken for a priest by a priest, and somehow I didn't think a real priest would find the idea either amusing or convincing. But this was my chance to shift into this reality, and I leapt at it. 'Yes,' I said. 'Just two days before I was supposed to come here a man came up to me on the metro platform at Kuznetsky Most and asked for directions to a church. He thought I worked there. It's the black clothes and the beard. When he realised I was a foreigner, he was very surprised . . . the strange thing is, though, he wasn't Russian, but a Kazakh and Kazakhs are Muslims . . .'

Father Grigory said nothing. It was obvious to him that I wasn't a priest, so if someone mistook me for one he was plainly an idiot. The detail about the Muslim, meanwhile, revealed just how preposterous the idea was. I should have skipped that part.

I ran out of words, I forgot how to speak Russian. It was a crap story, anyway, and I would never have told it if Edward hadn't pushed me to. It made me even more of an impostor, claiming a resemblance to the shepherds of a faith that wasn't mine. Edward should have used a better strategy. I looked up at the flypaper. There certainly were a lot of dead flies on it.

Edward, however, seemed satisfied that he had resolved the tension in the room; or perhaps he thought I had fumbled the ball so badly it was necessary to divert attention back to him. 'So Father,' he said, 'how are we to counteract the spreading influence of occultists in Moscow? What can we *do*?'

Suddenly Father Grigory stood up. 'Excuse me,' he said. 'I must leave now. We will discuss everything later. In the meantime, please relax. We have a television.' He walked over to the TV, switching it on. Gwen Stefani appeared on-screen, singing 'Hollaback Girl'. Father Grigory walked out of the room.

Edward and I sat there watching the video. It was shit, and the song was shit. Finally, Edward got up and switched over to a Russian news programme. Bad things were happening, all over the world.

Edward returned to the table. 'So,' he said, 'don't you think Father Grigory looks like Jim Caviezel?'

A POSTCARD FROM UKRAINE

The bathroom door
There's a picture of a girl kneeling, completely naked, in an inflat-
able paddling pool, tacked to the bathroom door. She is laughing
as she pours water from a red plastic watering can over her small
breasts. The style is American soft porn of the 1970s: the camera
lens is suffused with light, and the girl has a flicked hairstyle à la
Farrah Fawcett in Charlie's Angels. *But this is hardly a house for*
porn. And this nude is not an erotic image so much as an image
of freedom, of everlasting summer sunshine, of the West in the
days of the Iron Curtain. I have been in bathrooms like this
before, seen these pictures before, so full of sad, sweet longing.
An idea for a scholarly monograph: the meaning of photos of
naked Western girls in Soviet bathrooms in the 1980s.

16 The brood

I am not against children as a concept, but the noise and chaos they generate bothers me. Now I was in a home where there were fourteen units of human youth and no sooner had Father Grigory left than they started to appear, over by the doorway. One, two, three, four . . . boys, girls, another whose gender I couldn't determine . . . each of them bigger than the last one, as if they had all popped out of the same matrioshka doll.

They were just a few metres away, studying me, waiting for something. I eyed them uneasily. *Any minute now*, I thought, *they'll nail me to a board, poke my eyes out and then run around in the yard outside holding me aloft, before shitting in my mouth and stoning me to death* . . . For as anyone who reads the papers knows, children these days do that sort of thing. And who could hope to contain the life force of so many kids? With Father Grigory gone, I was pretty sure the scenario was going to degenerate rapidly into a *Lord of the Flies* style affair, and I had a bad feeling I was Piggy.

A toddler was the first to break the invisible barrier and charge forward. He was a little man with a head like a brick, and he was wearing a grubby one-piece romper suit with some dirt on it. He stopped his forward momentum by whacking his solid skull against my shin. He didn't cry, however: he was made of sterner stuff than that. He steadied himself by gripping my trouser leg, extended his other claw upwards, opened his mouth wide and said:

'*Auhhh . . . auuahahahhhh!!!*'

i.e.

'*Fooood . . . fooood . . .*'

I knew how he felt. I hadn't eaten for hours and I was getting pretty hungry myself. But whereas I could eat and be satisfied, I had a feeling from the sight of this solid little chunk of humanity that he could eat and eat and eat and never be full. After him came another toddler, a girl this time, with a head of thick black curls. She started crying for no reason. Some boys followed, dirty, grubby little urchins, who looked like they belonged in Fagin's gang, then a girl of about eleven, meek and retiring, yet curious. Finally there were seven or eight children circling around me, staring. The violence was about to start.

Edward tried to make conversation, but the kids ignored him. They were transfixed, hypnotised by the strange shadowy foreign manifestation occurring in the dining room. I was a phenomenon. My chances of merging into the furniture and attaining invisibility were slimmer than ever.

Suddenly, however, Father Grigory's wife limped into the room. Matushka ('little mother') was heavily pregnant. Clearly she and Father Grigory had got cracking on number fifteen almost immediately after the solid chunk of boy clutching at my trouser leg had entered the world. The current balance was seven boys and seven girls: soon that harmony would be disrupted.

It was hard for Matushka to heave that body forward. Her ankles were thick; angry-looking veins throbbed in her calves. Her eyes bulged slightly too, as if a pressure from within was pushing them outward, the new life growing within her bursting to escape. She addressed her children:

'Get the fuck oot ae it, ya wee shites, and stop bothering your faither's guests.'

Well, not quite, but you get the idea. The kids melted away towards the door and then vanished completely. Matushka was obviously not someone you disobeyed.

'Sorry about that,' she said.

Suddenly two young adults entered the room. Matushka directed them as they set out cups for Edward and me, and poured tea. Then she withdrew, leaving us with Rosa and Roma, whom I presumed were the oldest members of the brood.*

17

Rosa had just left school. She had pale eyes and rosy cheeks, and was built like a buxom collective farm girl in a Soviet mosaic. Rosa could have provoked sinful thoughts in a rock, but she wasn't aware of this. Edward liked her, but she didn't pick up on that either. Roma meanwhile had a shaved, square head, and muscles like wire wrapped around iron. Both of them looked like they could easily pop out another fourteen kids each, and without breaking too much of a sweat about it, either.

'So,' said Roma, 'what do you think of Ukraine?'

'Er . . . it's very beautiful,' I said.

'No, it isn't,' he said, wagging his finger at me. 'Let me tell you something – Ukraine is the most corrupt country in world.'

'Really?'

'Yes.'

'More corrupt than Russia?'

He shrugged. He hadn't thought about that. It didn't matter anyway; the corruption in Ukraine was what he had to live with.

'Even since Yuschenko? Nothing's changed?' asked Edward.

Roma waved dismissively. 'Yulia, Viktor, the Orange Revolution . . . who cares? What does it mean? Nothing has changed. Nothing will change. Politicians are politicians. They're all crooked, they're all out for themselves. They don't care about the people.'

'I voted for Yanukovych,' added Rosa with a giggle.

The conversation died, and we sat in awkward silence for a moment. I thought about something Dmitri the photographer had said to me on the steps outside the Digger's flat as he regaled me with tales of his travels around Russia. 'When you go to a village,' he said, 'you are a messenger from the outside world. You must bring stories, for that is what they are waiting for. Give them interesting information, things they do not know. They are hungry for it. If you do that, then you will make friends and all will be well.'

---

* Later I learned that Roma had married Rosa's elder sister, with whom he had produced Father Grigory's first grandchild, who was older than at least one of his uncles.

Yes, I thought, *that made sense. That's what I need to do here . . .*
Give these kids some stories. They were children of a village priest. I
had travelled, they had not. If I told some good stories I would be
accepted, and they'd stop staring at me. I'd be closer to becoming
invisible, to becoming the observer, rather than the observed.

'Where are you from?' asked Roma.

'Scotland,' I said. 'But I live in Russia.'

Roma nodded. 'I went to Russia once. The trees are so big there! I
couldn't believe my eyes.'

'The trees are bigger here!' said Edward.

'Eh?'

'Your black soil, it's much better than the soil in Moscow! It makes
the trees bigger!'

Roma shrugged. 'I don't know. The trees I saw in Russia were pretty
big. Bigger than the ones around here.'

Rosa shook her head. 'I thought the trees in Moscow were smaller
than ours.'

'Do you think so?' said Roma.

Rosa nodded.

'Yes,' said Edward. 'Rosa – it's Rosa, isn't it? Rosa's right. It's your
black soil. There are no apples greener than the apples that grow in
Ukraine! And your Poltavan strawberries, why they're the size of a
human fist! God has really blessed this land!'

Roma sat there nodding, but this wasn't what he wanted to discuss.
He had started with a question about Scotland and now he was listening to a lecture from a foreigner on the beauty of Ukraine. I understood how he felt. I don't like it when foreigners who have visited
Edinburgh castle and perhaps climbed a hill north of Perth wax lyrical
to me about Scotland. They know nothing, and seek to know nothing,
of pre-teens overdosing on heroin in Glasgow, of the grinding boredom of life in dreary scab-holes such as my native Dunfermline, or of
the irritation you feel when you're a teenager and a Gaelic-language
cookery show takes the place of the film with tits in it that's being
shown in the rest of the UK. Good for them: they are under no obligation to investigate that side of Scottish life. But there are few things
harder to stomach than a tourist explaining your own home to you:
other than cancer, rape, murder, genocide and anything else that actually matters, of course.

Roma waited for Edward to stop, then tried again:

'What religion are people in Scotland?'

I wanted to tell him that people didn't believe in anything much, but I knew he wouldn't accept the answer. He wanted a creed.

'Christian,' I said.

'Really? I heard they were . . . *Protestant*.'

The word escaped into the air like a puff of the gas used to kill the *Nord Ost* hostage takers. This was what Edward feared. Roma might as well have suggested I was a paedophile from a nation of paedophiles and he was about to reach for his pitchfork. Edward had to step in before the fact that there was an undesirable in the living room reached the ears of the exorcist: 'Yes, well,' he said nervously, 'the Scots are Protestants, but there are different sorts of Protestants don't you know . . . there are some Protestants who are practically Orthodox – take Daniel, for example, doesn't he look like an Orthodox priest? He's often mistaken for one you know . . .'

Edward kept going, tangling Roma up in definitions and redefinitions. Roma was irritated: he knew this was smoke and mirrors but was too polite to say so. The tone of the question had not been hostile, just curious. Edward's protestations to the contrary were too much, however, and now Father Grigory's son knew that something was amiss. He dropped out of the conversation altogether. Rosa stepped in with a question for me, but all I could catch in the mix of Russian and Ukrainian was this:

'You don't understand me, do you?'

I shrugged. I tried to say it was her accent, but I couldn't even find the words for that. My Russian, far from perfect at the best of times, had abandoned me completely. My opportunity to bring news from the outside world had passed.

I was completely isolated now, and entirely dependent on Edward. That was not reassuring. He was too deep in his own reality for it to occur to him that I might need help with translations in another one, or that he really ought to explain what we were doing in this family's house. He hadn't done that yet. I knew he was here to get more footage for his film, but no one else seemed to. So I was left on the outside looking in, watching as he interacted with Roma and Rosa.

From where I sat, he looked like some know-it-all from the metropolis: well meaning, but at once way too clever and way too naïve. An expert on the demonic he might have been, but I didn't think he understood life in a Ukrainian village at all, and Roma and Rosa knew it. I couldn't imagine how he was going to earn the trust of these people.

He may have understood all their words, but he was on the outside, too. He just didn't know it.

18

It was time for dinner. Father Grigory returned, said grace and then took his place in the centre of the T, with Matushka on one side and Edward on the other. Roma and Rosa stayed at the table, but none of the other children were permitted to sit with us. I was still out on the edge, next to a little bald guy who introduced himself as Viktor. He sounded and looked like Peter Lorre, the child murderer in Fritz Lang's *M*. He wasn't a member of the family, but some sort of assistant to Father Grigory.

The food was piled high in front of us, leading Edward to launch into another paean to Ukraine's black soil. Father Grigory wasn't saying much. Every now and then he'd grunt, and take another bite out of a piece of bread. Matushka had an ironic glint in her eye, as though she was enjoying Edward's performance and her husband's responses as some sort of weird spectacle. As for me, I didn't have much of an appetite. The world was swimming around me; I still hadn't found my place in it.

My eyes returned to the portrait of the mournful girl on the dresser. She had such smooth skin, and such sad, thoughtful eyes: she really was beautiful. I even felt I recognised her, though that was impossible. The picture was a sepia-tinted relic of a different epoch, the girl, perhaps, a pre-revolutionary progenitor of Father Grigory. But then, suddenly, I realised that the subject of the portrait was in fact Matushka before fourteen kids had clawed their way out of her body. I was stunned.

And then Viktor, who had been studying me out of the corner of his eye, started talking. He spoke Russian without a Ukrainian accent. I understood him perfectly. But that was the problem: I felt that he was somehow dangerous, that he wanted to grill me, to get to the bottom of what Edward and I were doing in the Father's house. He was not constrained by rules of hospitality, and nor was Edward there to deflect intrusive questions.

'Eat the chicken, it is good,' he said. I picked up a chicken leg from the plate, bit off a chunk, and chewed slowly. It was good. But I knew he was just breaking the ice, that he was working his way towards an interrogation. Viktor watched me eat. Once I had swallowed, he continued:

'Eat the soup, it is good.'

I slurped a little soup. Viktor nodded, approving. Then: 'Suck on the hard boiled sweets, they are most delicious.'

And now, having encouraged me to eat and thus established himself as a kind soul with my best interests at heart, he seized his moment. He leaned close, and asked very quietly:

'What are you doing here?'

Not: *What do you do?*

Or: *Who are you?*

But: *What are you doing here?*

I had known the answer; now I didn't. We weren't filming exorcisms or conducting interviews. We were just squatting in a village priest's house, eating his food, abusing his hospitality. Later we might get round to stealing some golden candlesticks and outraging his daughter, if we felt like it. I had no idea how to reply. And so, although I understood him perfectly, I said:

'Sorry, I don't speak Russian.'

He tried again, rephrasing the question, but I remained resolutely dense. Sometimes it's handy, being able to play the dumb foreigner like that. After a few more stabs at interrogating the pale-faced sphinx sitting next to him, Viktor eventually gave up in frustration.

19 Sacrilege

Father Grigory stood up; this signified that the meal was over. Everyone left their plates and followed as he walked to the back of the room, turning to face the crucifix hanging on the wall. He closed his eyes and began intoning a prayer in a high-pitched sing-song voice, crossing himself as he did so. Everyone in the room followed suit.

Everyone except me, that is. I had gone through the motions during the pre-dinner grace, but I just didn't feel like doing it this time. What was this after-dinner prayer? I'd never heard of the likes. And suddenly, just like that, I decided I'd had enough. I wasn't Orthodox, and I wasn't going to play along with Edward's mystifications. They weren't helping me, and I thought he was doing harm to himself and his film with them. If I was going to get anywhere with these people I would have to be honest: I was an alien, interested in ways of living and seeing that were unlike mine. That was all there was to it, and put like that, it didn't sound so bad. If they didn't like it, then I'd find a driver in the village to take me back to Kremenchug and I'd stay in a hotel there. Maybe I'd go and see the magic man who was going to cure all the sick people in town at the Palace of Culture. That would be interesting. As for the post-dinner grace, surely it was more respectful *not* to mimic an act that others held sacred, than to do it insincerely, in some feeble effort at leading them to believe I was 'one of them'.

Well, just in case you ever find yourself in a similar position in an exorcist's house, let me tell you that the answer to that one is in fact a resounding *no*. The prayer finished and when I looked up from my shoes I saw that everyone was staring at me, eyelids peeled back as far as they would go, jaws hanging down at their ankles. Even Edward looked shocked, as though I had suddenly yelped out a HAIL SATAN, *Rosemary's Baby* style. For the first time since I had met him he was lost for words. I knew he wasn't going to jump in there and conceal my crime under his customary fog of eloquence. And as for Father Grigory . . . well, that was anger I saw in his eyes. I had finally crossed 'the line'.

The air in the room felt dangerously unstable. Any minute now Father Grigory was going to grab me by the collar and throw me out into the plentiful supply of Ukrainian mud that surrounded his house. I had to think of some way to redeem myself, and fast. I searched through my vocabulary for some eloquent explanation, but I still couldn't speak Russian. All I could muster were single words: *Yes . . . no . . . potato . . . trousers . . . penis . . .* no, none of those were going to suffice. I needed a phrase, I needed something grammatical. Hm. Maybe: *Izvinitye – ya mudak.** No, that wasn't going to cut it. Come on, damn it, I needed something fast.

'Er . . . I'm tired,' I said.

Nobody spoke. Father Grigory continued to stare, though the anger in his eyes dimmed a little, and instead there was just that confusion again, that complete bafflement, that *Who the hell are you and why are you in my house?* he had been fixing on me ever since our arrival.

Then suddenly he grinned. He pointed at his arm. There was a white

* 'Sorry – I'm a cunt.'

patch on his black robes, where his sweat had crystallised.

'See this salt?' he said.

'Yes,' I said.

'It's to preserve my meat.'

'I'm sorry?'

'It's to preserve my meat! HAHAHAHAHAHAHA!'

Father Grigory may have been an exorcist, but he was a man also, and more than that, he was a man who understood people. He could see the weariness in my eyes, and understood that I wasn't there to ridicule him or insult his beliefs. So he had reached out to me with a joke; and once he started laughing, everyone else laughed. Viktor laughed. Matushka laughed. Edward laughed. Rosa and Roma laughed. Yes, everything was all right now. I wasn't a wicked heathen after all. Well, a heathen maybe, but not wicked . . .

'Come on,' said Father Grigory, taking me by the arm. 'I'll introduce you to my pet pig.'

20 Marilyn

Father Grigory led me outside, to the kitchen garden behind his house. Twilight was setting in, and great black flies were buzzing about in the approaching darkness. These were Ukrainian flies, and had sprouted from the rich waste that fed the black, black soil of their motherland: they feared no human. They didn't even try to fly out of my way as I walked forward. Walk into them and they bounced right back at you, *buzz, buzz*. The mud underfoot meanwhile was thick enough to suck your shoe off, and the stench of manure hung in the air. Somewhere in a marsh not too far off a squad of frogs were belching: it was a real symphony of the senses out there. *Ah, nature, my lovely, my sweet . . .*

'Here's the pig!' said Father Grigory.

I peered into the small concrete enclosure and saw a fat, blotchy, black and pink sow, standing in profile and doing what pigs do: snuffling away amid a pile of mud and straw.

'Her name is Marilyn,' he said.

Marilyn's black eye peeped nervously back at me, then looked away, then looked back at me again – before she finally dug her snout into the straw and concentrated on the mud. I think she was worried we had come to kill her and believed that if she just looked away and acted dumb, then we wouldn't notice her. I gazed at Marilyn's firm haunches for a few seconds, meanwhile swatting away the enormous black flies dive-bombing my face. Then Father Grigory said something that set Edward laughing.

'Did you understand?' he asked.

'No.'

'Sometimes the Father takes Marilyn for a walk through the streets of the village!'

Father Grigory was staring at me, nodding, beaming from ear to ear. An eccentricity like that was worthy of some response and he knew it. I tried to think of a follow-up question, but my mind was still functioning poorly. 'Good . . .' I said. 'Good.' He was hoping for more, but eventually gave up and started guiding me around the garden, showing me various green things sprouting out of the dirt, and some chickens. Father Grigory explained that all this was to feed his family, but now that he had fourteen kids and another one due any moment, he needed more land. There was a stretch of mud behind his enclosure that reached to the foggy horizon; he intended to annex that to his garden. It wasn't going to be easy, however, because the neighbours were jealous of his big house, his animals, and his crops, and so he expected opposition. Not all the villagers were religious; not all respected his clerical position. That hint at turmoil and dissension within his community hung in the air for a moment, but then he moved on, striding through the mud, his black robes billowing out behind him. At no point did he dip them in the filth at his feet.

The final point on our tour was another enclosure, but this one had a door, which was closed. Father Grigory pulled it open and I saw a pair of calves with beautiful, soulful, black eyes, standing in the cold, waiting patiently to become meat. The startling thing, though, was that there was a grubby, skinny boy of about nine or ten in there with them, perched on a wooden beam set above a pile of dung, clinging to the neck of one of the young cows as though it was his baby sister. He was the most ragged of all Father Grigory's urchins so far. There was fear, and an almost feral look in his eye.

Father Grigory registered the presence of his son in the shed, but immediately looked away. Strangely, he acted as though he hadn't seen the boy. 'So these are the cows . . .' he said. I stared at them for a few seconds, trapped in their dark little hovel. The boy caressed the neck of the one he was holding. 'Hello,' said Edward, cheerily. The boy did not respond. Then, realising there was nothing else to say about two

127

calves slated for the executioner's knife, Father Grigory closed the door of the enclosure again, leaving the boy in the dark with them.

The tour was over.

21

A small crowd of men and women were standing in the driveway of the house in the gathering twilight. Father Grigory greeted them warmly and then disappeared indoors. Edward told me they had come for a preliminary exorcism before the main one tomorrow.

'So what should I do?'

'Attend. Why not?'

'No,' I said. 'I don't belong here. I don't mind going to Father Grigory's church . . . I can stand at the back and be discreet, but this *really* feels like I'm intruding.'

'Come, come . . .' Edward laughed; he thought I was being ridiculous.

'I'm serious.'

'Tell you what, let me talk to Father Grigory and see what he says. Besides, I need to ask about the possibility of conducting an interview with him after the prayers. I should probably raise the issue and let him think about it before it gets too late, what do you think?'

'That's a good idea.'

And with that, Edward disappeared indoors, leaving me alone amid the gathering crowd.

22

Slowly, one by one, more villagers arrived. The men were big, big guys, champion eaters of pig fat (a delicacy in Ukraine), with shaved, square heads and black leather jackets; their women wore headscarves and long coats. They all knew each other, and were shaking hands, and laughing. It was a strangely convivial atmosphere for a pre-exorcism ceremony. I stuck close to the wall, staring into space, trying hard not to get involved in a conversation.

Never before had I felt like such a useless soft-palmed weakling. Standing there, I tried to remember the last time I had earned an honest day's wage from my labour. The best I could come up with was five days in 1993 when I creosoted a fence in Dalgety Bay, a suburb of Dunfermline, for fifty quid a day. I hadn't done a very good job of it though, splashing the creosote on some fancy white tiles the home-owner had installed just days before. Also, because I was a painfully slow worker, the job took me five days instead of the expected three. I got paid the extra, but I wasn't invited back when the fence was redone two years later.

In fact, I thought, *what use am I really?* If civilisation were to collapse tomorrow, these people would survive. They would still know how to grow crops and how to preserve them. They would know how to build houses out of wood, and how to purify river water. They could start a fire using sticks. They could kill invaders from neighbouring villages using boulders, and hang them from trees and stick forks up their arses. They'd be fine. In fact, they had already lived through the collapse of the USSR, the bankruptcy of their nation, and more hardship than most people in the West could even imagine: they had proven their resilience. But what about me? What would I do?

I gazed deep into my soul, looking for some kind of useful, elementary human skill I had picked up in my life up to this point:

Hm.

Maybe I'd missed it. I looked again.

Nope. Nothing there.

Eventually I decided that I could be a wandering bard, as in days of old, earning food and board with my song. But I was reaching: I'm not much of a singer and I can't play the lute either. And looking at these villagers, I doubted if they'd appreciate my style. They'd probably lob rocks at me.

There was one positive development, though. I had been in the village long enough to grow attuned to its atmosphere. I could feel its dirt on me, under my fingernails, on my skin and in my beard. This dirt was good. It helped me re-establish contact with my powers of invisibility. My face too had relaxed into its customary blank, unfriendly, unreadable expression. Nobody was taking any special notice of me. In fact, one guy came up, explained that he was new at these meetings and asked *me* something about Father Grigory. I shrugged; he said something else, obviously a joke, and I laughed. We shook hands and he walked off.

So: in a post-apocalyptic world ruled by talking apes I'd be worse than useless. But nobody here knew that. I had 'em fooled. I was on the inside now. The challenge was to stay there.

23

By the time Edward returned Father Grigory had already begun the evening ritual, so my participation was now a foregone conclusion. The exorcist was standing in the middle of the crowd of villagers, chanting the prayer in his high, sing-song voice. I bowed my head, but not too low, because I needed to see what was going on. No one noticed that I was taking my cues from my neighbour and crossing myself a second after he did, because almost all the villagers were doing the same, in a game of gesticulatory Chinese whispers that led back ultimately to the swift arm and hand movements of Father Grigory.

At first I thought that this rampant copying was down to the fact that the people in Salivki were strangers to their ancestral religion, still relearning its customs and habits after years of Soviet oppression. But fifteen years is quite long enough to pick up a few hand manoeuvres and chants, so perhaps the copying I saw has always been a feature of prayers in the Russian Church. There are thousands of pages in the Orthodox creed, after all – who has time to read all that? Better to just copy the priest, do what he says, and hope for the best. The language of the prayer, Old Slavonic, was almost as alien to them as it was to me. And so we were all, foreigner and local alike, united in our incomprehension of the sacred mysteries, our ignorance of the rite. Only two stood outside this communion of half-understanding: Viktor, Father Grigory's assistant, who had his eyes closed, but knew exactly when to echo his priest and when to cross himself; and Edward, who was standing next to me, fluidly following the ritual with a minimum of hesitation.

I waited for some of the strange phenomena from Edward's footage to begin. But nothing was happening. There were no sudden spastic movements; there was no cursing, no man with smoke pouring from his body. In fact, the atmosphere was very peaceful. The woman next to me – a peroxide blonde in her thirties – was weeping, but hers was ordinary pain – illness, or perhaps her husband was a drunkard, or maybe she had problems with her children. I wondered if Edward, in his hunger to see demons everywhere, had misunderstood Father Grigory's explanation of the prayer.

Once it was concluded, Father Grigory anointed the congregation with holy water. He had adapted a lip salve for the purpose, replacing the balm in the tube with water. This was more efficient: he didn't need to bother with splashing it on people, or repeatedly dip his finger in some kind of chalice. One by one he went through the crowd, drawing the shape of the cross on their heads with the lip salve. Finally he came to me, and hesitated. I stepped back to indicate that it wasn't necessary. I wasn't baptised in his church; I knew I was not entitled to these ministrations. But Father Grigory laughed, shrugged as if to say *Why not?* And then leaned forward, drawing the sign of the cross on my forehead.

I was anointed.

24 Vanishing act

Once the prayer was over, Father Grigory devoted his attention to individual members of the crowd. Some were laughing and joking with him; others were tearful and seeking reassurance. Patiently and with good humour he ministered to them all, even though it was darkening rapidly. The rising moon had brought with it a nocturnal chill that cut to the bone with wintry violence. I couldn't see anything clearly any more, and became conscious again of the chorus of frogs, and the mad flight of the fat black flies, crashing against me. Suddenly Viktor emerged silently out of the gloom to stand by my side: 'Was that interesting for you?' he asked.

'Very,' I said.

'Father Grigory is a good man, he is a good priest.'

'I can see that,' I said. 'The people really respect him.' If he had noticed the miraculous appearance of Russian language skills when earlier I'd claimed to have none, he made no comment.

'He gives everything to them,' said Viktor. 'He does not hold back, or stand aloof.'

I nodded. We stood there for a few moments, watching Father Grigory's massive silhouette in the dusk. He was leaning down to listen to the complaints of the woman who had been weeping next to me during the prayer.

'Where are you from?' I asked.

'Do you know Krasnodar? It is in the south of Russia, a warm place. That is where I was born. But I moved to Kiev many, many years ago. Decades ago, in fact. I forget that I am now old.' He laughed. 'I had many jobs during the Soviet time. First I was a journalist working for newspapers, then I worked in TV. I did it for many years, but I grew tired of that life. Who needs it? What does it mean, "a career"? What is the point of that nonsense? And so I came out here. Now I am studying in the seminary and I assist Father Grigory.'

I liked the simplicity and directness with which he dismissed all that striving after graven idols: as if upon waking up one day he had realised his life was dedicated to bullshit, and had stepped out of the race, just like that. But this was not some grating bourgeois tosh about leaving a career in the city and nipping off to Provence in search of vintage wine to drink, quaintly truculent peasants to condescend towards and juicy, dark-eyed farm girls to grope. No: this was hardcore. Viktor was abandoning his ego, his position in society, and dedicating himself to a life of discipleship and helping the weak.

I find living a bit of a pain in the arse myself at times, and so his words were poetry to me. Who is not tempted to turn his back on all that striving and aspiring and struggling and just vanish? I was jealous. But of course, what Viktor had vanished to was a life of unremitting toil, hardship and poverty, spent in harsh conditions. I didn't think I had it in me. And I didn't have his ascetic, mediaeval faith to help me endure it either. When I looked at the land I saw mud, flies, dirt, tedium. When he looked at it he saw the same stuff, but he knew also that it was part of a cosmic order, and that it was part of a larger, sacred soil that had produced Orthodox saints and holy men. I could never share in that.

Suddenly Edward appeared, towering over us: 'Yes, you made the right decision, Viktor. It's great out here. So beautiful.'

There it was again; Edward's postcard Ukraine, his rural idyll. But that wasn't what Viktor had been talking about at all. He shrugged. 'It's beautiful everywhere.'

'Yes, but . . . it's so *green* here.'

'It's green everywhere.'

Edward laughed, confused. He didn't know what to say. Viktor looked at me, smiling enigmatically. He knew that I understood.

25 *Nema*

After about twenty minutes the crowd dispersed. Viktor was the last to leave, going home to his wife. As soon as he was gone, Edward stopped Father Grigory on the step of the house and asked if there was time for an interview –

Nema, came the reply.

It was the one Ukrainian word I managed to learn during my stay in Poltava. Later I learned that it means 'there isn't' or 'there aren't'. But in the house it seemed to function well as a general negative. I heard it frequently, as Matushka addressed the children, or as Father Grigory responded to one of Edward's proposals. For example, later that evening we discovered that Rosa, the eldest daughter, had a bad cough, a consequence, she thought, of the fumes spewing from the death factory we had passed on the way into the village. Edward offered to put her up at his dacha, which he described as an astonishingly clean ecological paradise in the north of Russia. As Rosa put it: Thank you, but there's no way my father would let me stay on my own with a member of the male sex. And sure enough, Father Grigory had replied with one word: *Nema*. Well, actually first he stared at Edward in total disbelief, as though he'd just been asked if it would be OK for Edward to sell Rosa to some Chinese pimps who'd cut her arms and legs off, lock her in a box and rent her out to enthusiasts for stumpy women. Edward, unfazed, responded by suggesting it again, and then tossing in another request for an interview. *Nema*, came the response to both questions.

Written in English *nema* is *amen* spelt backwards. And so for me, at least, it gave Father Grigory's negatives an even stronger force. As in: absolutely never, young man.

Edward, however, was not troubled by any such association. And this was no doubt a good thing, if he was ever to get his film made.

VI

Exorcism on a Scale of One to Ten

1

Father Grigory was hunched over the wheel of his rusty old orange Lada Zhiguli; Edward was sitting beside him in the passenger seat, chatting away. I was in the back, rotten and filthy as a corpse in a ditch, struggling to wake up.

It had been a rough night. I was obliged to make my bed on a tiny two-seater sofa in the living room, and what sleep I managed to grab was spent being devoured from the inside by a threshing mess of parasites that had entered my system through the milk fresh from the cow's teat I had consumed just before bedtime. I had never drunk 'natural' milk before and doubted my system was up to processing chemicals the way God manufactured them. I am a creature of the industrial world: my organs prefer to interact with strings of molecules that have been abused by men in white coats. I drank it anyway.

Then, just as the parasites finished gnawing their way through my stomach lining, exploding onto the floor in a rush of blood, I felt a pain in my cheek and woke up to the sensation of a mosquito draining my life's fluid through the sharp proboscis it had inserted into my cheek. I tried to swat it away, but the pathways in my brain were slow to engage and I couldn't transmit a message to the appropriate limb. By the time I succeeded the creature was already engorged, and the first thing I saw that morning was the mosquito, its gut big as a golf ball, flying away, dizzy – drunk with my blood. Slowly the world crystallised around me, the unfamiliar surroundings became familiar and I remembered where I was. One word formed in my skull, like a fungus in a Petri dish:

Fuck.

Now I was staring at the back of the exorcist's head, trying to make sense of its place in this world: for Father Grigory was not only too big for the vehicle, but the whole reality it represented. The Zhiguli had trundled off a production line in Tolyatti in the 1980s, back when the Soviet Union was in its final, most toothless stage. It was a car for middle-class Soviet families, for mid-ranking Communist Party members, for managers at big factories producing substandard goods that were both ugly and uncomfortable. No one had ever intended it to carry a huge, bearded, pig farmer in black robes, who had fourteen kids and drove out evil spirits on Wednesday afternoons. And yet it was doing the job perfectly. We drove past the Death Factory, diabolical in the morning sun, and then entered Komsomolsk, where Father Grigory's church was located.

A POSTCARD FROM UKRAINE

The Komsomolsk real-estate explosion
Komsomolsk consists mainly of dirt, dust and decaying concrete, though some flesh has been incorporated into the mix also. Throughout the day humans can be seen standing around in abandoned yards and by the side of the road, willing their own brains to explode. The earth around them is crowned with fine white crystals: salt is choking the soil, killing off anything stupid enough to try and grow there. And yet even here, in such unpromising conditions, a mini real-estate boom is under way. A two-room apartment in an old Soviet block now costs $12,000 – a fortune by local standards. But who is buying? Those who have jobs work mostly at the Death Factory; and it would take a lot of labour at the lathe to amass that sort of money. Years would pass. The day you moved in, your body, aged and brittle, would be just strong enough to manoeuvre itself to the window, direct its eyes at the sorrowing world beyond the glass, suck a little poisoned air into cracked-leather lungs, and expire.

2 The secret lives of priests

Many Russian Orthodox priests are relative newcomers to their own religion, having followed radically different career paths in their communist youth. I had met one priest who was a former (Jewish) professor of

135

microbiology and another who had enjoyed a brief career as rock star during *perestroika*. Father Grigory's shift had been larger than most, meanwhile: he wasn't just a priest, but one that did battle with demons. Whatever he had been in his old life, this was a colossal leap. I asked Edward if he knew any details about Father Grigory's earlier incarnation.

'What do you mean?'

I thought the question was obvious enough.

'What did he do before he was a priest?'

'How would I know?' He laughed and turned away.

He wasn't even curious. And yet this was precisely the kind of detail I wanted to know, and had come in search of. It's what I would have included if I were making a documentary on exorcism: how the priest had entered this world of demons, and the psychological impact on an individual of waging war against the forces of Lucifer. It would provide people with a way into the story. It would draw them closer; enable them to identify, even, with the bearded, remote figures they saw on-screen. But then Edward didn't want you to identify with the humanity of the exorcists. Perhaps it was even wrong to think of them in that way, as men, outside their divinely ordained role.

His film was going to be a collection of testimonies from the possessed and priests on the effectiveness of exorcism as a tool for dealing with the demonic. It was almost utilitarian. He wanted to make you believe in devils, and then in Christ. It was a propaganda film intended to produce converts. The personal details of priests were trivial in Edward's eyes.

Well, that was his film, not mine. I persevered: 'Will you ask him?'

Edward had been discussing the occult. The sudden change in theme led Father Grigory to grow animated. He had been an electrician working in the Death Factory at Komsomolsk. In late *perestroika* he felt the calling to enter the Church, and had studied for several years in the early 1990s, including a stint in the seminary in Moscow. Then he returned to his home region to take charge of the cathedral.

'But why did you get involved in exorcism?' I asked.

But at that point his mobile rang. The ring tone was a Russian pop jingle, a track by a collective of oligarchs' girlfriends who usually performed in their underwear. He fished it out from under his robes. By the time he had taken the call the church was coming into view and the question was gone, a seed that had fallen on salinated soil.

Nothing would grow there.

3

The St Nicholas Cathedral, dazzling in the sun, stood on a hill across a stream that divided it from the industrial ruin of Komsomolsk. It was blue and white, set amid trees and, according to Edward, displayed clear signs of the influence of Polish baroque.* The church looked magical, as though the water separated not just two sides of the town but a whole other set of dichotomies besides – the material and the spiritual, the ugly and the beautiful, the sacred and the profane, the miraculous and the banal.

The car pulled up in front of the church gates. A crowd was waiting for Father Grigory; they greeted him with warmth. He wound down his window. A big lad, built like a butcher, with a shaven head called out: 'Hey, Father Grigory, when are you going to get a haircut?'

Father Grigory laughed. 'Never! I trimmed my beard once but I was scared of my own reflection.' He paused. 'Is Tatiana here?' He asked.

'She's over there.' The big lad indicated a frail woman in her thirties. I could make out a headscarf, narrow shoulders: that was all.

Father Grigory turned round.

'Watch this!' he said, grinning. He leaned out the window, cupped his hand to his mouth and started shouting: 'Tatiana! Tatiana!'

Suddenly the woman's legs gave way under her and she collapsed. Father Grigory turned back to me, his eyes gleaming.

'She's really badly tormented by her demon. It used to be that when I said her name she'd dance uncontrollably. Now she faints.' He laughed.

'She comes every day.'

4

Father Grigory went ahead into the cathedral while Edward and I stayed in the courtyard with the congregation. After about ten minutes a door in the back of the cathedral opened and the crowd began to shuffle up some steps that led to a dark, narrow corridor. I saw Father Grigory through grimy glass, standing tall and strong between the bare walls of an office that contained only a wooden table and one or two chairs. It was dark, dingy and cavernous in there. But it looked

* Poltava has over the centuries been held by Lithuanians and Poles as well as Russians and Ukrainians and was the site of a famous battle between the Russian Empire and the forces of the king of Sweden.

positively sunny compared to the atmosphere in the corridor. A queue was already forming in front of the door, a line of wailing women, all of them wearing different expressions of agony on their faces: so much suffering, and yet the day had only just begun.

I followed Edward up some narrow stairs, tumbling forward at the top through a small door into the main hall of the cathedral. There was room enough for a few hundred faithful in there, and the floor was split up so different services could take place simultaneously in different parts of the building. There were no chairs, of course, and the walls were decorated with murals, frescoes and icons full of meanings I didn't understand. But that was normal. There was, however, something murky and obscure about the cathedral's interior. The windows were small and had been placed way up on high, close to the ceiling. And what light that did manage to slip through the grubby glass stayed up there, as if reluctant to touch the soiled ground. The few stray rays that did approach served only to illuminate the dust, spinning in the air around us.

Slowly, slowly this barn of God began to fill up with multiple bodies, belonging to the lame and the halt, the sinful and the righteous, the pious and the unctuous – all the citizens of Komsomolsk who were troubled enough by the state of their immortal souls to attend church on a Wednesday afternoon. I found a space at the back where I felt relatively invisible and stood there holding Edward's camera tripod (though Father Grigory had given Edward a *nema* as far as filming the service was concerned, he was still hoping to get an interview on the church grounds later). Some of the parishioners would glance at me, but they didn't stare: they had seen me arriving in the car with Father Grigory so I was OK. I saw Viktor, nodded. He smiled and nodded back. I was still on good terms with Father Grigory's right-hand man. That helped me to relax.

A monk, pale and emaciated, was drifting about the cathedral, sliding from pillar to pillar, clinging to its darkest spaces. He was wearing long black robes, and had a wispy beard. His face was inscribed with the haunted look that comes from a life of excessive solitude and silence, as though he had stared into his own inner darkness several times too often. He was pale, gaunt, conspiratorial. Was he a spy, sent by the bishop to observe Father Grigory's exorcism, to see if anything untoward was taking place? No one else seemed to have noticed him, only me. I thought about warning Viktor, or at least asking him if he knew who the monk was.

In the end, I didn't. It was just too enjoyable, feeling my own paranoia bleeding into Edward's and Father Grigory's and Viktor's. I felt less isolated in the landscape: I had a stake in it now. And meanwhile the monk drifted, drifted, eyes darting to the left, then to the right. Speaking to no one, seen by no one: but studying all.

Suddenly Father Grigory entered the hall. He stood facing the iconostasis, his back to the congregation. A crowd formed around him. Then, without any explanation or a word of introduction, he started intoning a prayer.

Edward, who had been lighting a candle in front of an icon, walked up to me. 'This is the *moleben*, the prayer for the sick. It's not a prayer for deliverance. We're not going to see anything interesting here. It will last about ninety minutes. What do you want to do?'

I wanted to leave, but I didn't want it to look as though I was here strictly for the supernatural fireworks. That would have been crass. I shrugged. Fortunately Edward felt the same way as me, but was less bothered with questions of etiquette.

'Let's go outside,' he said.

A POSTCARD FROM UKRAINE

The beer kiosk
We crossed the bridge in search of nutrients, hoping that we might find some over on the other side. But there was no food there: only kiosks selling beer, beer snacks, and Shok chocolate bars.

The girl behind the counter of the first kiosk was beautiful, conscious of the power her beauty gave her over men, that ability to attract their admiring gazes and turn them into drooling idiots. It was hard not to stare, and she knew that, and yet gave no reaction to the eyes that roamed across her curves. But the gleam in her eye would soon be snuffed out, for I had been in many Komsomolsks before, and knew it was a grim hole that sucked the nutrients out of its people, transforming them into the salt that lay along the road, killing everything green. And so to admire her beauty was depressing. It was wasted, as she sold sweeties and bottles of beer to the assorted alcoholics and vagrants that made up her clientele.

In the kiosk next door, a woman about fifteen years older wore a drab blue overall that hung around her neck like her own life. There were various objects on sale in her shop but the main product was despair. I found a piece of bread. She charged me in roubles, though this was not so much an act of defiance against Ukrainian nationalism as a shrug of the shoulders, a denial that the changes wrought since 1991 had made any difference to the facts of her life.

Outside I bit into the stale bread. There was something hard in it: cherry stones. We sat by the bridge and stared at ants for about an hour, the blind eye of the sun burning a hole in the top of my head, baking my brain in its own useless juices.

5 Howl

Father Grigory was already at prayer when we re-entered the cathedral. It was a typical scene in an Orthodox church. He was facing an altar in front of the iconostasis, chanting in a high-pitched voice, reading from the Bible, surrounded by a small crowd of supplicants for God's mercy. *Is this it?* I thought. Edward had told me outside that Father Grigory carried out exorcisms twice a week, on Wednesdays and Saturdays, but that Wednesday was the special day, when the strongest manifestations occurred. This was a Wednesday. But it was hard to imagine that anything very terrifying could erupt out of this very normal scene.

And yet the air crackled electric with anticipation. I could feel it; I had walked into something, something that hadn't been there earlier in the day. And no sooner had we stepped inside than Edward left me and started roaming on the edge of the crowd, a small video camera under his arm, concealed in the folds of his jacket. Though he had been denied permission to film, he still wanted to be ready to record any strange phenomena that might occur. Nobody would be able to tell where it had been filmed, so Father Grigory would not be harmed.

Meanwhile Father Grigory went on chanting, for five minutes, six minutes, seven minutes. Eight minutes. I was hungry, bored, light-headed from the sun and heat. It was now five months since Edward had called me, almost seven since I had first met him in the Digger's kitchen. There had been so many trap doors and dead ends in that time it didn't feel as though I was looking for anything any more. I was running around in a labyrinth, seeking a Minotaur that had long since vacated the place: only a vague whiff of its shanks remained to remind me why I had entered. It was difficult to place myself inside the quest psychologically, to believe it was real, that anything was ever going to happen. The seeking had become an end in itself: there was no object any more.

And then I heard it: the wail, rising out of the woman's throat, uncoiling itself from deep, deep within her gut. And it came out from her, snaking outwards and upwards towards the top of the cathedral, towards the vaulted ceiling and the dim light trapped up there. And it just kept coming. And there was something to the tone, and the force, and the way that it just kept rising and rising and rising, uncoiling ever outwards, that was unutterably strange and chilling. There was no quavering; the voice did not grow weary or strained. It was unlike anything I had ever heard. The roots of my hair tingled; a bolt of cold, electrical fear burrowed from the nape of my neck to the base of my spine. I looked around and saw that the howl was coming from Tatiana, the woman from outside the church, the one Father Grigory had made faint.

It was the most anguished sound I had ever heard.

6 The Exorcist, part 1

The people in the cathedral froze, transfixed by the howl. Some stared into space, others at each other. Still others craned their necks to try and see the creature that was producing this unearthly noise. Most of them were not used to this, I could tell. How many, I wondered, had come as tourists, simply to listen, to see? Did they feel the fear? Were they breaking into a sweat, like me?

Two full minutes passed, and then the wail stopped. Edward came hurtling towards me, a dark gleam in his eyes.

'Did you hear that?' he asked, excitedly.

'I did.'

'Go over there. Something is happening. You have to see it.'

I got up and walked towards the crowd, all gathered in a tight circle around Father Grigory, huddling close, for comfort, security, or simply to get a better view. There were a few voyeurs in there, stretching their necks like spectators at a car crash – but hoping for what? Green vomit? A spinning head? A torrent of obscenities through cracked white lips?

It was a bit like being at a rock concert. Taller people, bigger heads kept getting in my way. Father Grigory was still chanting, with his back to the congregation. Wailing Tatiana was standing close to him. And then I realised that he was reading from a list of names, and that was what his chant was: the names of the possessed, of the sick, of the damned. When he reached the end of the list he would dip a cloth into a basin of holy water, then turn round and splash it over the people standing behind him. When he did this the crowd rushed forward, thirsting to receive more of the blessed H_2O.

Tatiana, the most tormented, received extra holy water. Father Grigory smacked her on the face with the cloth, positively drenching her in the stuff. The lads who had greeted him at the gate were helping him, holding the basin. They chortled merrily as he pelted her: they were really enjoying the spectacle. Even Father Grigory's eyes were sparkling with a wry humour.

This note of levity was startling. Where was the fear, the dark, grim fascination I saw in the wild, staring eyes of Edward?

I didn't think Father Grigory was mocking this woman. Rather, for him, performing an exorcism was a part of life that was integrated into his everyday experience, like working in the fields, disciplining his kids, or mucking out the sty. It all belonged in the same reality. His world was an earthy place, and he approached the business of expelling a demon in the same way: robustly, without great drama. Father Grigory had a keen sense of humour that lit up the world and made it lighter, but without making things trivial.

7

And so it went on. Father Grigory kept reciting names, and then periodically turning round to douse the people with holy water. But after that initial tormented wail, very little else happened. Slowly the electricity ebbed out of the crowd. The people around me grew listless. Formerly enthusiastic spectators drifted off to the outer regions of the mob. Some were beginning to look a bit bored, even.

I kept standing there, waiting, waiting for another wail, for someone to curse, to start smoking from their eyeballs. But: nothing. Father Grigory kept on chanting. The crowd occasionally pressed closer to him, then fell away again. Edward was nearby and I could see that he was talking to a woman. She was wearing a headscarf. He was earnestly debating with her under his breath . . .

At the forty-minute mark there was another outburst. An old woman in front of me cursed once or twice, danced on the spot, then collapsed. Someone caught her, picked her up, and Father Grigory splashed her with the holy water. After that, she was calm. Of course, I kept my eye on her, in the hope that something might happen again, but one splash was all she needed. And the same was true for Tatiana. She was standing by Father Grigory, her stare fixed at her feet. Whatever demon had been tormenting her, for now it was cowed, subdued. Father Grigory drew the sermon to an end and then the congregation formed a long queue in front of a metal tank of holy water at the side of the church.

Everyone in the building joined the line, except for me and the ghostly monk I had seen earlier. All this time I had been watching him, as he hovered on the outskirts of the crowd, somehow unseen by all the others. And although I was watching him, he was indifferent to my gaze: he didn't see me.

He took one final look round, drew up his skirts and headed for the door, vanishing as quickly as he could into the brilliant blue sky, the vast green earth, the white crystals of sand atop the dirt, the crumbling concrete.

8

After the monk disappeared I waited a minute and then stepped out of the gloom into the sunlight myself. It was a beautiful day on the top of the cathedral steps, and bright. So bright the light felt like needles inserted into my retinas. I was a subterranean creature that had surfaced too early, emerging into the late afternoon when it needed night and the moon and the cold darkness. I had to close my eyes and shut out the world the sunlight exposed: the towers of Komsomolsk, the vibrant blue sky, the lush, verdant green of the trees. The sudden change was jarring. It was hard to accept that this luminous reality had anything to do with the anguish and grief that had been unleashed within the walls of the cathedral: the rituals and prayers taking place in there could only be completely alien to it.

It was past three in the afternoon; we had been hanging about near the church for six hours. I hadn't eaten properly; I hadn't slept. I had been on my feet most of that time. I walked over to the wall enclosing the church garden to sit down and think for a few minutes, before Edward emerged from inside the cathedral. Slowly it dawned on me that I had just seen the very thing Edward had been preparing me for over a period of nearly six months. I had just witnessed an exorcism.

Hm.

I sat there for a few minutes trying to get some handle on it all. What did I feel? Was that really the end? Was that the climax of all these meetings and discussions, all that wandering in the labyrinth?

Yep.

What now? Where to next? What should I do? What should I think?

Suddenly I was overwhelmed by a dark, dark feeling. It's difficult to describe: I felt simultaneously hollow and yet heavy, empty and yet filled with a solid, dense darkness. My body ached, my thoughts were sluggish. But slowly they started to come, and to take on definite shape . . . forming into a question that can neatly be summarised as follows:

Is that it?

9

I'd come all this way to see the fully mustered might of the powers of darkness and the best they could manage was a sad woman wailing, and an old biddy doing a funny dance. If they hadn't been demons I'd have asked for my money back. The ones Edward had shown me on tape were much better, much more powerful. They made their victims lash out violently, curse, foam at the mouth.

But then I caught myself: what was I thinking? Did I actually want humans to be tormented by grinning devils, to see black hooks tearing scorched flesh apart in a lake of fire? No, I didn't, no more than travellers attracted to India or Africa 'want' poverty to persist in lands they would rapidly lose interest in if they were full of retail parks and office blocks. I was in search of something else: the same dark, surreal world Sergei had evoked for me the first time he had mentioned the Diggers, eight years earlier.

I recognised the strange, heavy yet empty feeling in my chest. It was a damp, bad feeling of hopelessness and futility. I kept believing the tall tales of cracked visionaries from a desire to see amazing things, and yet I always ended up disappointed. This was worse than the anticlimax of the Digger's tour through a sewer. I had never asked myself the question *What if nothing happens?* though it was always there, staring me in the face. But I couldn't ask it, because it's impossible to stay inside a reality if you start to question it. You undermine its foundations that way. But by losing myself in it, I was colluding in my own defeat. Was it a Catch 22? Or the Sword of Damocles? I didn't much care. I was too busy feeling empty and useless.

Edward stepped out of the church. He looked around for a few seconds and then spotted me sitting on the wall. As he walked over I saw that his eyes were dim, and his tread was heavy. He looked solemn. He wasn't feeling too excited about what we had just seen either.

'Did you see that woman talking to me in the church?'

'Yes.'

'She was a tourist. She had heard about Father Grigory's exorcisms and had come to see one for herself.'

'What did she think?'

'She thought it was hysteria.'

'I see.' It didn't seem unreasonable. Regardless of what 'hysteria' means, I knew what the woman was getting at. Sitting there, I knew that I was losing my grip on Edward's world – that it would soon be difficult if not impossible to remain there, to see things his way. In fact, Edward had raised the woman's doubts precisely because he feared that I was no longer viewing the war against demons through his eyes, but rather saw a sad, dismal manifestation of poverty and mental illness. He rushed to dispel that interpretation. 'But it's *not* hysteria! I asked her: did you hear how long that woman wailed for? Minutes! And without a break! That voice was not human . . . All the same,' he said, 'on a scale of one to ten, I mean measuring in terms of phenomena connected to the presence of the demonic . . .'

He raised the index and middle finger of his right hand. They stood together like sentries on duty, his thumb folded in on his palm.

'I'd give that a score of two.'

10 Crazy monk

An hour passed. We were still outside the church. Father Grigory was still providing spiritual succour to his parishioners. My depression was gradually lifting, though that had little to do with Edward's imitations of accents of the British Isles. He had been doing them for some time now, and he was particularly proud of his cockney. '*Olroit mite*' he said. '*Owz it goin'?*' I smiled weakly, hoping he would stop.

He didn't. Then he tried a new accent that I didn't recognise. It turned out that it was mine. He was picking himself up again, reanimating his soul, recovering from the disappointment of what we had seen in Father Grigory's church and preparing himself to set forth again with his hunting equipment, to trap a greater demon. Edward was resilient that way.

'Did I ever tell you about the time I was in Krasnoyarsk, in Siberia?'

'I don't think so.'

'I had heard there was a very powerful exorcist connected to a monastery there. So I travelled out to visit the priest. But when the chief monk of the monastery discovered what I was looking for, he locked me out.'

'What?'

'He didn't want me to talk to one of his monks. Of course the fact that it was thirty-six below and I was freezing to death out there in the snow didn't bother him. Mind you, he was a very scandalous fellow. A week before, he had got drunk at a wedding party and shot a gas gun at the guests.'

'What? The chief monk?'

'Yes. He'd had a bit too much to drink.'

'Did anything happen to him?'

'Oh no. He had friends in high places. Some members of the church hierarchy protected him.'

'Did you ever get to meet the exorcist?'

'No, not that time.'

A middle-aged woman, dressed head to toe in green, was standing nearby, listening to us speak English. Her face was puffy and red and the look in her eye was expressive of a life rich in suffering. She was trying to figure out who we were, and what we were doing in Komsomolsk. Eventually she summoned the nerve to approach us directly.

'Where are you from?' she asked.

'Moscow,' said Edward, pointing at himself. 'Scotland.' He indicated me.

The woman was startled. She was from some village located deep in the great void of deprivation and hopelessness. She hadn't expected to meet such interesting characters on the steps of a village church.

'Why are you here?' she asked.

Edward explained. Her eyes widened further. 'My . . . but that's very interesting.' Edward smiled, and then turned the attention towards her. 'And why are you here to see Father Grigory?' he asked.

She started to explain, now looking at Edward, now looking away. She had heard of Father Grigory, and knew that he was a man of God with experience of casting out evil spirits.

She was cursed.

11

The words rushed out of her, in a mix of Russian and Ukrainian. It was difficult to follow what she was saying, and Edward was not interpreting, but rather urging her to open up and tell him as much as possible. I remember a string of unfortunate incidents: one husband had left her, and another had appeared to take his place. But perhaps this new one had beaten her; one of them certainly had. There had also been a miscarriage. She had brought her daughter, a teenager, with her: the girl was newly married, but finding it difficult to conceive. There was too much bad luck in her life to believe it was simply accidental. Something was going on; something was not right in the fabric of reality.

Edward was leaning forward, giving her his full attention. She wasn't used to having people listen to her so closely. Emboldened, she continued. 'And then it started . . .'

'What?' said Edward.

'After the miscarriage I began building a new house in my village. But it didn't go well. Strange things happened . . .' She hesitated.

'Please,' said Edward. 'I'm listening. Don't worry. I believe you.'

'One morning I was inspecting the house. We were building a wall. And there, between the bricks, were cracked eggs.'

'What?'

'Eggs, all cracked, with the yolk and the white dripping down . . .'

'Strange,' said Edward.

'Yes, but that's not all. The next day I went out and the bricks had been rearranged. They were piled on top of each other, like a . . . like a pyramid. And then a few days later I found *clumps of human hair* between the bricks.'

This is what I thought:

Somebody is fucking with this poor woman.

But that wasn't what Edward was thinking. He looked back at me, raised his eyebrows, and continued probing for more details.

'Tell me,' he asked her. 'Do you ever feel a strange sensation in your spine?'

The woman looked startled. 'What do you mean?'

'Do you ever get a strange sensation in your back, right between the shoulder blades . . .?'

No Edward, I thought, *No, don't do this . . .*

'Well, I'm not sure . . .' she said, but I could see that she was thinking, *Actually, maybe yes . . .*

Edward turned to me, eyes wide open, nostrils flaring. *Proof!* 'Do you ever hear a noise like a mosquito, and then feel a chill? You see the demon, it takes a form of ether and then enters through the spine.'

If she hadn't felt it before, she was about to realise she had.

'I'm not sure, well . . . now that you mention it . . . Oh please won't you get Father Grigory to pray for me? He told me to come back on Saturday, that he's just too busy today! Can you talk to him, please? I travelled three hours to get here . . .'

But at that moment a nun came over and invited us to join Father Grigory for lunch. Edward told the woman he would talk to Father Grigory and see what he could do.

12

The nun led us to the refectory building off to the side of the church. A little doorway opened onto a set of stairs that took us to a small underground complex of rooms and narrow tunnels. It looked like the sort of place the Bolsheviks might have shot someone in. Lined up in the corridor were yet more women with expressions of misery and woe, women whose bodies and souls were mere sacks of suffering. They were everywhere, stuffed into every available nook and cranny of the cathedral complex. There had been men in the church, but most of those who suffered from possession were women. Where were the men? I suspected:

(1) At work

or

(2) Dead

or

(3) Dead drunk.

Edward and I were ushered into a small kitchen dominated by a table set for three. It was heaped high with food and drink: *pelmeni*, potatoes, salad, strawberries, pickles and conserves. Father Grigory sat down, said grace and then instructed us to tuck in.

Ministering to so many suffering women had given him an appetite. He wolfed down his repast while his eyes, alert and canny as always, sparkled with humour and mischief.

'Hey, foreigner,' he said. 'Why aren't you touching the fruit? Eat a strawberry.'

'All right,' I said.

'What do you reckon?'

It wasn't quite the size of my fist, but it was pretty tasty. 'Good,' I said.

'You're right. It's very good. Now try the *pelmeni*.'

Pelmeni are balls of soggy dough containing gristle and fragments of bone, a cocktail usually described on the package as 'meat'. I had eaten a lot of *pelmeni* in my time as I could usually boil up a bowl in ten minutes or so. I never enjoyed them, of course, but if I choked down enough it could kill the hunger long enough for me to get to sleep. These *pelmeni*, however, were unlike any I had ever eaten before.

'Notice anything strange?' asked Father Grigory.

'They actually taste good,' I said.

He looked at me for a second, wondering if I meant that the way it sounded or if it was an effect of translation. Then he continued:

'They contain fish.'

Father Grigory was fasting and so could not eat meat. His cook, however, had invented fish *pelmeni* as a tasty alternative to the 'meat' variety. Edward was impressed. Suddenly he launched into another lyrical flight about how fantastic life in Ukraine was. He wanted me to live here. 'Twelve thousand dollars,' he said, 'that's not so much. You could buy a flat here, Daniel, then you could visit Komsomolsk as often as you liked.'

'That would not amount to a great many visits,' I said.

'Sorry?' He looked startled.

'Nothing.'

Then Edward turned to Father Grigory: 'I mean, you have corruption here, but it's not *that* kind of corruption, not like we have in Russia . . .'

For the last forty-eight hours Father Grigory had just been listening, nodding his head, patient and quiet. Now, however, he interrupted Edward:

'There's a book of priests in the Ukraine. It lists details about every priest: where he's been, what he's done. In this book it says that I'm an alcoholic.' He stared at Edward, who was shocked.

'But that's not true,' said Edward.

'That's what it says in the book: that I'm a bad priest. An alcoholic.'

Edward hesitated. This had knocked him off course. 'But where did the information come from?'

'Some journalist. He never spoke to me, of course. He just came to the town, asked one or two people. Someone said I'm an alcoholic. And so it went in the book.'

'But that's terrible.'

'That's not all. Some people in the village think I'm a black wizard.'

'What? Why?'

'Because Marilyn follows me through the streets of the village.'

'The pig?' Edward laughed.

'Yes. The fact that she follows me shows that I have a supernatural control over the animal kingdom. I, therefore, am a black wizard.'

'Father Grigory . . .'

'It's true. And they steal from me.'

'The villagers steal from *you*?'

'Yes. They steal chickens, eggs.'

'But you're their priest!'

'They still steal. One time I waited up all night for the culprits to come. They came creeping over my fence at dawn, just as the sun was rising. There were two or three of them. I shot a flare gun at them. That scared them, I can tell you. They haven't been back since.'

'That's terrible.'

'Other people in the village have threatened to report me to the authorities, because I deliver my children myself. They say it's against the law, that I'm endangering the health of my wife and children. I told them: go ahead. Call the State Prosecutor, if you like. I don't care.'

Edward was reeling. This was not his Ukraine. This was some other place, somewhere nastier. Father Grigory was describing a world inhabited by poor, spiteful, lazy, greedy, envious bastards. That is to say, by the same shining specimens who live everywhere else on our beautiful planet. Edward was finding it difficult to process: 'But Father Grigory, why?'

'Envy,' said Father Grigory simply. 'I work hard and I have a big house and land. There are people in the village that don't work at all. They just sit around drinking all day, doing nothing. They are waiting until I improve the land. Then they will call the police and try and take it off me. They don't want to work: they just want to steal what I have done. That's why I'm building a tall fence around my farm. I have three people working on it for me, right now, even as we are sitting here, talking: because I can't trust my neighbours.'

13

Edward sat in silence for a moment, thinking of what to say. Suddenly he remembered: 'Listen, Father, I met a woman outside –'

'I'm too busy. Let her make an appointment.'

'No, wait – it sounds like a serious attack of the demonic.' He reiterated the symptoms the woman had described to us.

Father Grigory shrugged. 'It doesn't sound like she's possessed to me.'

Edward blinked. 'But Father, what about the eggs?'

'Someone's messing her about. They bought eggs at the market, and cracked them over the bricks.'

'But the hair?'

'Someone pulled his hair out, and put it there.' He bit off a chunk of bread.

'But the rearranged bricks?'

'Someone rearranged the bricks, too,' he said, spitting crumbs as he chewed on the bread. 'It's not hard.'

Edward was shocked. 'But really, Father!'

Father Grigory gave the earnest young man from Moscow a look. 'Are you married?' he asked.

'Not yet,' said Edward.

'How old are you?'

'Twenty-nine.'

'Then it's time you found a wife.'

Edward laughed. Father Grigory did not.

'Get yourself a *hohlushka*.* They're good girls, pretty girls. And then have some children. But not less than four. Four is the minimum.' He wagged a finger. 'Now excuse me, I must return to my parishioners.'

Father Grigory got up to leave. But Edward was not to be deflected

---

* Colloquial term for a female Ukrainian. A man is a *hohol*. Can be offensive, depending on whether it's a Russian or Ukrainian using it.

so easily. I heard them debating in the corridor. Finally, he succeeded in getting Father Grigory to talk to the woman.

14

Father Grigory still had some work to attend to, so after dinner we went above ground and went for a walk amid the forest behind the church. Edward was moved by the beauty of nature:

'Look at the birds singing,' he said, 'at the flowers growing, at the sunlight spilling through the leafy canopy overhead, casting dappled shade upon the ground. When you see this, then it's clear that our Creator is kind, and that he has made for us a kind creation. Why then do people rush to see violent movies? Why do they fill their heads and souls with such rubbish? Why?'

He was genuinely puzzled, but then, he lived in another reality in more ways than one. Edward liked folk music and mediaeval chant. He was a reader of the Bible. He was a good, kind man, who struggled to emulate Christ the way Christians are meant to: many times I had seen him empty his pockets and give all his cash to the poor, even if he was left with no bus fare home, or without money to buy food.

I, however, thought of all the microscopic beasts at our feet. At that moment they were either engaged in some form of drudgery or torturing and eating one another. Elsewhere, bigger animals were doing similar things. Meanwhile Edward had recently witnessed a woman howl for forty minutes owing to what he believed was a demonic presence in her soul. If, at that moment, I had wanted to argue for the essential kindness of the Creator, I wouldn't have looked to nature for proof of it.

I'd come to Ukraine in search of exorcists and the possessed, expecting I'd find people creating and inhabiting private realities, people like the Digger. Now, suddenly, I realised I'd been looking in the wrong place. Father Grigory may have inhabited a world very different from mine, but nevertheless it was grounded in tradition and philosophy and theology, in a set of values and beliefs that were held communally, and that hadn't been invented by any one individual. His exorcisms took place in an overall worldview that allowed for the existence of the demonic, but also allowed for human folly and weakness. Father Grigory had strong opinions, but he wasn't credulous or naïve. He didn't believe in every claim of demonic possession; he applied it to a system he had inherited first, and knew well that many of the people who came to him were sick or suffering from more earthly causes. He believed in the demonic because his faith instructed him to, and because he had seen it at work in its victims, and because he had seen the alleviation that came from his exorcisms.

There was something robust and earthy about what he did, therefore. In fact, in his hands, the rite became shockingly unfantastic, pragmatic, almost practical. Tatiana came every week for some sort of controlled relief from the demon that haunted her. But it could never be cast out once and for all. Demons or no demons, Father Grigory knew that he was relieving pain, and making it easier to live with wretched poverty, with illness, in a place where the people had benefited little from the actions and machinations of the country's elite. For him, performing an exorcism was part of the world, like healing a sickness, like milking a cow, like delivering a baby. It was natural.

15

Edward, however, was different. And only now did I see how different he was. Everywhere he looked, he saw demons. In sickness, in depression, in misfortune, he was always ready to jump to the magical answer first. It was an exciting world he inhabited, but a terribly isolating, and dark one.

Did anyone believe in demons as much as Edward? Even the priests cared less. And was it not a small part of the Bible? But he spent all his energy and money on this film, travelling around Russia with his camera, recording these confessions, trying to get the demons on film, believing that if he pinned them down like that he could persuade people, and finally get them to share his view of the world, to commit to its truthfulness and tangible existence.

This was more than just the missionary impulse, the urge to proselytise that comes with any deeply held belief. It was more radical. Because if he was different from the priests, if he was more obsessed, more possessed even by the idea, if even among them he was isolated, then what else could he do but try and persuade other people that he was right? It's hard to carry a reality around inside you and just keep it there. You want to share it. Why else had the Digger cast around for followers, and invented all his schools of thought and science? Why did he *need* to take his world, with its creation myth, rituals, art and philosophy, out of his head and make it communal? Because if you don't share a reality, and get others to agree with you that it exists, then what are you left with? Solipsism, psychosis, alienation, madness.

Edward was not egoistic like the Digger. He didn't need to be the absolute monarch of a tribe. But now I understood better why he had been so keen to involve me in his travels, even after I had told him I had no useful media contacts. He didn't want to convert me to Orthodox Christianity, but to something more personal: he wanted to convert me to his *reality*. Hence the books and films, the long disquisitions, the endless accounts of horrific manifestations over cups of coffee, this tour through Ukraine in pursuit of evil: he wanted someone in there with him, seeing the world the way he saw it, giving aid as he did battle with demons.

16

Later that evening we returned to Father Grigory's house. Kids were crawling everywhere. I was more used to them now, and they paid less attention to me, as if we had come to some sort of accommodation of each other's existence. Rosa was holding one of them, the original chunk of boy that had been pawing my ankles on my first night in the village. Too young to realise I was no longer of any significance and about to exit his reality entirely, he stumbled towards me in search of more food, but fell just before he reached his target, and whacked his skull off the table leg. He didn't cry though. He just screwed up his eyes, rubbed his forehead, and then got up. This kid was indestructible.

Matushka stomped in.

'So you saw the *otchitka*?'

'Yes,' I said.

'Did you like it?'

I didn't know what to say to that.

VII

In the Spring of Revolution, Comes a Head like Fresh Meat

A POSTCARD FROM UKRAINE

Future Ukraine
A strange vision in this dirty, broken-down world where Europe is so far away. All around me: nothing but fields, and aging Soviet housing. And yet here, looming out of the night, on the road to Kiev: modern petrol stations, gleaming in the night, a mirage, a reflection of an image from the future, once Ukraine has become a modern country, leaving its past as a Russian vassal state far behind. Dazzled, I write down the names of these oases of hope, not forgetting to include their colour schemes:

UKRUAT (orange)
KBITI
NAFTA (white/orange/black)
BAT KIPS (blue)
TNK (electric blue)
EKOIN
ANP
LUKOIL
UKRNAFT (yellow/blue)

Strange acronyms, bold neologisms from a newer, better world. Then I drift off to sleep, and in my sleep I have a dream, of the future children of Ukraine, eating burgers in a shiny McDonald's and filling up their small modern cars with clean, sleek futuristic fuel. They are happy, so happy, and so united. But then I wake, and coming into Kiev, in rude daylight, I see a banner strung across the street that reads: Samsung Welcomes Eurovision 2005.

And seeing that, and then later, the T-shirts and mugs and the pride related to the capital's hosting that crock of shit, well, it becomes harder to believe. Imagine that you came from a nation proud to host Eurovision, that you yourself saw this as a great achievement for your country. That, more than any number of think-tank reports, or newspaper editorials, or scholarly books, will give you some idea of how hard a time Ukraine is going to have forging its own path in the world . . .

1

The night bus from Kremenchug pulled into Kiev coach station at about 5:30 a.m. The city planners had thoughtfully located it far from a metro station. We caught another bus north, and then leapt onto the first train of the day that propelled us through the earth until we reached our stop. Above ground a mongrel bitch was suckling her puppies in a cardboard box in the underpass. Nothing else lived. It was nice to be surrounded by that vast, empty, silent space; as if I had arrived in a world after the neutron bomb. The concrete towers looked pleasingly dead. I was back in a world I could dissolve into. That lunar suburb of Kiev was beautiful that morning. I wanted to stay.

By midday, however, Edward was pacing back and forth in his room, intoning a prayer. He was restless. Father Grigory had declined to be interviewed, and so the only footage Edward had left Poltava with consisted of a few establishing shots of the church. It was a long way to travel for so little, especially as he had been there before – a complete waste of time and precious resources, in other words. But he was less worried about that than he was about my attitude. He met me in the kitchen and started chattering rapidly, nervously, reassuring me that he really had seen a man emitting fumes from his flesh in the north of Russia; that he really had heard the infernal growl of Satan's voice rising up from the throat of a teenage girl. He couldn't understand why we were having so little success now.

He insisted that we go out again. I thought it was a bad idea, we were both exhausted, and I wanted a break. But Edward was adamant. He knew an exorcist on the outskirts of Kiev, a Father

Varlaam. His deliverance services were powerful. We rushed to the bus, Edward once again neglecting to call ahead or make any plans or even check that the priest was there. Then we travelled for thirty minutes until we were deposited in a strange wasteland, where one-storey wooden huts with chickens in the yard faced off against a gleaming air-conditioned business complex enclosed by an electrified fence that was covered in signs warning the locals to keep out – the future thus notifying the past that it wanted absolutely nothing to do with it.

Just before we reached the church I suggested to Edward that we invent a cover story for me this time, perhaps that I was his camera operator, to make the priest feel more at ease with me than Father Grigory had been. But if he heard me, it was in his own way, and by the time the words had reached him they had changed their meaning entirely. He responded with a paean of praise to the greenness of the neighbourhood: 'Look at this!' he said. 'You'd hardly think it was a capital city, now would you? It's more like a village. Life goes on here as it always has done. And yet it's only thirty minutes from the centre of Kiev!'

Father Varlaam refused to speak to us.

2

And the following three-hour trip across town to the Vidubitsky Monastery, where a contact had told Edward powerful deliverance services were held, also ended in failure. Satan, the Great Trickster, had evaded us again.

3 The absence of lightning

When I was a child, during thunderstorms I would run outdoors onto the backdoor step and wait for forked lightning to rip out of the clouds and set my neighbour's house on fire. I would stand there, whipped in the face by wet icy winds until gradually boredom and a realisation that real life was not like the movies set in. Eventually, tired of waiting, I'd go back inside with a mild feeling of disappointment to continue playing or drawing.

A similar process was happening in Ukraine. But I had been standing out in the storm for some time, and unlike in Komsomolsk, where I felt depressed, I was now at the point where I had accepted nothing much was going to happen. I was ready to go back indoors and watch

Monkey on BBC2. It was about time; I had been following Edward for almost six months, after all.

Now I suspect that these non-events and anti-climaxes actually happened more frequently than Edward realised. He usually went demon hunting on his own, and on those occasions would be deep inside his own perceptions and thus able to experience everything he saw as a titanic manifestation. But now I was there and he had another pair of eyes to see through – like when you show a film you love to someone who hates it, and suddenly it looks unconvincing to you too. Maybe I was the problem. I hadn't expressed any scepticism, but I knew that he was worried I was slipping out of his orbit. And perhaps this fear was bleeding into his own perceptions, and he was seeing these non-events as failures when usually he might have seen them as smaller links in an epic narrative. But at the same time, I wouldn't push the idea too far: I remember his films, and he had recorded some extremely violent reactions to the priests' exorcisms. Perhaps we were just unlucky.

I had to step out of Edward's world for a while. It could get oppressive in there. A walk around Kiev, I thought, pursuing my own obsessions with trash, rot, decay and urban nothingness would do me the power of good. Besides, it wasn't just the demonic that had lured me to Ukraine. I wanted to absorb the triumphant atmosphere of the Orange Revolution, before it dissolved into bitterness and rancour. Komsomolsk and Kremenchug had seemed to exist outside these epochal changes, and I knew that I was missing the spirit of the moment by trailing along behind Edward as he went from closed door to closed door. It was time to breathe deep of the sweet air of freedom, to step into the golden democratic future, before it vanished once and for all.

DIGRESSION: A WALK IN THE AUTUMN OF *PERESTROIKA*

I *Kreschatyk*
A little history: Kiev is not only a Ukrainian city. For centuries it was the
capital of the Kievan Rus, the centre of the ancient Russian civilisation
– but then the Mongols arrived and turned the Slavic princes into their
vassals, thus displacing the centre of power. Kreschatyk, the central
street, derives its name from the word for baptism in both Russian and
Ukrainian. It is the eastward route to the river Dnepr, where the Grand
Prince Vladimir's subjects were baptised into Christianity in 988.

That happened over a thousand years ago, however, and since then
many invasions and revolutions have swept through Kiev, bringing
with them upheaval, disorder, death. In the three years following the
February Revolution in 1917, for example, Kiev was the seat of no
fewer than twelve different regimes. The Orange Revolution was not
the first time the country had cried out for rebirth.

The most terrible devastation occurred during World War II, after
which Kreschatyk was entirely rebuilt in the Stalinist Gothic style. The
most striking building on the street was a stunted Stalinist 'wedding
cake' skyscraper about a third of the way along. There are seven of
these in Moscow (eight, if you count the plasticky one recently added
to the city's skyline by Mayor Luzhkov and his cronies in the construction industry). The other buildings, meanwhile, were similar to
those lining Tverskaya Street in central Moscow, the start of the road
that leads north from the Kremlin to St Petersburg. There were
grandiose arches ornately decorated with such motifs as sheaves of
wheat, hammers and sickles, and a Soviet Ukrainian touch: plaster
friezes of mining equipment, a reference to the workers of the country's industrial Donbass region.

Kiev, however, had an unreal, otherworldly appearance in my eyes.
It was hard, in fact, to 'see' it; because Kiev was a weird, parallel city,
a shadow, an echo, an expression not of itself but of Moscow's conception of what it should be. Efforts had been made to expunge this
influence, but there's not much you can do with stone short of tearing
it down. Everywhere I looked, there was still Moscow. The impres-
sions of my first ride underground on the metro were only reinforced
above ground. Even the modern, post-Soviet Kiev was indebted to the
old capital. The design of the street signs was identical to the one used

in Moscow, the logo for the metro was identical, the newspapers, magazines and novels on sale in kiosks were mostly Russian publications, the celebrities advertising mobile phones on billboards were Russian, and of course, almost everyone on the street was speaking Russian.

Still, the government's language policy was as visible here as it had been on the metro when I arrived. There was no Russian signage, and all the government offices had plaques in Ukrainian and even in English on them, thus favouring a foreign tongue over the first language of many of the country's citizens. The English signs were a gesture towards modernity, an expression of the will to Westernise, even as the very object of Yuschenko's desire, the EU, was giving mixed signals: issuing praise for Ukraine's new democracy on the one hand while simultaneously muttering warnings that it would be a 'long time' before the country was ready to join.

But gradually, Kiev did begin to appear through the monumental Soviet façade. It was in the trees that lined the street, providing dappled shade, and it was in the cafés set up on the pavement, taking advantage of the temperate southern climate. I walked around, reading advertising posters, losing myself in the laid-back rhythm of the city: one announced that Moby was bringing his brand of anodyne dinner-party pop to some stadium or other. *Sin City* was coming in a month's time, as was *Batman Begins* and the Spielberg remake of *War of the Worlds*. The banners heralding Eurovision still hung across the street, sad like old balloons, slowly leaking air. Street musicians were playing jazz, folk music, heavy metal. Beautiful girls were parading along in cheap T-shirts with messages in English:

I can't wait I get better looking every day.

I'm not a bitch
I'm THE bitch
And that's Miss Bitch to you.

Kreschatyk wasn't overdriven like downtown Moscow, but it wasn't as dilapidated and dull as the centres of most provincial Russian towns either. It hovered somewhere in between. I liked it, and spent all my subsequent evenings in the city drifting up and down the street, watching the street performers. One night I even caught an Italian 3-D horror movie in the Kino Orbita, a dark poem from another age: it was easy to imagine that here, amid the chandeliers, red velvet seats, and marble pillars, the weary proletarians of communist Kiev had come to watch Stalin's favourite movie, *Volga Volga*, and later, perhaps my neighbour Vasily Lanovoi, stoically suffering for love in *Officers*. Even the dust had been preserved, lying undisturbed for decades.

The city, with its quiet shabbiness, appealed to me. It was an ideal place to spend time if you wanted to rot, unseen, among pleasantly decayed buildings.

II *The Maidan*

The climax of the walk along Kreschatyk was Independence Square. This was the place I had seen on TV months earlier: crowds camped out in sub-zero temperatures in December, Yuschenko with his scarred face, his running mate Yulia Tymoshenko with her ice-cold grimace, and Ruslana, the feisty winner of the Eurovision Song Contest, all standing up for democracy against ballot stuffing, all declaring that they would defend the autonomy of the Ukrainian nation from Russian interference.

It was as if Ukraine had been born at that moment. Until then, as far as the rest of the world was concerned, the country was just an appendage of Russia. Its name even sounded very close to the Russian for *on the edge*, as if to say it was not something in itself but rather a place on the edge of somewhere else, i.e. Russia. Fourteen years of independence hadn't much altered this perception. Its most famous city, Chernobyl, achieved fame due to a nuclear accident, and yet how many people knew or cared that it was in Ukraine? And in fact, the disaster poisoned far more Belarussians than Ukrainians. I knew one man who had lived in western Ukraine for a while, which, until Stalin annexed it after World War II, had been a province of Poland. This was the most nationalistic part of the country, and he told me that Ukrainians there were morbidly sensitive to questions of their national dignity. They were (understandably) incensed by those Russians who maintained that Ukraine was not a real country, that it was still Russia, that the two countries were too closely bound together by culture, history and language for an 'independent' government in Kiev to make any difference.

But by standing up at that moment, Yuschenko had gone against this trend of nothingness, and had finally established Ukraine in the consciousness of the watching world. He had created an identity that was separate from (or at least opposed to) Russia's. Even the Russians had to face its reality now. If nothing else, he would be remembered for that.

Some guy on the square had a monkey on a string. I had my picture taken with it standing on my shoulder. There was also a long pole, topped with a golden wedding-cake ornament, that I presumed represented Ukraine or liberty or something like that. Similarly tacky statues occupied the spaces left by departed Lenins on Independence Squares across the former Soviet Union. I much preferred the cheesy digital clock on top of the building across the way. It had probably looked really modern in 1981. Beneath the pillar there was an underground shopping centre that contained a few rubbishy boutiques selling rich man's crap.

I crossed the street. They had preserved some pro-Orange graffiti on a column of the central post office by placing a square of protective plastic over it. I understood the motivation behind this, but even so, it stuck in my craw. The Revolution had occurred only a few months earlier and this rush to declare it a success before the team that had come to power had actually done anything struck me as a sham. If you had touched down in St Petersburg in March 1917, a month after the Tsar had been deposed, you would have been struck by the dreams and idealism of people who later turned out to be saps, fools, thieves, baby-rapists and mass murderers.

III *Is God Ukrainian?*

In front of the post office, some women were standing to attention at a line of wooden tables covered with souvenirs. Almost everything on sale was connected either to the Orange Revolution or Eurovision, leaving me to wonder what they had been selling six months earlier. There were DVDs of Eurovision 2004, orange mugs with *Tak!* (*Yes!* – the slogan of the Orange forces) written on them, and green mugs with the legend *Eurovision*. There were orange T-shirts, cards, pens and portraits of Yulia Tymoshenko alongside photos of Ruslana and her 'Wild Dancers'.

The photos of President Yuschenko, however, were as tragic as they were celebratory. Most of them dated from before his poisoning, as though his supporters could not bear to look upon his ravaged features. They preferred to remember him as a young, confident, strong man, and not the damaged wreck that looked like Two-Face, Batman's second-best villain after the Joker (though Two-Face was only half-disfigured). Then there was an English pamphlet titled 'How It Was Done'.

An American, the middle-aged beneficiary of a rich, well-organised society, walked up to the table and started leafing through the pamphlet. He was tall, handsome and still athletic. The stallholder, on the other hand, was a dissolving heap of flesh and rags. A misshapen hole flopped open in the bottom part of her head and she barked a few English words at him. 'It tell story of Oranzhevaya Revolution.' He nodded, smiled, flashing a neat row of burnished white teeth at her.

Remarkable, I thought. *I've never seen one of these before.* Though of course, it made sense that they existed. Here was a freedom tourist, come to see the new, independent, happy Ukraine. Indeed, I had read about a team of Canadians who had travelled throughout the country during the stand-off between the blue and orange camps, promoting the Orange cause. These lovers of liberty had actually gone into pro-Russian strongholds and lectured the Yanukovych supporters on how wrong they were. Apparently it hadn't gone down too well. Even the Orange side was reportedly a bit baffled by these rubbery, exfoliated humanoids telling them how to run their country.

I left the freedom tourist to it. He couldn't read the Cyrillic alphabet, so he didn't know what the books on the other side of the table were about. One of them was called *The Jewish Yoke*. Another was called *The Yid Conspiracy*. And let's not forget *Masons*, and my favourite, *Russian Gods*. Later Edward told me that this last one revealed that Christianity was a Jewish invention intended to separate the Slavs from their true pagan gods and thus weaken them, so that the Jews could do all those things that diabolical Jews like to do, such as drink the blood of Slav babies, slaughter Slavs in huge numbers, that sort of thing.

Numerous pogroms swept across Ukraine during the Tsarist period, and evidently there were still plenty of foaming anti-Semites around. That didn't surprise me. I was, however, a little startled that no one had thought to clear this stuff from the centre of town. It might put some of the freedom tourists off, if they ever managed to decode what the covers of the books next to the orange *Tak!* mugs said.

The crone saw what I was looking at, and realised I understood. She cackled.

'I just came from a meeting,' she said. 'We were debating: is the God of the Jews Ukrainian?'

IV *Tent city*

I followed a path that led up a hill to a monument of Soviet workers standing under a metal rainbow. Beyond this, the path twisted round into a wood. I crossed a bridge, passed through some more trees and then stumbled upon something startling – a tent city. What were tents doing up here? The revolution was over, and the Orange side had won. There was no need to camp out any more. Then I realised that these tents were not orange, but blue. They belonged to supporters of Yanukovych.

This was startling. Tent cities of the Orange forces had been reported in the Western press, but the continued presence of Blue protestors had not. It was, of course, inconvenient for the George Lucas-derived Rebel Forces vs. Evil Empire framework our news media favour when reporting on struggles in galaxies that are far, far away. The life of a foreign correspondent is very exciting, after all. There's always a war or disaster going on somewhere, so you are constantly parachuting into strange lands you know little about. Then you have to establish an easily understood context for the people watching at home who know even less. Then, as soon as the drama is over, you have to parachute into the next famine/revolution/war/alien invasion, and quickly cobble together some more footage of devastated corpses and exploding cities. There's no time to reflect or analyse. Besides, that might bore people into switching over.

I walked through the tents. They were all empty, but the settlement was not abandoned. There was still a presence at each encampment, someone watching over them, as if the tents were only temporarily unoccupied and would soon be filled again. Or perhaps the protestors had gone home to make money, but had left their tents behind, to perform a virtual protest for them. At one encampment I spotted nuns praying for union with the Holy Rus that had been torn away from them by Yuschenko's victory.

The slogans posted around these Blue tents declared again and again that the election had been stolen from them. Robbers and capitalists were taking Ukraine in the wrong direction. Yuschenko was a stooge of the US, spreading prostitution, drug abuse, strip bars and thievery. Before, in the Soviet period, there was sport, a space programme, Ukrainian cosmonauts, a good education system and friendship with Russia. Then there was the 'Grand Hotel Yanukovychgrad',

Vanquished Yanukovych supporters prepare to lay their human rights to rest

a simple blue tent, but next door to it a cardboard coffin was suspended from the trees. A sign on the coffin mourned the ascent of the Orange forces which had brought about the death of democracy, law and human rights in Ukraine.

It was interesting that so many of the protests of the Blue side were identical to those of the Orange. I would not presume to get involved in proving or disproving the truth or falsity of these claims; I was hardly there long enough for that. But at the very least it suggests a great, unreported other half to the story of the events of December 2004: a murky world of accusation and counter-accusation, of complexity and greyness.

And later, of course, Yuschenko was forced to accept Yanukovych as his prime minister anyway – mixing orange with blue, which, if I recall correctly, creates brown.

V *Kunstkamera*

Back on Kreschatyk I followed a series of signs that led me to a wax museum of horrors that was located in the basement of a Stalinist building. The guide wore a little baseball cap with a Ukrainian flag on it, and his eyes were bulging out from behind the smeared glass of broken plastic spectacles. The wax models in the display were replicas of real freaks of nature. He looked as though, when no one was around, he liked to rub them against the naked blubber of his torso.

Slowly, very slowly, he led me through the display, holding the dirty dummies out to me, inviting me to touch their yellow, brittle forms. It was hot and difficult to breathe down there with the freaks. With each freak came a story, and if he'd been speaking Russian I would have made my apologies and left. But his mangling and splintering of the English language led to a weird, broken poetry that fascinated me. It was as twisted as the limbs and bodies of his exhibits; terse, brutal, and somehow evocative:

'Zis is nature's Siamese twin.'

'Zis is nature's hydroencephalic.'

'He born in Poltava two years ago, live two days, then go dead. His mother drinkman. His mother drugman. Zis Cyclops with one eye, penis on head and no *cherep*.'

'You mean skull.'

'*Cherep* skull?'

'Yes.'

'Sank you. Zis one, he let's go work in circus. People smile. He let's go work in army. He live thirty-two year. Then take gun and flash in head. Go die.'

Some teenage girls joined us. Our guide handed a fossilised six-week-old embryo to them. It was not wax; it was real. 'Go, touch, feel,' he said. They squealed, and ran outside. My guide continued, merciless, moving from freak to freak, offering each one to me also, that I might leave my own fingerprints on the filth-encrusted effigies.

'Zis man have two heads, one big, one small. Big head drank tequila in circus. Big head no get drunk but small head smile. People very like how small head smile.'

'Zis man fish man.' He took the wax dummy and demonstrated it swimming. 'He let's go work in circus. People go smile.'

'Zis little girl from Semipalatinsk in Kazakhstan. Many radiation. One head, two bodies. Live three minutes then dead.'

'Zis three-headed baby from New York. Lived three hours. Parents give names Peter, Paul, John. And zis Grace McDaniel, most ugly woman in planet. She had head colour of fresh meat . . .'

I was particularly struck by the little girl from Semipalatinsk with two bodies. Semipalatinsk is an area in Kazakhstan from where the

Soviets tested nuclear weapons. She had lived for three minutes only and yet here, thousands of miles away, that tiny story was being retold in a strange basement. She even had her own little wax monument. I suppose that the three-headed baby with biblical names that lived for three hours was more sensational, but that happened in New York, and sensational things are always happening there. In Kazakhstan they are less commonplace.

The memory of the little girl had been preserved because of Ukraine and Kazakhstan's common history as Soviet republics. The wax museum too was an echo of the Kunstkamera in Leningrad/St Petersburg, a collection of real freaks. These cultural links were part of a past from which the Orange Kiev above ground was struggling to break free. Standing in that basement, I was glad that for now, they persisted. For the little girl's sake, at least: because if they were erased, then the memory of her short, tortured life would be erased with them.

VIII

Satan

A POSTCARD FROM UKRAINE

Magic on the metro
There are TVs on the platforms of the Kiev metro. Sometimes
they show pop videos, though you can't hear any music for the
screaming of steel wheels. I was watching a girl pop singer seduc-
tively mouthing the words of her song when suddenly the image
gave way to one of two feet sticking out from under a blanket, a
thin river of blood flowing from in between them. It was a TV
show rounding up all the car crashes, fires, corpses they had
found that day in Kiev. They have the same programmes in
Russia, but they don't broadcast them on public transport. I
stared at the feet for half a minute as trains pulled in and passen-
gers rushed towards the escalator. Without the voiceover, it was
as if the director was waiting for something to happen, as if the
legs might twitch, and the corpse resurrect itself. It didn't. The
body was just lying there, quite dead. The corpse vanished,
replaced by another image, I can't remember what. Then my
train arrived. I stepped on board and left the dead of Kiev
behind. Someone else would have to watch over them from now
on: I could no longer.

1

We had spent a couple of days apart. Now we were on the metro, travelling to see Father Roman, the priest Edward had called on our very
first morning in Kiev, the one who had invited us to his church but was
not there when we arrived. This time Edward had agreed in advance

the time of our meeting, and been given confirmation that Father Roman would grant an interview.

Edward wasn't interested in where I had been or what I had seen. He was busy filming the horoscopes on the TV screen in the carriage. People were staring. I found it embarrassing.

'Edward,' I said.

'Shh!' he said. 'I'm filming. Do you see how deeply the occult permeates society? Look: it is here for everyone to read, to influence all their thoughts. And they are all just sitting here, as if it is normal. They don't even notice what is being done to them, right in front of their eyes.'

I was going to say that horoscopes are derived from the ideas of an ancient people who also believed the world was a flat disc floating through space supported by four elephants standing on the back of a giant turtle. It was better to laugh than treat them as a sinister conspiracy, and needlessly alienate viewers. But Edward's eyes were gleaming. Once again I collided with absolute faith. He was deep in his world again, where it was very straightforward: the occult was the occult. Evil was on the loose, and the people were being misled, and if he had to scare people into believing, then he would do so.

He kept on filming.

2

Father Roman's church was in central Kiev, in an area that resembled an embryo of North London, that bleak hinterland of bingo halls, retail parks and housing estates. There was a car showroom, its window full of sleek Japanese vehicles, way too expensive for most of the city's residents; and diagonally across from it, a giant crane standing guard over the concrete skeleton of a future office block. The first time we had visited, it had been very jarring to be seeking an exorcist in this landscape. A short walk led to a TGI Friday's, a statue of Lenin and then downtown. Now, however, it seemed almost commonplace. Perhaps I had been with Edward long enough, and knew that with him I would find the demonic everywhere. He had seen it in the villages, on the train, on the outskirts of town, and now, opposite a car showroom. The demons did not hide in dark corners, but rather, worked their evil in the open. They were granted a great freedom by their invisibility, and the refusal of most people to even countenance their existence.

The church stood on top of a hill. It was new, made of orange-brown brick. This is not uncommon with Orthodox churches built since 1991. They are rarely plastered or painted, giving them a weird, half-finished look.

Edward grabbed a medal hanging round his neck. 'I have to hide this.'

'Why?'

'It's a St Benedict medal. It provides good protection against evil spirits. But it's Catholic. Father Roman is a good Russian Orthodox priest. He would not be pleased if he saw it.'

Edward, in his element but still on guard, tucked his medal away, and then we passed through an iron gate to take a set of stone steps to the top.

3 A psychedelic God-house

Next door to the church there was a traditional Russian *izba*, a two-roomed wooden house with ornate carvings around the windows. But this *izba* was covered in vivid, naïve paintings of disembodied heads attached to wings, surrounded by emaciated angels that looked like famine victims gone to heaven, wearing feathers and white robes, but still with cavernous cheeks and haunted eyes.

'What's that?' I asked.

'It's the church, of course.'

'Then what's that?' I indicated the new brick church.

'That's also the church. Before it was built Father Roman held services in the *izba*. It is consecrated and so functions as a place of worship.'

Father Roman was in a meeting, so we sat on a wall and waited. A nun with a simple, kind expression was sitting beside us, collecting money for the church in a metal tin with an icon taped to the front. She explained that it was a church of healing, staffed by 'Sisters of Mercy' who cared for the sick and destitute, those with nowhere to go, and nobody to look after them.

On our first visit the place had been abandoned; today it was busy. Ill, pale people were slowly dragging their fragile carcasses up the hill to the little *izba*. Women, men, heaving their bodies along with them, forcing those twisted cages of flesh and bone to comply just long enough to reach the doors of the psychedelic God-house, where one of the sisters would receive them and welcome them in. As they passed, the sick would stare at Edward, stare at me. They were moving so slowly they had plenty of time to scrutinise our features, and it was clear that we were total strangers, that we had no place in this world.

4

Edward pulled his camcorder out of the bag and switched on the little screen. To my surprise I saw Father Varlaam's church, and there, sitting in front of it, was the exorcist himself. He was an even more imposing figure than Father Grigory: a bald head sat on top of muscular shoulders, heavy and blunt as a boulder. A long snow-white beard flowed across black robes draped over a swollen gut, upon which rested a massive gold crucifix, heavy enough to drown a baby.

'I went back,' said Edward, 'and asked him to give me a message for today's youth. He did not refuse this time.'

Father Varlaam was speaking about a boy, a scrawny, withdrawn creature, who had retreated completely into himself after playing too many computer games. He had sent the mother away at first. The boy then went to psychologists and psychiatrists, but they couldn't do anything. By the time he was brought back to Father Varlaam he had acquired superhuman strength and it took four men to hold him down. Father Varlaam was certain some kind of demonic force had entered him. And so he had set about praying for the boy. Weeks had passed. He was getting better, but he was not healed yet . . .

There was no explanation; there was never any explanation. There was just a reality, described, endured, struggled with. It brought me all the way back to the books Edward had given me to read in the earliest stages if our friendship. I had expected a deep analysis of the demonic, some metaphysical probing. But instead the chapters piled up on each other: repetitive, endless lists of spasms and torments that were meaningless, and overwhelming. No one ever reached any deeper than the surface manifestations. The authors were satisfied to stay there.

Then Father Varlaam spoke about how he had become involved in exorcism. It was an interesting story. Unlike Father Grigory, who had come to the Church after the Soviet Union had fallen, he had been a priest since the mid 1970s. And it was while he was studying in the seminary that he had stumbled upon some prayers relating to demons. He asked the senior priest about them, why they didn't study this part of God's word.

'Forget about it,' said the priest.

But Father Varlaam didn't have that kind of mind, able to shut out inconvenient facts for the sake of his career and smooth passage through the world. If God had given this information to us, then there was a purpose in it. So Father Varlaam had made a private study of the prayers and started to incorporate them into his services. He had been doing so since the last days of the Brezhnev regime.

Most people are not like this. They prefer an easy life, and are concerned for their careers and prefer to get on well with superiors. They are good at cancelling out voices. But others – like Edward, like Father Varlaam, follow their logic to the end, regardless of the consequences. They can't live in violation of their conscience, of what they know to be true. And if it means that they have to change the way they live their lives, then they will change their lives. These people are radically honest, and radically consistent. Some people may label them obsessive, or worse, lunatics: I admire them.

5

It was a good interview. But there was one thing missing. On our first visit to the father a few days earlier, an old woman had come running out of the church as he refused to be interviewed, waving her arms above her head.

'Father!' she cried. 'Anya said that I drank the communion wine but she's a lying old pissbag and a cunt! A cunt, I tell you! Cunt! Cunt! Cunt!'

'Masha!' barked Father Varlaam. 'Cross yourself and pray for forgiveness.'

Immediately the old woman whimpered, looked down at the ground and crossed herself. She started praying, moving her lips together and mumbling away to herself.

Edward would have loved to have captured that manifestation on film; but when he visited the second time, Masha was calm.

A POSTCARD FROM UKRAINE

Metro fauna

*A blind accordionist is standing at the head of an escalator lead-
ing to a metro platform. As the throng surges forward, he strikes
up a tune, an old war song – I have heard it before, in an old black
and white movie on Russian TV. An old woman scuttles past:
half-crippled by back pain, she can no longer stand up straight.
She drops some money into his tray, and then steps onto the escalator, which transports her to the depths. Once she is gone, a man
with a droopy moustache walks past, then loops around, com-
pleting a circle. He has a sign around his neck. It reads: I KILL
COCKROACHES. The blind accordionist plays on, his military
waltz filling the air. I stand there, listening to the music and
watching the endless circling of I KILL COCKROACHES, until
suddenly a head appears at my waist. It is a man with no legs, pro-
pelling himself forward on a trolley. He zips onto the escalator
and is then also carried off into the underworld.*

*Three songs later, and I KILL COCKROACHES is still touting
for business. No one has yet spoken to him. But what's this?
Another man wearing a sign around his neck has appeared, and
he goes one better. He is wearing a red and white Ukrainian peas-
ant shirt, and the shaky scrawl on his piece of cardboard pro-
claims:*

I CURE CANCER.

6 A comparison of facial hair

Eventually, Father Roman emerged from a door in the side of the new,
brick church. He was a little tree stump of a man, rapidly moving forward under a black hat shaped like a cylindrical drum. He walked
straight past us.

Edward leapt up from the wall and dashed over to catch him before
he vanished. Father Roman recognised Edward, but he was distracted,
agitated, and kept looking sideways around him as Edward explained
his mission again.

Unlike Father Grigory or Father Varlaam, he didn't wear a wild,
prophet's beard, and it was hard to imagine him living on locusts and
wild honey. (It was hard to imagine Father Varlaam, with his expan-
sive gut, living on locusts and honey also, but his stupendous beard

was still grand and biblical.) Father Roman's facial hair was neatly manicured, and there was something worldly, almost harried in his eyes. He only had twenty minutes to spare, but he kept to his word: he would grant Edward an interview.

We followed Father Roman round the side of the big cathedral, away from curious eyes. Edward had the camera and microphone ready in about a minute, and then immediately set to conducting the interview. Father Roman checked me out briefly, but there was no suspicion in his eyes. He was much too busy to care who I was; and that was good, because I didn't care who I was either. I was inside Edward's world again, a pair of eyes and ears only, disembodied, phantasmal. It was a good feeling. I hovered near the camera, playing the part of technical assistant.

Edward's interview technique was simple. He didn't attempt to get the exorcist to talk about himself, or the personalities of the possessed, or what demons actually were. He wanted Father Roman to elaborate on his idea that demons were real, ubiquitous, and a threat to everyone. It worked. Soon Father Roman was in full flow, speaking in a hurried, agitated fashion. However, unlike Father Grigory or Father Varlaam his thoughts were less focused on the problems of individual souls but of a more socio-political nature. He saw the demonic at work on a more ambitious, even global level, possessing the institutions and organisations that moulded society. Here, in the twenty minutes he granted us, is what I learned:

(1) Diabolical forces are active in many levels of Ukrainian society. Politicians and businessmen alike hire black wizards to cast spells on their rivals. Father Roman believed that this was happening at the highest levels of power.

(2) Advertisers also utilise occult forces. For example, hidden frames are placed in advertisements to manipulate minds at the subliminal level.

(3) Sects were at work in Ukraine, and they were free to evangelise and do evil without any interference from the authorities. For example, Evangelical Christians and Jehovah's Witnesses were very active in seeking converts. These were satanic movements that led people from the true path of salvation. When Evangelicals spoke in tongues, we had to wonder what force moved people to produce these ecstatic utterances. Was it the Holy Spirit? Of course not:

though it may well be a spirit, it was certainly not holy . . .

(4) Lastly, there was a spirit of divisiveness at work in the Church itself. The Ukrainian Orthodox Church had declared itself autonomous from the Moscow patriarchate in the early 1990s, rather as if the Irish had created their own pope and seized control of the biggest cathedral in Dublin, tossing out the Roman cardinal. Edward had told me that the Kiev patriarchate also rejected the use of Church Slavonic in services and addressed their congregations in Ukrainian, something anathema to the traditionally minded Moscow Church. And now, according to Father Roman, it was 'seizing' the congregations and property of the Moscow Church in Ukraine. The new nationalist government was in collusion with this strategy. The Ukrainian Church had even tried to grab his building, although it had been constructed and paid for by the Moscow patriarchate. The world was very evil; we were living in trying times. He had even heard that monks in the Kiev patriarchate got married. Married monks! Can you believe that? And the Ukrainian Patriarch Philaret, well, he liked to drive around in a big limousine. He was interested in earthly power, not the Kingdom of God.

The sky was starting to drizzle down on us. Father Roman hitched up a long black sleeve and looked at his watch. 'That's twenty minutes,' he said. 'Is that enough?' The question was a courtesy; we knew it had to be. Edward declared himself delighted. 'Good. God bless you, my son.' With that Father Roman left us, darting over to the consecrated house.

Edward set about examining the film he had just shot. He needed to check that everything had recorded, that the sound and light levels were good. I stood in the background, thinking about Father Roman's interview. To me, it didn't sound exactly like what Edward was after. Father Roman had spoken about political power and issues pertaining to Ukrainian nationalism, not the redemption of individual souls. But perhaps Edward had heard it in his own way. He could edit it later.

After a minute or so he turned to me and, in a very blasé voice, as if it were an afterthought, said: 'By the way, Father Roman is performing an exorcism now.'

'Now?' I said.

'Yes. Why don't you go in and watch?'

And suddenly, after I had given up, there it was again: the possibility of dark magic, of surreal mystery. Was it only when I stopped knocking that doors would open?

7

The church was located in the front room of the *izba*. It was overwhelming – crammed full of glittering icons and vivid frescoes, silver censers, incense, smoke, candle-light and gold, so much gold. The room was writhing with light and colour and tormented human flesh, flesh that stood elbow to elbow, thigh against thigh, nose pressed up against nape. I made my way through it to the back, where there was a little more space to breathe and move, until I found myself standing next to an icon of the infant Jesus emerging from a goblet of wine. The look on his face was calm and infinitely wise, as though he were staring straight out of the picture and into my soul.

As before, the congregation was mostly female, but up here, at the back, there were a lot of men. They had all made their way back here because they were less familiar with the ritual, and were seeking a place to hide. The man on my left, pale and sweating profusely, pain chiselled on his features, was casting around, looking at the icons and the candles, as if he couldn't decide whether to stay or not. He decided to stay. The women, meanwhile, were waiting with grave expressions on their faces. They weren't distracted by any of the gold trappings of the room: they were staring straight ahead, or at their feet, lips pressed together. The light in their eyes was inward. They were preparing themselves for what was to come.

This time there were no voyeurs, no suspicious monks lurking in the dark corners. There were no dark corners. The place was tiny, and there was nowhere to hide. Everyone was pressed together, in sin and sweat and fear. I inhaled the scent of pain and desperation, mingling with the heady stench of the incense. There were eighty of us in there. And yet the room continued to fill up, as more and more women with troubled expressions came through the door . . .

Father Roman entered. It was hard to see him, as he was smaller than most of the women in the front row. I caught a brief glimpse of him as he passed in front of the open space between two heads. Unlike Father Grigory he did not laugh, or set people at ease. His expression was extremely severe. But then again, he was about to challenge the might of Satan: what else could you expect?

8 The Exorcist, part 2

Father Roman's ritual was very different from Father Grigory's. He started with his back to the congregation, chanting. When he paused the congregation would cross themselves and respond: *Lord Jesus Christ, forgive us our sins.* I joined in with them and after a few minutes could predict when the crossing and the chant would come. It was quite calming, as I lost my sense of self and merged with the rhythms and gestures and poetry of the service. My sense of self-annihilation grew, as the lack of air and stench of incense made me light-headed. And then, after about ten minutes of floating in space, I heard something strange, a guttural snarling that shattered the atmosphere of peace and contemplation and drew me back to earth. It was a few seconds before I realised that it was a woman.

'CUNT PUS FUCK!' she said. 'Fucking wanker!'

Her voice was strained and strangled. Words were interspersed with barks. A weird rasping: rats' feet over broken glass. *Ah,* I thought. *Just like in the movies.*

'Cunt! AAAARGGHHHH! Shit! Shit-eating CUNT!'

A shudder ran through the congregation; but this crowd was prepared for these manifestations, and continued praying. I looked up, above the rows of bowed heads: there she was, writhing, jerking about in front of the iconostasis, lashing out at the priest as he advanced towards her. She had a thick mane of dark curls and was in her early forties. For a brief second I caught a glimpse of her features: twisted, vicious, disfigured by bestial hate.

'Shit-eating CUNT!'

Father Roman, still praying, remained composed. He turned to face her and placed a huge metal crucifix against her forehead. Then with his other hand he took a bushel of leaves and, still chanting, dipped it in a basin of holy water held by an assistant. He stepped closer and suddenly had the woman trapped in a kind of spiritual wrestling hold: his left arm moved suddenly to place the crucifix directly between her shoulder blades, while with this right he set about thrashing her violently on the face with the dripping bushel.

The woman howled, snarled, spat. Father Roman continued thrashing, chanting: *Let God arise and all his enemies flee before him.* A handful of people were jostling to get a better view, but most were still, eyes focused on the floor. This was not new for them, this was not shocking. On the contrary, they were steeling themselves for something, staring up at the ceiling, or at an icon. I saw sunken cheeks, and haunted expressions . . . then, suddenly, the woman fell silent. Father Roman blessed her, and began chanting again. Someone else stepped forward to receive prayer and a thrashing in the face. A woman, flustered, rushed past me to grab a plastic bag that was sitting on the floor next to me. This was the exorcised woman, the one who had been screaming and cursing thirty seconds earlier. I wouldn't have looked twice at her in the street. Once she was out the door she would melt into the crowds of Kiev easily, slip on a train in the metro and disappear behind a door in a high-rise block of flats somewhere. The city would go about its business, oblivious to what had occurred inside this little house, on the floor of this strange little room. Nobody would know of the struggle between the forces of dark and light taking place in her soul . . .

9

And so it continued, with people coming forward for prayer, getting thrashed, and then leaving. Some snarled and tried to wrestle the crucifix from Father Roman's grip, but most willingly accepted their beating. These were meek devils; they accepted that they deserved their punishment for tormenting mortal souls. A woman next to me, quite young, was nervously jogging about on her feet, and the next thing I knew she was at the front, spewing obscenities. She lashed out at Father Roman, but he was used to these attacks and dodged her blow with ease.

It was so strange in there, surrounded by the heat and the flames and the screams. I felt as though we were sealed off from the world outside, inside some strange glittering spacecraft, hurtling through the cosmos, and that we had left earth and Ukraine far behind. Set the controls for the heart of the sun: we were heading for the Eye of God, and Father Roman was excising the demons because you must be pure before you can gaze on the shining face of the Almighty. And it was at that moment of vertiginous disorientation that I looked down at my feet and realised that I was standing on the same linoleum I had on the floor of my kitchen in Moscow.

Suddenly the whole experience came much closer to me: some kind of invasion was taking place. I felt connected to these people, and not only them. All over the former Soviet Union, people were standing on that creamy yellow and brown linoleum. It stretched from Moscow to Kiev and beyond, into Central Asia, right up to China. What could it mean?

Not much. It was a coincidence, of course. But it was a coincidence like seeing my colleague acting in the film on the bus to Kremenchug, or like Edward phoning me as I walked past the Digger's flat. It *ought* to indicate a meaning beyond the rather obvious one: that there weren't too many linoleum designs in the Soviet Union. But what could that other meaning be? And who could I tell about it? And what did it matter?

Anyway, I quickly stopped worrying about it, because at this point I noticed that Father Roman was exorcising an extraordinary number of people. At first I had thought that they were moving towards him one by one. But as I watched him coming nearer and nearer I realised that this was not the case. In fact, it was he who was moving through the church, making his way slowly through the congregation, towards me.

Suddenly Edward appeared in the doorway. Seeing me, he pushed his way through the crowd, then leaned over and muttered in my ear: 'Father Roman is exorcising everyone in the church. If you don't want it, just say *no thanks*.'

I wasn't convinced. Father Roman was getting closer and closer, and everyone he passed was getting thrashed in the face. The whole room was caught up in a fever. I thought he might already be giving me a damn good thrashing before I managed to get the 'no' out. It was time to get out of there.

I ran: the Sisters in the hall didn't seem surprised to see me making a dash for it, either.

10 St Theodora

On the way out, however, I was stopped dead in my tracks by the fresco painted over the door. A woman was flying through the sky, and as she went she was tormented by hundreds of little black demons, swarming in the air around her. This was the sort of religious art I liked – full of hell and torment and anguished cries for mercy. Twenty minutes later, when Edward came out, I asked him what it was.

'Oh,' he said. 'That's St Theodora's journey through the Aerial Toll-Houses.'

'The what?'

'You know, the twenty stations in the sky where demons lie in wait for us. When you die, and you ascend towards heaven, they try to stop you by reading a list of your sins. If you have committed a sin, they get to keep you and torment you until the Second Coming. You don't know about this?' He was surprised.

'No.'

'Why there's a toll house for adultery, one for sorcery, one for murder, another for sodomy and so on. St Theodora died and passed through each one and then returned to earth in a vision to tell Gregory the disciple of Holy Basil what she had seen . . .'

'Hm.'

'It's all right, though,' Edward said. 'She made it to heaven in the end.'

I loved the way Edward talked about this. I loved that he did not strain to believe, or persuade. It always caught me off guard, the way these demons were as real and as present for him as the clouds that drifted overhead, as the birds crapping in the trees, and the rain pissing on our heads.

I should mention that Edward's face was red and wet. Bits of leaf were sticking to it.

'How do you feel?' I asked.

'Good' he said. 'Very good. There are some aesthetically pleasing features to Father Roman's deliverance service.'

'Yes,' I said. 'It's very dramatic.'

'Dramatic! Yes, that's the word!'

'Very different from Father Grigory's . . .'

'Don't discount the efficacy of Father Grigory's ritual . . .'

'I'm not saying it wasn't effective . . .' (But I did wonder what ranking Edward would have given it on his scale of one to ten. Now wasn't the time to ask, however. Edward was supercharged on God.)

'I said I'd show you something remarkable!'

And then, immediately, he was striding forward, leading me to the centre of town, seeking the next satanic encounter, as if he had already forgotten this climax.

A POSTCARD FROM UKRAINE

Lost property
We arrived at the central train station to buy tickets back to
Moscow. Suddenly Edward vanished, as he often did, without
explanation. I was left standing by the stairs to the lost property
office. After a few minutes he returned. But he didn't see me. I am
good at disappearing, at becoming the invisible man, lost in the
mob. I watched him for a while, towering far above the crowd,
looking for me, turning his head this way, and that way, like the
revolving beam in a lighthouse seeking ships lost in the night.
Eventually I stepped into the line of his vision.

'Where did you get to?' he asked.

'Nowhere,' I said. 'I've been here all this time.'

'And I didn't see you?' Edward was incredulous.

'I know how to avoid being noticed. Sometimes I project
myself, other times I'm good at sucking in my aura.'

Edward stared at me, alarmed: 'Never get involved in the
occult,' he said, very, very seriously.

THE STRANGE DREAM OF SERGEI TOROP

I

Traffic-Cop Messiah

1

Back in Moscow, Edward gave me a few days to recover and then resumed calling, summoning me to more summits in McDonald's. He had plans, so many plans. We had to go to Odessa, of course, and then Siberia, and then, and then . . .

Edward already had enough material for his documentary. He kept filming because he didn't want to finish it. Because however much the film was intended to be a way of infecting other people with his vision, it was also a way of keeping Edward inside it. Edward created his world by the act of filming. And for as long as his life was devoted to amassing information for the film, he could ignore that other world, the one that loomed, threatening, outside – where you are required to find a wife, and a job, to pay rent and car insurance.

He was already hatching plans: he told me that when he did eventually finish his movie, he would then make another film, and another film, and another . . . each one homing in on a new detail, or elaborating on a fact, or the life of an exorcist. A series of footnotes to the ur-film he was currently working on, that would carry him safely to his grave.

2

I wished him well with it. But there wasn't much room for me in there. Besides, on my last day in Kiev I had returned to the Vidubitsky Monastery, the site of one of our abortive demon-hunting expeditions, to witness one last exorcism. On our first visit I had checked the timetable of services and seen that a *vichitka* (the Ukrainian word for exorcism) was pencilled in for Saturday morning.

The Vidubitsky was one of the oldest monasteries in Ukraine, erected on a hill, surrounded by high white walls, above which peeped out brilliant green and blue domes and golden spires. As is traditional for many Orthodox monasteries it was difficult to reach, except in this case it was not a remote location that separated God's house from the temporal world but rather lethal traffic hurtling up and down a motorway. It was run by the breakaway Kiev patriarchate, which is why I went alone: Edward, although extremely open to all confessions of Christianity, nevertheless had some reservations about entering a Ukrainian Orthodox church. It wasn't that he was opposed to them, but he was concerned about how they would react towards *him*.

This is what happened: the priests chanted, the congregation prayed and crossed themselves, then the priest said something in Ukrainian and everyone got into a straight line. I joined them. The priest said something else, and everyone dropped to their knees. So did I. Then a long cloth was unrolled over our heads, and the priest started chanting. At the end of our line someone started screaming.

I was used to this by now, though. So I just kept my head under the cloth and waited for it to finish. It lasted about five minutes, then we all got to our feet and the congregation started lining up to get splashed with water and eat bread. I left, and caught the metro into town where I ate a burger. And that was that. I knew then that I had gone as far as I could.

Besides, I now had a new problem to deal with in my own reality. A visa I needed for my 'original' second book, the politico-historical epic that would have explained everything about a certain country in the post-Soviet sphere, had not come through. Without it, the projected follow-up to *Lost Cosmonaut* was impossible.

The strange thing was that I didn't really care. Something had changed – some force had taken possession of me in Ukraine. I knew I was already on another path, and that I had to follow it to the end. Meanwhile the next stage lay right in front of me.

3 The secret heart of the universe

Remember *Residential Property Shit*? Well, I have an admission to make: I had written for the publication in question.

Allow me to explain. After university I spent several years writing strange short stories that I never showed to anybody. Naturally they were brilliant, but at the same time, there was never any obligation on me to follow rules or make sense to anyone except myself. So when I decided to start writing for an audience I thought it would be good to submit to an external discipline for a while. I wanted to write things that were extremely tedious and in direct opposition to my own interests. In short, I wanted to commit a few acts of violence against my own soul.

That's where *Residential Property Shit* came in.

Their contributors were mostly Russians with a shaky grasp of English, so it wasn't difficult to get hired. I wrote some crappy articles to order that were bereft of style or any point of interest. The money was laughable. I found it hard at times to deal with the self-loathing. The only pleasure came from inventing ever more unlikely pseudonyms: my favourite was 'Becky Chambers', a former cheerleader who was enthusiastic about everything.

But every now and then I would suffer a lapse and try to slip something through that interested me personally. For example I had an idea for a story set in a barren wasteland called Uglich. Though it was only 200 kilometres or so from Moscow it took ten hours to get there by bus because the main roads and railway lines had passed it by. And once you arrived there was nothing to see except a church, some water and one or two old factories. The government had never got round to paving more than a couple of streets and so the citizens stood around ankle-deep in mud, gazing into space. The cinema had shut down; the only shop I could find sold rubber balls and a metal bucket. Wait, I tell a lie: there was also a sex shop. I went in and saw a row of dildos and butt plugs standing upright behind a glass cabinet. The girl at the counter asked if I wanted to buy anything.

'Just looking,' I said.

'Like everyone else,' she said.

I had come to write about a family that had turned their living room into an alternative-history museum, dedicated to Uglich. After wandering round for a few hours I stumbled upon their little wooden house. Inside there was a bizarre display of life-size *papier-mâché* dummies representing various deranged tsars and tsarinas with real or tangential connections to the town, as well as junk they had found lying in the mud: an old arrowhead, a piece of metal, a rotting camera. Bizarrely there was also an original edition of Diderot's dictionary sitting in a glass case. The father delivered an impenetrable lecture explaining that Uglich was the centre of the cosmos. Then he and his children dressed up in period costumes and enacted scenes from the history of the town.

I was there with Semyon, who had helped organise the interview with Vadim the Digger. The performance left him feeling depressed; he said the family was insane. I agreed that they were strange, but thought this was probably a good thing. Their madness had filled the world that surrounded them with meaning and symbolism. It gave them satisfaction. Instead of feeling hopelessly stranded, as many Russians in the provinces do, they felt absolutely central. 'Madness' was the best and most rational response to their situation.

I wrote this story up for the magazine, doing my best to cut out all the best stuff. But even so, no matter how boring I tried to be, I was never quite boring enough. They kept postponing publication until finally I knew it had been spiked for good. Then one day the editor said to me:

'Hey, have you heard of Jesus of Siberia? That's exactly the sort of thing you're interested in.'

'Jesus of Siberia?'

'Yeah. He's an ex-traffic cop who believes he's the Second Coming of Christ. He lives up a mountain somewhere in Siberia, surrounded by followers. You don't know about this?'

'First I've heard.'

'Well, about a year ago a guy went out there for us. He actually managed to meet him and conduct an interview. He wrote a story about it. A pretty good one, in fact. Didn't run it, though.'

'Why not?'

'It was too interesting.'

I shit you not: that's actually what he said.

4

And now, a year later the details of this conversation came flooding back to me, and I was suddenly filled with the urge to find out more about this 'Jesus of Siberia'.

Instinctively, I knew that he belonged with Vadim the Digger and Edward and even the family in Uglich, who I now understood were part of this same secret movement that I had been following, this group of unaligned radical outsiders who sought to supplant the 'real' world with one of their own imagining, to replace our drab molecules with better, more radiant ones. Like them, this man also sought to spread his ideas and convert others to belief in them.

But this Messiah went much further, in every way. If what the editor said was true, then here was a *literal* builder of an alternative reality. Vadim claimed he had followers, and Edward had sought to create them with his film. The Uglich family proclaimed their truth from their living room. But the Siberian Christ was not only possessed by a vision, he'd actually brought it out of his skull and into the world, and now people lived in it, as his followers, at the base of the mountain. It was physical; it existed. You could touch it.

I went out on the net to look for traces of this Jesus. It didn't take long to find some.

5 Traces

I

The newspaper interview wasn't very detailed. I learned that the Siberian Christ had been born Sergei Torop in Krasnodar, a city located in Russia's warm south, but had grown up in the Siberian town of Minussinsk, where in the early 1990s he had realised he was the Messiah. 'Torop' was interesting. I had never seen this name before; it didn't sound Russian. Better yet, it was true that he had been a traffic cop, an interesting career choice for a future Saviour of Mankind. Jesus was a carpenter: that profession has an appealing symbolic simplicity. A mangy rat-fuck copper employed in the most despised branch of a despised organisation, hitting up drivers of clapped-out Ladas for a few grubby, well-thumbed rouble notes as bribes, does not.

Aside from this, I learned that this Christ's name was not Jesus but Vissarion. Vissarion, like Torop is an unusual name. Its most famous bearer was a nineteenth-century literary critic, an early champion of Dostoevsky who was famous for his criticism of autocracy. Stalin carried it sandwiched between Josef and Dzugashvili as his patronymic. Apart from that, I knew of no others.

Vissarion said that he and Jesus were the same person, though not in any ordinarily understood sense. They shared some sort of cosmic soul essence, but Vissarion himself said it was difficult to understand. He and his followers lived in Krasnoyarsk, a vast territory ten times the size of the UK. Many dissidents had been exiled to this land, or had chosen to go there to escape state oppression. Vast, empty, full of forests and hiding places, it was a good place to build a new reality.

And now there was a new group of dissenters out there. According to the article there were *four thousand* Vissarionites, living in a hundred villages surrounding Vissarion's home on the mountain, which was called the Abode of Dawn.

II

The Son of God's own website was more thorough.

He had the right look: the beard, the straggly long hair, the slightly beatific smile. In some pictures he wore blood red robes, in others white. His head was usually cocked off to one side, as if it was too heavy to hold perfectly upright. The overall impression was warm and welcoming; but there was an *otherness* too. It was hard to pin down, but it was there, residing in his eyes: something enigmatic I didn't recognise.

Living on the mountain with him was Vadim the Chronicler. Vadim had shoulder-length curly black hair and a very long face. In another life he might have been a member of a particularly spaced-out Eastern European prog-rock band. But Vadim was the main scribe of Vissarion's Word, entitled the *Last Testament* (although there were some sections the Teacher had written himself, in his own hand). Everywhere Vissarion went, Vadim followed, recording the words and deeds of the new Christ for the generations to come: Matthew, Mark, Luke and John rolled into one.

Vissarion's followers were pictured en masse, in white robes, usually against a backdrop of green trees and lush grass. In this Siberia, it never snowed, and skies were always blue: life was an eternal festival. Women had garlands of flowers in their hair; men wore headbands. I saw some acoustic guitars. They reminded me of modern Druids, but without the defensive pomposity. The Vissarionites were unselfconscious, and totally beyond the fear of appearing ridiculous. The look of delight and happiness on their faces was like that of the Hare Krishnas you see dancing in high streets, handing out books with colourful covers: blissful, slightly vacant, alien.

I recognised these people. Over the years I had met many of them, though in writings about Russia today they are rarely, if ever, mentioned. There is a reason for this: the Yeltsin era of unbridled greed and violence very nearly obliterated their culture, and cast them into the outer darkness of poverty and total irrelevance, where they remain under Putin's steelier, more restrained helmsmanship of the Russian state. Nowadays they skulk, lost and lonely, scrabbling to survive like insects trapped in the cracks of Moscow's concrete vastness; or slowly starving to death in the provinces, wailing and gnashing their teeth as they try to make sense of what has happened to them. A few have given up and gone on to compromise with the state, or taken jobs as editors of (for example) *Playboy*. The vast majority, however, have been left out of Russia's new wealth entirely.

I'm talking about the massed army of dreamers, artists, hippies and musicians that arose during *perestroika* espousing a philosophy of crystals, the Beatles, Pink Floyd, mediaeval history, Tolkien and barely digested Eastern mysticism; who idolised the West as the home of freedom; who devoured long-suppressed books on spirituality; who read the works of Soviet dissidents when they were first published; and who mixed this jumble of ideas and a fractured conception of Russian religion and history with their own deep impulses: a sense of the Russian soil as sacred as well as tragic, and a desire to reject materialism and embrace the 'spiritual'.

They were the people who, for a brief while, had thought they were going to inherit the Soviet Union and make it good and holy. Had they been born ten years earlier they would not have been infected by the ideals of *perestroika* and could have retreated into nostalgia for the Soviet Union fuelled by bitterness. Had they been born ten years later they would have adjusted more easily to the cynicism of the nineties. But it was too late: they had been born into an era that died just as it was getting started. Suddenly the children of freedom were faced with a grim realisation: 'liberty' and 'democracy' had already come and they did not matter a fuck, either at home or abroad.

Sergei Torop was born in 1961. He came of age in the late seventies/early eighties, a period of stagnation and decline, and was a young man during *perestroika*. He was just the right age to have drunk deep of the ideals and images of this epoch. And it looked as though, deep, deep in Siberia, he had codified and formalised them, blending veganism with environmentalism and a late-Soviet hunger for all forms of 'spirituality'. The result was a creed that appeared to be the opposite of the governing ideologies not only of Russia but also of Western culture, however much it pays lip service to these concepts. And then, to top it off, he had declared himself not only supreme leader of the movement but God-born Saviour of all Mankind, establishing an authority that went way beyond the earthly.

And so out there, the children of *perestroika* could triumph – because it was not AD 2005 but 45 ED (the Era of Dawn). The cosmic clock had been reset with the birth of their Messiah. They had turned their back on the civilisation that had raised them up into the light only to cast them out into darkness. Now they were somewhere else, somewhere better, finding miracles in the earth, in holy stones shaped like bears and hearts, in new festivals and music, and most of all in Vissarion's word and luminous presence. Soon the end would come, washing away the civilisation that had wounded them.

After that? The new era, the new earth – and they were going to be at the heart of it.

6

I had walked in the darkness of the Underworld; I had heard the screams of souls tormented by devils. Now it was time to ascend into the light and encounter Christ. I became obsessed with Vissarion: I had to penetrate his community in Siberia, and not only that but seek out the Messiah himself, stare into his eyes and hear him speak.

The English-language pages of his site showed that he wanted to connect with the world outside Russia, and so my status as a foreigner would be an advantage in dealing with him: contact with me would give him publicity abroad. But at the same time, there was a lot of room for madness, strange demands and sudden reversals. After all, the Digger lived about a mile from my flat and it had taken three months to organise the septic tour. Edward never stopped phoning me with proposals, but still it had taken us over four months to reach Kiev, which was a mere sixteen hours away by train. As for Vissarion, he was thousands of miles distant, living on top of a mountain in a region where even the major cities were notorious for the poor state of their rotting infrastructure.

And being the Son of God, he was probably quite busy.

7 The quest for answers

I drafted an exceedingly respectful letter. Semyon translated it into exceedingly elevated Russian. It fell into an abyss.

I sent it again; the abyss was still hungry.

Next: phone calls to a remote room. I pictured a small cube, a single wooden chair, an old bed, an oriental rug on the wall, darkness. The old, black, Bakelite phone sat ringing on a battered and scratched table.

On the first day, it went unanswered.

On the second day, it went unanswered.

On the third day, it went unanswered.

But on the fourth day –

A woman, startled by the sound of her own voice, as if she had not expected to ever speak on the device she was holding in her hand. She had no answers, only another number. Semyon took it, and this time the call was answered immediately.

'It was some guy,' he explained to me, sitting in a café several hours later, 'called Vadim. Not the gospel writer. He was too old. This Vadim is some sort of personal secretary to the Teacher. He had a lot of questions about *you*.'

'Really?'

'Yeah. He'll need to talk to Vissarion, but I think he wants to help.'

'How did he sound?'

'What do you mean?'

'Suspicious? Paranoid? Like a paedophile?'

'Not at all,' said Semyon. 'He sounded very positive. My impression of him was very good.'

8

The obligatory stage of negotiations and counter-negotiations, proposals and counter-proposals followed. I wanted to meet Vissarion in his home on the mountain, and also to spend time among the believers in one of the villages, moving around physically in his reality. Vadim had no objections, but Vissarion was about to embark on a six-week tour of Russia, moving from city to city, accompanying an expo of photographs and text about life in the community, displaying his paintings (he was an artist in addition to being the Messiah) and also holding personal meetings. So if I was going to meet Vissarion on the mountain I had to leave immediately, or wait six weeks.

It was late September. In six weeks it would be early November. I had zero desire to climb a mountain in Siberia in temperatures of minus 40 or less. But there were few English speakers in the community, so if I went immediately I couldn't be guaranteed an interpreter, and, having read some of Vissarion's writings, which were prolix and convoluted, I knew I would need one.* But Semyon had a wife and a baby and a job in an office selling ATMs. The possibility of escaping that third feature of his life for a few days made him keen to go, but he couldn't leave at such short notice.

This led to proposal two, which was:

– Meet Vissarion in Moscow, the first stop on his Russian Messiah tour. This fell through, however, as Vissarion mysteriously disappeared a few hours after his arrival in the capital. Semyon phoned, reached a harried Vadim who was unable to speak, and then heard nothing for twenty-four hours. When Vadim called back the Messiah was sitting on a train heading north. For unexplained reasons he had decided to abandon the Moscow segment of his tour.

This led to proposal three, which was:

– Meet Vissarion in St Petersburg. Vadim offered to show me some photos so I could get a sense of life in Siberia, and a personal audience with the Teacher. But by this time I had experienced a shift in my thinking. I knew now that I had no choice: I needed to go to Siberia. An hour grabbed at the back of the Metallurgist's Palace of Culture in St Petersburg was not going to reveal very much to me. I not only needed but *wanted* to see Vissarion in his own environment, the one he had forged himself out of the great void, where he was at his most powerful. This was something remarkable, a grand achievement that was worth witnessing. More than that, I was suddenly glad, grateful even, that it should be difficult to get there. The path to salvation is always narrow and hard to find. Let the way forward be strewn with traps and snares: I was now ready to welcome physical exertion, madness and starvation.

Anything else seemed like cheating.

---

* Unlike Jesus, who favoured simple language and parables, Vissarion liked to elaborate at great length on his ideas. His *Last Testament* stood at seven volumes and was still growing. And even allowing for the problems of a bad translation, it was convoluted and difficult to follow. Try this single sentence on for size, from a section called 'The Last Hope': 'Then there comes the period of the disintegration of the force outlines which lasts for a certain number of days, after that all the information connected with the former organism joins total information which is kept by the more powerful Strength of Mother-Earth.'

And so on and so on for many, many pages.

II

Destination: Dreamland

1 Transition

I

Vnukovo is Moscow's oldest airport. I had never flown out of it, but I had heard plenty of stories – about wild dogs roaming free and pissing in the corners, that sort of thing.

This information was outdated. Vnukovo was now home to Putin's presidential terminal and Mayor Luzhkov, the man Vadim the Digger had considered his arch nemesis, had taken the rest of the place under his control. He was very busy transforming it into a metaphor for his personal vision of Moscow, though whether or not his wife's firm was directly involved in the lucrative reconstruction work I did not know.

The old airport was still there under the surface, even if concealed now by marble and plastic cladding to give it the appearance of modernity. To complete the effect the old kiosks selling stale bread and tea had been swept away and replaced with gleaming glass ones occupied by sullen women selling thimbles of coffee for $4 each. Shiny surfaces, crap service and low quality at high prices: ah, progress!

Luzhkov, a terrible snob, clearly wanted Vnukovo to compete with Moscow's largest and most modern airport, Domodedovo, and offer flights to exotic holiday destinations and sterile, 'civilised' locales like Stockholm or Helsinki. Alas, it was still servicing outposts of the apocalypse. We arrived late, under cover of night. The destination board read Mahachkala and Abakan. The first of these is the capital of Dagestan, a federal republic that borders Chechnya, home to a mountain-dwelling people feared throughout Russia for their perceived violence and criminality.

The second is the capital of Khakassia. This is the birthplace of the

Turkic tribes that swept westward to Constantinople, leaving behind them the cities and peoples of the states of Central Asia today. Though the land is littered with remnants of this ancient culture – including four thousand burial mounds and many standing stones – the Khakass themselves are nowadays outnumbered in their ancestral home. Ninety-nine other nationalities live there with them, though many did not come by choice.

And in addition, it is the gateway to Vissarion's brave new world.

II

We sat under the announcements board. Nobody was going to Abakan except us. It was bizarre: Vnukovo was a ghost airport, ferrying invisible people to invisible cities.

'I read an interesting story in the papers recently,' said Semyon. He was already half-sloshed on a carrier bag full of hooch.

'What was that?'

'It was about a Russian pilot who let his sons fly the plane.'

'*What?*'

'They were just boys, nine, ten years old.'

'What happened?'

'The plane crashed. Everyone died.'

I was sceptical.

Western newspapers are not the only ones containing poorly researched horror stories about life in Russia. Russian papers have them too.

'Are you sure that's true?'

'Yes. The investigators found the – what do you call it in English – "black-box recorder"? They could hear the boys' voices. They were laughing and having a very nice time – until they hit the ground, of course. The father was probably drunk. Russian pilots like to drink.'

'Are you scared, Semyon?'

'No, no . . . I just think it would have been better to take the train. It would have been nice, to ride the Trans-Siberian. We could have seen Russia . . .'

'We would have seen the inside of a railway carriage, more like,' I said. 'What's the point of sitting on a train for three days? That's why God gave us planes.'*

* A note on the Trans-Siberian Express: after living in Moscow for many years I had never met a Russian who had travelled on it, or would even consider travelling

III

We had to remove our shoes for the security check, but it was hard to imagine who would want to blow up a plane to Abakan. After all, if Semyon's story was to be believed, the pilots were perfectly able to take care of terror in the skies themselves.

The departure gate was downstairs: Luzhkov's remodelling was yet to reach this part of the airport. Here the green and white plastic of the original Soviet design persisted. The toilets too were 'authentic' communist holes in the ground.* Soon, however, it too would all be covered up with marble and plastic.

This vanishing corner of Soviet Moscow had a certain charm, and I was glad I had seen it before Luzhkov and his cronies got their hands on it. It was probably good that it was going: few people would lament it. But, like the final strains of a smallpox virus kept in a test tube in a lab somewhere, I didn't want to see it destroyed once and for all . . . how would we ever really understand its existence in future if we were to do that?

I wasn't the only one who preferred this rough and uncomfortable environment to the sleek façades upstairs either: this was where all the passengers were waiting. They knew that the dream airport under construction above their heads was not for them. The men wore black leather jackets and flat caps, the uniform of the Russian provinces. The women, mostly heavy set, had on thick fur coats. They were all clutching bags of treasure purchased in Moscow's shops. But none of them were Muscovites heading east; they were all citizens of Abakan returning home.

There was no tannoy. A fat old woman standing next to the glass doors leading to the landing strip barked 'Abakan'.

We got to our feet and shuffled forward. She collected our tickets in her hand.

---

on it, unless he was too poor to buy a plane ticket. The notion that it contained some romance was exclusively the province of foreigners. Those I knew that had made the trip reported seeing: (1) fields, (2) trees, (3) mountains and (4) poor people drinking copious amounts of vodka to escape the crushing boredom. Brilliant!

* Though at least they had doors. Traditional Soviet crappers were so communal they were open to the view of passers-by.

IV

Deeper into the darkness we went, deeper into the past. The view from the landing strip was classic Cold War: night, mist, planes of Russian officials, including the Atlant-Soyuz plane of the mayoral administration. It looked like something out of a film I had dreamed long ago, before I had lived in Moscow: about icy, mapless and unsmiling life in the Soviet Union.

Our plane was a TU-54. I had been on one of these before, but that plane had been retired and was in an open-air museum. I remembered, under glass, a display of tubes of cosmonaut food: pâté and cottage cheese in a tube.

It wasn't very comfortable. There was no leg room. I couldn't sleep. I irritated the woman in front of me by continuously bumping my knees against her seat. The little Khakass boy next to her got up on his knees to stare at me. He was wearing a woolly hat with bear features on it. It gave him an extra set of eyes. He stared at me with all four of them, impassive and wise. He looked like a miniature shaman.

The flight took six hours. I spent all of it gazing into the black nothingness of the window oval. Only once did I see the lights of a settlement in all that night, a floating, fragile cluster of luminous, cold coral in that vast deep ocean of darkness.

And then it was morning. We touched down and I disembarked onto cold concrete. I looked around and saw some sheds. In the distance: a couple of low, purple hills.

We were in Siberia.

2 Concrete mirage

I

I collected my bags and went into the arrival hall of Abakan airport. It was dark and cavernous. Something drew me over to a list of regulations, frozen behind glass on a marble pillar. The letterhead was adorned with a hammer and sickle and the legend CCCP. I was in a zone where rules issued in a country that had ceased to exist fourteen years earlier were still valid. Was the TU-54 not an aeroplane at all, then, but rather a time machine? And then I paused, mesmerised, in front of a destinations and arrivals board that jammed once, a long time ago. From Abakan you can fly to the earthly paradises of:

Moskva

Kyzyl
Vladivostok
Novosibirsk
Norilsk.

Don't forget your bucket and spade.

II

The Hotel Druzhba* looked like a giant dog-eared library book, split open and stood on its end, engulfed by dead sky and concrete. We went inside: the air molecules in the lobby, so rarely disturbed, bristled at this intrusion. It took a few seconds for my eyes to adjust to the darkness. Then I saw the receptionist, sitting behind a glass barricade, her skin milky as the eyes of a blind subterranean. We approached. She looked up.

'There's a better hotel in the centre of town,' she said.

'I'd like to stay here,' I said.

'Our rooms are horrible. Theirs are nicer, and cost the same.'

But I didn't believe in Abakan quality. I knew that would mean rank mediocrity at ludicrous prices. I wanted a bad hotel, a room someone had slit his wrists in: a place with atmosphere.

'That's OK,' said Semyon. 'We'd rather stay here.'

She shrugged and took our passports. She started copying out the details. But then she saw that mine was foreign. She handed it back.

'Really, you shouldn't stay here. Go to the Khakassia. It's better, and it's the same price.'

'But I want to stay here,' I said.

'You *mustn't* stay here. I'll call a taxi for you, if you just promise you won't stay here . . . Please . . .'

She was ashamed. She didn't want a foreigner to see how people lived in Abakan. She picked up the receiver, and started dialling.

I let her.

III

A serial killer was prowling Druzhbi Narodov Street. Next to a plaque commemorating a Great Khakass Painter I saw this poster for a missing person:

* Friendship.

Ludmilla Baturina
Born: 1959

Last seen 29th October, 1400 hrs, leaving office in Siberia hotel.
Looks about 35, blonde. Any info as to whereabouts, please
contact . . .

Above this text: a grainy, black and white headshot for a passport
or identity card. But the features were so blurred it could have been
almost anyone, even a man. There was something haunting about this,
as though the missing woman's face was dissolving, and with it, the
memory of her.

Four days had passed since Ludmilla's disappearance. The notice
was soggy, peeling off the wall.

The next one I found was already in the gutter.

IV

Abakan's shopping district lined the major highway leading into the
centre. Cars and buses rattled past the storefront windows.

There were a lot of mobile phone shops, and also one or two
designer boutiques: Mexx and Benetton. I preferred Lidya, however.
There you could buy not only detergent, pirate DVDs and school notebooks but also a suit of armour, a snip at $1,000.

It was very shiny, and it had a plumed helmet.

V

In the city centre there was a busy street lined with Stalinist neo-
classical houses. Some were painted pink, others yellow: very pretty.
One was home to the Union of Khakass Writers, a holdover from the
Soviet Union when all the county's nationalities were provided with
literary and musical organisations to bolster the state-approved versions of their cultures. I was surprised not only that the Union still
existed, but also that it could afford to maintain an office in such a
central position of the town. Meanwhile, two banners hung across the
street: one for a circus featuring 'Algerian lions' and another for DJ
Groove, who had been popular in Moscow ten years earlier.

It felt strange. I was looking at the same faces, and listening to the
same voices having the same discussions, as if I'd driven thirty minutes
out of Moscow to Zelenograd. But Moscow was four time zones

away. If I'd flown the same distance in the other direction I'd have wound up in London.

No, something definitely wasn't right here. I felt as though I was staring at a replica of something. Did this city belong here? Did these people belong here? How had they wound up in Abakan, so far from the centre of their culture? To me they looked marooned: Abakan was a remote island of Russian civilisation surrounded by vast oceans of land, and these people were doing their best to copy a world that was known to them only from the messages beamed to their radios and TV sets. The trees, the buildings had all been arranged to replicate these signals as best as possible. Whatever the true reasons for constructing the city, or why people had moved here in the first place, it all seemed forgotten.

VI

The tip of the ten-foot concrete penis had a happy face; beneath it there were various geometric designs; at the base was a keyhole. Behind the penis there was a boxy subsidiary monument, also decorated with geometric patterns. Nearby were some bushes, with multicoloured rags tied to the branches for good fortune. The whole ensemble was located in front of a building site.

A Khakass woman, the first I had seen in Khakassia, saw us studying the penis monument. She ran across the street to join us. She was wearing multiple jackets; her long steel-wool hair was worn in thick plaits. She flashed a smile at us, revealing a half-rotten chessboard of brown teeth and gold implants.

'Young men!' she said, pointing at the monument. 'What's that?'

'A monument,' said Semyon.

'But what does it look like?'

Semyon shrugged. I looked blank.

'No need to be shy. You're grown men . . .'

'We know what it looks like . . .'

'Out with it, then!'

'I said we –'

'It looks like a big cock, doesn't it? And what about the thing behind? If that's a penis, then this must be . . .'

'We get the picture,' said Semyon.

She tutted, exasperated by our modesty. 'Why, it's a lady's minge of course!'

She talked about cocks and minges and the creation of the universe. I couldn't keep up. Semyon didn't want to. He just nodded, staring above her head. Then suddenly I understood her perfectly:

'You know, here on this spot, four thousand years ago, there was a White Yurt. Do you know the White House, in America?'

'Yeah.'

'Well, here in Khakassia there was a White Yurt. And Adam lived in it. That's Adam over there, the one who looks like a cock.'

She pointed at Adam.

'Yes, Adam. The name has its roots in the Khakass language. So does *Rai*.* So does Jerusalem . . .'

'Thanks, but we have to –' said Semyon.

'And who was Adam's father?'

Silence.

'The King of Heaven! Well, Adam was a hunter, and all women loved him. But the problem was that no woman could get near him, because he was so fast and he was so busy hunting all day. But there was one girl who was clever and she had the idea that she'd put antlers on her head so that she'd look a deer and trick him into hunting her. And sure enough, when Adam saw her, he followed in hot pursuit. She ran and ran, but then he shot an arrow and wounded her, and when he caught up with her, well, here was a beautiful woman, just lying there, naked and all aquiver with her hot little snapper exposed, just quivering and moist . . . Adam had never seen anything like it. He –'

'I get the picture,' said Semyon.

'He cried out to God, his father, the King of Heaven – please cure this girl, so that I, the Great Hunter might know love! And then God looked down and – but wait, that's not all. Look closely at the face. Those great big eyes, that nose like a potato, the lips like a *lepyoshka*:† who does it look like?'

'I don't know.'

'Those great big eyes, that nose like a potato, the lips like a *lepyoshka*!'

'I still don't know.'

'I'll help you: doesn't he look Russian?'

'I suppose so.'

'Doesn't he, in fact, look like a Russian actor? Doesn't he, in fact,

* Russian word for heaven.
† A type of Central Asian bread.

look like none other than the great Pugovkin!?!'

'Actually, he does a bit . . .' said Semyon.

'Who's Pugovkin?' I asked.

'A Russian actor with a funny face. He made comedies. He's dead.'

'Now, at the base of the Adam cock . . . do you see the keyhole?'

'Yes.'

'It's the keyhole to paradise. But the problem is – there is no key. Now President Putin . . .'

'Yes?'

'Does he have the key?'

'I don't think so.'

'Exactly! Putin is going the wrong way. You know the Pope of Rome?'

'Yes.'

'Putin follows the Pope of Rome. That is the wrong way. Now what about me? Who do I look like?'

'OK, thanks for your time, but we have to go . . .'

'No, wait, one last question. Who do I look like?'

She played girlishly with her braids. She looked like a pagan witch, an old medicine woman, a female shaman, skin dried as leather by rituals performed in the howling gales of the steppe.

'Why, the Virgin Mary of course! And Mary, too, is a Khakass name in origin . . . Clearly this spot is the centre of the universe. Civilisation was born here, on the site of the White Yurt . . .'

We made our excuses and left. Of course, the Virgin Mary was outraged that we didn't want to hang around for further enlightenment. But it was starting to snow, and the cold was gnawing at my bones.

VII

Just beyond the Adam cock: a row of dilapidated wooden barracks. They had been slapped together as storage for assemblages of human bone and flesh in the 1930s. Seventy years later, assemblages of human bone and flesh were still living in them. Someone had daubed the legend 'Down with the slums' on one of the shacks.

Next door, vicious dogs prowled the brick house of a rich man.

Next door to that, stood the striped tent of the Novosibirsk Circus that promised Algerian lions and illusions. But the lions were silent, and a sign tacked to the *kassa* window announced that the circus was cancelled.

Beyond the circus, meanwhile, lay a vast park, where goats grazed and a metal tower built on the edge of a river commanded a view of the whole city.

The tower was unoccupied.

VIII
MONUMENT TO THE VICTIMS OF REPRESSION

I stared at the title for a long time to be sure that I had interpreted it correctly, that it was not dedicated to the war dead, or the White Army's victims. But no: it was definitely about the Great Terror. Apart from a rock near the old KGB (now FSB) headquarters in Moscow and some bad sculpture hidden behind the enormous New Tretyakov Museum, I didn't know Russia had any memorials to Stalin's victims. One was too many for Semyon, however. It offended his sense of patriotism: 'Anti-Soviet propaganda,' he muttered.

I went closer. The monument was a black wall, like a giant tombstone, incorporating the outline of a weeping female figure and a long list of names. More than 60,000 people had died in Khakassia, among them representatives of all one hundred nationalities in the republic. It was a remarkable list of names: Russian, German, Korean, Khakass and others I didn't recognise. The monument was so shocking that I wrote some of them down, as though later I would need to prove to myself that I had actually seen it; or perhaps I was reinforcing the knowledge in myself that there was a person behind each name:

Grek F. G.
Dementiev M. P.
Domozhikov G. S.
Shestak S. N.
Suetin N. T.
Penkin S. A. & S. A.
Kim Chen Bek
Kim En Mu
Doppert N. Ya.
Bahmanin V. F.
Veide E. K.
Van Sek Hak
Gaidai V. A.
Gogenberg H. I.

Gusev N. P.
Bekker F. B.
Abashin S. E.
Aeshin F. A.
Chydrgashev E. I., T. V., F. B., A. E., A. M.

There were many others.

IX

The prehistoric standing stones were embedded in dirt on the pavement outside the state museum. Khakassia was the birthplace of the Turkic peoples, after all: here were traces of those long-vanished ancestors. Unfortunately it was getting dark, so the details of the carvings rapidly dissolved in the gathering night.

A few minutes later we stumbled upon Victory Square. By the light of the sputtering eternal flame I was able to decipher the markings on another set of monuments that had preserved the idea and practice of ancestor worship when the shamanistic forms indigenous to this region were outlawed: the graves of fallen Heroes of the Soviet Union.

X

I ended my tour of Abakan with dinner in a Soviet snack bar and the movie *Doom* in the Nautilus Cinema. It had been a good day. Now, however, I had to change my thinking. Tomorrow I was going to travel to the village of Petropavlovka, 200 kilometres away from Abakan.

The rules would be different there.

3 I'm a stranger here myself

I

I awoke in a world grown much colder. Winter, so long postponed, had finally arrived. The slushy, late-autumn snow underfoot was now lethal black ice; the wind, raw and Arctic, scraped at our eyes. We half-walked, half-skated to the taxi rank. The journey that had taken twenty minutes the day before now took forty-five.

Vadim had reassured Semyon that all the taxi drivers would know Petropavlovka. But none of them did. Everyone we spoke to just scratched their chins: 'Nah, mate. Never 'eard of it.'

'Er . . . do you know Vissarion?'

Everyone knew Vissarion. Quickly we had a car organised. It was a 'customised' brown Lada Zhiguli with no rear-view mirrors or door handles (except on the driver's side), and, as a final touch, a piece of polyethylene in lieu of a rear window. The driver also pointed out an admirable feature I had missed: 'I don't have any snow tyres either. The weather was good yesterday, y'see.'

Although none of the cars was especially roadworthy, this one was unquestionably the worst of the bunch. In fact, it looked like a mobile death-hastening device.

'What the fuck,' I thought.

I climbed in.

II

We had been driving for about ten minutes when the driver said:

'Two hundred kilometres without snow tyres . . . hmm . . . not sure I'll make it.'

Which he quickly followed with:

'By the way, lads, have you got a map?'

III

The driver wasn't a fan of Vissarion. In fact, he thought we were wasting our time. 'Fuck that wanker,' he said. 'You should go to Krasnoyarsk. The city I mean, not the region. Now that's *really* interesting.'

'What have they got there?'

'A hydroelectric power station.'

'Really? That sounds fascinating.'

'It is. And they've got a fucking big dam, too. Biggest in the world.'

'That's true,' said Semyon. 'My dad's seen it. He said it was fucking big.'

'Maybe next time,' I said.

Nevertheless I did manage to draw some Messiah-related information out of the driver. I learned:

- Vissarion lives like a king, on money derived from the sales of his followers' houses, which they are obliged to give to him. He is driven around in a gleaming black Land Rover which can occasionally be seen in Abakan.
- His followers eat only vegetables. As a consequence they are pale, sickly people, prone to illness. The children are particularly unhealthy. They die.

- The Vissarionites are forbidden to use modern technological devices such as TVs and radios. Music is banned.
- Those who violate the rules of the community are cast out and exiled to the taiga, where they starve to death or are eaten by bears or die from exposure.
- The whole thing is a trick to con people out of their money. Vissarion's agents show people films of Siberia in summer. The films are full of images of beautiful landscapes and idyllic village life. Duped into believing they will enter a pastoral paradise, they sell their houses and then give Vissarion the money.

'And what do people in Abakan think about him?'

'We don't care. Everyone is too busy trying to make money. Just staying alive is a struggle for us. We're more worried about all the fucking Chinks coming over the border and taking over our markets. I mean, this is Russia, for fuck's sake. Why are we so poor and everyone else so rich? It's our fucking country.'

'But are there many people from Abakan living round the mountain?'

'He's taken everyone he can from round here, so he isn't interested in us any more. His followers are outsiders, city folk, arsewipes from Moscow and Nizhny Novgorod and places like that. He prefers to avoid Siberians. We're suspicious by nature. We don't fall for his kind of shite so easily.'

But, local or not, I doubted the driver's reliability as a source of information. It came to a head while we were discussing the Khakass. He had lived among them all his life, but he knew nothing about them.

'What religion are they?' I asked.

'Christians,' he said.

'Really?' I was startled. 'Who converted them?'

'Uh . . . I think it was Stalin. Yeah. Stalin converted them.'

IV

Minussinsk was a grim concrete outpost of Russian civilisation, whipped by snow and dirt. But this was where Sergei Torop had grown up, where he had worked as a traffic cop, and where he had received the first intimations from God that he was the Messiah. I tried to superimpose this knowledge on the reality I saw through the grimy taxi window. It wasn't easy: like trying to perceive a toilet plunger as a magic wand.

Outside Minussinsk the view was of old, low, tired hills – just like the ones you see driving from Fife to Glasgow. But I was in Siberia, so where was the sense of vastness? Why, if I was in the geographic heart of Asia, did it look so much like central Scotland? I kept waiting for the 'real' Siberia to appear – some mountains, a bear, a type of tree I had never seen before even: but nothing.

Gradually, however, some new features did begin to manifest themselves in the landscape. Periodically the hills would vanish, then reappear. Sometimes they had snow on them, at other times not. There was one area where the field was green but the road adjacent to it was buried under deep snow. Then we arrived at an area with no snow at all; then an area where everything was entombed in the stuff. There were fields; there was emptiness, a river. One moment a blizzard, then a clear blue sky: neither lasted long.

Human settlements were scarce and scattered. Occasionally we'd pass a grim village, rotting in the snow, and you could practically smell the human-flesh barbecue. They were the kinds of places where kids are found playing football with a human head.

Then we'd pass a lonely human, standing by the roadside, far from any village. What was he doing, I wondered, surrounded by so much snow and emptiness? Sometimes the humans were just standing around, black dots against the vast whiteness. Others were walking, but where to? We drove through a corridor of tall trees and spotted the figures of a father and son (or perhaps a paedophile and his victim) shuffling ahead of us. I expected them to flag us down. They didn't, but I still felt guilty as we drove past. Nobody should be out there, I thought, on the road, on their own. The space might eat you. The silence might breathe you in. And yet they watched us go by so blandly, as if we were a comet in the distant sky they could never hope to touch.

Three hours after Minussinsk the driver was starting to think he was lost again, so we stopped and spoke to one of these stranded humans. He was staggering along a remote country road running between the vast spaces of two empty fields.

'Hey! Where's Petropavlovka?' asked the driver.

'Where?'

'Petropavlovka! Are we on the right road?'

The man shook his head, smiling: 'Sorry, friend. I'm a stranger here myself.'

V

After about four hours we came upon a big carved wooden sign announcing that we had reached Petropavlovka. Instantly I knew that we were somewhere totally different from all the other villages. An old woman walked up. The driver wound down his window. 'Who are you looking for?' She was exceedingly cheerful.

But I was suspicious. This woman, trapped deep in the great void, abandoned by her government, should have been full of anger, bitterness and suspicion. I know I would have been. But her eyes were bright and her smile was honest and open: it just wasn't natural.

Semyon had been told to ask for Andrei and 'the German House'.

'You have come to the right place,' she said, smiling. Then she leaned in through the window. 'But what brings you to our little village?' she asked, staring directly at me sitting in the back.

I didn't answer. We drove on.

VI

The village was set in a flat plain enclosed by a wall of dark forest that ascended to crown a series of low hills in the distance. This was the beginnings of the dense and impenetrable Siberian taiga. Above that thick green line the world was a brilliant blue, beneath it, a dazzling white. It looked as though we were driving through the crater of a frozen volcano.

On our right, a half-frozen river, on the left – houses. Some of them were dilapidated, miserable shacks like those we'd seen along the road. But dotted among them were the frames of future homes, other buildings almost completed, and still others with roofs and windows that were light and bright and hadn't suffered from exposure to the elements. These were buildings intended for a future life, and not relics of an old one. They were startling and strange and alien.

Ahead there was a little hexagonal pagoda, and beyond that a big wooden building, about three floors high, with many windows and a pointed roof. I couldn't tell what it was for – it was too big to be a house, but nor was it a shop, or a shed, or a barn for keeping animals in.

It looked fantastical, like something from the pages of E. T. A. Hoffmann, the German romantic who wove grotesque tales of living puppets. Inside, a dead-eyed marionette was waltzing up and down the stairs. At night it would creep out from a cupboard and kill children with a pair of sharpened scissors, stabbing them through the ear as they dreamt in their beds.

The driver stopped the car and we got out. Just beyond the German House was a wooden church, all spikes and points, with a thin spire emerging from the bristling mass of subsidiary roofs like a wizard's hat. The cross on the church was not Orthodox. It lacked the two extra bars – one at the top and one slanted at the bottom. Instead it was enclosed in a circle, like so:

A wizened, mangy-looking guy was leaning against the fence of the German House, staring at us. 'Is Andrei here?' asked Semyon.

'Yes,' he said. I caught a flash of gold teeth.

'Can we speak to him?'

He looked us up and down.

'Depends. Who's asking?'

VII

It was an awkward moment. I had just invaded another world. The people here were perfectly content being unknown to us. What could we want from them? Why didn't we just fuck off?

And sure enough, Vissarionites started arriving at the house. They greeted each other with expressions of joy, with hugs, and kisses – and then walked right past us, beaming blissfully as they approached the entrance. We were invisible.

Only the mangy little guy with the gold teeth reminded me I had not blinked out of existence. He would not lift his suspicious gaze, as if he was worried I was going to make a dash for the doorstep, drop my jeans and commit a terrible act of blasphemy.

I managed to restrain myself. Suddenly a smiling hippy in a head-band emerged from inside. He looked like Bjorn Borg and spoke as if he had some seniority. That didn't mean he had heard of us, though. He hadn't.

'And not only that,' he said, 'but no one in the house knows anything about you either, ha-ha! Isn't that funny? You came all this way and nobody has the faintest idea who you are!'

Semyon explained that we had spent two months arranging the meeting with Vissarion. Bjorn Borg listened, nodding and smiling. 'I'm not saying I don't believe you, oh no. But there's a problem, you see – the Andrei you want is nowhere to be found!'

'But he does live here?'

'Oh yes. He's just gone AWOL. I haven't the foggiest where he is!' Bjorn Borg chuckled.

'What about Vadim?' asked Semyon.

'Vadim's in Krasnoyarsk right now. He won't be back until midnight. So you see, it's simply impossible to check your story or confirm exactly what you agreed upon with anyone! Isn't that funny?'

'Not really,' said Semyon.

Bjorn Borg wiped away a tear of laughter. 'Tell you what,' he said. 'I'll find you a place to stay in the village, and you can just hang around until Vadim gets back. If everything is OK, you can go up the mountain and meet Vissarion tomorrow. Just let me make a phone call.'

He disappeared back into the house. A minute later he reappeared.

'I've managed to put you in a house with English speakers. I'm not going to promise their English is great, but it's the best you're going to get! Ha-ha!' He paused.

'By the way, do you have a torch?' He was very serious all of a sudden.

'No.'

'Well you're in trouble! The village disappears when it gets dark.'

And with that he turned away from us and re-entered the German House.

VIII

Our driver had been standing in the background all this time, studying the proceedings. Semyon settled the fare with him. But he didn't want to leave: he was worried for us. 'Listen, lads . . . that guy was a fucking loon.'

Semyon shrugged.

' . . . a complete knob-end. He couldn't find his own cock in a blizzard, unless you tied his hand to it.'

'Maybe,' said Semyon.

'Take my number. Just in case. You never know what these fuckers might try.'

We duly noted it down.

'And if you make it back to Abakan . . .'

'Yes?'

'Let me know what happened, eh?'

He climbed back inside his car, slammed the door shut, and drove away.

We were marooned on planet Vissarion.

III

News from Nowhere

1

In Russian folktales there's a recurring character called Baba Yaga, a witch who lives in a log cabin that stalks the forest on enormous chicken legs. In some tales she helps, acting as a guide; in others she eats children. Tatiana's House was like this, only bigger, and some giant had cut its legs off and dumped it on its arse and left it there, stuck like a cripple in the snow.

Tatiana's House was the tallest wooden building I had ever seen: three storeys high, and terminating in a sharply vaulted roof. It had been constructed with love: elaborate carvings framed the windows, and just beneath the roof, between two peacocks with long, fabulous tails, was a heart. There was also a grinning sun. Sun-carvings are not uncommon on wooden houses in Russia, but this one seemed closer to the pre-Christian origins of the symbol than most.

The strange thing is that I cannot now see this sun in the pictures I took. Is this to be explained by the fact that I didn't photograph the house from every side, or did I just imagine it? Or is it something else – did my experience of the reality itself engrave that symbol on my memory, placing in my skull an object that wasn't there, but should have been?

2 The library at the end of the world

It was not what I'd expected to find in a tiny village entombed in the great Russian void. The room, though small, was lined with shelves that heaved under the weight of expensive coffee-table art books: volumes on Modigliani, Michelangelo, the Russian landscape painter

Levitan and many others. There were also Soviet-era 'complete editions' of the Great Writers, among them Tolstoy, Pushkin and Dickens. Then there were colossal dictionaries and encyclopaedias, medical and scientific manuals, school textbooks and piles of magazines. It felt not so much like a reading room as an archive, an essential record of accumulated human knowledge for life after the apocalypse.

Vissarion was waiting for us behind the door; in a photograph, that is. He was standing in the taiga, holding a staff that terminated in a ram's head. It hadn't been carved: the shape was natural.

I hadn't seen the Messiah for a while. He hadn't changed much. His hair was still long and parted in the middle. It still looked unwashed. His skin was still pale.

But something was different. I stared at the photo for a long time, trying to extract the right meaning from it. In Moscow, an image of Vissarion was just an image, something freakish and strange. It had no power. In this room, however, it was a totem, part of a mystery, something with a secret strength of its own I was not privy to. But it was very real to others, who were all around me, even though I could not see them. I stared at it, trying to access that power. I couldn't. The picture was jarring, alien, strange.

I was already deep inside a dream, much deeper than the Digger or Edward had ever been able to get me in theirs.

3

There was a creaking of floorboards, then the sound of feet descending a wooden staircase. An elongated Tatar appeared in the doorframe, bowing so as not to crack his head. This was Rashid.

Rashid had a pointed beard and arched brows, giving him the look of a wise poet in the Khan's court. But the effect was undermined by his woolly jumper, which was too big, and trousers that were too short; in addition, he was half-deaf and walked with a limp. His English, meanwhile, was stilted and emphatic, gleaned from poring over books with a dictionary rather than interaction with native speakers.

Rashid introduced himself and explained that we were in the Vissarionites' cultural centre, which would soon be transformed into a girls' school. Then he invited us to join him for lunch in a wooden hut a few metres away from the house, where Tatiana, the founder of the cultural centre, lived.

We got up and followed him out. It was just a few steps through the snow to the hut, and then we found ourselves in the entrance vestibule, a kind of airlock designed to separate the external cold from the living quarters. We took off our boots and stepped into the kitchen. It was a very narrow room, warm, cosy and dominated by a single sturdy wooden table. Soft Arab music was wafting through the room, emanating from a shiny silver CD player on a stool: so much for our driver's claims that music and technological devices were banned. But then, I had never believed him anyway.

'Come in, sit, be comfortable, ha-ha!" said Rashid. 'This is Natasha! She is from St Petersburg!' Natasha, a shy, smiling little woman doled out soup and buckwheat into big bowls, then retreated, waiting eagerly for us to partake of the delicacies.

I stared grimly at the buckwheat in front of me. *Of course*, I thought, *not only are the Vissarionites vegetarians, they're Russian vegetarians.* Until this point I had forgotten what that meant. In Russia, except for among the devout Orthodox, vegetarianism ranks about equal to eating raw human testes as a culinary option. As for buckwheat, I might feed it to a horse. If I wanted to sell it for glue later, that is.

But I was starving, so I spooned a mouthful into my hanging maw and started to chew. 'Hmm!' I said. 'Very delicious!' Natasha beamed like a little girl awarded a gold star at school. 'Yes! This is our new style kitchen,' said Rashid. He meant 'cuisine'; it was a mistake common to Russian speakers of English. 'Without meat. We love our animal friends – ha-ha!'

4 Rashid's story

Rashid came from Kazan, the capital of Tatarstan. He was proud of this, explaining that it was an ancient city, boasting 1,000 years of history to Moscow's paltry 858. When I told him that I had been there twice, and even written about it, he was delighted. 'And where are you from?' He asked. 'Dunfermline,' I replied. I decided to skip the reality and cut straight to the romance: 'It's the birthplace of kings, the ancient capital of Scotland.' 'Excellent!' he said. 'Then we are both the citizens of great capitals!'

In his old life Rashid had been an English teacher, giving private lessons to children in his flat in Kazan. However, after encountering Vissarion's writings he became very attracted to the Teacher's ideas of living 'harmonically' with nature and realised he had to change his life. He sold his flat and moved to Siberia. He had been in Petropavlovka for about one and a half years now, working as the 'manager' of the cultural centre. He was planning to bring his parents, both pensioners, to join him in Petropavlovka soon.

'What we are building here,' he said, 'is an "Ecopolis", where we will put the Teacher's ideas into practice, giving back to the planet what we take from it, and taking no more than we need. And these are very exciting times. At a big environmental conference in Germany at the end of this year, we will extend an invitation to people of all faiths to join us here in this work.'

'Did you say that *anyone* will be able to live here?' I asked. That seemed incredibly open for a hitherto closed community located in the middle of oblivion.

'Anyone. For the last fifteen years we have worked in isolation, but this was necessary so that we could develop our ideas and institutions. But now we are ready to end this period. Hindus, Muslims, Jews . . . all will be welcome. They must only respect our beliefs, and understand the importance of living harmonically with nature. Do you know Mutti Erde?'*

'No.'

'It is a big environmental movement in Germany. Recently its leader announced her intention to join our community. At first she was interested only in Vissarion's ideas about the environment. But now her spiritual journey has led her to full belief in the Teacher . . .'

Germans, of course, are the funniest people in Europe. I especially like it when they do strange things, like open nudist butcher shops, or live in wig-wams, or eat people they have met in chat rooms, that sort of thing. Consequently, I found Rashid's news quite exciting.

'Is she here yet?' I asked. I had wild hopes that she would be an ex-Baader Meinhof Group member, with tattoos of various methods of coitus on her beefy forearms.

'No,' said Rashid.

Damn.

---

* Actually, Mutter Erde.

5

Rashid, of course, was stressing how *normal* the group's beliefs were: as if all these thousands of people had decamped from Russia's cities to some of the most inhospitable conditions on earth from a simple desire to eat vegetables and be nice to animals. I was familiar with the technique. A few years earlier I had taken the group tour at the Scientology centre in Hollywood, where a perky girl had led us around an exhibition dedicated to the life and times of the mighty L. Ron Hubbard. The way she told it, Scientology consisted of some simplistic psychological theories and a grab-bag of entirely unoriginal ethical teachings, all very pragmatic. Of course, if you know you are holding some unorthodox ideas and want to attract followers, then you really ought to get your listeners nice and comfortable before you break out the stuff about Xenu, leader of the Galactic Confederacy.*

Suddenly a young girl came in to the room, a gust of freezing air following on her heels. She was blonde and thin, and pale to the point of translucence: without clothes, you would have been able to see the organs beneath her skin. Her English was flawless and for a second I thought she might be British or one of those remarkable Scandinavians who speaks the language almost as well as a native. In fact she was Tatiana, daughter of Tatiana, the founder of the cultural centre.

Rashid continued talking. 'Here boys are trained to become master craftsmen. We make beautiful and useful things, but not for money, for love . . . We give them to each other . . .'

Rashid seemed to think that was he was describing was new, and not an enactment of scenes written down in numerous utopias written over the preceding centuries. I felt like William Guest, the traveller in William Morris's *News from Nowhere* who one day awakens in a future cod mediaeval paradise of skilled craftsmen and beautiful maidens. Taken to the market, he is presented with a beautifully carved pipe for nothing; the craftsmen here work out of love for each other and the thing they are making and not for money. Tatiana undermined

* Evil alien overlord who 75 million years ago transported billions of people across the cosmos to our planet, where he lined them up around volcanoes and then dropped hydrogen bombs on them. Their disembodied spirits cause a lot of problems on our planet to this day, apparently. For more information, visit your nearest Scientology centre.

this impression, however, smirking as Rashid talked; amused perhaps by his naïveté, or his stilted English, so inferior to hers. He was aware of it – his speech stumbled once or twice before skittering to a halt entirely. Tatiana took over:

'So, what's your book about?' she asked.

'Er . . . modern developments in spiritual life in Russia,' I said.

Enlightenment did not shine in her ice-crystal eyes. That was good: I didn't want to talk about my theory of alternative realities. At the same time, I had not lied. I was absolutely certain that these new mutations of the spirit would have been impossible except in the very last stages of the USSR. They were thus inextricably connected with the birth and life of post-Soviet Russia. But I didn't think she'd be very interested in all that, either. I waffled on vaguely about exorcism and Ukraine instead.

6

The word was now out that there was a 'foreign journalist' in Petropavlovka. The village filmmaker arrived. He informed me that he had made several documentaries about life in the Vissarion Community, one of which was in English: perhaps I would be interested in viewing it in his multimedia studio later?

I accepted the invitation and he left. Then a Lithuanian entered. The Lithuanian wanted to see me because, like him, I was an outsider in Russia. In this world, however, he was very much an insider. He had been in the community for eight years, and was breathless about the change he had seen. 'We have built so much!' he said. 'Our community is growing all the time.'

Up until this point I had been too aware of the gulf between my worldview and that of the people around me, worried that if I opened my mouth I might somehow destroy my chances of meeting Vissarion. I was particularly worried about Tatiana: her English was too good; she was receptive to nuance, and I thought she was suspicious of me. However, I couldn't sit and nod in silence for ever, however loquacious the Vissarionites might be. My reserve was confusing them: they had expectations of a 'foreign writer' that had to be met.

'Was this village built by the Vissarionites, or did it exist already?' I asked.

'No,' said the Lithuanian. 'It existed before we came here.'

'So what did the original inhabitants think when you arrived?'

He laughed. 'They thought we were an evil cult.'

'Really?'

'Yes. In the past we had struggles with our neighbours. But now we live together in harmony.'

'What about Vissarion?' I asked. 'Does he come to the village often?'

'No,' said Tatiana. 'The mountain, where he lives, is about forty kilometres from here. He says the mountain was the birthplace of Aryan civilisation – that long ago our ancestors set forth and spread out across the world – but now it is time for us to return home. The mountain is also special because nothing was ever hunted or killed there; and it is also a centre of ancient energy lines – if you know what I mean . . .'

But then she broke off, as if she was aware of how this sounded. It was supposed to be fact, not a folktale. But Tatiana had been abroad. She had studied in a diplomatic academy, and had lived in England and America. She was attuned to alien perceptions.

'But Vissarion says he's coming down from the mountain,' she said.

'Really?' the Lithuanian was startled.

'Yes,'

'Well, well, well . . .'

'Did he say why?'

'No, just that it's going to happen.'

'When?'

'Soon.'

'What's life on the mountain like?' I asked. I found it difficult to imagine. Tatiana told me that the Vissarionites had built an entirely new village up there, a community within the community who lived close to the Teacher, thousands of feet above sea level.

'The conditions are harder up there, but not primitive,' she said. 'Oh, no! They have electricity. And they also have an excellent dentist's cabinet.'

'Really?'

She whistled. 'State of the art. There used to be a big cathedral up there too, but it burnt down . . .' she cast her eyes at the floor. 'But our people don't like to talk about that.'

Then she started to complain about the 'black PR' that circulated about Vissarion in the media. The Orthodox Church, she claimed, paid journalists to write articles accusing the community of brainwashing people, of stealing their money, of sickness and suicide in the villages. It is a common practice in Russia for businesses to pay journalists to write negative articles about their competitors, but even so, I doubted the Church was really behind this. If so they were naïve: the media needs little encouragement to write bad things about self-proclaimed Messiahs who gather thousands of followers around themselves in isolated regions.

Tatiana was convinced, however. And that wasn't all the Orthodox Christians did: for example, when Vissarion toured Russia, the halls he rented for his meetings often became 'unavailable' at short notice. What lay behind this mystery? Not so much the hand of God as the hand of the local Orthodox bishop, holding a telephone and instructing the authorities to stop this dangerous heretic from leading the souls of honest Russians to damnation.

Knowing how the Orthodox treat mainstream Christian confessions, that one I actually did believe. Tatiana broke off the conversation, though: the theme made her too angry, and she didn't like that.

7 Foreigners

I

Tatiana then started to list all the foreigners that had passed through Petropavlovka, to help me realise just how boring and ordinary I was in her eyes: it was part of her charm.

For example, I was not the first Scot to visit Petropavlovka. No, he had arrived in the village a few months earlier, while backpacking across Siberia. Intrigued by a sidebar in the *Lonely Planet*, he had taken a detour and spent a few days in the village.

'Ah, Scotland,' said Rashid, suddenly coming to life after a long silence. 'I love the film . . . what's it called . . . the one with Mel Gibson . . .'

'*Braveheart*?'

'Yes! It is great. About the wars between England and Scotland . . .'

'Stop!' snapped Tatiana. 'No stories about war and killing! I am sick of violence, sick of it.'

Rashid was silent.

II

Three years ago the BBC had come to the village. Tatiana was proud: in Siberia, the BBC was still a name to conjure with, an institution worthy of respect. And yet she was concerned: 'They promised to send the finished film' said Tatiana, 'but nothing ever arrived. 'Did you see it?' she asked.

I had my own ideas as to why the producers might have wanted to keep the finished product to themselves, but I declined to speculate. 'No,' I said. 'I haven't lived in the UK for a long time.'

'It is very strange . . . they promised . . .'

I said nothing.

III

A few days earlier a pair of Austrians had swung by, just to have a look.

IV

The best foreigner of all time, however, was 'the African', a woman from Côte d'Ivoire. I was impressed: had word of the Teacher's message really spread that far?

But 'the African' had come via Europe. Her husband was a politician who had fought corruption in his homeland, and after making too many powerful enemies, he had sought refuge in Germany. But the path from Germany to Petropavlovka was well travelled. Rashid had said there were several German Vissarionites, and the *Last Testament* had also been translated into German. And so 'the African' seemed less than astonishing to me.

But Tatiana was proud. 'She will return,' she said. 'And the next time, she will bring her husband.'

8 Tatiana's story

We had been sitting in the kitchen for two hours. Rashid and the Lithuanian were long since gone, and Tatiana wanted us off her hands. 'There's also a Belgian living here. He grows bananas. I'll take you to him.'

We went out into the snow and started tramping through the village towards the Belgian's house, following Tatiana. I asked her how she had come to leave her comfortable life in Moscow and move to Siberia.

'My mother converted first. I did not believe but still I would come here to visit her. And each time I came, I learned more about the community, and more about Vissarion's teachings. I liked what I heard . . . so one day I decided to stay. I was very nervous of course, and sad to leave my friends, but I've been here for several years now, and I don't want to go back.'

'But what do you *do* here?'

'I used to teach English, but I gave up. If the pupil doesn't have talent then I don't want to make the effort. What's the point? I still have one or two students but only the very best ones. Our children follow the standard Russian curriculum and take all the state exams, but we also add extra classes in the arts and crafts to bring out their creativity. So now I teach dance. I like it much more.'

But I was confused by Tatiana: she was in her early twenties, cosmopolitan, a product of the new Russia. She had travelled widely and lived abroad; she spoke foreign languages fluently. By any standard, she was privileged. That did not mean she was exempted from a spiritual hunger or feelings of emptiness, of course. But even so, I had expected to meet *perestroika*-era hippies in the village: Vissarion's ideas were more tailored to her parents' generation.

'But don't you miss your old life?' I asked.

'No,' she said. 'I never miss the world. I've done all that. What's the point of travel, of going to places just to stare at some old bricks and pictures? I don't miss Moscow either. Everyone is so concerned about money and status there. But why *pay* someone to chop wood for me, when I can do it myself . . . the Teacher says –' she broke off. 'No, I don't get bored. I am always busy. I am happy.'

And then her words just stopped, and the conversation dried up, as it always did.

She was happy.

Good for her.

9

We arrived at a futuristic-looking house with solar panels on the roof. This was the Belgian's domain. The Belgian wasn't in. His bananas would remain for ever unknown to me.

He did have nice digs, however – the best I had seen, in fact. Tatiana explained that when you sold your house 'in the world' the community used the money to build a new one for you in the village. However, the more money you had in your old life, then the better a house you would have in Petropavlovka, or wherever you were settled. 'And so we cannot live without the outside world completely,' she said. 'Old divisions of wealth and poverty remain.'

This was strange: I would have thought it simple to implement a rule whereby the profits of house sales were pooled collectively so that everyone starting a new life could be given the same size of house and same amount of land. Vissarion, for some reason, had decided against establishing this sort of equality in his Ecotopia.

'What about people with no money?' I asked.

'They get a smaller house.'

'No, I mean, people with absolutely no money?'

'They are given old houses, or a room.'

Tatiana led us back to the cultural centre. 'You mustn't think that all our villages are like this, with cultural centres and banana plantations,' she said. 'Petropavlovka is our "capital". It has more amenities. The others are . . . simpler. But now I must leave you. I am travelling to Moscow tomorrow and I have a lot of preparations to make. Goodbye.'

And with that, she was gone.

10

It was the middle of the afternoon. We were in a Siberian village. It wasn't immediately clear what we should or could do next.

We returned to the library. I didn't know much about Modigliani, so I picked up that book and tried to read the introduction. But I couldn't concentrate. Fortunately Semyon found some less cerebral reading matter: English-language magazines that had been acquired on a trip to the US in late 2001. Reading them in late 2005 was a strange experience. They had not been intended to endure, and seemed to come from a lost age. The editor of *Maxim* fired a few words of defiance at Osama Bin Laden from his comfy chair, but *Celebrity Hair*, *Movieline* and the *National Enquirer* were indifferent towards that particular apocalyptic event.

I read about Michael Jackson's secret baldness and Whitney Houston's impending death. Meanwhile a few little girls came in and sat down to read books and draw pictures in silence. They took no notice of us; they were too busy adding culture to their young minds. We might as well have been houseplants.

It was strange though. Two foreigners would never be left unguarded in a roomful of preteen girls in the UK, where, as anyone who reads the papers knows, every bush and shadowy corner conceals a slobbering, deranged pervert. The news had not reached the Vissarionites, apparently.

It grew dark. Every now and then the ceiling or stairs would creak, but nobody came to check up on us. Was it trust? Innocence? Freedom? Or had we had just been forgotten?

I didn't care. I was bored. We went out, leaving the girls to their education.

11 Secret meat

The village had disappeared, just as Bjorn Borg had promised, leaving a dark void in its place. There were no street lights, and the moon could not break through the clouds to illuminate the snow. Sometimes a meagre light would dribble from the window of a house, but die in the all-engulfing shroud of darkness before it touched the earth.

According to the Lithuanian, there were two shops in the village, one run by the Vissarionites and another that wasn't. I wanted to find that second shop and buy something that Vissarion had banned, like a piece of raw meat. I wouldn't eat it, though. Instead I'd carry it around in my pocket. It would be especially nice if it were bloody, and it started to soak through my clothes, so I could walk around stained with the blood of a murdered animal. Maybe I would sleep with the meat under my pillow: it would be my own, secret meat.

I explained this to Semyon. 'Why?' He said.

That was a tricky one. 'I don't know,' I said. 'I just feel an urge . . .'

We fumbled our way through the darkness to the shop. It was little more than a shed: a woman with gold teeth stood behind the counter, mistress and guardian of her meagre supplies – sweetened bread cakes, sugar, washing powder and a chicory coffee substitute. There was no meat, but I did see lard. That would do: I could slip some in my pockets, get it on my palms and under my fingernails . . .

The man ahead of us in the queue was chatting with the shop assistant. She replied in a mix of Ukrainian and Russian, her gold teeth flashing. *Nema*, she said, *nema*. I thought of Poltava, green fields, Father Grigory declining Edward's last request for an interview: it all seemed to have happened so long ago.

Nema, of course, means *there aren't any*. That is to say, she didn't have what her customer was looking for. But he wouldn't get out of the way and let me get my lard. Instead he stood there, chatting, about the village, about this person and that person. They were friends, fellow villagers: they had known each other forever in this village on the edge of forever. They measured time differently from me.

We stood in line for fifteen minutes, then left. Outside it was still Petropavlovka, and it was still dark.

What were we going to do now?

The night did not answer. We trudged back through the snow to the cultural centre. It was just after five.

IV

First Steps Towards Enlightenment

1 Tatiana Sr's Story

Some hours later the older Tatiana arrived. I put down *Celebrity Hair* and went into the hall to engage her in conversation. She was a solid, middle-aged woman with red cheeks and a blonde bob. Where Tatiana the daughter was cold and aloof, Tatiana the mother was warm and open. 'Have you toured the building yet?' she asked. 'No,' I replied. 'Then let's go!'

She led me upstairs to the computer room. Rashid was in there, staring intently at a monitor. The centre had internet access, and I was welcome to use it. Then I was shown the room where the girls of the village enhanced their femininity through sewing and weaving. But now Tatiana was so inspired by the poetry and beauty of life in Petropavlovka that she seized my hand and, staring directly in my eyes, started to tell me her story.

'Before I came to Petropavlovka,' she said, 'I had many professions. I am a trained philologist, and a qualified librarian. I worked for the newspaper *Sovietskaya Rossiya* – do you know that paper? I was the editor. And my husband was a film director. Because of my work I had many opportunities other people in our country did not. I have been to thirty countries. I have never been to Scotland, and that is a pity, but I have been to London five times! I love London, especially – what's it called – St James's Park! Have you been there?'

'Yes,' I said. 'It's beautiful.'

'So beautiful! But let me tell you – I suffered from bad health in the early 1990s. I was hospitalised five times. And I was so ill that I saw no reason to go on living. I didn't care then about parks and careers and travel. What was it all worth? What did it all mean? But when I heard of Vissarion and his teachings, everything changed. I recovered from my illness and I started to see a reason to live again.' She paused, took a breath, then leaned forward so her nose was almost pressed against mine. 'There are five thousand books in my personal library. *Five thousand!* And yet, I would give them all up for Vissarion's seven. There is such wisdom in the *Last Testament* – it's like nothing I've ever read before! And I am not uneducated, or gullible, you understand? I am a trained philologist and a professional librarian. People say, "Vissarion is Christ, he is the Messiah" – and all that *blah blah blah*. Is he Christ? Who can say? All I know is that he is an incredible man . . .'

2

The ground floor was a communal TV room, doubling as a dormitory for workers from Vissarion's mountain posted temporarily to the village. Two of them were in there, watching *Back to the Future*. One of them was a dark-eyed dwarf with enormous shoulders who was holding a cheese grater in his hand. Tatiana introduced him to me as Ali, from Dagestan. 'He is a Muslim!' she said, especially proud of the fact that a member of this particular religion had converted: the prophet decreed death for apostates, after all. The second worker was a young guy in paramilitary fatigues. Tatiana didn't introduce him, or even look at him.

A photo of Vissarion and several paintings were hanging on the wall. One of them was a muddy landscape Tatiana had bought with her first ever wage; another was a bright painting of slender girls of varying ethnicity dancing and banging tambourines. The painting was a carefully sexless 'tribute to the beauty of the young girls of the community'. She mentioned the artist's name. 'Do you know him?' she asked, as if fame in Petropavlovka amounted to fame beyond the borders of Vissarion's world.

'No,' I said.

Tatiana was disappointed. 'A pity. He is very talented. We have so many talented artists and musicians in our community. You know, before we came to this village there was nothing at all. It was dead, like all the others you saw on the way here. But now, with the money from the sale of my flat in Moscow, I have built this school, a dance hall and my own cottage. But I am not finished: I dream that this is the beginning of what will one day be my art gallery . . .'

Suddenly she turned to Ali and Camouflage Boy. 'Right, you two, out.' There was a pause. Nobody moved. 'I'm going to show Daniel a film.'

'Excuse me?' I said.

'It's all right, they don't mind.'

Ali got up and left, taking his cheese grater with him. Camouflage Boy was slower to get to his feet.

'Oi! Get out!'

'Really, it's not necessary –'

'Oh, don't worry about him,' said Tatiana. 'You're our guest.' Camouflage Boy exited, grumbling as he was cast into the outer darkness. Tatiana slid a DVD into the machine. The sound of ethereal bells ringing in the heavens filled the room, and then the screen lit up with a revolving gold cross, its four points enclosed in a sparkling circle, and the narrative began . . .

3 Film 2005: the Vissarionite community in Siberia

Intro

Mountains, forests and shimmering Tiburkul, 'God's Lake', in Khakass: beautiful as a dream, bearing so little resemblance to the bitterly cold tomb-world I had just been wandering around in. Children are laughing, couples are smiling. The narrator echoes young Tatiana: 'The Aryans lived here, and are preordained to return to fulfil the Will of the Almighty . . . the heart of the earth is right here.'

Data

There are tens of thousands of members of the church in Russia and abroad. Of the four thousand that live around the mountain itself:

39.5% are men
60.5% are women.

The average age is between 30 and 50. Of these:

36% have higher education
31% are graduates of colleges or trade schools
33% have school certificates only
85% of the community members are Russian
15% are 'other' (comprising thirty-four nationalities).

There are 830 children under the age of sixteen; the population of the community is growing nine times faster than the Russian average.

Lifestyle

There is no ban on the consumption of dairy products, but they are not recommended. Animals are not eaten, but horses are kept for haulage. Sheep's wool and goat's hair are used to make warm clothes in winter. The community grows a variety of crops, including rye, oats, buckwheat, and potatoes. They strive to keep technology to a minimum and plant by hand. And yet, even operating under these restrictions there are greenhouses where the community's farmers are successfully growing crops atypical for Siberia – tomatoes, sweet peppers, cucumbers, aubergines, and even grapes! All of this is being combined to create interesting new culinary experiences.

Transformations of the soul are under way: a computer technician learns rod-weaving; a chauffeur becomes a potter; a metallurgist is now a blacksmith. City dwellers are mastering traditional arts and crafts.

The goal is to become an entirely self-sufficient settlement. At the moment, however, the community is still attached to world economy, and its craftsmen sell furniture and other works of the hand at festivals and fairs in the Krasnoyarsk region to raise funds.

The mountain

The Abode of Dawn is being built on Mount Sukhaya, 1,000 metres above sea level. This is where Vissarion lives. At the moment the buildings are made of wood, but as the skills of craftsmen develop it will be transformed into a city of stone that shall endure for ever. The town is divided into 120 plots, fourteen streets radiating starlike from the centre. It will not grow beyond these limitations, for cities are dehumanising. The other members of the community will live together in a network of villages radiating from the mountain.

Men and women

One man and one woman, living together in a bond of love that produces children. A believer will never leave his family of his own free will.

Children

Boys are raised as master craftsmen, while girls are trained to be feminine, skilled hostesses, who care for the home. The creativity of children is encouraged, their imagination is fostered, but no negative or destructive images are permitted. Only the good in a child's soul should be strengthened. Petropavlovka has a media studio that produces 'Magic Box' comics, concerts and activities for the children according to these principles; and so children are exposed only to kind, gentle stories, that they may grow up the same way.

Communion

In some of the villages, all possessions are held in common. The aim is to overcome the personality, and forge new types of relationship devoid of ego and fear. Problems are discussed together and resolved together. Sometimes the people of these villages meet, link arms and form a circle for communal singing and dancing, singing the new songs written by the musicians of the community.

Outro

The ethereal bells return and the Messiah, in blood-red robes, walks through a crowd of adoring followers. The camera follows him for a full two minutes, mysterious, silent, acknowledging the love showered down on him with a smile. His eyes are half-closed, giving him a dreamy expression: he is present, yes, but also elsewhere, someplace higher and brighter. Vadim the Chronicler is on Vissarion's left, while on the right another man, wearing an altogether graver expression, is gently guiding the Messiah forward, a hand at his elbow. The camera focuses on the Teacher's blissful expression, and the happiness of his followers.

Vissarion does not speak. He keeps his revelation to himself. But you see the beauty he is creating, don't you? And though you do not believe yet, surely you are at least curious . . .

4 Ali's story

The film finished. Camouflage Boy returned, Ali behind him, cheese grater still in hand, and he had also now acquired a turnip. Ali started telling me his story, and the video I had just seen played a central part in it. It wasn't easy getting the details out of him though: Russian was his second language, and he answered questions briefly, in short sentences that stood alone and came to a definitive end, never opening up any other thoughts or associations, always looking down or away as soon as he was finished.

Ali was from the mountains. I had read about that life: remote villages where men lived as tribal patriarchs with four wives and enormous families. I had read too that Wahhabism, the strict Islamic sect promoted by the Saudis, was spreading, radicalising the populace. Ali didn't say anything about that, though: he had lived for years in Mahachkala, the capital, running some businesses: shops, cafés, a gym. It was in the gym that he had first heard about the Teacher, from a Vissarionite who used to come in a few times a week to train. Like Ali, he was a power lifter. ('Because I am small,' he said, 'I have always had to fight.') The Vissarionite talked about his beliefs; Ali liked what he said. Then he gave him some videos. Ali liked what he saw. After that he visited the community twice and had three meetings with the Teacher.

'Personal meetings?' I asked.

'Face to face,' he nodded, keen to make me understand how close he had been to the Son of God. 'I was impressed by the Teacher's words. And so I decided to sell my things and come here.'

Now he lived on the mountain, close to the Teacher, alongside the most deeply committed believers. His new trade was that of a stonemason, and he made steps for the path that led to the temple on top of the mountain, so that in the future it would be easier for the faithful to get up there. He worked day and night, but he was too busy to complain. ('And anyway, because I am small, I have always had to fight.') Life was getting a little easier too: they now had electricity, not from a grid but from solar panels. They gave power for only a few hours a day, but it was enough for his TV.

It had been question–answer all the way, the most excruciating sort of conversation. But then suddenly, apropos of nothing, he looked me directly in the eyes and said, 'I have a four-month-old daughter.' He paused; that wasn't all. 'And my wife is Russian.'

In the Soviet Union the leaders of non-Russian republics had frequently married Slavic wives; it was a mark of status. Ali wanted me to know how far he had come, how much he had gained by abandoning his old life of struggling against mockery, derision, bullies. Now he struggled for the future. In Siberia, and only in Siberia, had he found meaningful work, acceptance, family, love, status.

And it was all down to Vissarion.

5 Eavesdropping

Meanwhile Camouflage Boy had switched *Back to the Future* back on. He wasn't interested in talking and sat facing away from us. I took the hint and went upstairs. But noise carries in wooden houses, and a few minutes later I heard arguing.

Male voice: I can behave how I want!

Tatiana's voice: Not in my house, you can't!

This wasn't the first time I had overheard mutterings of conflict. Earlier, whispered voices had travelled up the stairs:

They're calling a meeting to discuss the relationship between the two girls . . . Masha and Lena . . . they wanted to live together . . . but they fight all the time . . . they're going to be told that they have to become friends or they'll be separated . . . sent to live in different houses . . .

Meanwhile the meeting under way in the German House when we arrived was also about resolving conflict between two men. The whole community was getting together to discuss possible solutions.

Were we already uncovering the dark truth behind the façade of bunny-petting, vegetable-eating loveliness?

6 The inevitability of a fiery death

Well, maybe. The tone usually adopted in writing on modern-day saviours and their followers is extremely negative. The miniature apocalypses of David Koresh and Jim Jones are world renowned, but there are plenty of other, smaller ones too. Just the day before flying to Abakan I had read an article about an American organisation called the Family: I had never heard of them, but the allegations were truly horrific, detailing sexual abuse so bad that one of the victims, who was actually the group's chosen Messiah, had rebelled and sought out his mother, the Family's 'spiritual leader', in order to kill her. He failed, but not before stabbing her lieutenant to death and then retreating to an abandoned car park, where he shot himself in despair.

And what about 'brainwashing'? Semyon's father, a high-ranking Soviet engineer, was outraged his son was accompanying me to see

Vissarion. He was concerned that the group might somehow be in possession of a magical, hypnotic technique for separating the weak and gullible from their money. This was a common view: why else would anyone be so stupid as to believe a traffic cop was Jesus?

And then there were the comments of the taxi driver, which I later found repeated in the Russian press, that Vissarion was working a scam, that the children in the villages were undernourished and infected with tuberculosis, and that his followers might one day commit mass suicide. There was never any evidence given to support this claim other than that it had happened before, in other countries, under other Messiahs.

There are indeed a lot of Christs out there giving Messiahs a bad name. But I have purposefully avoided the word 'cult' in this narrative, not out of some spirit of equivalence, or approval of what Vissarion is doing, but simply because it is such a loaded term that it gets in the way of seeing.

I was wary of looking for evil. I knew that I was actively *seeking* cracks in the façade, that I *wanted* them to be there, like someone staring at a grainy photograph of a blur in the sky, willing it to be a UFO, when really it's a smear on the lens. But I was equally determined not to do this: it's good to be on the alert, but being overly suspicious is no better a way of approaching a phenomenon than being overly credulous of it. The Vissarionites had fights: what was shocking about that? They didn't claim to have attained perfection. Not yet, anyway.

I was there to listen, to record, to try to understand; interpretation or judgement could come later. I resolved then to resist the (admittedly powerful) urge to prophesy impending fiery death based on whatever angry words I heard. Not every Messiah is David Koresh or Jim Jones.

7 Inauguration into the mysteries

I

After she had finished castigating Camouflage Boy, Tatiana invited us to join her in her house for some supper, where Natasha had prepared some more 'interesting new culinary experiences', this time in the form of oats and salt, for our delectation.

I studied the room again, seeing it more clearly. The painting of the dancing girls in the TV room was reproduced here as a calendar. The year was given as 45 ED, that is to say the Era of Dawn, which had begun with Vissarion's birth. Underneath there was something about ancient Chinese methods of healing and an alphabet of 'magical' words: I tried to memorise them, but when I came to write them down later they had all merged into each other – variations on *bright, clear, magical, wonderful* and so on. Magical words, it would seem, lose their magic when placed in close proximity to each other.

It was time to inaugurate me into some of the mysteries. Tatiana was holding some framed photographs of Vissarion behind her back; one by one she brought them forward to reveal unto me the changing face of the Messiah.

Portrait #1 consciously mimicked Catholic iconography. Vissarion's head was bowed, and his eyes gazed inwards at some terrible torment, as though he were suffering terrible agonies on the road to Calvary itself. This Vissarion was not so much the God-man as the man-god, a mortal struggling with the divine part of his being. Could he carry this burden, this terrible responsibility?

Portrait #2, stark, black and white, had been taken in Israel. Vissarion's eyes were still haunted, his features were still gaunt, but there had been a change. Now he was looking up towards a sky we could not see, and an illumination had touched his face, giving it an ethereal quality.

Portrait #3 revealed the Christ Triumphant: Vissarion sitting on a throne with a gold crown on his head. Thorns and roses were inter-twined in the metalwork, the Teacher acknowledging pain, but merg-ing it with something new and brighter, with beauty and hope and love. Vissarion was smiling too, having attained harmony with the divine aspect of his being. He now wore white: last year he had cut up his old red robe and gifted squares of it to his followers.

'Did he cut it himself?' I asked.

Tatiana looked puzzled. 'I don't know,' she said. 'It's not important. Look! He is a king! And doesn't he look like Christ?'

'Yes, he does.'

'It's not a coincidence! For two thousand years this face was pre-pared. On his first trip to Israel, people asked for his autograph . . .'

Tatiana had obviously made up her mind since we'd spoken in the house. Vissarion most certainly was the Christ, and she was out to prove it to me.

II

Next, Tatiana pressed a Vissarionite cross into my palm.

'This is a symbol of Vissarion's mission on earth: the four points of the cross represent the world's four main faiths: Taoism, Buddhism, Christianity and Islam. The circle encloses them because the Teacher has come to unite all religions under the banner of the *Last Testament*.'

'Why those four?' I asked. 'Why not include Judaism? It's the source of Christianity and Islam. And Hinduism is older than all of them.'

'Er . . . those are OK,' said Tatiana, 'but they're not that important . . . they're just branches off the main tree.' She changed tack: 'Do you believe in reincarnation?'

'It can't be proven either way,' I said.

'The Teacher says that we all live many times.'

'Hm . . .'

'Listen to this uncommon wisdom: in the *Last Testament*, Vissarion asks whether we should love both the good man and the evil man, or only the good man.'

'Christ commanded us to love everyone,' I said.

'That's a good answer,' she said, before promptly launching into a long speech I couldn't follow. Semyon, blank-eyed and miserable, had given up interpreting: theological discussions just weren't his thing. I think she said that as the soul is eternal, you can't measure an individual by his actions alone, but rather have to consider the state of his soul throughout its existence in many bodies and forms throughout time. What I definitely understood was her conclusion: 'What Vissarion says that is startling and new is that we must love the good *within* the evil man. No one is entirely evil; everyone has good characteristics. Maybe the evil man is hurt, or afraid. So we should love him.' She sat back and smiled, beaming at the Teacher's wisdom.

Hate the sin, love the sinner: not exactly revelatory. Although this old proverb differs from Vissarion's formulation in that it doesn't ask you to believe the rather naïve proposition that all wicked men are secretly scared children within.

III

The scales had not fallen from my eyes. I wasn't quite responding with the awe that Tatiana had hoped for. It was time to break out the heavy weaponry. She disappeared into her room and then returned, weighed down by six fat red volumes with gold embossed lettering on the spines. She laid them on the table slowly, one by one, with reverence.

At first she was silent. I needed time to fully appreciate the wonder that lay before me. Then she spoke: 'This is the *Last Testament*.'

'Yes.'

'It is printed in St Petersburg.'

'I see.'

'There are seven volumes, but only one to four and number seven have been printed . . .'

'Why's that?'

'Er . . . we didn't have enough money to print volumes five and six.'

'I see.'

She indicated the tome lying on top. 'This is volume seven. It is of especial importance.' It was a big book; indeed, they seemed to be getting bigger.

'It's on the internet,' she said, 'in English. Have you read it?'

There was such hope in her eyes. In fact, I had made a sincere stab at it, carrying it on the metro and reading passages between stations. I remembered some stuff about the outer space mind; some seemingly contradictory statements to the effect that God was the essence of love but also that God didn't care about us; that the ego was bad and that only Vissarion was absolutely without ego . . . and also that the Jews had a 'special mission'. But how it all came together I had no idea.

'The translation . . .' I said.

'Yes?'

'It's . . . problematic.'

She looked crestfallen; but it wasn't a surprise. She knew. 'But I did agree with Vissarion about the ego – that we must struggle to overcome it . . .'

'Yes, yes, but all religions say the ego is bad. Vissarion is the first spiritual teacher to say it can be overcome! For there are three testaments: the first, the Old Testament, is about faith. The second, the New Testament, is about hope. And the final one, Vissarion's *Last Testament*, is about love . . .' She cracked open volume seven: 'At the beginning there is an open letter from Vissarion to the Patriarch, and to Putin.'

'What's in it?'

'He explains how to save Russia.'

'Did he get a response?'

'No.'

IV

Tatiana was God-intoxicated. Her thoughts moved at a bewildering speed, making connections that were obvious to her, but less so to me. I knew she would jump on my brain until I surrendered.

'There is so much wisdom in this book! People are sceptical, of course. They say: if you're the Christ then why don't you die? The Teacher replies: the times today are less hard. Then people ask: if you're the Christ, why do you have five children? But the Teacher has an answer for them also. Jesus was only here for thirty-three years. It's irresponsible to produce children if you can't raise them . . . But I will be among you for a long time. What else do you need to know? Ah! He is strongly against money. Money is the root of so much evil . . . there is no lending or borrowing here. If money is given, then it must be forgotten. It's better still not to give money, but to buy the needed thing for your neighbour, leave it on the doorstep, and forget you bought it.'

Then she told me the story of Vissarion's trip to England: he had been denied a visa by the British embassy, as he was expected to declare his salary and job and employer. Vissarion, being the Son of God, had none of these. He spent five days in Tatiana's flat in Moscow eating buckwheat and salt. Eventually the BBC was persuaded to vouch for him and an invitation was issued.*

At the mention of the BBC a look of anxiety came across her features. 'They came here and made a documentary about the Teacher,' she said, echoing her daughter. 'They said they would send it but they never did . . . Did you see it?'

'No.'

'But why wouldn't they send it? It's so strange.'

In fact, the missing BBC documentary was a source of much confusion. I was asked about it repeatedly in the coming days. What had the BBC said about the Teacher that was so bad they wouldn't let the community see it?

---

* Vissarion stayed in a B & B in North London, not far from my brother's flat. So we had something in common at least – the experience of waking up in the shithole of Hendon, if not the jumbo sausage breakfast at the King Café. He clearly hadn't made any converts, however, or I would have been introduced to them by this point.

237

V

Tatiana's anxiety sobered her up quickly. A deathly silence descended. To clear the air, she put on a CD by Vadim Redkin, a.k.a. Vadim the Chronicler. For in addition to a library for the preservation of human knowledge after the apocalypse and a film director, Petropavlovka also housed a recording studio. Tatiana skipped past the first couple of tracks, and then stopped: 'This one is lovely,' she said. It was a ballad in the style of late-eighties hair metal. The lyrics were to the effect that there was a road ahead, and it was very, very, *very* long.

'Vadim was a member of Integral,' said Tatiana.

Semyon snapped out of his torpor: 'Really?'

'Oh yes.' She was pleased that she had finally caught his attention. 'Integral were a really famous band in the early nineties,' said Semyon. 'But then their leader, Zhenya Belousov, died. Many teenage girls were upset.'

'And did you know that before he died, he too was about to give it all up and follow the Teacher? He said that to Vadim.'

Semyon nodded. He didn't believe her, and she knew it.

'That's not all, though,' said Tatiana. 'My neighbour is Svetlana Vladimirskaya —'

'What?' Semyon raised his eyebrows. Now he was really impressed.

'Who's that?' I asked.

'She was *extremely* popular in 1994 or 1995. I mean, one of the first real pop stars in post-Soviet Russia. Then she just disappeared.'

Tatiana asked him to translate what he had just said. She glowed. 'Yes. Well, now you know where she disappeared to.'

VI

The CD's cover image was Vadim's long face beaming an enormous grin; its title was *Hey! Hey! Cheer Up!* In the liner notes he explained that he had recorded the songs in the few spare moments he had between writing the *Last Testament* and working as Vissarion's private secretary. Then I noticed one of the song titles: 'The Cathedral Had Already Burned Down'.

I remembered Young Tatiana's words about the great cathedral on the mountain that fire had erased from the face of the planet, and her warning: *Our people don't like to talk about it . . .*

'Hey, Tatiana,' I said. 'What's this song about?'

A shadow passed over the elder Tatiana's features; she hesitated. But

I had asked directly, so she had to answer. I didn't get any new information, she just confirmed that there had indeed been a big cathedral on the mountain, and it had burnt down. 'It was a very sad day for all of us . . . Vadim wrote the song as a memorial. Would you like to hear it?'

'Sure.'

I had heard that Vadim was a big Whitesnake fan. I couldn't detect much influence. A mournful voice crooned to a plangent keyboard accompaniment: O, *we went up with big buckets of water to save it, but it was too late: the Cathedral had already burned down, the Cathedral had already burned down, the Cathedral had already buuu-uuurned dooooooooooown!*

Tatiana was uncomfortable. I wasn't sure if she actually liked the song. Then again, perhaps it was simply the sad memories making her grimace. Once it was over she skipped to the upbeat title track.

'You simply must visit us again,' said Tatiana. 'Our villages are not at their best during the winter. Come on the 18th of August. That's the date of our biggest festival – the Holiday of Good Fruits. We have wonderful music and dancing, and you will be able to see how creative the members of our community are. We have one village, for example, Cheremshanka, which is full of jazz musicians, folk musicians, classical musicians . . . it's simply wonderful! August is also good because it's the only month in summer when you won't get eaten alive by mosquitoes.'

'Really? You get bad mosquitoes?' I hadn't seen those in the film.

'Terrible,' she said, then continued: 'Next year's festival is going to be extra special because it will mark the fifteenth anniversary of Vissarion's "preannunciation". For it was on the 18th of August 1991, not far from the city of Minussinsk, that the Teacher first openly proclaimed the fundamentals of the Teaching of the United Faith, revealing that he had come to unite into one all people who strive for Love, Good, Truth and Happiness, irrespective of their denomination, nationality or language. More than that, it was also the day Vissarion revealed that there is not one God, but two . . .'

'Wait, wait,' I said. '*Two* Gods?'

'Yes, the God of the Universe who created the planets and stars, and God the Father who created souls . . .'

Tatiana's eyes flashed. She had relocated herself, and was ready to take flight again on wings of heavenly revelation.

Unfortunately for her I had had my fill. It was past midnight, and I was exhausted. I cut her off. It was time to sleep.

VII

But sleep didn't come easily. I was thinking about her words, the jumble of ideas taken from other religions and mixed together wholesale. I was particularly suspicious about the omission of Hinduism and Judaism: had Vissarion really read and absorbed all the texts of these religions *before* he had his revelation? It seemed unlikely, especially as he had grown up in an officially atheist country where such texts were hard to come by.

In fact, I saw another religion lying hidden and undeclared in Vissarion's thinking, and its influence was crucial. It was, of course, possible to find analogues in numerous places for his beliefs, but the call to live together, sharing everything, the attempt to abolish money and differences in status, the desire for one world government under one ideological banner, the insistence on peace and pacifism, the cult of physical fitness, the demand for clean, enriching entertainment, the search for personally fulfilling, noble labour, the idealisation of nature, the sacrifice of the self for a future paradise that would be located on earth, and especially the settlement and terraforming of Siberia, growing fruits and vegetables that went contrary to nature, resembled nothing so much as the state religion of communism that Vissarion had grown up with, in its pure, idealised form. Perhaps even Vissarion's position as supreme leader was made easier to accept by his followers' long acquaintanceship with the personality cults of a totalitarian system; certainly they decorated their homes with photographs of him in much the same way ideologically correct Soviets had approved of the portraits of the various general secretaries of the party that had festooned their cities.

Below me a wizened old woman was sitting in the front room of the cultural centre, hunched over the TV, watching a traditional Russian dance ensemble. This had been a staple of the Soviet variety shows people of her generation had enjoyed for decades. The sound of balalaikas followed me as I drifted in and out of sleep. At some point I started to dream that I was in the room myself, floating in the corner like a disembodied spirit, watching the TV with her, receiving signals from a dead world that could so easily be summoned back to life, in the feelings and imaginations of so many other aging men and women hunched, just like her, over flickering blue screens located across the vast territory of the former Soviet Union.

V

Two Gods Are Better Than One

1

I became conscious. Rarely a pleasant sensation for me, that morning it was worse than usual. My neurons sent out exploratory probes to my limbs and organs, but met resistance. I had barely slept since leaving Moscow, and my body was angry. It didn't want to obey my commands. When it did, it was crudely, as if my brain was jerking the strings of a puppet it wasn't practised in manipulating.

A 'vehicle' was coming at 8 a.m. to transport pilgrims to Vissarion's mountain. We had received clearance to accompany them late the day before, but I had been warned that if I was late, the driver would leave without me. It was a forty-kilometre journey, all off-road, so it took several hours, and he had to return to Petropavlovka the same day.

I dragged my sawdust-stuffed carcass outside. The night was gradually receding: its blackness had turned navy blue, and the sun was burning red at the foot of the hills surrounding the village. Soon it would fill the world with cold light. I wasn't wearing a jacket, but I didn't care. The climate was dry, so the sub-zero temperatures felt relatively mild in comparison to the same ones in Moscow. I plunged my hands into the snow and rubbed the night's crystals on my face, trying to shock my nerves into life. Feeling returned to my fingers, and the skin on my cheeks burned, scalded by tongues of icy fire. The shock did help me to wake up, only to become aware of the profound silence exuding from the watching taiga. It engulfed the village. Nobody was about; no animals or birds could be heard. I was the last living thing on earth.

I didn't like it. I went back inside.

2

At 9:30, two and a half hours later, Tatiana *mère* made some phone calls to see what had happened to our 'vehicle'. Nobody knew anything. There was a chess set under a pile of encyclopaedias. Semyon and I were just finishing our second game when Bjorn Borg appeared in the doorway.

'Lads!' he cried, rushing in to shake our hands, 'I'm so sorry, but the bus was full! There was no room for you – too many pilgrims heading up the mountain to see the Teacher!' He grinned: *We believed him, didn't we?* Not really. I thought we'd been forgotten, or the driver hadn't been informed of his extra passengers.

Bjorn Borg continued: 'Tomorrow, however, we will provide a bus *especially* for you! Then you will be able to ask all the questions you want and get everything you need for your book. In the meantime you have a free day. Why not explore the village? You can visit our cathedral, which is always open. Or you can go to the Minussinsky Dom, and speak to the priest, or look at the exhibition of the Teacher's amazing oil paintings . . .'

Bjorn Borg left, but we didn't go out immediately. Instead we hung around the cultural centre playing chess, to kill another hour. I had already been awake too long, and those extra hours of consciousness weighed heavily upon me. I didn't know how I was going to use the time we had in Petropavlovka. I wanted to move among people, but Tatiana had left for Moscow, and everyone else I had met in the village had also disappeared, presumably to work.

So it was up to me to occupy myself. It was strange to be left to my own devices like this. On the one hand, it showed evidence of openness and trust. But on the other, it was rather like being let loose in an abandoned Disneyworld where all the rides were shut off. I was free to walk around, but I couldn't really *do* anything.

3

We trudged through the village, violating its air of desertion. So many of the houses were unfinished, without windows or even, in some cases, walls. It was difficult to tell if they were still under construction, or if they had been abandoned. The sound of our own footsteps crunching the snow rang out in the silence. And, aside from the smoke rising cautiously from one or two chimneys signalling the presence of unseen life, Petropavlovka appeared to be ours and ours alone.

But then I heard a third set of footsteps crunching the snow, approaching from behind. They came closer and closer, until Camouflage Boy suddenly appeared at my shoulder. He tramped past with a snarl, hands stuffed deep in his pockets.

'He hasn't forgiven you for interrupting *Back to the Future*,' said Semyon.

'That's wrong,' I said. 'Vissarion would want him to.'

But as I watched him charging ahead, I knew that his anger went much deeper than the events of the night before. It was a weekday; he was from the mountain; he should have been working. But he didn't appear to be going anywhere. His frame was hunched and lonely and his walk was dizzy with anger and frustration. Petropavlovka, after all, was not the sort of place you just went walking in. There was nowhere to go, nowhere to hide; the whole place was visible; there were no surprises.

4

The cathedral, 'always open', was closed. We walked around it, up to our knees in snow, trying to peer in through the windows. I couldn't see anything.

Ahead of us, the taiga loomed, dense and silent, like the massed ranks of a huge army just waiting to march on the village. 'Don't walk in the taiga,' Bjorn Borg had said. 'It is too easy to get lost. You might wander into it and never come out again. And there are bears.'

'Let's walk in the taiga,' I said.

'OK,' said Semyon.

5

I started trudging forward. It was only twenty metres to the point at which all tracks disappeared. A lagoon of sparkling white crystals separated us from a long, low hill that reared up ahead of us, bristling with trees.

One step: the snow rose up to my waist. A few steps more and it was under my nipples. The hill wasn't getting any closer, and it was exhausting work constantly displacing my own mass in snow.

'Fuck this,' I said. 'It's just a lot of trees anyway.'

We turned back towards the village to find a dog had materialised. It was watching us quizzically, as if wondering who the two idiots wading towards the taiga were. Didn't we know it was dangerous? It did not deign to bark or wag its tail, choosing instead to hold its distance and watch us warily.

Semyon kicked snow at it. The dog looked surprised and hurt.

'What did you do that for?' I asked.

'Look at him, just standing there, trembling in the snow. He's a gay dog. He's useless.'

'I thought you liked dogs.'

'I do, usually. But this place is doing something to me. It's the atmosphere. It's unnatural. It's too quiet, too trusting. In my mother's village they wouldn't just let strangers walk around like this. Someone would kick the shit out of us. And where's the rubbish? Russian villages are dirty. There should be a broken-down motorcycle in front of that house, a drunk lying in vomit over there . . .'

I understood him: while playing chess I had seen an earwig crawling along the floor of the library, trailing its arse-pincers along behind it. I had felt an overwhelming urge to kill it. Then, when Camouflage Boy had stormed past us, I had fantasised about joining up with him and setting fire to a house for no good reason, or grabbing a chainsaw and cutting down a tree, or maybe jumping a Vissarionite and giving him a beating. My desire to buy meat and carry it around in my pocket was part of the same impulse. I wanted to cross the lines Vissarion had drawn delineating what was acceptable behaviour and what was not, because though I was not a member of the community, still I could feel them, invisible and yet tangible, restricting my steps, or guiding them in another direction. It was in the air, part of the reality he had built here. He was that powerful.

Petropavlovka looked like a fantasy village from the pages of a folk-tale. In some of Vissarion's literature, it was referred to as 'Dreamland'. But though it may have been a dream that had brought it into being, it was an enormous act of conscious will that kept it there. That act began with Vissarion and was echoed in the souls of all the people in the village, who were vigorously policing themselves for bad thoughts, attending meetings to resolve conflicts peacefully, struggling to live 'in harmony' with nature. Sustaining this took a lot of effort and energy.

I looked back at the taiga. Out there the indifferent violence of nature was under way: growth, death, toil, slaughter. Beyond it lay cities that had been constructed purely to rip resources out of the earth because it would not yield them willingly. They were built on the bones of human sacrifices: yet that too had been done in the name of a dream.

The peace and silence of Petropavlovka was not relaxing but oppressive. It was suffocating. It was conducive to violent fantasies. I wanted to rebel, to set the world on fire. I knew I couldn't, however: that would mean crossing a border, and once I had crossed it I didn't think I'd be able to get back again, to where I had been, among the Vissarionites. And I was not yet ready to leave. I still had to climb the mountain.

Semyon kicked more snow at the dog. It ran away.

7 Minussinsky Dom

Minussinsky Dom was another name for the German House we had arrived at the day before. It was a structure of some historical significance: in the early years immediately following the 'preannunciation', the house had stood in Minussinsk, and Vissarion and Vadim the Chronicler had occupied adjoining rooms upstairs, while the lower parts were used for worship by the first believers. When the Teacher and Vadim moved to the mountain, the house was taken to Petropavlovka and reconstructed there. It was now used for many purposes. In addition to meetings, this was where the village filmmaker worked in his audio-video studio; this was where the Vissarionite newspaper and Magic Box children's material were produced; and this was also where some of Vissarion's oil paintings were on display in the village art gallery.

A caretaker was shovelling snow in front of the gate. He was a little man, in his fifties, with a pointy grey beard. He ignored us. Eventually two women appeared out of the snow, chatted to him for a minute and then entered the building. That opened the possibility for us.

'Excuse me,' said Semyon.

'Yes . . .' He looked up at us, unsmiling, waiting to get back to his shovelling.

Semyon explained who we were. 'Is it possible to go inside and look at the pictures . . . ?'

'And maybe,' I added, 'could you help us find the priest? I'd like to interview him.'

'I am the priest,' said the little man.

He was called Sergei: that was all. There were no patronymics in the village.

8 Art show

Sergei led us into the entrance hall, where we took off our boots. I placed mine next to a pair of felt *valenki* – the footwear Russian peasants have worn throughout centuries of winter. Sergei then rushed into the warmth of the building's labyrinthine interior. There were lots of rooms and openings, but no time to take them in. I peered through a crack and saw part (I was unsure which) of a human; it was withdrawn; a single eye peeked back at me. Then Sergei opened a door and we followed him into a small, unfurnished room where a few portraits hung on a wall.

The paintings were hyper-realistic studies in oil. Sergei guided us through them: the young teenager was Roma, the Teacher's eldest son. Then there was a self-portrait and a portrait of Sergei himself . . .

He fell silent when we came to the women. There were two, flanking the self-portrait. One was middle aged and a little overweight. Her smile was weak, as if she was tired from raising her kids and working a bad job simultaneously. She was probably Vissarion's wife: she was the right age, and wore the right expression. The other woman, however, was much younger – about twenty. She had a dazzling smile and sparkling, feline eyes: she looked as though she was about to leap out of the frame. 'And who are the women?' I asked.

'Er . . . she's my wife,' Sergei indicated the young girl. 'The older one is Vissarion's.' So Sergei was married to a fox? He didn't look the type. I was suspicious, especially as he wanted to get us away from these pictures as quickly as possible. He ushered us into the second room of the exhibit, where there was a painting of a woman in robes walking on clouds towards a sunset. I felt there was something missing: a winged unicorn perhaps.

'These are actually reproductions of the Teacher's works,' said Sergei. 'The only Vissarion original we have in our collection is this one.' He indicated a life-size painting of a woman standing in the desert, her head in her hands, an animal skull at her feet.

'This is what will become of humanity if it does not listen to the Teacher,' said Sergei. 'So, shall we talk? Please, take a seat . . .'

My feet were tired. My eye moved towards an elaborately carved wooden throne, upholstered with red velvet, in the far corner. It looked extremely comfortable. Sergei panicked.

'Except for that one! That is the Teacher's chair; no one can sit upon it except him.'

9 Sergei's story

Sergei was a scientist by training, a military officer by vocation, and a priest by calling. After gaining his first degree he had planned to study aeronautics in Ukraine; but an invisible hand had written his name in another ledger, and when he arrived at the institute in Kharkov he was compelled to enter another faculty, one that inaugurated him into the mysteries of rocket construction and the destroying fire that falls from the heavens. Suddenly he found himself embroiled in state secrets, and he could not back away from the consequences of his knowledge. He entered the Red Army, and eventually came close to an awe-inspiring power, closer than almost anyone else in history. For there was a secret room, and in that room, Sergei sat, waiting for the telephone call instructing him to apply his finger to the button that would launch the final storm, extinguishing civilisation once and for all.

But the call never came, and he was lecturing at a military academy in Moscow when the reality he had grown up in collapsed. After seven decades of enforced atheism, religious creeds started erupting in the city, like mushrooms after rain. Intrigued, Sergei started to study them. He wanted to believe in something, but he kept finding contradictions, this one above all – that in all religions, however much people preached love and goodwill, there was always conflict. How could that be squared with all this talk of peace?

Sergei did not like contradictions. He was a scientist, a man of research, evidence and logical deduction. But he didn't give up hope, and continued to search for a creed he could believe in. It was at that point, in 1991, that Vissarion arrived in Moscow for the first time: 'I saw him preaching on Lobnoye mesto,'* he said, shaking his head at the memory of Vissarion's youthful audacity. 'Then I saw him again,

---

* A thirteen-metre-long stone platform in front of St Basil's Cathedral on Red Square. Popular legend has it that many heads were severed there, while tedious historians claim that it was simply a place from which important proclamations were read.

preaching in an old, disused church. I thought: *But he is very young, what does he know?* But as I listened I realised that the Teacher had not only united all religions in one and removed all contradictions between them, but he had also reconciled faith with science for the first time in history. Through him, people who had never believed in God before could find answers and believe.'

Suddenly Sergei found himself embroiled in Truth, and he could not back away from the consequences of his knowledge. Vissarion invited him to Siberia, where he and his followers were just starting to establish what would later become a community of four thousand. Sergei accepted the invitation.

For the first two years there were only fifty believers, living together with the new Christ in Minussinsk. Then they moved to Petropavlovka. But the citizens of Petropavlovka did not welcome the new arrivals. The village was home to many Old Believers, devout adherents of the pre-reform Orthodox creed. They had been living in the area for centuries, suffering oppression first under the tsars and then the communists.

It was clear to them that Vissarion was the long-prophesied Antichrist, come at last, and his followers the servants of Satan. Armageddon was close at hand. The non-religious locals also responded to the new settlers with fear and loathing. Rumours spread through the village: the Vissarionites didn't buy meat in the local shop – why was this? Obviously because they had their own supply of flesh: they ate children! No one would sell a house to the Vissarionites. The villagers attacked them in the street and shot at them; one man was even burned to death in his house while he slept.

But the Teacher's leadership was strong, and the Vissarionites grew in number, inspired by the Truth. More and more came to Petropavlovka and the surrounding villages. The violence and persecution meted out to them by the original inhabitants was not having any effect. Then one day the leader of the Old Believers had a vision: he received word from the Lord that he and his community were to leave Petropavlovka and move to a new place, a pure place on the river Lena, in . . . Siberia. Conveniently enough, the vision also allowed them to sell their houses to the Vissarionites. Since that departure, relations had improved between the Vissarionites and the unbelievers in the village. The Vissarionites tried to help their neighbours, and had a shop where they sold goods to them at the lowest prices possible. But still, it had been a long, hard road, and Sergei confessed that at times he had harboured doubts.

'In those first years, it was so difficult. The Teacher forbade the use of chainsaws and petrol and other technology. So we cut down trees with simple axes, moving stones and roots and planting flowers by hand. We were all city people: few of us had the skills necessary for this kind of work, and so everything we have now, we first had to teach ourselves as we did it. The Minussinsky Dom, where we are sitting, was the first thing we ever built. Then we built the church, which you saw outside. Then we started work on the mountain. We were eaten alive by mosquitoes as we advanced up its slopes, felling the trees one by one. And sometimes I asked myself: *Why is this so hard? Am I mistaken? Is he not the Christ after all?* But the Teacher was strong, and through the faith we triumphed. We have shown that it is possible to live in harmony with nature, and live good lives. Our goal is to return to the technological level of the eighteenth century. These were not primitive people; they could do almost everything, but without harming the environment.'

'But you use modern technology,' I said. 'You use cars, you use petrol . . .'

Sergei sighed. It was a bad point, a journalist's point, provocative, designed not to illuminate but to undermine. It was the most obvious and quickest method of getting an 'angle' on Vissarion – by trying to catch him out in a contradiction when he claimed to have resolved all of them. But this was an asinine, lazy approach. The believers would have got there before me, and would have constructed an obvious rationalisation. Besides, unlike Sergei, I did not think the presence of contradictions necessarily negated an idea. If that were the case then the intellectual history of mankind would never have got very far.

And yet something compelled me to say it, to provoke the answer I knew Sergei was going to give me, and which he knew that I knew he was going to give me: 'But they are just to help us build a basis. We will live without them in the future. We are trying to create the full range of production with what we have here in Siberia. We work with the trees and we build houses, so that in the future we will be able to live together, entirely self-sufficient, in this place. But it must not become a city. Cities breed alienation and unhappiness. Petropavlovka will be the centre of an interlinked network of villages.'

His eyes shone.

'For Siberia is a clean place, a new place,' he said. 'It is virgin soil. All the people who were sent here, or who have decided to come here, rejected society and its rules. From the Old Believers, who disagreed with the reforms of the Church, to the Decembrists who opposed the Tsar, to all those who disagreed with the Soviet regime – it's a place for dissidents, but it is also a place of brotherhood, where every man must cooperate with his neighbours, regardless of belief or ideology, if he is to survive. For having experienced evil in the world outside, the people who come here do not want to repeat those bad deeds they experienced in their old lives . . .'

'Yes,' I said, remembering the myth that young Tatiana had told me about Vissarion's mountain. 'I heard that nothing was ever killed here . . .'

'Oh no,' said Sergei. 'Many things were killed here. On the film Tatiana showed you, it looks beautiful, of course . . . but they did hunt, and they exploited the taiga until we came. They cut down the trees; they set fire to the forest. Death was abundant. There were no animals here, there were no birds. The forest was weeping. But we changed that.'

Sergei had spent fourteen years with Vissarion in total. After the first year he had been appointed an elder in the community; for the last six he had been a priest. He was one of two – the other was an astronomer from Alma Ata in Kazakhstan, who lived on the mountain. Sergei explained that the Vissarionites rejected hierarchy: his priestly status was simply an indicator that he was more knowledgeable about the *Last Testament* than most of the other believers. But all men were obliged to know the *Last Testament*, and all men were equally qualified to perform the rites. Sergei's role was to help, to guide, to answer questions – but not to govern.

Only the Teacher governed.

10

In most books or TV documentaries about 'cults' there is a wealth of information as regards totalitarian leaders and their penchant for child rape, polygamy, murder and apocalyptic mass suicide, but very little detail as regards what the people who follow these leaders actually feel or believe, other than that their chosen guru is God. This approach, entertaining as it is, thus leaves the actual followers of these Messiahs blank, empty ciphers, incomprehensible and alien to us.

They become subhuman – weak-willed lost souls, or victims of 'brain-washing' – essentially not worth understanding, they are instead victims to be pitied or laughed at. Intentionally or not, it serves simply to make a strange and confusing phenomenon easier to dismiss, not understand.

But people, whether secular or religious, believe all sorts of strange things for all sorts of different reasons, and the application of reason is only one of them. As for Sergei and Tatiana and the priest on the mountain, it was difficult to dismiss them as weak-willed losers. They were all highly intelligent, driven individuals who had been successful in their old lives – not washed up *perestroika*-era hippies at all, and now in their new reality their old talents had revealed themselves again, and they had risen once more to positions of leadership. Their conversion stories, meanwhile, were similar to those of anyone who has been converted to any belief system.

Sergei was a small, unassuming man, shy, modest, entirely without charisma, and yet strangely fascinating. He discussed Vissarion's ideas coolly and methodically, measuring each word and phrase. When he spoke it was not spontaneous, rather it was more like a catechism, a recitation of articles of faith as if some other voice was speaking through him. Precision was all important; there was none of Tatiana's emotional effervescence in his speech.

Indeed, he was so dispassionately logical that it was only about ten minutes into his detailed explanation of the Vissarionites' belief system that I realised exactly how strange the content of his speech was, and that he wasn't advancing these ideas in a half-apologetic hypothetical way, but rather as a collection of established facts that he believed in as much as he believed in the existence of his own body. That Sergei Torop was Christ wasn't a tentative notion, a Pascalian wager, or a vague belief in some ill-defined 'spirituality'. He and the others were committed to this idea with a force that is extremely rare, and that, of course, was why they had been able to give up so much and submit themselves to so much hardship. Torop's Christhood was absolutely real, as real as the trees and mountains, as waking and dreaming and cutting wood. This was not a game, or a show put on for visiting writers to fill their books with. This was a life that was lived every day, every night. It had been going on for a long time before I arrived, and would continue after I left. It is going on now, as you read this.

What follows over the next few pages is a (highly) condensed account of what the thousands of Vissarionites living in Siberia actually believe. The data is given in italics as a courtesy to those readers who fear words such as 'consciousness', 'reincarnation', and 'energy waves'; they may skip ahead to page 261, where normal service will resume. On the other hand, readers who are intrigued by words such as 'aliens', 'Lucifer' and 'nefarious Jewish plot', or who want to know the precise nature of the 'uncommon wisdom' that has led rocket scientists and astronomers to live on salted porridge in some of the most inhospitable terrain on the planet may wish to read on.

A CONDENSED GUIDE TO THE REVELATION OF VISSARION CHRIST

I *Gods*
Long ago, *the first God created the universe and everything in it. After
that he withdrew to monitor the processes essential for its continuing
existence. But he does not intervene in human affairs: he is absolutely
indifferent to whether we live or die. The Vissarionites do not worship
him.*

*The second God was created by the collision of energy waves of
earth and space. After coming into being he gained consciousness, and
his consciousness was even higher than that of the first God. This God
has no name, but his nature is pure love. The Vissarionites call him
God the Father, even though he is a young God, younger than the
human race, in fact. His essence is like light, brilliant as the sun, but it
is a light that doesn't burn, which is cold and white and tender and
gentle.*

*Even at this early stage humanity, emotionally immature and prone
to violence, was in a sorry state. God the Father wanted to help us, but
as he is not physical, he cannot influence the physical universe.
Fortunately mankind is a suitable vessel for souls, so he created souls
from his energy and placed them in mankind, to try and influence us
through that.*

II *Qualities of the soul*
*The soul is eternal. If you kill the body, the soul will live on, and will
be born again in another body.*

*The soul is connected only to our feelings. It has nothing to do with
the mind. If someone claims God is speaking to him, he is lying,
because God doesn't speak directly to our reason. He works through
our feelings.*

*To get to the next level of consciousness, we have to learn how to
control our feelings. But there is a problem: when souls were placed
within mankind, our feelings had priority over our intellect. Man was
like a child, and unable to control his emotions and so the negative
ones predominated. This has been the situation for millennia. That is
why this is such a difficult period for humanity.*

The soul is supposed to improve through each incarnation. For example, if I kill in one life, I will learn that this is wrong, the lesson will be inscribed on the record of my soul, and the next time I am born I won't be able to do evil in this way. So each time we live, we should accumulate experience and knowledge, and the soul should grow, until it returns to God the Father and is then passed to another human being. Over time, the soul should develop immunity to evil. When it reaches this perfect state, it goes into a sort of 'soul storage' – what is commonly referred to in other traditions as 'heaven'.

But there is a problem: the common soul has grown hard, and so it no longer receives the vibrations of our Heavenly Father as it was intended to. We receive them, but as if through a wall, with difficulty and without clarity. In this imperfect state, the soul can deteriorate. Even if it wants to be better, circumstances might make the soul worse. For example, if it is born into such bad circumstances, if it is surrounded by killing, and evil, and there are no positive examples for it to learn from, then the soul will not develop, but rather will sink and sink through its incarnations, until it enters the storage of broken souls – what is referred to in other traditions as 'hell'.

The situation is not without hope, however. Though the soul is eternal, hell is not. The record can be erased, the soul released, and the cycle will start again.

III Evil

Satan is real, but he is created by us. He is the sum total of the confluence of human evil. For there are 'channels' through which our negative and evil thoughts pour out: they don't stay locked in our skulls. And these negative thoughts, when they meet, mingle and create Lucifer. He is primitive: his nature is pure evil, and he exists only to cause pain. He knows the thoughts of all men, and can return to us by the same channels through which our thoughts pour out.

Damned souls are located close to the Devil. The Devil will die when the record of their sins has been wiped clean, when there is no person left who can provide him with a source of negative energy. So far that hasn't happened; but Lucifer knows that it will and that he will die and so lives like a prisoner due to be shot tomorrow – instead of repenting, he inflicts pain on his cellmate out of pure malice. He lusts for maximum violence, rape and so on. And the closer to the end, and we are very close to the end, then the more violent he will become. Violence, pain, misery are pure pleasure for him.

Lucifer would like to kill us but he cannot because like God, he is immaterial. So he sits at the centre of the channels of negative thoughts, listening to our thoughts, and whispering to us, and that is how he manipulates us, forcing us to pour out our negative energy and make him stronger . . .

IV

' . . . like in *The Matrix*,' said Sergei. 'Have you seen it?'

'Er, no,' I said. So far we had stayed close to Gnosticism, Hinduism, New Age talk of 'energy', and there was also an appealing smattering of Dostoevsky in the description of the condemned man's psychology: nothing too startling. The pop-culture reference was jarring. I looked for a twinkle of irony in Sergei's eye, a sign of an appreciation of the absurdity. It wasn't there.

'Well you should watch it,' he said, solemnly. 'Because that's how Lucifer works.'

V *Aliens*

There are also alien civilisations. Like God the Father, they were created by energy waves clashing in space. Now they live on alien planets.

There are two types of alien civilisations: good ones and bad ones. The good ones try to help us. They come to earth as the gods and gurus of religions – Krishna, or the Buddha, for example. They try to help us by working through our reason. The problem is that they do not know the rules of the soul perfectly. And so even though their intent is good, and their words may contain truth, yet they become distorted. Humans build temples and organisations, and by the time the message has reached the common mass of people, it has all gone wrong. And so these religions do not succeed in solving our problems.

The second group of aliens are ruled by Lucifer, and like him, they want to wipe us out. They whisper to us, giving us aggressive feelings, alcoholism, and providing us with dark knowledge – of how to produce weapons, for example. But we're the ones who actually make them.

Their most powerful weapon, their most diabolical invention, however, is money. For money divides people. The rich are an intermediary between these dark forces and mankind. They have been given special knowledge by the dark forces about how to use money and how to control people through it. They chose the Jewish people in particular,

255

isolated them, trained them in mastery of money and then dispersed them all over world, so they would rule our societies, and spread the doctrine of money everywhere.

VI

'Wait, wait – the rich are intermediaries between the evil aliens and us?'
'Yes.'

'And the Jews have received special training from them in the mastery of money?'

'Yes.' Sergei looked irritated. He didn't like being interrupted, and didn't like being challenged.

I decided to let the sinister alien–Jewish conspiracy slide; for the moment, at least.

VII *The end*

And so, the current state of mankind is abysmal. So much hate and greed and violence and egoism: if we don't destroy ourselves, then the planet herself will wipe us out.

For the ancient pagans were right when they said that the planet has a life force; their prayers were not in vain. Though she is not sentient, the earth feels, and can respond, if you are in harmony with her. And therein lies the problem – for we can compare the earth's situation today to that of a man tied to a tree in the taiga. Every bad thought we have is to our globe like a bite from an insect to this man. She will kill us to survive: it's a natural instinct. The earthquakes and tsunamis we have been experiencing recently are efforts by the earth to remove the sources of the negative energy that so afflict her.

But that is only the start of our problems. For the soul is immortal, and so if the earth destroys us, and all human bodies die, then the souls will whirl around in space for ever, never being reincarnated. And that will be a real disaster . . .

VIII *Good flesh*

So with this situation looming, we need to find a solution rapidly. And that's where Vissarion fits in. In fact, if the Teacher hadn't come, then we'd already be gone. But he brought hope, and for as long as there's hope, then the earth postpones Armageddon. It will surely come, but now, thanks to the Teacher, not everyone need be eradicated. The only question is: how much flesh will be left?

We need to develop a field of positive energy if the world is to survive, and if there are to be bodies left for souls to reincarnate into. That is why we need more and more people here in Siberia, so we can build a critical mass of goodness to ensure the human race's survival.

All religions say that you will sin; that it is inevitable. But Vissarion turns this on its head. No, he says. It is not inevitable. We must try to live without sin, if we are to survive. We must be completely non-aggressive. We cannot even think ill of other people. It is not easy, of course. It is a fight within man's soul, as fierce as Armageddon itself. And if you want to fight, you must learn how to fight, methodically.

But it can be done.

For example, here in the village we have lots of people from different walks of life, different jobs, different positions, and yet still they managed to find the true belief, and to come here. And even though everything is bad in the world, some souls have reached perfection, or have come close enough.

And the Christ, the Living Word of God too has come. So there is hope.

IX *Origin of the Son of God*

Vissarion's body and his soul were specially prepared for his mission. Until the age of 30, however, the nature of his soul was concealed even to him. He had to live among men first. He had lots of jobs. He was in the army, then he was an electrician, then he was a traffic policeman. But he was always interested in people's behaviour, and throughout this time he was watching people and studying them.

His awakening took place when he was working as an artist and he received a commission to paint icons for a church in Minussinsk. He had never painted icons before; he was not even religious. So he started reading books, researching the commission so he would know what to paint. While he was doing this, Vissarion felt a new feeling being born inside him. He didn't understand it at first. But although icons are painted according to strict rules, the Teacher started painting according to his own vision, and depicted St Nicholas and the Virgin Mary walking on the clouds.

The priest saw the difference, but he accepted the icon, and paid the Teacher for his work. Later there was a meeting, and some other priests complained that the Icon was non-canonical. They told the priest to tell him to paint it again, or take the money back. The priest asked the Teacher: can you repaint it? But Vissarion had painted what he had felt, so he said no, and returned the money. The next day he had a sense of illumination. It took him six months to get used to this new state of consciousness. He preached for the first time on 15 August 1991.

The first Christ came two thousand years ago. He came to stop the Jews' destructive programme of money, and was thus born in Israel . . .

X

'Wait, wait – did you say he came to stop the Jews' destructive programme of money?'

'Yes.'

I had been enjoying the unfolding doom that faced our planet: I was almost looking forward to it. In particular I appreciated the twist that Vissarion had come to preserve flesh, and the way it flowed logically from his cosmogony. It was a weird inversion of Jesus' mission, which had been to save souls.

But there was the stuff about Jews again. After all the talk about living in harmony with nature, and avoiding aggression, it bothered me. It seemed out of place, an intrusion from an older way of seeing the world into Vissarion's New Age talk of environmentalism and 'energy waves'.

Sergei continued.

XI *Characteristics of the second Christ*

. . . but this Christ was killed, and His gospel was corrupted. Now the second Christ is here.

The characteristics of the second Christ are as follows: like all men, he has a soul, but whereas man has freedom of choice Christ does not. His soul has been specially prepared and is pre-programmed. He cannot act against God's will. For he has been sent to us in a dark time as the direct voice of God – whereas ordinary souls are hard and resistant to God's vibrations, his soul is different. It is fluid; he can hear God.

Christ's second feature is that in an emergency he can access the super-consciousness of the Father. That way he can get any information he needs about the laws of the universe, or about human behaviour. And thus the Last Testament *reveals to us exactly what we should do in every situation. It is the book of foundations for the sixty-one basic situations we face in life, according to the sixty-one rules of the soul.*

The first volume of the Last Testament *gives the basic rules; the following volumes apply them to all sorts of situations. Before Vissarion came, no one knew the sixty-one rules, so we don't even have words to describe the new feelings we have.*

XII

'Why sixty-one rules?' I asked.

Sergei was irritated by my interruption.

'Because there are rules and there are sixty-one of them,' he snapped.

XIII *Characteristics of the Second Christ continued*

Our bodies have one billion sensors through which we can feel the world, its emanations and its energy. Vissarion, however, has ten thousand times that number. He feels what the whole of mankind feels. If you have a question you can go to him and ask, but before you ask, he feels your problem, your attitude to it. It helps him to resolve the problem properly.

Vissarion's goal is to change man's inner nature. You can compare this work on the soul to changing the stars in the sky. The Teacher is changing the constellation, one by one. In the future, the picture of the sky will be completely different.

For now we see the world through the prism of egoism. We need to see it through the crystal of Living Spirit. Vissarion is here not just to show us, but step by step to live with us and guide us by example. He went through all the steps of life – he was an ordinary man; he had troubles in marriage; he has children. He does not perform miracles, or at least, not in the sense that outsiders would understand. For us, though, there are miraculous events. He leads not just by example but by feeling. In his reactions he communicates his internal state to people.

In the past, when the community was small, if you had a question you could ask the Teacher directly. Now, however, there are many of us, spread out through a hundred villages, and the process has changed. The people living on the mountain have weekly meetings with the Teacher, but we have to learn to be self-sufficient. Fortunately, everything we need to know is written in the Last Testament.

The Last Testament *is not just a set of general principles. It deals with specific situations. It is based on the questions people ask at meetings with the Teacher. Everything is recorded on a dictaphone, edited and then written down.*

It is the School of Life: read it, and do what it says. Whatever your problem is, there is probably already an explanation in the book.

XIV

'Can you give me an example?'

'It is difficult to pick just one. It is about everything, I mean, even very tiny questions. For example,' he said, laughing a little, 'there is one question: *If my wife forces me to clean my boots before I enter the house but sometimes I forget and leave traces of dirt in the house, what should I do? Ask her to forgive me, or ignore it?*'

'It's that precise?'

'Yes.'

This sounded less like Christianity and more like Islam, where two books, the Koran (the direct word of God revealed to Mohammed) and the Hadith (reported sayings of the prophet), combine eschatology with exceedingly thorough legislature on moral, social, commercial and personal matters. The Hadith, for example, contains not only descriptions of the Day of Judgement but also instructions on the correct way to dispose of a date stone. Centuries of Islamic thinking have been dedicated to annotating these two books, producing untold millions of pages of instruction for every aspect of life. By the time of the Iranian revolution in 1979 the Ayatollah Khomenei himself had written eighteen volumes on Islamic jurisprudence and philosophy, and yet with all that learning seemed unable to decide whether God approved of chess or not. At first it was banned in the new Islamic republic; ten years later he lifted the prohibition.

But then Sergei seemed to reconsider. He didn't want to focus on Vissarion's remarkable attention to detail; that was a dangerous angle. 'Well . . . perhaps that is a bad example. There are only a few basic laws, but they are applied to lots of different situations. But ultimately the Teacher reveals that at root, egoism is hidden in *all* these situations. He helps us to overcome this, to triumph over the ego.'

'I see.'

'You see, whenever we do the wrong thing it leaves a negative imprint on the soul. To erase it . . . you have to warm up your feelings, and then do the right thing. That will make a good print on the soul, instead of a bad one. Yes, in our life man tries to do the right thing, but he is always thinking of doing bad. He wants to do good, but he can't. It is extremely difficult. But it *is* possible. I know. In the last ten years, I have seen so many changes in the internal world. We *can* do it. We make mistakes, but step by step, we *are* changing the arrangement of the stars in the sky, we *are* reordering the constellation . . .'

11

His voice trailed off. I had asked too many questions, disrupting the flow of precisely memorised perfect knowledge. When Sergei had to respond off the cuff he became anxious; he wanted to return to precision, to recitation, revelation. Vissarion's teachings were ultimate and finished. That being the case they were difficult to explain, as 'close enough' was not permitted. That, after all, was one of the main problems with all the world's other religions, why they were not to be trusted. They were all flailing around in the dark, right about some things, wrong about others. Vissarion had come to do away with vagueness, to administer life perfectly and absolutely, to shine a light into every dark corner and issue an instruction that had to be followed, for God (the second one, that is) cares how we wipe our shoes.

Sergei took us to see the church. The Keeper of the Church, a bearded man in a mediaeval gown, was waiting for us at the gate; he opened it and let us in, smiling a blissful, gentle, slightly vacant smile. He loved his job.

The exterior owed a lot to the traditions of Russian wooden architecture; there was nothing original about it. But the atmosphere inside was very different from the murky gloom of most Orthodox churches, with their images of glowering Christs, solemn saints and the likes of St Theodora being tormented by hundreds of black demons. In fact, it was very feminine: pink and powder-blue banners and streamers hung from the ceiling, and baskets of flowers were positioned next to circular windows. Sergei explained with a slightly sheepish smile that the village's women had done the decorating.

There was a small Vissarion by the altar, the same image I had seen on the walls of the cultural centre. Candles were burning under him, as if the photograph were a sacred icon. Sergei pre-empted my question:

'We do not pray to Vissarion, of course. He is not God. But he is close to God, and so he is close to the holy altar.'

The church ultimately was not very spectacular. We stood there for a minute or two, mainly because it would have been rude to leave too quickly. Sergei thought of something to say. 'Anyone can pray here, according to their own ritual. Hindus, Muslims, followers of Krishna . . .'

'But do they come?' I asked.

'Everyone comes,' he said. 'Except the Orthodox.'

I was sure Sergei was telling the truth, but even so I found it difficult to accept that anyone who took his religion seriously could pray in Vissarion's temple. To do that would be to ascribe spiritual authority to Vissarion and thus (to some degree at least) validate his claims. But most religions don't have room to accommodate other beliefs claiming to supplant them. And this is not unique to religions, but is a feature of almost any ideology which is deeply held: Evolutionists and Creationists never attend each other's conferences except to bark at each other; Communists don't go to Nazi rallies, and vice versa.

As for the Orthodox, their hostility was understandable: there could be little more blasphemous to any Christian than Vissarion's claim he

Vissarion: close to the altar because he's close to God

was the Second Coming. But according to Sergei, the Orthodox Church's reasons for not reconciling with the new belief were far more worldly – 'They will not recognise our message, because to do so they would have to give up their big hats, and their power. They have their system, their hierarchy, power and influence in society. A lot of money is attached to it, and so they resist the truth. Not only that, they try to obstruct our work. We don't blame them, though – we are not angry. Once an archbishop came here for round-table talks with Vissarion. It led to nothing, of course. It's a question of belief: there can't be any compromise. But the Orthodox do steal from Vissarion's teachings. We know that they study the *Last Testament* and use it in their sermons. Unofficially, of course . . .'

I had an idea. Two years earlier I had met a pagan priest, an encounter described in my first book, *Lost Cosmonaut*. His beliefs required him to kill animals for God: chickens, rabbits, and every five years, a horse. Would the Vissarionites have allowed him to kill a rabbit in the temple, I wondered?

But I was falling into the same trap that had opened up in front of me when I had overheard the arguments in Tatiana's house. It was a trick question, designed to provoke, and not to illuminate. I knew the answer would be no, and that there would be a rationale for it, so why bother asking? To watch him squirm?

We left the cathedral and walked over to the Minussinsky Dom. Sergei stopped at the gate to shake my hand 'How long will you be here?' he asked.

'A few days,' I said.

'That is not enough,' said Sergei. 'You will need to stay longer to *feel* what we are doing here . . . feeling is the most important thing. That is where true understanding comes from.'

12

Back at the house, the little girls in the cultural centre looked different. They were the first generation to receive these ideas as facts, to not have to unlearn old ways of thinking, who had not 'chosen' but were born into it, who knew this world before they knew any other. Whose bodies had their souls inhabited before? What was Satan whispering to them? Around them, energy waves were flowing in and out, my negative ones going to form Satan. God the Father was trying to whisper to their hard and unresponsive souls. On the mountain, the unseen mountain that I found hard to picture, Vissarion was amassing his good flesh to stave off total annihilation of the species. I was in the midst of a heroic struggle of cosmic proportions.

Hungry and light-headed, I tried to process everything Sergei had told me. There were definitely some things I liked about Vissarion's belief system: the fusion of science fiction elements with traditional religious concepts for example, the depiction of the Devil, and especially the all-pervasive apocalyptic tone. The necessity of building up a 'critical mass' of 'good flesh' was raw, wild poetry to me. But there was other material that was harder to digest. For example:

1. In spite of what Sergei had said, there were obvious contradictions, or at least inconsistencies in his explanations of Vissarion's beliefs. If Vissarion had direct access to the mind of God and knew everything already, then why couldn't he speak to me in English? If they were seeking to return to eighteenth-century conditions, then why were they not just using modern technology as a temporary stop-gap, but actually *increasing* their dependence on it (a radio antenna was under construction so that all the believers would soon have mobile phone coverage, and as Ali had said, even on the mountain, close to Vissarion, there were TVs, powered by solar panels). But I hadn't pursued this angle. I knew there would be a rationalisation and I would simply irritate him and make him defensive.

2. Vissarion's numbers – from an aesthetic point of view, they were very disappointing: sixty-one rules of the soul; two Gods; fourteen points on the astral street plan. They were numbers without beauty or significance, asymmetrical, obsessive, clumsy, and deeply banal when compared with such timeless classics as the Ten Commandments, the Holy Trinity; the Ninety-nine Names of God and the Number of the Beast. On the other hand, their inelegance was good evidence that Vissarion was absolutely sincere. Anyone cynically constructing a religion would surely have chosen better ones. I would have, anyway.

3. A return to the eighteenth century did not seem very attractive, especially if we were talking about Russia, which at the time was a pre-industrial society where the vast majority of the population lived in serfdom. It was also the beginning of the large-scale environmental despoliation of Siberia as the Russian Empire expanded eastward in search of fur, establishing prison colonies and attempting to convert the indigenous nationalities to Orthodoxy along the way. Meanwhile

the intellectual and scientific revolutions that Sergei opposed were already under way: Russia's greatest scientist, Mikhail Lomonosov, walked from the village of Kholmogory on the White Sea to Moscow, enrolling at the Slavo-Greco-Latin Academy there in 1731. The good news: there were printing presses, so it would still be possible to produce the *Last Testament* in sufficient quantities.

4. And then, of course, there was the collusion between Jews and evil aliens. It hadn't shocked me in Ukraine: over there, Yid-bashing is a venerable tradition. But I had hoped for better from the Son of God.

13 The souls were prepared

But I was succumbing to the old temptation again. Critiquing Vissarion's ideas was a dead end; it could only propel me out of this reality he had created. I had to stay close to the believers, to see through their eyes if I were to travel deeper into their world and understand not only what had brought so many people to such inhospitable conditions, but what had kept them there.

It wasn't the environmentalism, even though this is a movement with deep religious underpinnings. Because whatever the science says, its emotional drive is derived from Christian eschatology: the sins may be committed against the planet instead of God, but the end times are still nigh and the pending apocalyptic catastrophe remains in place. We live wrongfully, we shall reap what we sow and be punished for our wickedness. Only sincere repentance and atonement can prevent this calamity from taking place.

In environmentalism, however, 'sincere repentance' usually amounts to wallowing in guilt and 'atonement' to recycling the odd bit of rubbish. Any changes that would entail a real cost for the individual are usually avoided. The Vissarionites on the other hand required the believer to embrace a life of backbreaking toil, of relentless self-criticism, and of striving in some of the most inhospitable terrain on the planet.

Maybe, then, it was something deeper, perhaps something in the dark side of Vissarion's teachings, that held them there. Once you got past the strangeness of the imagery, all the talk of Lucifer and bad energy and evil aliens orchestrating cosmic conspiracies amounted to a thoroughgoing expression of a profound despair, a certainty that man, childlike, seduced and manipulated by unseen forces, whether

Jews or aliens or Satan, was unable to avoid evil. Consequently he had to be destroyed.

But as Sergei had said, the intellect was not enough – feeling was the key. So it wasn't enough to *think* this. The believer had to feel this deeply. And perhaps then, once you really did feel it, the only sensible option really would be to flee the world, and escape to another one, where you could build another, better life. Then all that backbreaking toil and suffering would make sense, and as an extra benefit, you'd be living as close to God as was possible.

Tatiana and Sergei had both said that Vissarion's soul had been prepared for years, millennia even. His was not the only one: his followers' souls had also been prepared, by an individual and national experience, to accept his beliefs. Russian history seemed designed to make it easier to adopt them: the country had already experienced several apocalypses in the twentieth century, so it was perhaps less difficult to believe in another, final one just round the corner. The proximity of Siberia was also key: Vissarion's belief required a vast, epic landscape to disappear into, and construct something new. If it hadn't been there, what would he have done? (Similarly in the nineteenth century another vast and largely unsettled area, the USA, contained multiple utopian communities comprising those who had withdrawn from the mainstream in pursuit of perfection, and even now the tradition continues in desert cults.) His rejection of the intellect half-echoed a poem known to all Russian schoolchildren that declared their country impossible to understand with the mind, and insisted that it could only be 'believed in' (though Vissarion, of course, talked about feeling instead of faith, and applied it to his God and not the country; but the dismissal of rationalism was still there). And finally, his followers needed to be prepared to accept severe hardship. Russians are masters at this, and have a high tolerance for suffering.

Vissarion seemed more and more like an exclusively Russian Messiah; it was hard to understand how his message could ever become universal. And later I was told that the Germans, coming from the materialistic and individualistic West, were hampered in their spiritual growth by their inability to speak Russian. They were too analytical, too systematic. They tried to grasp the revelation through thought rather than feelings. It was necessary to understand Russian to truly grasp Vissarion's ideas; once you could think *in* Russian then you could start to think and feel *like* a Russian, more accustomed to collective living, to sacrifice and toiling towards a greater aim. And thus, though unhappiness is universal, Vissarion was a thoroughly Russian Messiah, and redemption could only be found here, on Russian soil . . .

So behind all the smiles and openness lay a great shadow: the certainty of doom and death and colossal bloodshed almost built into the DNA of a people. It was a grim business contemplating all these souls so despairing of hope that they would come here, where in the past only prisoners and outcasts could be settled by force . . .

14 Natasha's story, part 1

Or at least that's how it seemed sitting in the cultural centre at that particular moment. But almost immediately I had another experience that seemed to undermine these ominous musings, pointing out clearly how varied individuals' reasons can be for believing what they believe.

Natasha, our cook, offered to show me the workshops where the Vissarionites were developing the crafts that would eventually see them become independent of the world, and with the dominating Tatiana gone, she suddenly opened up, giggling and chatting away.

She was from St Petersburg; she had had a nice flat there, and run a business that was 'more or less successful', but none of it fulfilled her. Then a friend gave her some videos to watch: 'It looked so beautiful, like something out of a storybook! I didn't know such places could exist in reality! Ever since I was a little girl I had wanted to live in a village like that!'

Then the Teacher came to St Petersburg. Natasha listened to him talk in a palace of culture; at the end he spoke to her personally. And immediately she knew that she had to move to Siberia. And that was that; Natasha's motivations were shockingly naïve, even touchingly so. She became more and more childlike as she spoke about her new life, and I became less sure about my doomy speculations. Natasha seemed to have come to the village in pursuit of innocence. Motivations began to seem enigmatic again, and what lay behind the phenomena once more started to slip away from me.

'It's wonderful here,' she continued. 'You know, you can wear any clothes you like and nobody will judge you. What matters is the spirit, what's inside . . . Yes, it's magical here. It's a pity you came in the winter. In the summer I always dress in eighteenth-century costume!'

You know, last summer a couple came here to get married: he was English and she was Australian. A Dutch company came to film them. And the TV people, well, they filmed me, because of my dress . . . they liked it. They thought it was beautiful. Some of our girls wear mediaeval gowns. It's so creative, so free here: there's no snobbery, not like in St Petersburg. And you know, the Teacher says that we should have nothing in our houses that is not useful . . .'

15 Natasha's story, part 2

But Natasha was not without sadness. Suddenly her story took a darker turn.

'Yes,' she continued. 'I left everything to come here. My business, my flat and . . . my son.'

And how that final sentence hung in the air: like a sudden insertion of real, adult darkness into a fairytale, shattering the carefully crafted illusion.

'Why did you leave your son?' I asked.

'He didn't want to come, and I couldn't make him. So I left him with his father. He's fifteen.'

'Do you ever see him?'

'Oh yes. The Teacher is very strict on this. We can't just throw away our families when we join the community. We must return to the world, and visit those we leave behind. So every year I return to see him.'

At the thought of these compulsory reunions, Natasha's eyes grew darkly reflective. Did that separation weigh on her like a sin, I wondered, or was she so in love with her new life that the necessity of going back to the old one was a burden she resented?

Suddenly Camouflage Boy appeared, stomping past us, driven by a wild energy. He looked as though he was continuing the same hopeless walk he had been on earlier in the day.

'We're moving! We're moving!' he said, giggling nervously as he passed us.

'Him!' Natasha snarled under her breath. 'Let me tell you about him! You know, his parents accepted the faith and came to the village. He did not, but they brought him with them anyway . . .'

The boy was from Yaroslavl: hardly St Petersburg, but still Paris in comparison to Petropavlovka. Stuck out here, unable to get drunk or fight or chase girls, surrounded by lentil-eating lovers of God, he had to be one of the loneliest and angriest boys in the world. Now I understood his mad walk: he was trying to kill time, and not only that, but to kill his youth and energy. I thought of Natasha's son, growing up in St Petersburg, abandoned by his mother for life in the storybook village governed by the Son of God. That could have been Natasha's son, if she had forced him to come with her. But there was no sympathy for the boy in her soul:

'He is an idiot. He has nothing in his head.'

16 The Three Stigmata of Vissarion Christ

Natasha showed us knives, baskets, wooden eggs and clay pots. The basketweaver looked bored and resentful that she had the most tedious craft, the wooden-egg girl was keen to sell me an egg with a unicorn on it; the clay-pot guy was enthusiastic, but barking mad. He was convinced that the Teuton in Lederhosen standing on two crossed bars of a fence on his mug was symbolic of a German desire to subjugate Christianity. As for the knife-maker, he was dead. The only stuff I liked was the furniture.

The furniture-maker was a dark, bearded giant with a voice deep and resonant enough to liquefy the internal organs of Humboldt squids darting around in the depths of the ocean. He explained that he tried to capture the natural feeling of the wood and follow the forms that the pieces themselves suggested to him. And it did look as though the roots and branches had grown into these shapes of their own accord, as though his furniture wanted to be sat on or slept in. It was beautiful stuff, and popular: all of it was sold in the markets in Krasnoyarsk and he received a lot of private commissions. It wasn't a very efficient economic model. A single chair took three men a day and a half to make; a bed, two weeks. To meet demand he worked from dawn until eleven every night, like a Stakhanovite, one of the famous shock workers of Stalin's day, working inhuman hours for the sake of the leader, for the sake of the future, for the nobility of labour itself. Like everyone else in the village he had never practised his craft before; like Ali he was not worried by the absence of objects and distractions in his world. This was not a problem as he had so much work.

He was relaxed and affable and communicated warmth. I had a weird, inexplicable sense that I had met him before; in fact I had, sort of – I later realised that he was the narrator of the Vissarionite recruitment video. We could have stayed; I think he wanted us to. But there was nothing left to talk about, not unless we were going to get into the thing that was underlying everything, the thing that was strange, and awkward, and that after talking to Sergei, I understood a little too well. My growing familiarity with the new belief, ironically, was placing a distance between me and the people I met, even as they became more open towards me.

Because it was Vissarion who had brought all this to pass, it was Vissarion who had summoned this beauty out of the void; it was Vissarion who was necessary for this world. Vissarion was inside them, and they were inside his reality. Wherever I looked, whoever I spoke to, Vissarion was staring back at me, with his weak smile, greasy hair and that strange, unidentifiable glint in his eyes.

VI

The Holy Mountain

1

At some godforsaken hour the next morning I crawled out of bed and went to the window: the promised vehicle was already sitting outside the cultural centre in the snow. It was an old UAZ minibus, a dark blue tin cigar that teetered on top of enormous narrow wheels. *Hm.* I had been hoping for something a bit more modern, perhaps a vehicle from Vissarion's alleged secret fleet of stylish SUVs, with a TV built into the back of the headrest and those bouncy wheels you see in rap videos. No matter: we went down, shook hands with the driver, a young hippy in a headband, and then climbed inside. I perched myself on the edge of a bench that had been repaired with black masking tape and tried not to sneeze, in case the whole thing fell apart. A metal plaque stated that the UAZ had been built twenty years earlier in Ulianovsk, birthplace of Lenin. And now it was ferrying pilgrims to meet the Messiah. I smiled, but only briefly. It was an irony of the sort of which there is perhaps rather too much in Russia, and I quickly came to accept it as normal, natural even.

Nobody else from Petropavlovka was going to visit the mountain that day, so we set off immediately. I let Semyon sit next to the driver, ostensibly so that he could enjoy the view but really because it was too early in the day for me to listen to hippy blather. Semyon was no keener on it than me, but I was leader of the expedition, so I had privileges.

2 The secret Jew

The oceanic night receded, leaving a few villages washed up on the shore of the new day. We stopped in one (a hotbed of musicianship according to the driver) to pick up a young girl who was coming to the mountain with us; her name was Antonina.

We drove on. By the time the sun had fully ascended all signs of habitation had fallen away, and only a mud road remained, cleaving a path between rows of trees that seemed to lead to nothing and nowhere. The old UAZ, however, was bearing up well: it could take any crevasse, any pit, and just keep going. It was a real Soviet war horse: fine as long as you didn't object to the violent vibrations in your internal organs.

After an hour the world beyond the grimy window began to change: the wall of trees dwindled to nothingness and the sky opened out above us, held up on the peaks of mountains covered in thick forest. It was beautiful, but forbidding: the kind of landscape that warns you off as being too steep, or impenetrable, a solemn, silent nature that threatened death.

We drove and drove. It seemed as though we were plunging deeper and deeper into the wilderness, but of course, our penetration of the territory was in fact pitifully shallow. I knew that this realm of mountains and forest stretched on and on with appalling tedium; that we were just playing with it . . .

And then suddenly the UAZ stopped. There were a couple of shacks standing at the foot of a hill. They looked like prospectors' huts from the California gold rush. The driver informed us we had arrived at the foot of the Holy Mountain. Then I discovered that he was not a true Vissarionite but a double agent in the employ of the same sinister aliens who had been training the Jews in the mastery of money, because he swiftly ripped me off, making something like 1,000 per cent profit on the cost of fuel. I didn't have much choice but to pay him, however, as I was relying on him to drive us back in two days' time. As soon as he had the notes in his hand, he grinned, jumped back in the van and drove off, his extraterrestrial masters no doubt well pleased with their good and faithful servant.

I didn't fancy his chances of surviving the apocalypse.

3 God's will

It was a six-kilometre walk through taiga up the mountain to where Vissarion and his closest disciples dwelled. There was a path, but it was easy to lose as it had been buried in snow and deceitful pseudo-paths snaked away from the main one, tempting the naïve visitor to go *this* way, or *that* way, and thereby encounter death by hunger or by cold. Antonina, however, had been to the mountain before: she knew the true route to the city of mankind's salvation.

Antonina was a small, pale, odd woman in her early thirties. She had first encountered Vissarion and his ideas through videos while studying English at the pedagogical institute in Ryazan in southern Russia (she spoke the language, but in a stilted, ungrammatical way). His was the message she had been waiting to hear all her life, and she was converted almost immediately. But it was the 1990s and life was hard; she could not afford to move to Siberia. Thus she had been forced to finish her degree and after that work for several years, slowly scraping together enough cash for the move. But in all that time her dream had not wavered, she had remained faithful to the word and finally she had done it. She had now been living in the community for about five years.

Recently, however, she had separated from her husband. Vissarion did not permit divorce if it broke up a family, but Antonina and her husband were childless, so it was permitted, if not condoned. Even so, her position in the community had changed.

'The Teacher says that women are to be homemakers for men, but now I have no man to care for. But I am not allowed to do nothing either. Vissarion says that I must work, and be a useful member of society.'

'So what are you going to do?' I asked.

'I am going to live on the mountain.'

'But what are you going to do there?'

'I am going to teach English to the children in the school.'

It struck me that that was a job only marginally more useful than sitting on the sofa at home and counting the hairs on her arm. Why were they teaching English on the mountain? It made little sense, except as one more reflection of the religious influence the Vissarionites did not acknowledge: millions of children in the Soviet Union had been educated in European languages they would never have any call to speak, considering that the vast majority of citizens in that socialist paradise were forbidden to travel abroad. The purpose of the language was not pragmatic but rather to demonstrate how enlightened and humane the Soviet education system was, and how fully rounded Soviet citizens were.

'Are the children interested?' I asked. 'I can't imagine they have much use for it.'

She shrugged. 'It's what I must do.'

4

The mountain climbed steadily, slowly, constantly upwards, but at such a low gradient that I didn't realise how high above sea level I was: it was the thinness of the air that let me know I was ascending towards the heavens. Antonina was accustomed to it and soldiered on regardless; Semyon wasn't bothered either – clearly he was a lot healthier than me. But suddenly I found myself gasping for air and physically exhausted for no apparent reason. Antonina slowed the pace a little, and then started asking questions. She seemed to think I was a follower of the Teacher. I rapidly disabused her of the notion.

'Do you eat meat?' she asked.

'Yes.'

'You shouldn't. The Teacher says it is bad for our souls.'

'So why are you wearing leather shoes?' I asked.

'There is no alternative.'

Nonsense, of course: there are a great many alternatives – shoes made of cloth, wood, felt, plastic or rubber, for example. But I didn't press the point: I wanted Antonina to open up, and give me an insight into some of the aspects of community life that were still shrouded in darkness – especially the 'meetings' that always seemed to be going on, where the Vissarionites resolved their problems collectively. I had learned a little more about them: the gathered believers would discuss moral problems, relationships, the construction of the village, the book, everything – though always under the guidance of an elder and with reference to the *Last Testament*. Nothing was off limits at these meetings; all topics were open to group discussion. Sometimes tempers flared, and conversations grew uncomfortable – but if the majority agreed to go on, then the meeting had to go on, until a consensus had been reached and the issue resolved.

It sounded like another echo of the old state religion, though this time it came from the earliest, most *avant-garde* days of communism: the re-engineering of the soul of man; the abolition of the individual in pursuit of an ideal and harmonious collectivism. The Vissarionites were trying to construct a city of transparent houses, where every citizen would be continuously visible to his neighbour, but need never fear because nobody ever felt the urge to sin. The Vissarionites after all were reconstructing man's soul like the stars in the night sky, moving them around one by one, until his nature was changed and he was perfect, having conquered the ego and now living instinctively in accord with the multitudinous rules laid down by the Great Benefactor, Vissarion.

It sounded like a monumental struggle. I wanted some kind of illustration from Antonina: for example, what if a member of the village harboured a passion for his neighbour's underage daughter? By the rules of the meetings he would have to reveal these thoughts, and 'work through them' with everyone, including the father of the object of his desire. But Antonina didn't seem to have much of a theoretical grounding in her own beliefs. She couldn't tell me much about this or anything. She wasn't even able to say what it was about Vissarion's teachings that had won her over and became exasperated when, out of boredom, I asked her about Vissarion's stance on the theory of evolution.

'Why don't you read the *Last Testament*?' she asked. 'There is an English version on the internet . . . the Teacher answers many questions there.'

'It's just an introduction,' I said.

'Oh.'

'And the translation is awful.'

'Really?'

'Yes. Unreadable: like someone who doesn't speak English went through it word by word with a dictionary.'

'Oh.'

She was silent for a minute.

'Well, you might be able to ask lots of questions tomorrow at the *sliyaniye*.'

'What's that?' I asked.

'Every Sunday, after the holy liturgy, we have a meeting with the Teacher on top of the mountain, and he answers some of our questions directly. If you are lucky he may answer yours . . .'

5 Mountain security

There was a security guard at the top of the ascent, sitting in a wooden cubicle with a ledger, keeping track of everyone who came and went on the mountain, just as though it were an office building in Moscow. He wrote our names into his book, then radioed ahead to say we had arrived.

I walked behind his cubicle and found a few dismal huts. They were abandoned, tiny and primitive: ancient Old Believer settlements, perhaps, or the last remnants of a White Army refuge dating from the post-revolutionary civil war. But in fact these hovels were little over a decade old. This was where the first Vissarionite pioneers had lived as they set forth to tame the taiga.

Beyond the huts was the peak of another mountain. Its sides were thick with trees like all the others, but towards its peak there were several alien elements: a futuristic circular building, and above that a house that stood suspended between abyss and void, looking out over the vast wilderness. This was the Heavenly Abode of Vissarion himself, the Eagle's Nest, the mountain eyrie of the man with direct access to the father-mind of God, he who knew all that went on above and below, and who had revealed the true origins of the cosmos and the sixty-one rules of the soul for the first time, leaving his followers without words to describe the magnificence of his gift.

What was he doing now, the Son of God? Usually we encounter Messiahs in heavily truncated form and get only the best bits, edited highlights specially selected for our edification. We don't get to hear about them moving from room to room, stealing a lazy moment, eating, farting, suffering through an afternoon's ennui or watching TV. But right now, Vissarion was operating in real time, and a hidden camera placed in his rooms might well have revealed just such a moment of nothingness.

And standing there, I wondered not for the first time if there wasn't something about the Vissarionites' life on the mountain to envy, in spite of all the physical hardships, the isolation, the endless toil, the dismal food and the strict moral instruction. After all, they were so close to their Messiah that they could see him, and talk to him, and listen to *his* words in *his* voice, uncorrupted and unmediated by interpretation. They had a direct line to God; their faith was instantly rewarded and confirmed for them, and so their lives had a solid metaphysical purpose. There could be no dissent or doubt: the truth lay open all around them. Very few people in history had been in their position . . .

6

Sergei had spoken of 'miracles that only we understand': the story of how so much territory had come into Vissarion's stewardship might have been what he was thinking of; it had certainly baffled me. There was timber on it; it had to be worth money. Land is always worth money. More than that, in the early nineties, when the community had been formed, private ownership of land was illegal, and yet Vissarion had managed to get his hands on an entire mountain. It seemed uncharacteristically generous of the state to just hand out so large a gift to such an extremely unorthodox belief.

In fact, Vissarion didn't own the mountain. Later I learned that the community had leased the land from the government for eighty years as an 'experimental ecological settlement', without referring to the religious nature of the group. At the time Vissarion had not yet declared himself Christ: that didn't happen until a few years later, at a press conference, when he was asked directly by a journalist.

It still seemed incredible: so much land, for nothing, for no profit, for the most idealistic of goals. And it wasn't just bizarre in Russia: it would be bizarre anywhere. And some Vissarionites did take the event as proof that Vissarion really was fulfilling God's will.

But there was another, less magical explanation. Vissarion had started his mission during late *perestroika*, and this was extremely significant. It was a period of unprecedented openness and change in Russia and the Soviet Union, both commercial and spiritual. One Vissarionite had put it like this: 'Conditions came together at that precise moment that had not existed before then and do not exist now, and we were able to take advantage of that and make real something that would be impossible now.'

And Vissarion knew he had been the beneficiary of a remarkable moment in Russian history. He was very careful not to provoke the new regime. Although the mountain was remote, he obeyed all the laws of the state, opening up the community to the authorities, permitting the emergency services and safety inspectors to perform regular checks, ensuring that the children studied the state curriculum and took state exams. The governor was invited to their festivals. Vissarion may have created a reality, but he was aware its continued existence depended on the goodwill of the larger, more earthly reality surrounding it.

7 Alim

A tiny figure emerged from the wall of forest, distracting me from my thoughts. He walked towards us, slowly growing larger and larger until finally he was standing at full height under my nose. His name was Alim; he had Asiatic features subverted by piercing blue eyes. Like Ali he was from Dagestan; like everyone else we had encountered, he knew nothing about me. More than that, he was in a rush. I was distracting him from his important labour and he was keen to return to it. 'The first I heard about you was this morning, when they radioed us from Petropavlovka,' he said, as he raced back towards the trees, retracing the path he had just cut out of the snow. I half-walked, half-ran to keep up, answering the questions he tossed over his shoulder as he tried to figure out how to get me off his hands as quickly as possible. Alim didn't know that I was supposed to be interviewing Vissarion. Like Antonina, he suggested I could ask one question during the *sliyaniye* the next day. 'Everyone will be asking questions, though. A face-to-face meeting is impossible.'

'No, it isn't,' I said. 'That's what I'm here for. That's what we agreed with Vadim.'

'With Vadim? You've spoken to him?'

'Many times,' said Semyon.

Alim's tone softened slightly. 'Well, it might be possible. I'll radio the Heavenly Abode, but I'll need to see a list of questions first. The Teacher has given many interviews, he has answered many questions; he's tired of it now. Nowadays when Russian journalists come we turn them away. You might be lucky because you are a foreigner. What do you want to ask him?'

I paused a moment, thought, then realised: *I had no idea*. It was startling. In all this time, during all these preparations, dating from my first efforts at contacting Vadim back in Moscow to this very moment, I hadn't once thought about it. But then, it didn't seem to matter. I wasn't interested in getting Vissarion to prove himself to me, or in trying to provoke him with lazy, niggling questions . . . I just wanted to meet the man possessed by the strange vision, who had ended up creating a whole reality in such extreme conditions, and attracting so many intelligent people to follow him. I knew that he would be ready for anything I asked him; he was a master at explaining himself. I wasn't going to get much truth or understanding from his words. My instinct told me that his power, that what made him remarkable, was not to be found there anyway. No: the interview was a pretext. It was standing in his presence that was my goal.

'I'll write them down once we arrive in the village,' I said. Alim seemed satisfied with that. We pushed on into the forest.

8

The taiga opened up into a wide circular clearing. There was a sculpture in the centre: two wooden angels standing back to back with their arms raised, bells hanging from their wings. A globe emerged from the space in between them, topped by a star with so many points it looked like a particularly cruel mediaeval weapon – something homosexuals might be made to sit on while the villagers pelted them with muck and old turnips, hooting with delight.

I was still carrying my memory of the furniture from the night before, and the knowledge that, in some people at least, the act of surrendering their will to Vissarion had unleashed remarkable talent. So I was surprised to see that the centrepiece of the holiest village in the community was a piece of syncretistic New Age crap that had raided the chest of religious symbols but failed to synthesise them in a convincing way. It was kitsch, yes, but not the entertaining kind.

'We are forbidden to walk up to this monument unless we are praying,' said Alim, leading us in a wide circle around it.

'What does it represent?' I asked.

'Nothing much,' said Alim. 'We'll put something better there later.'

9 City of the Shining Star

And then, at last, after so much planning, so many preparations, I was finally in the Abode of Dawn, the village on the mountain, where those closest to the Messiah lived, those most righteous men and women Vissarion had hand picked from among his followers to live close to his divine light. Over the years the village had been named and renamed: New Jerusalem, Town of the Sun, Town of the Masters or simply the Town, or the Town on the Mountain. On 14 August 1998, however, the leaders of the village had made a decision to call their settlement the 'Abode of Dawn'. The fourteen streets had then also received their names, and they were, according to the church's official information:

Milky Way
Children's Dreams
Moon Flowers
Tender Dreams
Eternal Quests
Solar Winds
Diamond Dew
Crystal Gates
Forest Spirits
Naughty Rains
Twinkling Mysteries
Silver Springs
Chanting Mountains
Star Fields

Ahem. God the Father may have been the embodiment of pure love but he clearly didn't have much power to stop his followers from succumbing to utter tweeness. And for all the florid poetry of the names, the village didn't look like much. There was a lot of snow, and some wooden houses. They weren't as primitive as the ones I had seen next to the security guard's hut, those dark, pokey holes in which the early settlers had huddled together, sheltering from the taiga. Some of them had high vaulted roofs, and looked quite comfortable and spacious. One had a vaguely oriental design. My eye was drawn upwards, however, back to the futuristic circular building I had seen earlier (Alim explained that it was going to be an art gallery containing Vissarion's paintings and those of his most talented disciples), and above that, the Teacher's own house, that stood in the heavens like a second sun; visible from every angle and with a clear view of everything beneath. But in fact the Teacher's domain was better than the sun: it was closer to his people and its light could never be obscured by clouds.

Alim stopped at one of the smaller huts.

'This is where you'll be sleeping.'

10

It was good to stop walking, to get inside, into warmth, and to sit down. I took off my boots and my socks, soaked all the way through, hit the wooden floor with a wet slapping sound. We were in a workshop with a kiln, where Yura, Vissarion's brother-in-law (he was married to the Messiah's younger sister) made little clay coffee cups that the community sold at the Krasnoyarsk markets. His elegant creations lined one wall: they were small, dark and unvarnished, and each one had two raised beans close to its mouth. A workbench ran along the other wall, decorated with a photograph of Vissarion, some books and a row of tapes by Phil Collins, Enya, Enigma and Deep Forest: the aural equivalent of the street names of the village. Yura, a tall, gentle man, offered to put on some tunes: I politely declined.

As he busied himself in another room, making us cups of coffee, I tried to think of some questions for Vissarion that were not too obvious or banal. I couldn't take too long about it, though, as I wanted Alim to think I had a master plan and not just that I had turned up for an idle chat and cup of tea with his lord and saviour. Fortunately some switch in Alim's brain had been flipped; his previous indifference towards me vanished and the enthusiastic convert in him started to uncoil, randomly spitting out facts and ideas about the new life on the mountain.

He spoke about the weather, which was so extreme, and surely mitigated against building a settlement here; which made it look like madness in fact. But the cold wasn't so bad. The climate was dry, so if it was minus 15, like today, then he'd work without a coat. In Dagestan, he had lived on the coast and there minus 1 was more unbearable than minus 15 in southern Siberia. On the other hand, the current temperatures were uncharacteristically warm. Usually it would be minus 40 by the start of November. The last couple of years had been like this. Winter came quickly. It just happened, suddenly, at the end of October. One day you'd wake up and there'd be snow everywhere. Summer was the same, you'd just wake up one day and it would be 40 degrees and there would be mosquitoes everywhere, eating you alive . . .

11

Alim was far more confident talking to me than anyone in Petropavlovka had been. There was no hesitation; he knew exactly what it was that he believed. But then, he lived literally a kilometre from the Divine Truth, so that wasn't surprising. His speech about the climate came to an end; I hadn't finished my questions yet, so I tossed him a question to keep him occupied.

'How do you decide who gets to live on the mountain?' I asked.

'In the past Vissarion himself decided, but the number of believers is growing, and there are too many people now. So if someone in one of the villages around the mountain applies, then a panel selects. However, there are some extra rules: women can't just be homemakers if they want to live here. They must have some useful skill – whether it is sewing or teaching or working in the fields.'

He stopped, almost panting, ready for another question. I tossed him one: 'Are there any special privileges for people living on the mountain?'

'No. In fact, life is harder. There are no extra prayers or worship. Our only benefit is that we live closer to the Teacher. After the liturgy he comes to a special place on the mountain where we meet with him as a group; I told you about that. But he doesn't always come. Usually, he does, but you can't take it for granted. You can ask anything, and his answer will be recorded and put in the *Last Testament*.'

'Is it possible to have face-to-face meetings with the Teacher?'

'That's our other advantage. If there's a problem, we can radio the Heavenly Abode, and we can get our answer faster. But you can't just go to him with any problem. We have a system. First, you should read the *Last Testament*. Vissarion has already answered many of our questions; you just need to know where to look.'

'How do you find out where to look? People are very busy, and there are seven volumes.'

'If you can't find the answer, then you should take it to one of our community meetings, then to one of our priests. Only then, if the problem is still unresolved, should it be taken to Vissarion, who will decide if it requires a personal audience . . .

'It's amazing what's happening here,' Alim continued. 'Before we came it was just wilderness. And now, there's a village. And two hundred people. There are families, young people. And it's all because of the Teacher, because we've been given energy by his teaching. Life here is hard, of course, incredibly hard. It would be impossible without the Teacher, and not everyone can cope with it. Some people have to leave, and go back into the world. But look: you've arrived late, and yet the village is abandoned. Everyone is out working in the forest. That's how motivated we are.'

I was almost finished my list of questions now – I just needed him to talk a little longer. Fortunately he broke into a lament, and it was the same lament Sergei the priest had made in the Petropavlovka at the end of our interview.

'You're not going to be here long enough to get the feeling. You need to meet the people, to talk to them, to *feel* them, to understand . . .'

I let the issue of 'feeling' pass away in silence. I had 'felt' something in the furniture-maker's studio the night before, and I had 'felt' something in Ukraine when talking to Viktor, who had abandoned his television career to serve Father Grigory. But I had felt a lot of things in my time, and anyway, inner feelings come and go.

I finished writing down my questions. They weren't brilliant but they weren't embarrassing either. There were even a couple on the list that I thought rather original and that would probably hook the Messiah's interest. Alim looked them over: 'Not bad,' he said, and then dashed out the door to radio the mountain. He wasn't gone long. Yura had just served us coffee and was talking about his brief sojourn in LA in the early nineties when Alim returned. He was impressed.

'Well, lads, you're all right. You can go up.'

12 An audience with the holiest man on earth

I

Our guide, dressed in white and pale as a phantom, emerged out of the snow, only to immediately start drifting away from us, like a filament of spider's web caught on a breeze. He had no name; he asked no questions. He led us in silence through the village to the foot of the path that led to Vissarion's house, and without a pause, began the ascent.

The air was very thin now, and I felt like an old man climbing the steps to some abandoned place where he had decided to die. After only ten minutes I had to stop, to lean against a tree, to inhale deeply.

The ghost-guide smiled: I was too young to be struggling like this. Perhaps it was evidence of my life, lived badly amid the corruptions of the world beyond. I ignored my exhaustion and resumed walking, but very soon I had to stop again, and then again, and then again.

'I need pollutants,' I gasped. 'This air is too clean for me. It doesn't have the chemicals my system requires.'

'What's he saying?'

Semyon translated. The phantom didn't crack a smile. There was nothing good about pollutants. The Teacher had said so.

II

By the time we reached the top, the dusk was drifting in from the corners of the sky, shrouding everything in a murky haze. There was a guardhouse and a fence, behind which a huge dog was leaping up and down, barking and snarling and slobbering with a lust for violence and the taste of blood.

The phantom floated through the fence to get the gatekeeper to call off Cerberus. I thought about the dog, which was there to plant fear in souls. Was the Messiah afraid of intruders? After all, there had to be some terrifying loons among his four thousand followers. Was this enhanced security a precaution, or had it emerged as a response to something that had already happened?

Vissarion's house was just above us now. It was bigger than the buildings in the village, but not extravagantly so. Beneath it, the stumps of dead trees thrust out of the snow, like so many headless necks. I recalled Sergei talking about those early days, when the Teacher and two men equipped only with axes and saws and the intoxication of a new revelation had ripped out an opening in the taiga for the Teacher to inhabit, as mosquitoes tore at their flesh: madness, divine madness.

But it had paid off, for Vissarion had one of the most beautiful views on earth. When he awoke in the morning it was to the peaks of mountains, crowned with trees, dreaming beneath a vast silent sky. That way lay Russia, that way China, and over there, Mongolia. But here, here was Vissarion. This was the sort of place where the top of your head could fly off and signals from space and messages from angels invade your sense of self. Indeed, it might be hard to prevent it happening, to shut the messages off, even if you wanted to. But then again, it wasn't here that Vissarion had had his revelation. No: that had happened in Minussinsk, a smear of dirt on the face of the earth, while he had been working as a traffic cop. From industrial hellhole to mountaintop, surrounded by worshippers, bathed in sky: God #2 had been good to his boy.

'Russia . . .' said Semyon.

'Yes,' I felt an impulse to wax lyrical, to spout some shite about a mystery wrapped inside an enigma or something like that. I waited for him to finish his thought.

'It's big.'

'Yep.'

There was nothing else to add.

III

Vadim welcomed us at the entrance of the Teacher's house. I had the
jarring sense that I already knew him, because I had seen him before,
in the video Tatiana had shown us, and in photographs online, and on
the cover of his CD – and so the 'old' Vadim Semyon had spoken to on
the phone in Moscow was in fact also the prog-rock apostle I had read
about on the site. He was tall and thin, and his face really was as long
as it had looked in all those two-dimensional reproductions.

There were a lot of people moving around in Vissarion's house: I saw
the grandkids of God, and also the divinity's daughter-in-law, whom I
recognised from the oil painting in the Minussinsky Dom in
Petropavlovka. She was tired and flustered. A staircase directly in front of
me led upwards: I knew who was up there. I wanted to slow time down,
so I could drink everything in, but Vadim was eager to get started:

'Shall we go up?'

IV

Vissarion was standing there, just a few feet away from me, smiling
and nodding in his long white robes, his lank hair down at his shoulders, his eyes half-closed, his beard, all as they had appeared in the
film and photographs. And yet he was much taller and physically
stronger than I had expected, and his presence was overwhelming, like
nothing I had ever encountered before. He needed the mountain and
its sky simply to *be*, and here, cooped up in a little wooden room, he
looked as constrained as a lion in an enclosure at the zoo.

Back in Moscow I had wondered: *How do you greet the Son of
God?* In Russia, men always shake hands when they meet. I had
picked up the habit myself and now did it all the time. It seemed a bit
forward, though, shaking hands with Christ. So what should I do?

'Hello,' I said.

He nodded; smiled; then nodded again. There was a look in his half-
closed eyes, as if he were dreaming this encounter, and neither of us
was actually in the room at all. I was just a shadow moving across his
eyelids as he slept, or lay hypnotised somewhere else.

The Messiah didn't step forward. He didn't extend his hand. He sat
down. I did the same.

Etiquette problem solved.

V

We talked about things I already knew – the end of the world, the need to accumulate a critical mass of good flesh. Vissarion confirmed that he was in constant contact with the Godhead and had access to all knowledge; when someone entered the Krasnoyarsk region, for example, he knew what that man wanted, and could feel the troubles in his soul. He did correct me as regards one misunderstanding, though – the 'global situation' was not necessarily going to get worse. It didn't need to; things were already bad enough. And I was struck by one other clarification: according to Vissarion, Russia's traumatic experience in the twentieth century actually gave Russians an advantage. For the Bolsheviks' slaughtering of priests, demolition of churches and suppression of faith had actually been to Russia's advantage. By obliterating the traditional beliefs of the people, their minds had been cleared of dogma. Russians knew little about Christianity or any other religion, and thus they were more ready than anyone else to accept his new belief and be saved. And so, once again, the exclusive Russianness of his belief was driven home to me, this time by its very originator, albeit in a slightly perverse form.

But otherwise, Sergei had taught me well. I didn't even need to listen that closely, as I knew what was going to come. His voice was fascinating, however. It was a soft, weary whisper almost without modulation. I was glad I was recording it: I knew that if I didn't then I would forget it, although the *sound* of that half-chanted speech was important, essential even. It was connected to the hypnotised look in his eyes, and, I felt, contained as much meaning as his words. I stopped listening for meaning and listened only to the music of his speech, and there was still something there, in the air that he sucked in and expelled again, modified by his God-designed lungs and vocal cords.

Meanwhile, I made a mental inventory of the contents of his room. There was:

a sword on the wall;
a large selection of oil paints;
a gold crown (sitting on a shelf);
an easel;
several canvases (turned away from me so I couldn't see them);
some tapes, but they were too far away for me to read the spines;
a parrot, squawking away in the background – I could see the edge of its cage, but not the beast itself.

The most confounding object in the room, however, was a young girl of about twenty, who was sitting next to Vissarion and smiling nervously. Her clothes were tight and sexy, and she had flashing cat's eyes. After a few minutes I recognised her too: I seemed to know everyone on the mountain. She was the other woman, the younger girl with the inappropriate gaze in the portraits in the Minussinsky Dom, the one that Sergei had seemed to claim as his own wife. Perhaps I had misunderstood him: she must have been Vissarion's daughter.

But still, what was she doing here? She looked bizarre, sitting at the side of the Teacher, whose eyes were closed, and whose head tilted slightly to one side, as if it contained thoughts too heavy for any human skull, and whose extraordinary presence filled not only the room but was flowing out through the windows, down the mountain-side and into the village below. It was like staring at an icon, only to notice someone had added Betty Boop.

VI

Vadim was sitting to the left of Semyon recording the interview, as every formal utterance of Vissarion was precious and not to be lost. Perhaps the Teacher would produce some new wisdom during this meeting. But Vissarion wasn't interested in what he was saying. It was nothing new; he had said it all thousands of times before. He didn't care if I believed or not. He had said that himself: he wasn't concerned that his base was in such a remote location, and he wasn't going to send out missionaries. If people were ready for his message, then they would come, though they needed to hurry, for time was short. If I wasn't ready, that was my problem.

I needed to do something before we both fell asleep. I decided to abandon the information-gathering approach and strike right at the heart of the subjective experience of being Christ. That was what interested me most: what did it *feel* like, to be responsible for human destiny? 'In the New Testament,' I said, pausing for a moment, 'in the Garden of Gethsemane Jesus cried out to God that his mission was too difficult. Is your mission a burden – or is it a joy?'

Vissarion paused. I had just stepped across a line. Something had changed. 'Excuse me?'

I repeated the question. He laughed: 'I can't imagine any work harder than this.'

'But do you ever cry out?' I continued. 'Do you ever cry out:

"Father, relieve me of this burden"?'

He shook his head; warming to the theme he continued: 'It's useless. You can't make it easy. While you're on earth you're inside a body that can experience feelings and sorrow. My mission is to be open, not distant from people. If I didn't have feelings, I wouldn't be able to understand what was happening inside man. Of course, my mission makes me tired, but I can't stop it . . . some Eastern spiritual leaders talk about meditation to transcend the self – but that's not for me.'

'What about the end?' I said. 'Christ's mission on earth lasted three years, you've already been among us for fifteen. Do you know when you will leave?'

'No,' he laughed again. 'But I will know close to the time.'

Vissarion had changed. He was alert, and listening, and enjoying himself, cracking gags and laughing. I had touched directly on his Christhood, and he liked that – it had transformed him into quite a lively Messiah. Then I asked about Mohammed, Buddha and Krishna. If he was a direct continuation of Christ, but had come to unite all religions, then what was his relationship to these other teachers?

And now Vissarion really took flight. This was one of the 'major themes' of his thought, but difficult to explain and 'very delicate'. He placed the New Testament higher than any other holy book, though they all had validity. The problem with the New Testament was that it contained not teaching so much as a 'good message'. In fact, he had special praise for Islam: for the Muslims had analysed the problem with Christianity, detected its incompletion, and by adding long lists of rules and directions had produced a finer message, which even Jesus hadn't managed to reveal.

Vissarion, however, had arrived with the final word on everything. And then suddenly, like Sergei the priest, he was talking about alien civilisations, critiquing systems based on reason and not faith and emotion, but unlike Sergei, who had been recollecting a catechism, Vissarion was speaking from inspiration, from his essence, with a force and inspiration that was unstoppable. The time was coming soon when conditions would lead people to reject dogmas. It was coming, but it had not yet arrived. The earth was changing, there was movement from one step to another. It wasn't God's will, but it was coming, and only a few people would survive the calamities ahead and become 'the basis of future mankind'.

He spoke these words with total calm, as if the apocalypse was good. After it, mankind would leave earth behind and move into the universe, which was the purpose for which we had in fact been born: to constantly change the laws of the material world by love. 'But we must understand ourselves first, and become one nation, with one belief. Only then will people have the qualities that will help them leave the earth in ways different from how they do it now. And then we will settle other planets.'

VII

He had me in his power, in the grip of his reality. By talking to him as Christ I had placed myself in the position of acolyte, which, of course, was how he related to everyone around him. Infused with energy for prophecy, he was ready to 'Vissarion' at me all day. The interview was getting out of control. I tried to undermine him a little, to throw him off.

'Christ was physically resurrected,' I said. 'But you teach that we are reincarnated.'

Vadim's eyes became thoughtful and he nodded, as if he hadn't resolved this contradiction for himself either. For a second I wondered if I had asked a question that was going to enter the *Last Testament*.

'Yes,' said Vissarion.

There was a pause. The parrot squawked. I'd been hoping for a bit more. Eventually, seeing that I wasn't satisfied, Vissarion continued:

'It's basically the same thing . . .'

Then he lost me in a long disquisition on the nature of the body, and the nature of the soul.

It wasn't exactly an answer. It wasn't an answer at all, in fact. You might even call it an evasion. Vadim didn't look any more enlightened, either. No, this conversation wasn't making it into the book.

VIII

Vissarion was still talking. But now I wanted to look for Sergei Torop, to see if I could find him somewhere concealed beneath the robes and beard and glittering eyes. I tried to steer him into discussing his past, his life before the revelation.

'Before you were thirty, did you have any indications in your soul that this destiny was waiting for you?'

'Yes, I felt it. But at that time I couldn't understand it perfectly. If I had, I couldn't have been silent. But at that time it was forbidden to believe in something so unorthodox.'

'So your revelation happened at the right time?'

'The hour was prepared: it had to be at that time, and that time only.'

It wasn't working; his answers were short and matter of fact, leading to nothing except their own conclusions. So I tried again, with questions about art, and questions about his children to get at Sergei Torop; it didn't work. Anything that even hinted at his old life drew a blank, or led to a lecture on something else entirely. I didn't think he was evading the questions: he simply did not understand them. They referred to someone else, someone who didn't interest him. Sergei Torop's DNA had long since fused with Vissarion's; the sleeper could not be awoken from his dream. The dream in fact had taken over – devouring him and all those others camped out around the mountain, awaiting the end, their final vindication. Perhaps if I had had access to other methods, say involving rubber tubing, crocodile clips and a car battery, I might have been able to locate the traffic policeman, but even then, maybe not.

I ran out of juice. I'd been there for about an hour, it was pitch black outside and I was hungry. I thanked him for his time and switched off my tape recorder.

IX

But Vissarion didn't want me to go. He was enjoying himself. I even think he liked me.

'Stay,' he said. 'Ask anything you like.'

But I knew now that I was just going to receive more wisdom, and I had had my fill of it. 'Can I ask about the parrot?' I asked.

Vissarion laughed. 'Yes.'

'How long has it lived on the mountain?'

The girl at his side answered. 'One year,' she said in English, thrilled by the sound of the alien language exiting her mouth.

'Does it speak?'

'Name,' she said, before adding something in Russian.

'It imitates the sound of the telephone,' said Semyon.

Then Vissarion himself took the initiative. He spoke about the body's 'informational field', which did not die with the body, but rather persisted over days, slowly fading, until the now disembodied memories it contained vanished completely. Only the soul was deathless. 'But in the future, people won't change their bodies so often. For the body may live for hundreds of thousands of years. It will still die, and the soul will change bodies, but it will keep a record of acts in previous life . . .'

But I wasn't listening. He talked a little longer, and then stopped. Without a willing audience, the revelations dried up.

X

I asked if Vissarion would pose for a photo with me.

'What for?' he asked.

The mock confusion struck a false note, the first time I had felt that he didn't believe himself. It was a gesture towards the total annihilation of the ego he preached, but nothing more. Considering the number of portraits I had seen hanging in homes in Petropavlovka, and the picture by the altar in the cathedral, it was clear that he knew exactly what photographs were for, and then he posed happily for multiple shots anyway. As soon as they were taken, however, a curtain fell. Vissarion turned away and began a conversation with Vadim. I was still in the room, but I was no longer in his presence.

The girl saw us out. At the foot of the stairs she spoke:

'I stady Eengleesh,' she said, staring at me, waiting for some practice.

'Very good,' I said. 'So what's your name?'

'My name Sofia . . .'

'And whose daughter are you? Vissarion's or Vadim's?'

She giggled.

'I . . . not daughter.'

Eh?

'I . . . wife Vissarion.' Her eyes flashed.

I wasn't sure what the next question was. Or rather, I couldn't ask it. Something else came out instead.

'And . . . how long have you lived in the village?'

'Long time,' she said.

So Vissarion had known her since she was a child.

Well, well, well . . .

XI

The phantom was waiting at the door. I had been with Vissarion for almost an hour; he was impressed.

'It went well?' he asked.

'Very,' I said.

We went out into the night and then down the mountain, weaving between trees, cutting through the darkness. It was much easier going down than up; I didn't feel tired at all. It was still necessary to concentrate, however, to stay on my feet. But that was difficult: there was just one thing on my mind, and it was young and nubile and spoke English badly. Antonina had said divorce was forbidden, and I had seen Vissarion's first wife in the house. Was it really what it looked like? Because it didn't look good.

'Let's ask our guide about Sofia,' I said.

'I don't think we can,' said Semyon. 'It's not polite . . .'

'I'll be discreet. Ask . . . ask when Vissarion married Sofia.'

Semyon was reluctant, but he asked.

'I don't know,' said the phantom.

He stepped up the pace a little. I tried to think of another question, one that would be harder to evade. After a few minutes stumbling down the path, I had it:

'If Vissarion is the highest spiritual authority in your community . . .'

'Yes . . .'

'Then who performed the marriage ceremony?'

'Eh?'

'Well, no priest can do it,' I said, 'because the Teacher is higher than a priest.'

He paused for as moment, then spoke: 'We believe that when a man and woman start living together, that is marriage. We have a ceremony, but it is not necessary. Love is all that matters.'

After that he retreated into silence, and it was permanent. The topic made him uncomfortable. I enjoyed that discomfort, and knew that I was onto something. But I decided to leave it for the moment; I had pushed him as far as he would go.

It didn't matter anyway. A few hours later Yura told me directly that Vissarion had two wives, and as for the dog, yes it was there to stop crazy people getting in. An incident had taken place in the past that had necessitated the step. And that was that – he wasn't ashamed, he didn't attempt to conceal anything. But at the same time, he didn't exactly elaborate on the themes either, and it was clear to me that I was not supposed to ask. Because his acquisition of a second, younger wife suggested that he had entered a new stage, one common to men who believe themselves prophets or half-gods, when they start according to themselves sexual privileges that none of their followers have;

because, of course, no one else had two wives, let alone a young and nubile one. The *Last Testament* stated that a family should consist of one man, one woman and children.

Well, that no longer applied to the Messiah it would seem. And now he had crossed that line, would he stop at just two? What would happen when Sofia grew old and his ardour for her died? Would another young girl from the Abode of Dawn graduate to life on the mountain with the Teacher himself?

It was an ominous sign.

13 Panopticon

I walked through the village, back towards the statue of the two angels that marked the centre of the settlement. I wanted some time away from watchmen, from guards, from observers. I had received only hospitality and warmth from the Vissarionites, but that in itself was oppressive. Since my arrival on the mountain I had never been unseen, except on trips to the outhouse; and even then it didn't take much imagination to deduce what I was up to. I craved darkness, invisibility.

Once I was at the statue, though, I stopped. I had seen the view from Vissarion's mountain, and knew that from his vantage point he could see everything. The clearing was a circle from which multiple paths stretched outwards, the centre of a fourteen-pointed star. Even now, the moon illuminated the path clearly enough that from up there I was probably a small black dot, visible if the Messiah chose to look. Real disappearance would require me to enter the taiga.

Antonina had told me about a child who, in the early days of the community, had done just that, wandering into the trees, never to return. It was hard to imagine a more terrifying death. He would have spent days stumbling from tree to tree, hungry, thirsty, terrified of sounds and shadows, always expecting his parents to appear and save him. The Vissarionites had notified the authorities, and an emergency party had been sent out to search for him, but to no avail: he was lost for good, food for all the scavengers, the insects, the birds, mice, rats and maggots. They would have started with the soft, exposed parts first, the eyes and the tongue, before moving on to his meat and internal organs, reducing him to a skeleton over a period of weeks. And now, somewhere out there, his bones were lying under the moon, half-buried in dirt, picked clean. And so there really was no invisibility to be had out here, for invisibility meant death. Life could only exist in the village, under the watchful eye of Vissarion.

Slowly, silently people started to materialise from out of the void, returning from their work in the forest, from their war on the forest, for it was obvious that life on the mountain was absolutely precarious, and that only by constant vigilance, and by constant and unremitting acts of violence against nature, could the taiga be held back, and the village that had been dreamed into existence by the Teacher continue to exist. These warriors fighting against their own obliteration walked right past me, asking no questions, paying no mind to the presence of an intruder in their midst. Some said hello, but without any tone of suspicion or query. On the contrary, they were friendly, knowing that if a stranger was on the mountain there had to be a good reason for it. They had faith in the vision of the Messiah on the mountaintop, the one who saw and understood all, and through whose will, all this had been made real.

14

It was difficult to sleep that night. As soon as I closed my eyes, Vissarion appeared, and he was so solid, so vivid, it was as if he had been hiding at the back of my retinas all this time, ever since I had left his house. He didn't say anything, he didn't move; he just sat there, grinning, staring at me.

But of course, he was just an illusion, an impression, a series of private actions taking place inside my skull. Yet even so, there was something in that gaze of his that this miniature phantom Vissarion had retained from his corporeal double on top of the mountain. It was something I had never seen before, something overwhelming.

Something very strange had happened to Sergei Torop: I had no idea what it was.

VII

WE

1

Yura crept into the workshop the next morning at five, starting the potter's wheel on which he moulded wet clay into cups. He wasn't concerned about letting us sleep, and as he worked he listened to the radio. A voice from some faraway studio was mumbling about Paris, where a series of riots were entering their second week. The youth in the *banlieues* were setting fire to cars, smashing windows and attacking the police, and the excitement of this destructive rage was too much to contain: the voice on the radio informed us that the fires and violence had now spread to Italy and Belgium.

The riots had started while I was still in Moscow, exposing to the world another France, one far removed from the images propagated in art films or holiday brochures. For decades grim suburbs had been forming on the edge of Paris and other cities, holding French citizens descended from North African immigrants who were less assimilated than their parents had been. A film about this world, *La Haine*, had made a splash in the early 1990s, but after that – nothing; nobody, as far as I was aware, had ever bothered to report on this shadow France.

I was fascinated by the unfolding revelations, but now realised that I literally hadn't thought about the riots from the moment I had arrived in Petropavlovka. And there was something slightly alarming about the ease with which I had forgotten the world beyond, and not only that, but the ease with which I had forgotten I had forgotten. Had anything else slipped my mind? Unless it was also reported on the radio, how was I to know? Did I have children I didn't know about? Was there perhaps an unremembered diagnosis of an incurable disease, a fat, greasy tapeworm swelling in my belly? No, no . . . I didn't think so. The amnesia wasn't that bad. But I was impressed: Vissarionites came here to disconnect from the world and build a new one. It was working on me too.

Yura switched to the weather forecast. Why should he listen? The radio transmissions might as well have been describing events on a different planet. And besides, there was nothing shocking for him in these riots taking place in rich, civilised France. He knew the end was on its way; that it was already here, in fact.

Whatever was going on in Paris was just another sign, one among many.

2

Meanwhile, the children of the world to come, those who would one day cast off their bodies and colonise the planets, were gathering in the centre of the Abode of Dawn, on the perimeter of the circle, around the sculpture of the angels. They stood facing up towards Vissarion's house. I added my flesh to the mass, but kept my distance, standing on the opposite side of the statue with my back to the Messiah.

I recognised some of the faces in the crowd: Antonina was there, along with Bjorn Borg, Alim and a man called Adrian, at whose house I had eaten dinner the day before. Alim and Yura called him 'Castro'. He was an astrophysicist from Cuba, a balding, mild-mannered man with multiple degrees from prestigious universities, fluent in Spanish, Swedish and Russian, and competent in English besides. Remarkable, certainly, but I was accustomed now to the extraordinary CVs to be found among the Vissarionites. In his new life he was the headmaster of the school on the mountain. He wouldn't tell me whether Vissarion's children had any brains or not. His silence, of course, spoke volumes.

Alim nodded to me. Hanging back from the main crowd, his eyes darting left and right, he looked like a bouncer at a nightclub, waiting for trouble. Suddenly a man in a hooded green cape appeared at his side; Alim brought him over to me: 'This is Sanya,' he said, 'our village chronicler. He knows everything about our history. He will explain the mysteries of our new rite to you . . . And by the way, you owe me four hundred roubles.'

'Eh?'

'Food and lodging, man, food and lodging.'

It was a bit jarring to be hit up for cash in such a holy place, just before the start of so sacred a ceremony, but at the same time the sum was very small so I didn't think Alim was under the tutelage of aliens, as the driver had been. I paid him and he returned to his place on the outskirts.

Sanya was a little man with sharp, shrewd eyes and a pointy red beard. His cape made him look like a character from *The Hobbit*. 'In the world' he had been a sculptor, working in all media. He wondered if I knew his work.

Eight years earlier I had toured the Yusupov Palace in St Petersburg where Rasputin was murdered. In the basement there was a bizarre display of wax dummies, representing the mad monk and the various aristocratic conspirators who had shot, poisoned, stabbed and drowned him in their efforts to stop him causing the downfall of the monarchy. They didn't look human at all, but rather like a group of alien body snatchers that had hatched out of their pods before they were ready, with bulbous fingers and noses, crude straw hair and glass eyes that shone with dementia, frozen for ever in pointless acts of savagery.

Sanya was the artist responsible for this glittering tableau of cruelty.

3

Alim and Yura had both spoken of the liturgy as if it would be the climax of my experience in the community, even more so than my interview with Vissarion himself. I would hear beautiful new songs and prayers, witness the ritual, see the wonderful temple at the peak of the mountain and then be present for the villagers' weekly meeting with Vissarion (assuming he turned up, that is, for, as Alim had said, he could not always be relied on to manifest himself). Then I would listen as the Teacher responded to the questions that had been burning in the souls of his disciples, answering them definitively for inclusion in the *Last Testament*, so that future generations would know exactly how to deal with these situations, and there need never be any ambiguity and doubt on earth ever again.

At last, the priest arrived, and the choir with him, entering the circle and walking up to the angels. They were all dressed in white; my ghost-guide from the day before was among them. The priest walked up to the statue and pulled a cord, ringing the bells suspended from their wings. The chimes drifted out into the cold morning air, over the trees, towards the mountain, killing, so the Teacher said, all harmful organisms in the air. The vibrations slowly diminished and then silence returned, rushing in to fill the space around the statue, the trees, the assembled fleshly bodies of the congregation, hovering around us, an almost tangible presence. The whole village held its breath. And then another bell, from way up on the mountain, responded. The choir burst into song. The villagers stepped into the circle and dropped to their knees. The liturgy had begun.

The priest moved among the kneeling worshippers with a bucket of warm water, and they washed their faces and hands. 'They are not washing away sin,' said Sanya as Antonina purified herself, 'but rather cleansing themselves symbolically of negative feelings.' The liturgy was celebrated twice a week, on Wednesday evenings and on Sunday mornings, but it was only on Sundays that the full ceremony was performed. It took several hours as the community ascended the mountain, starting in the centre of the village and slowly making their way up to the peak, stopping fourteen times along the way to sing the praises of the Father God. 'Fourteen is a significant number for us,' said Sanya. 'The fourteen stops mirror the fourteen points of the Star of Bethlehem that you see above the angels; and our village also has fourteen streets.'

'Why fourteen?' I asked, though it was certainly in keeping with Vissarion's curious penchant for numbers without any strong symbolic resonance.

'Because the teacher was born on the 14th of January!' said Sanya. So in fact, there was symbolism; it was simply lost on anyone who was not a believer.

4

'For a guy who claims to have absolutely no ego, he's got a nice personality cult going here . . . his picture's everywhere, they started counting time again from his birth, his birthday is a holiday, and now fourteen points on the star because he was born on the 14th?'

Be quiet, Lucifer.

5

Cleansed of their negative feelings, the gathered worshippers began singing one of the community's oldest hymns, based on a prayer written by Vissarion himself. Musically it sounded very close to traditional Orthodox chant. This was not strange: every new revelation must start raw, and base itself on established forms, only slowly developing its own styles as it matures and grows in confidence. In fact, the more I thought about it, the more I was amazed that there were no anthropologists in the Abode of Dawn, because here was an opportunity to study the formation of a religion as it happened. The Vissarionites were open; I didn't think they would turn away someone who came in a spirit of enquiry. If anything, they would like the attention.

The song finished, the assembled villagers rose from their knees and started trudging through the snow towards the Holy Mountain.

The first stage was over.

6

Slowly, very slowly, we climbed towards the peak. This time, however, I didn't grow tired, as the pace of the congregation was slow and the stops came frequently, each one lasting several minutes while the Vissarionites prayed and praised, singing slow, sacred and ethereal paeans to God, light and Mother Earth.

Semyon, Sanya and I lurked in the trees, shivering in the cold like the unclean excluded from the temple. I had chosen to stand there because I wanted to respect the privacy of the believers, although in truth nobody would have cared if I had been two miles away or breathing over their shoulders. Just like the night before, when I had stood by the statue of the angel and the Vissarionites had emerged from the taiga, glances passed straight through us, or registered us as part of the scenery only. To the assembled villagers, secure in the omniscience of the Teacher, we didn't really exist.

Meanwhile Sanya talked about the liturgy, stressing openness and flexibility as its central virtues. Although two hundred people lived in the village, only half were present. Attendance was not compulsory, though it was, of course, better to attend; but Yura, who was the brother-in-law of the Son of God, had decided not to bother, and was spending the morning working on his clay cups. As for the content of the liturgy, Sanya said it was a creative process, and it was always changing, unlike the hymns and rituals of more established religions, and thus superior. Every year they added something new. 'We don't sing the same songs. For the Teacher says that a fixed canon stops development, and that dogma is the beginning of death. Life is movement,' he said, smiling.

The villagers finished a hymn and moved upwards. The gradient became steeper; remembering my struggle the day before, I thought of the older members of the community. This climb had to be difficult for them.

'Yes,' said Sanya. 'Some people do ask, "Why do we have to climb? Why is the liturgy so long. Why does the Teacher make it so hard for us?"' But Sanya brushed these objections aside: 'As we climb the mountain and pass from stage to stage we clean ourselves of our negative emotions, and we become spiritually renewed. We regain our inner harmony, as we move away from civilisation and closer to God . . .'

'Sounds like a lame excuse to me,' said Semyon.

7 Chronicles

Sanya was a good storyteller, easy to listen to. There was nothing rigid or incoherent about the way he spoke, and he didn't just repeat the facts I already knew, but embellished them as we moved upwards. No one had died in the Abode of Dawn yet, for example, and only a few had succumbed to bodily decay in the greater community. The believers were still young and strong, and growing in number all the time. As a result they had not yet developed any fixed funeral traditions, though death was considered a cause for celebration. Vissarion condemned grief as a sin. It was an expression of egoism, a pity for the self, not the deceased, whose soul had been released to continue its growth and ascent upwards. Not only humans grieve of course; elephants and apes do too. No matter: this was another part of nature that had to be overcome if we were to successfully reorder the constellations.

He spoke about the Old Believers too, though in more positive terms than Sergei. If the ones in Petropavlovka had waged war with the first believers, in the taiga they had actually helped the constructors of Vissarion's Holy City, showing the strange tribe of displaced metropolitans the paths through the forest and which nuts and berries were edible and which were not. Without their help the early settlers would not have survived; but now the Vissarionites were inheriting the forest from them: 'They are fading away,' said Sanya. 'They drink wine and marry outside their community, and so become assimilated to mainstream society.' He said this with sadness; he respected the dissidents who had preserved their faith for centuries in the wilderness.

Then we reached the Heavenly Abode. A wooden cross I hadn't seen the day before marked the point where the *really* sacred territory of the mountain began. Sanya explained that from here to the peak, everything was considered 'the temple'. There were three levels, the first of which contained Vissarion's house and those of the families that served him. Beyond that was the area where the villagers had their meetings with the Teacher after the liturgy. And then finally there was the actual temple building, located on the peak, one kilometre above sea level. Somewhere in that area there was also a small house to which Vissarion withdrew when he needed to be alone. That was where he had written the *Last Testament*.

The other inhabitants of the mountain were: the gatekeeper, who with his dog kept a watchful eye over the home of the Holiest Man on Earth; a gardener; a housekeeper; and, of course, Vadim, his amanuensis, who lived in the smaller house beneath the Teacher's. Sanya explained how Vadim had got the job of disciple #1 and gospel writer. It was a very prosaic tale:

'Er . . . in the early days, the Teacher held "auditions" for the post. A bunch of different guys followed him around and tried to write a chronicle of his actions. Vadim's was the best. He got the job.'

8

The first villagers reached the gate and the dog ran out barking and snarling, threatening to liberate their souls from their bodies. The Vissarionites laughed at this fierce display, and waited for the gatekeeper to call off his hound. I looked up at Vissarion's house, where I had been less than twelve hours earlier, and wondered what he did while his closest and most devoted followers were camped outside, waiting eagerly to commune with him. Were there any special rites that he performed to prepare himself for this moment? Did he pray, or read from holy texts other than his own? Or was he busy chasing Sofia round the bedroom, hoping to get a swift one in before he had to step out into the cold?

No, no, I thought, *resist. That's the bad voice, the evil voice again. It will eject you from this reality. Don't listen to it. Stay inside, just a little while longer. You will be free soon enough.*

Sanya indicated a tree that split into four equally thick branches. Like the soul and body of the Teacher, it had been prepared especially, by God or nature, or both: 'When the Teacher first saw this, he realised it marked this mountain out as a special place, for it is a symbol of the world's four great religions . . .'

Then we turned around to gaze at the mountains in the distance. I could see much farther than I had the night before, and in the daylight the landscape was even more stunning, the kind of view that in an easier world you might be content to spend a lifetime gazing into.

So long as you didn't look down, that is, because the paths and houses of the village sprawling on the plateau beneath were ugly in the daylight, like weird, jagged patterns shaved into someone's scalp as a drunken prank at a party. Sanya, of course, saw only beauty: 'Journalists lie,' he said, 'and claim that we call this the City of God. That is not true. When it is finished it will be in the shape of a star, with only fourteen streets, radiating outwards from the centre. And because of that it is called the City of the Shining Star.'

That was news to me: I thought it was called the Abode of Dawn. But then it had had many names; like the liturgy, the process of identifying the village was also fluid.

The gatekeeper called off the slobbering hound. It was now safe to go up.

9

The atmosphere was almost festive as the Vissarionites passed through the 'temple zone'. We reached the stone steps laid down by Ali the Dwarf, and the ascent became easier. Sanya said that one day they would reach all the way to the village, and everyone, young and old alike, would be able to reach the top without *too* much struggle.

It was here, where Vissarion's Christhood was most established, that I suddenly remembered the enigma of Sergei Torop, the lost dreamer, and decided to push for more details. Sanya had been here from the very beginning; perhaps he remembered a Vissarion less sure of himself, more of a Torop and less of a Christ. I couldn't be too aggressive, however. He trusted me now, but it would still have been very easy to alienate him if I didn't phrase my enquiries very carefully.

'I heard that the Teacher's mother lives in Petropavlovka . . .' I said. Natasha had pointed out her house to me two nights earlier, on our walk to the artisans' workshops.

'That is correct,' said Sanya, instantly tense. I was getting away from the message, straying into shadowy territory where it was unsafe.

'What about his father?'

'He lives in Krasnodar, where the Teacher was born. His parents divorced when he was young. His mother raised him here in Minussinsk.'

'Are they followers? It must have been strange for them, to live their entire lives in the Soviet Union and then discover their son was the Son of God.'

Sanya hesitated. Then, phrasing his words with obvious care, he said, 'His parents are trying to understand what happened.'

I wasn't going to get any further. For a Vissarionite this was not relevant, or perhaps even worse – it was dangerous. As if to contemplate Sergei Torop after all was to somehow deny Vissarion, to move away from hagiography to the dangerous and murky reality of biography. Sanya was silent for a while as we continued walking upwards. We passed a boulder sheltered under a red umbrella: this was where Vissarion sat when he met with the villagers after the liturgy. The congregation stopped to sing again.

'What about the Teacher's wife?' I asked. 'She must have been shocked when she discovered she was married to the Christ.'

'Yes . . .' said Sanya.

'But she followed him? She believes?'

'She came, but not immediately. She followed about three years after his announcement.'

'It must have been difficult for her.'

'It was.'

'What about his children? Were they born before or after he was Christ?'

'Two of them, Roma and Elisei, were born before. Slava was born during, Svetogor and Dasha came after . . . and recently he adopted a baby daughter, Nastia.'

I knew more about Nastia than Sanya was telling. Yura had told me the night before that she was the daughter of a mentally disturbed girl who had 'caused a lot of problems' before eventually leaving the community, abandoning her own child on the way out. Vissarion had adopted her legally, filing all the papers with the authorities.

And then I had an idea: was she the cause of the savage dog, planted at the entrance to the Heavenly Abode to keep out 'crazy people'? Had she perhaps burned down the temple? Was that why the Vissarionites were so reluctant to talk about it? After all, an accident was an accident. It was nothing to be ashamed of, nothing to conceal. But if a member of the chosen people had flipped, and lashed out in rage in a community that abhorred violence, burning down their most sacred building – well, that was something you might not want to talk about. It might lead to questions, about nigh-on impossible pressures, and the difficulty of reordering the constellations

There was no way I could talk to Sanya about this, however. I knew I wouldn't be able to get much further with my current line of questioning as it was: if I kept going out there, the ice beneath me would collapse, tipping me into freezing waters. But there was one burning urge left, a topic I just had to raise. I really wanted to watch Sanya react to a question about Sofia. Sergei had panicked in Petropavlovka; the ghost-guide had lapsed into silence; Yura had been matter of fact but very brief. The Messiah's second bride made believers exceedingly uneasy. And so I guided Sanya towards her slowly, by a winding path.

'Sanya,' I said, sounding terribly naïve, 'you know the Teacher's private house on the top of the mountain, where he withdrew to write the *Last Testament*?'

'Yes?'

'Is he always alone there?'

Sanya gave me a quizzical look. 'I mean are other people allowed to join him? Like his wife, for example?'

'Yes, sometimes Lyuba comes.'

'And his children?'

'Yes.'

'What about Sofia?'

And now I had stepped right through his ear into his skull and was curled up next to his brain, like a devil, listening to his innermost thoughts: *He knows! He knows!* But Sanya immediately pushed me out and I was back on the mountain again, standing in the cold, beneath trees that were ready to tip wet snow onto me. 'Yes, sometimes Sofia comes also.'

And that was that. But this was a fascinating area in the Vissarionite consciousness: because Vissarion could never be wrong. And yet they understood that the second wife was something that needed to be concealed. Was this just an awareness of how it seemed to outsiders? I didn't think so. The obvious panic, the way the Vissarionites seized up when I prodded at this tender spot was something visceral and involuntary, as if they were wrestling to justify it to themselves, and didn't like to be reminded of it.

The bell rang fourteen times. We were at the top now. A stone lay by the side of the path. 'Look!' said Sanya, steering me back onto safe ground. 'It has a cross on it! The symbol is natural, it was found here . . .' Another sign, like Vissarion's beard and hair, like the tree divided in four – this site was sacred, it had 'been prepared'. Prepared or not, it was nothing compared to the beautiful gate that the Vissarionites planned to erect at this point in the future, and the cross-stone was but a marker, a sign to believers to create grandeur in their heads.

When the Vissarionites passed through this invisible entryway they not only crossed themselves but drew an invisible circle in the air afterwards, uniting the points of the four world religions. I had seen the sign before, in Petropavlovka, but now that everyone was doing it, the gesture looked like a parody. Nobody was laughing, however. On the contrary, the atmosphere was extremely solemn: the next phase of the liturgy was about to begin.

11

The 'temple' was a frail wooden structure, little more than an altar under an onion dome, crowned by the Vissarionite cross. Inscribed on the side of the dome was the legend 'Glory to the Living God' and the date of construction, year 38 of the Era of Dawn. Like the sculpture in the village below, like Ali the Dwarf's stone steps, and like the stone marking the notional gateway, it was just a sketch towards a future construction that would be so much grander, in this case a cathedral that would be made not of cedar but of granite, and which would stand here, so close to the sky, for centuries, throughout the golden days that would follow once the wicked kingdoms of man had finally fallen.

Sanya decoded the shrine for me. It stood on another mystical stone, this one symbolising harmony between heaven and earth, and its four sides represented the four major religions. There was a set of bells under the dome, and beneath them, five wooden cherubs circled the fourteen-pointed 'Star of Bethlehem'. The cherubs, however, were not just cherubs but rather represented the 'five origins of universe', which according to Vissarion were the Absolute Creator, the Material Spirit, the Heavenly Father, the Holy Spirit and maybe Mother Earth, I can't remember. Fatigued by the excess of symbolism, the almost decadent lust for appropriating all signs and then reinterpreting them to suit the needs of the new Messiah, I had tuned out.

And so as Sanya babbled on I watched the priest, a former astronomer in an observatory in Kazakhstan, take the cords of the bells in his white-gloved hands and tug gently. The bells chimed, softly, tunefully, sending out invisible sonic pulses to the heaven he had once gazed at through a telescope in the steppe. Now he could communicate directly with that world which, when viewed through a contraption of metal and glass had seemed so dark and cold and empty, but which he now knew to be bright and brimming with love.

He was a lucky man.

12

The Vissarionites had lifted the format of the ceremony from Russian Orthodox ritual. The priest faced away from the huddled believers, chanting, and periodically he would stop and break into song, at which moment the villagers would join in. But where Orthodox believers always stand in the presence of God, many of the villagers were on their knees. There were no strict rules, Sanya explained, invoking once more the great virtue of the liturgy – its flexibility. Anything else meant dogma and dogma, of course, was death.

'However,' he added, 'most choose to kneel.'

Thus liberated from rules, each worshipper responded as his spirit prompted him. One man might close his eyes, while the woman next to him kept hers wide open, but turned upwards, towards the sky, her gaze burning through the clouds into another, higher reality. One man might lift his arms up and stretch out his palms towards the sky, while another might let his lie by his sides and rest his hands on his knees. One woman smiled blissfully; her neighbour had his face set in solemn concentration. And even up here, at this most intimate moment, in this most sacred spot, I did not exist. It was the light and warmth of God the Father that was real. Me? I was just a phantasm, an illusion, part of a reality that was soon to pass into oblivion.

'We are now nine hundred and sixty-five metres above sea level . . .' said Sanya. He had run out of symbols to interpret and was moving on to geographical features. Nobody exercised the flexibility of the ritual more than him. He hadn't crossed himself once, and felt no need to pay even lip service to the ritual. 'And three kilometres from our set-tlement . . .'

He pointed me in the direction of Lake Tiburkul, the Sayan mountains, the Altai, Mongolia, and China. 'You could fit several Europes in here . . .'

I stepped away from Sanya and listened to the words of the hymn the Vissarionites were singing. The themes had not changed noticeably since the start of the ascent: 'Holy Father, your warmth, your spirit, your breath . . .' they sang. All around me I saw expressions of bliss, of tranced-out ecstasy, of drugged joy. Truly, they were loved up. A lot of the women wore the same semi-glacial Hare Krishna smiles I had seen months earlier in the photos the community had posted online, and beamed with that same alien joy it was difficult not to be suspicious of. Antonina's expression was like this, only more so: eyes turned upwards, and hands out-stretched, she looked as though she was having an orgasm, but a supernatural one, where the ecstasy was caught, suspended, strung out in time.

13

You mean she's getting fucked by the Holy Mountain, Satan whispered, utilising once more the invisible channels through which thoughts and feelings flow in and out of human heads.

No, I thought, *that's the bad voice again. Resist it. Resist!*

14

I went behind the altar, and turned my back on the ceremony. In the distance, beyond the dense taiga, I could see the grey smear of Lake Tiburkul. It didn't look very inviting, though I had heard that the fish there did not fear humans and in the spring would swim alongside the believers. Then I turned back to the Vissarionites, and noticed that in the midst of this joyous communion there was one who seemed excluded. A middle-aged man with a black beard, an engineer I had met the day before, was rocking back and forth, but not in ecstasy. He was casting around nervously, totally out of sync with the other worshippers, looking this way and that way, unable to concentrate. I couldn't understand what he was doing there; how you could reach this point and not be totally inside Vissarion's world. He looked ridiculous on his knees.

'Father God,' sang the priest, '*happiness and love are Your creation, and the light on Earth is Your creation, our Father, O Father God we sing to you.*'

And then the priest led the Vissarionites in a final prayer, this time to Mother Earth, and Adrian, the Cuban astrophysicist at whose house I had had such a pleasant meal the day before, and who had struck me as an exceptionally thoughtful and generous individual, and whose wife and two little boys were so beautiful, and charming, leaned forward, as if he were about to kiss the ground –

15

Oh fuck, no. That's just embarrassing, said the Devil.
I turned away.

16

Now it was time for the *sliyaniye*, the 'merging' with the Teacher. Eyes were closed, palms raised to the skies, and souls troubled and blissful alike reached out to the shining, radiant warmth of the man-god they all hoped was waiting on the lower stage of the mountain. It looked like meditation, which Vissarion, of course, had said he was opposed to.

'No,' said Sanya. 'Meditation is about leaving life, whereas the Teacher stands for living life, the right way. He says that if you meditate, certainly you will feel the breath of the universe – but you shall not develop spiritually . . . Here, in the *sliyaniye*, our souls communicate with the Teacher Himself!'

Sanya continued, but the explanation became very involved so I left it at that, where I just about understood him. The *sliyaniye* lasted a full minute, then the kneeling Vissarionites got up, shook the snow off their legs and boots and crossed and circled themselves. 'You can cross yourself any way you like,' said Sanya, 'from right to left, left to right, up, down, whatever. We have no canon, no dogma . . .'

'"Life is movement,"' I said, finishing his thought for him.

'Exactly!' He beamed.

'But Vissarion hasn't been crucified.'

'And?'

'So why the cross?'

'The cross is an ancient symbol,' said Sanya. 'It pre-dates Christianity. Long before Jesus came it represented positive energy . . .'

'So what is it for followers of Vissarion? Symbol of Christ's death and resurrection or positive energy?'

'Er . . .'

'Christ or pre-Christ?'

'Ah . . .'

Sanya looked flummoxed. For the first time I'd hit him with a question he didn't have a ready answer for. I decided to help him out. After listening to all his talk of tolerance and flexibility and freedom from dogma, it wasn't difficult. The solution was simple: 'Or is it both?'

'Yes!' he said, smiling. 'Both, both.'

And that's how I made my contribution to the rich iconography of the Vissarionites.

The Vissarionites had all descended, leaving only Semyon and me, neither of whom really existed anyway, standing at the altar alongside two more substantial inhabitants of Vissarion's reality. One of them was Sanya; the other was a man still kneeling in the snow, gloved hands resting on his knees, head tossed back, an ecstatic grin glowing in the centre of a sprawling beard. But he was only partially present. His soul, set free by the *sliyaniye*, was elsewhere, drifting deep, deep in the warm light of his Messiah, lost to itself in a state of pure bliss. For some reason, though, the sight of him made me feel depressed. Perhaps I was wrong to feel that way; but I took a photograph, and over a year later, nothing has changed. Something in that smile still strikes me as tragic when I look at it today.

We descended back towards the second level of the 'temple zone', where the Teacher met with his followers. I had just about managed to shut off the channels through which Satan whispered to me, but it was a struggle. I was bothered by the relentlessly ethereal, positive tone of the Vissarionite liturgy. Every song was about love, warmth and light. There was no reference to struggle or hardship or sacrifice, of which there was a great abundance on the mountain or in the community at large, not to mention the world beyond it. Aesthetically it was as ephemeral as a double CD of dolphin song marketed to office workers in need of an aid to chilling out, man.

It needed more. It needed pain. It needed awe. I thought about the Old Testament and the psalm that, after praising God for his gifts, his beneficence and wisdom, nevertheless cautioned the worshipper to beware, for 'Fear of the Lord is the beginning of all wisdom'. I put this to Sanya, just to see how he would respond. He laughed.

'The Teacher says that only a fool or a child would fear God. The Old Testament is talking about the first God, God the Creator, not God the Father. Our God's nature is pure love. What is there to fear?'

Of course: I'd forgotten Vissarion's great revelation, that there is not one God but two, and that it's the second one who loves us. It was a neat solution to the theological 'problem of evil', dumping everything dark and confusing on the shoulders of a demiurge, leaving the second God free of all responsibility for the violence and chaos of creation. He had come along later, like a medic at a pile-up on the motorway, surveying the twisted mess of metal and protruding limbs, the soup of blood and organs seeping outwards, the chorus of shrieks and howls, and now he was working on a plan to extricate as many survivors as he could from the carnage. This God was as innocent of our suffering as a baby, and the Vissarionites responded to him with a corresponding innocence. It was the one great, simple, pure idea of their otherwise exceedingly complex cosmogony.

It was also utterly conventional Gnosticism, an idea nearly as old as Christianity. And yet Sanya was starry eyed at the contemplation of this Truth; and suddenly I remembered the similarly enraptured Tatiana Sr discussing the uncommon wisdom of 'love the good in the bad man'; Sergei's remark that the pastiche of science fiction clichés in *The Matrix* was a valid representation of spiritual reality; and everybody's lack of concern at the demotion of Hinduism and Judaism to positions much lower than the religions they had given birth to.

Vissarion thought that the obliteration of Russia's religious culture had been a good thing, that it had cleared away 'dogma' and made people more ready to receive his ideas. It had seemed a bit sweeping at the time, but now it really did look as though he was right. At the very least, it had cleared away any framework of comparison, and left his followers like innocents gazing upon a garden for the first time, believing that the flowers they saw grew here and nowhere else.

18 The prohibition

Below us, the villagers had all dropped to their knees and total silence had descended. It could mean one thing only: Vissarion had come.

Sanya motioned to me to stop. 'We can't go any further,' he said. 'Unbelievers are not permitted near this *sliyaniye*, but you may stand among us at the next one. For the next nine minutes we must be silent, while the people commune with the Teacher.'

This sudden prohibition came as a relief. All the ostentatious tolerance and openness had been getting on my nerves, and I could hear Satan pounding at the wall I had erected. I ignored him; but every time Sanya mentioned freedom from dogma I remembered seven fat volumes with thick red spines that dictated in astonishing detail exactly how to live your life, including how to wipe your shoes in the way that God recommended. Maybe that was considered 'teaching' and not 'dogma', but for me the line was blurred. So I was glad that the Vissarionites were finally openly excluding me and reserving a privilege for the believers, like every other belief system in the world, religious or otherwise. After the haze and confusion of altars where any rite could be performed, it gave me something solid to hang on to, to orient myself by. Now I knew where I stood, and it was firmly outside, among the unbelievers, the damned. And thus defined, I was at last seen; I did indeed exist.

And so I stood there, in the snow, in the cold, shivering as, down below, Antonina, Bjorn Borg, Alim and all the others closed their eyes and sent their quivering souls out towards the warm pulsating light of the Teacher. There was no wind, there were no birds. I didn't have any new thoughts. I was a waiting organic thing only, and the longer this thing stood still, the more the cold infiltrated its outer garments. Periodically I would shift my feet and crush some snow, or listen to my own intake of breath, or watch my breath drifting away in white clouds . . .

And then, just as the cold was beginning to kill the feeling in my toes, the *sliyaniye* finished. Through the trees I saw an arm drop, a head turn. The man at the foot of the slope waved us on. We resumed stumbling downwards, digging our heels into the snow so as not to slip. It wouldn't have been any good to arrive at this most sacred moment sliding on my arse.

19

'Now the people will have an opportunity to ask the Teacher for advice regarding the situations and problems in their lives,' said Sanya. 'But we must formulate our questions very precisely before asking, as if we are describing our symptoms to a doctor. For the wrong question will lead to the wrong answer. As Vissarion says, in learning how to ask the right question we learn how to live.'

I stored the formulation away in my memory banks, as a saying to be used in the future, forever prefaced with 'As Vissarion says . . .' Then Sanya notified me of a second prohibition:

'The people will pass the microphone among themselves and ask their questions,' he said. 'And all the Teacher's replies will be recorded and edited for inclusion in our book. That is why we must forbid you from recording what you hear today. For there cannot be two versions of the Teacher's wisdom in existence. We must be very precise, and ensure that there is only one official Word of God. There must be no schisms, no debates, as there have been in other religions. There must only be clarity . . .'

The following account of the meeting therefore is not based on verbatim recordings, but was put together twenty-four hours later, using Semyon's memories and mine. I have done my best to capture the essence of the petitioners' questions and Vissarion's replies, but what follows is of course incomplete, unreliable and absolutely non-canonical, as mere human memory cannot hold all the intricacies of Vissarion's wisdom, which is rarely expressed with anything even remotely approximating brevity. Anyone looking for an authoritative account of the Teacher's answers to these profound moral problems should therefore track down a copy of the relevant volume of the complete and unabridged *Last Testament*, taking a few years to learn Russian first if necessary (so no nuances are missed), and then consult it directly.

20

Vissarion was sitting on the boulder at the foot of a wall of solid rock. He looked very regal in his long red robe, although the woolly gloves and the tea cosy on his head detracted from the effect somewhat. A red velvet cushion protected his semi-divine rear from the boulder's roughness, and a bright crimson umbrella shielded his head from any conspiracies the clouds might have been involved in, as if the slightest upset might cause the Teacher's bones to shatter and internal haemorrhaging to begin. But then he had said in the *Last Testament* that he intended to stay on the planet for a long time, to teach his children all they needed to learn. The Vissarionites weren't taking any chances.

The believers were also separated from their Messiah by thirty metres of untouched, sparkling white crystals. Was this for added safety, in case there was a maniac in their number, like the mother of Vissarion's adopted daughter? The Teacher would have time to make a break for it if anyone came lunging at him, after all. Or was it simply to intensify the sense of numinous 'otherness'? It was a far cry from the first Christ walking amid lepers and washing the feet of his disciples, that was for sure. The tableau shrieked: *Do not come close, do not touch, stay there, in the distance, and gaze in wonder!*

Most of his followers were on their knees, and rightly so, because he was the absolute monarch of both the physical and spiritual realms, the bringer of laws, the arbiter of truth and knowledge, the representative of God on earth – Moses, Jesus, Mohammed, Buddha, Zarathustra rolled into one. He was the fulfilment of all their dreams. But I couldn't stop thinking about the man I had been chatting with less than twenty-four hours earlier – the guru with an eye for young girls, a knack for gags and a pet parrot that could repeat its own name and mimic the sound of the telephone.

It seemed obscene, kneeling before this man. There was no denial of the ego here, but rather a monumental inflation of it. I felt an urge to rush forward, to sully that expanse of white snow that separated the divine from the human and grab the hem of his garment – not to be healed though, but rather to stain it with my unbeliever's touch. Would he retain his divine calm? And what about the Vissarionites? Would they remain committed to non-violence if they thought the Messiah was threatened? Alim was lurking in the trees near the boulder and once again he looked to me like a security guard or a bouncer, ready to deal with trouble.

But then I calmed down. I was here to watch, to listen, to record, not judge: I was not off the mountain yet. For now I had to let the Teacher unveil his truth, to allow even, that he really might have access to the uncommon wisdom Tatiana had spoken of, or at least that there might still be one or two good ideas up his robe. The *Last Testament* was being written in front of me. Perhaps, even at this late moment, I would discover some secret, final element that had been eluding me, and I would understand why so many intelligent people, who were far more accomplished than Sergei Torop the traffic policeman had ever been, believed this man to be their saviour. And then I might also dream a little of the dream that had devoured him and so many others.

I had forgotten the sound of Vissarion's voice, those soft and soothing, sing-song tones that made every utterance sound like a lullaby, and which mirrored the dreamy, otherworldly look in his eyes. Yet at the same time, there was weariness in there, as if being the Christ really was the great and heavy burden he said it was. But the weariness too was hypnotic; so hypnotic in fact that I forgot to listen to the content of his speech, and let the whispered vowel sounds, the hushed, softened consonants soothe and seduce me . . .

Semyon stepped forward. 'Do you know what he's saying?'

317

'No,' I replied. 'I've just been listening to the sound of his voice.'
'He's pretty angry.'

21 Divine wisdom

I

The first question had come from a man kneeling in the front row. He
wanted to know whether the Messiah thought it was acceptable for
his wife to leave the mountain so she could take a job and earn money
to pay for vital dental work. Her teeth were causing her a lot of pain.

Vissarion saw the question as an opportunity to address another,
larger issue: 'In the past,' he said, 'many women have left the mountain to earn money. This causes problems for the husbands left behind,
who have to keep house *and* work. But it's worse when men leave,
while our town is still under construction. *That* amounts to criminal
negligence.

'Until now, I have given you a lot of freedom in letting you come
and go. You did not appreciate how free you have been. You abused
it. But from now on I want to stop it. I am going to be much stricter.
And when I am strict, you are not to ask why, only to accept it.'

The crowd was silent, accepting this admonition, some with heads
bowed, others looking forward. The Teacher had spoken, and to dis-
agree would be to question the rightness of God. The questioner took
the microphone in hand again, and asked, 'Will the committee decide
who can leave, or will it be you?'

'In the first days of our life on the mountain it was I who decided.
Then I delegated to the committee. Now I shall be the one to decide
again. In some cases, such as emergency dental work, I shall make
exceptions. But too many people are leaving the town. This must
stop.'

Things were about to change in the Abode of Dawn. The free and
easy days were over.

II

A woman in the third row took the microphone. It sounded like
Antonina, but I wasn't sure: the microphone distorted the voices,
making them loud and abrasive.

'Teacher, if someone tells me an offensive joke, should I tell them
that they have offended me?'

Vissarion answered calmly and decisively. 'No. If you take offence at a joke, it's egoism. Confronting the joker will only create antagonism. You should look for the good in the joke.'

That sounded reasonable; but the questioner's voice rose in pitch. She wasn't satisfied.

'But Teacher, what if it's *really* dirty! I mean –'

Vissarion cut her off: 'Then you are to go away, and think carefully, and look for the good in the joke, even if it's difficult.'

'But it was filthy!'

Vissarion then entered into a lengthy, universalising discourse about jokes, something to guide both those inclined to be funny and those who would laugh. I lost the middle of it but heard the conclusion clearly:

'We must be careful what we joke about. But you are not to confront the joker.'

III

So far the questions had been fairly straightforward, and it was strange that they needed to be resolved here, by the Teacher, and not collectively at one of the meetings, or through consulting the book, or even through the application of common sense. The reasons for the stupendous length of the *Last Testament* were becoming clearer than ever, however. But then, just as I was wondering if all the questions were going to be so mundane, a woman in the second row took the microphone.

'Teacher,' she said. 'My four-year-old son asked if he could play with my breasts. I let him, for about fifteen minutes. Then he asked if he could play with them for another twenty minutes. Should I let him?'

Yes! I thought, *That's more like it!* This was the kind of thing I'd been hoping for when I first arrived in Petropavlovka, my ear pressed to the walls of the wooden cultural centre where clandestine whispers and hissed admonitions travelled so easily. But I'd stopped myself then, knowing that if I sought out the bizarre and dubious I would find it. Now perhaps, it had come to me . . .

'How old did you say the boy was?'

'Four.'

'Let him play. There's a difference between four and thirty-four, after all.'

Vissarion chuckled; his kneeling followers chuckled too. There was nothing strange in this advice for them. As for me, it was the first time he had stepped over the boundaries of common sense into dubious territory.

I wanted more.

IV

Suddenly Semyon stepped up to me. 'I think we should stop this.'

'What do you mean?'

'It's blasphemy.'

Semyon had been my friend for five years; in all that time I had never heard him express a single religious thought. I thought he was joking. But then he continued, and I could see in his eyes that he was serious. 'I'm worried. Like, maybe we're gonna go to hell if we don't do something.'

'There's nothing you can do,' I said.

'I could run in there, make a lot of noise,' he said. 'Fuck their shit up.'

'They'd just jump on you and beat you,' I said.

'Maybe,' he said. 'But at least I'd have done something.'

'What? It wouldn't work. They're used to being rejected by the world. They'd just see you as another heathen, someone misguided, who has failed to grasp the importance of the new belief. If anything, you'd entrench them in their belief. They'd know they were right because they had provoked such a strong reaction in you. You would confirm for them their status as righteous outsiders.'

'Hm.'

He wasn't convinced. But the moment of violence had passed. He stepped back again. I had missed a question, however. Now I listened to the next one, to find out what burning issue was awaiting resolution in the soul of another of Vissarion's most righteous men. It was the most bizarre one thus far.

V

'Teacher, if I ask my hostess for extra helpings at dinner, but she says, "No, won't you explode?" And then I say, "In that case, stand back!" – will I get the food?'

This was a reference to a popular Russian TV ad in which a little girl gulped down buckets of fruit juice: a boy walks up to her and asks,

'Won't you explode?' To which the little girl replies, 'In that case, stand back!'

Vissarion thought, perhaps communed with the Godhead, and then answered.

'Yes.'

And that was that.

VI

The believers were not exactly testing their Teacher. Next the bearded engineer who had looked so out of place at the *sliyaniye* took the microphone: Lyuba, Vissarion's wife, had been at a meeting in town the night before, and according to her a certain brand of washing powder, hitherto banned, was now acceptable to God. 'Is this true?'

'I never said that,' said Vissarion. 'It is not OK to use that washing powder. You are *lying* to me.'

The engineer shrank back, nodding vigorously, eager to receive his chastisement, so that it would end all the sooner. Vissarion, however, still sounded half-hypnotised: a non-Russian speaker would have had no idea at the anger implied by his words.

VII

But the issue of which detergent was pleasing to God remained unresolved, and now a woman risked provoking Vissarion's wrath further by picking up the theme. She asked if it was permitted to use cleaning products that contained chlorine.

'Yes,' said Vissarion.

'But I seem to recall that in 1995 or 1996 you said it wasn't . . .'

And that was a mistake, because how could she challenge the originator of the *Last Testament* over what was in its pages? What a sinful display of the ego! And Vissarion was indeed agitated, and answered in a voice different from before, with more animation and less languor.

'I did not say that. Categorically, I state that I never said that. You may use products with chlorine, but you should always study the chemical constituents of the powder, and be mindful that whatever you pour out you will eventually drink again!'

VIII

If doubts still remained over which washing powders were acceptable, no one now dared to raise them. Instead a woman, sitting not far from the one who had asked the consanguineous breast-fondling question earlier, took the microphone.

'Teacher, my fourteen-year-old daughter is dating an older man. They say they love each other and are ready to be married. They are becoming more intimate. They have already kissed with tongues. Is this acceptable?'

Now that was interesting: following his advice on the son/mother + breast issue earlier, was he going to stray into yet more unorthodox territory? He had two wives, after all, and I had wondered if he was preparing to cross more new boundaries: but the answer was no.

'This is not good,' said Vissarion. 'She's too young to make these decisions. They may meet, and talk, but they must not touch or kiss. How old is this man?'

'Twenty-seven.'

'He should be spanked in public.'

The crowd laughed. And of course, they all knew who she was talking about. There were only two hundred people in the village, and they all shared their problems at meetings throughout the week, and lived in transparent houses, bathed in light. Perhaps this 27-year-old was even present; or perhaps he was hiding in the village below, working in the forests, hoping his actions would remain unseen, though of course, the Teacher knew and saw all . . .

IX

A man in the middle of the kneeling audience took the microphone.

'Teacher, if I eat only once a day, will this act of self-denial help me to forget the taste of something I used to enjoy in my old life, but am no longer permitted by our community's rules to eat?'

'You eat only once a day?'

'Yes, but I eat a lot.'

'Won't you explode?' said Vissarion. The villagers laughed. Vissarion laughed too; then he continued. 'No, this is not right. You shouldn't try to forget the taste of something you once liked. It was a positive experience and it's imprinted on your soul, so be grateful for it. Also, unless there's something wrong with you and you have to force yourself to eat and once a day is the most you can manage, then you shouldn't live like this. You should eat more often. It's bad for your health otherwise.'

X

And then after this specimen of perfectly reasonable, humane advice, a woman, kneeling right in front of me took the microphone.

'Teacher, if I let my neighbour keep her horses and goats in my barn, and then when she takes them out again, there's shit on the ground from her animals, can I use it to fertilise my field? Or should I give the shit to her? Is it my shit or is it her shit? Can I use the shit?'

Vissarion shrugged.

'Use it.'

22

The meeting had lasted about an hour, and now it was over. Vissarion was blessing his children, rising from the boulder, and waving as he walked away, towards the pines, where some men were waiting for him. He reached them, and then the whole group followed the Messiah into the trees. And just like that, the whole procession vanished. The Divine Light was gone, not to shine again for another week.

The kneeling Vissarionites got to their feet, brushed the snow off their clothes and started the descent back towards the settlement, chatting about the *sliyaniye*, repeating Vissarion's jokes and his comments on washing powder, as though they were walking home after watching a good play at the theatre.

'What did you think?' asked Semyon.

'If I'd been on the boulder I'd have said the same things . . . except for the one about the four-year-old boy fondling his mother's tits. That was very questionable. What about you?'

'What do I think about fondling my mother's tits?'

'No, about his advice.'

Semyon shrugged. 'Nothing special.'

And it was precisely that 'nothing special' quality about Vissarion's moral advice that had me fascinated.* Never mind Tatiana's 'uncommon wisdom'; never mind lifting freely from Gnostics and Buddhists and Christians and communists – this was nothing, nothing at all. And that was good, I supposed, because he couldn't do much harm if all he pronounced were obvious truisms.

---

* And in fact, a year later I consulted the *Last Testament* directly to check for accuracy and discovered that I had misheard this question. The son was not gripping his mother's tits but rather his aunt's; and so even this answer was more banal than it seemed.

But now I was more confused than ever. I was on the edge of something; there was something misshapen and ugly lying under the surface of this apparent nothingness, and it was something disturbing I couldn't quite grasp or articulate fully, except as a question that kept coming back to me: if these people were all intelligent and earnest and had dedicated themselves to leading a good life, if they read the *Last Testament* every day and worked hard to perfect themselves morally, why then did they even need to ask Vissarion such simple questions?

VIII

Exit Dreamland

1

But there was no time to reflect; I had an appointment for tea with Vadim. Sanya led us back down the hill quickly, and envious eyes followed us as we crossed the narrow ledge that led to the house of disciple #1, the gospel writer.

Once I was there, though, I knew that I was already finished, and that it was too late for this meeting. The door was closing on me and I would soon be outside this reality, whether I liked it or not. So although his wife had prepared the most delicious meal I had eaten in the community, with berry tea, home-made blackberry jam and mushroom soup, and although Vadim was very hospitable and his two daughters were very charming, I had no enthusiasm left in me: I was saturated. We discussed bears, wolves, Germans, the amazing achievements of this community of former urban sophisticates in Siberia again, but it was rote, mechanical, for both of us. His questions and my answers quickly dried up and tasted like powder in our mouths. It was disappointing, because I liked him, and I think he liked me. But there was nothing to be done. As soon as was polite I made my excuses and Sanya led us back down the mountain, racing towards the Abode of Dawn, and each step was a step into a world with a greater supply of oxygen, and it became easier to breathe.

Back in the village, the chronicler stepped into his house and, after a minute, emerged holding a clay crest that displayed the shrine on the top of the mountain.

'A gift for you,' he said. 'And when you get back . . .'

'Yes?'

'Say hello to the world for me.'

Hello, world.

2

Adrian the Cuban took over from Sanya, leading me through the taiga further and further away from the Teacher. He was travelling to Abakan to apply for Russian citizenship. The old world and his old identities were completely closed to him now. He was not going to take his family anywhere, so why go through the problems involved with maintaining and renewing a residence permit when, thanks to his marriage and the years he had spent in Siberia, he was entitled to a Russian passport?

I could think of several reasons, most of them connected to the future of his two young sons. In his old life he had lived as a scientist in Sweden long enough to qualify for citizenship, which he had taken; but Mother Russia demands unconditional love from her adopted children, and if they are to come to her breast, they must renounce all other ties. Adrian therefore was about to toss away not only a Swedish passport but also his children's right to a free passage to a prosperous, free country, sentencing them to a hard and brutal life in Siberia instead. At one time that was the exclusive fate of condemned criminals and political dissidents and the guards who watched over them; now it came about as the act of a loving father.

It was a Very Bad Idea. Or that was how it seemed to me, at least; Adrian had another perspective. You know what it is.

3

The pathway was busy with girls and boys, all trekking up towards the peak, towards the centre of the dream, to continue the work of building the new civilisation. They greeted Adrian with warmth and love, and he explained again and again why he was leaving and re-assured them not to worry, that he would be back.

They made me think of the 'shock brigades' of the 1930s that had rushed to overfulfil Stalin's Five Year Plans, and of the students that Khrushchev had later summoned to settle the 'Virgin Lands' of Siberia and Central Asia in the 1950s. Sergei thought the Vissarionites were continuing in the tradition of the Old Believers, the Decembrists and the intelligentsia repressed by Stalin, that they were dissidents and exiles. But in fact they had just as much in common with the atheistic, fanatical true believers of the Soviet regime, for, like them, they had come here of their own volition, and were enthusiastically continuing the work that their atheistic forebears had begun, constructing something new out of a 'blank slate', transforming the hostile landscape into a paradise on earth. Cheeks freshly scrubbed, enthused by an ideal, these apostles of the new Christ were also the inheritors of the work started by one of the great devils of the twentieth century, whether they realised it or not.

About two-thirds of the way down we found an older woman with curly hair and red cheeks who had stumbled and was lying in the snow, unmoving, staring into the gathering darkness and breathing heavily. Adrian stopped: he was concerned.

'Are you OK?' he asked.

'Yes,' she gasped, '. . . I just . . . just need to rest.'

But she had barely started climbing, and there was a look in her eyes, something dazed and delirious, like the gaze of an alcoholic collapsed in the street in Moscow. The God-intoxication had infused her with a ghost strength that had vanished as soon as she put it to the test. The reality of her old body was keeping her from the dream the young people were rushing so eagerly towards. Twilight was setting in: soon it would be dark. That was not a good time to be alone in the taiga. There were bears and wolves out there. Adrian didn't want to leave her.

'Are you really OK?' asked Adrian.

'Yes, yes,' she said, waving, exhausted, staring into space. 'They won't . . . I'm OK . . . I'll be fine . . .'

There was nothing he could do: the bus was waiting, he had to make his appointment with the Russian state to sever his links to the outside world. We continued our descent, leaving the crippled woman behind as she slipped into the darkness, into invisibility.

4

The twilight forest was full of murder and torture: silhouettes of men forced to their knees, of death by rape and strangulation, knifings and disembowelment. So many people out there lost, dying violently and in excruciating agony. Except they weren't: I was staring through the window of the bus at the shapes made by branches weighed down by wet snow in the darkness, seeking suggestions of ever greater atrocity, like a half-drowned man emerging from the ocean to gasp for air. The images came easily.

Adrian, unaware of the shadow plays unfolding in the closed chamber of my skull, started talking. 'The Teacher says that in the West people live together in peace not because of any moral superiority or a state of enlightenment but simply because material conditions are good. There is nothing inherent to the condition. It will only last for as long as material prosperity continues. Take that away and people will be at each other's throats, or there will be severe repression to stop it.'

'That's reasonable,' I said.

'That's why we're on the mountain. We are learning to live together as family even in the most extreme conditions, so that when the apocalypse comes, we'll be able to thrive. We will have already passed through the fire. We are forging the spirit of a family which *must* spread across world. The world *must* unite, it *must* become one nation, it *must* become one family, with one religion . . .'

And then suddenly I grasped something that had been staring at me in the face all along but that all the rhetoric about living in harmony with nature and the video footage of green pastures and the talk of bananas in the taiga had obscured. Vissarion was teaching his children how to live in hell, and like it; because that was what lay round the corner.

'But families fight.'

'I know that,' he said, irritated. 'It's just an image. I mean, we must live together like a happy family. But this feeling of family must come from the heart,' he said. 'Not from the head.'

'But you have so many rules to learn. You have not escaped the head at all.'

He became impassioned. I didn't understand; when they read the book they took the *Last Testament* into their hearts. Gradually, their natures would change, and then they wouldn't even need to think; good would flow naturally from them. He wasn't just explaining, however: he was making a last ditch attempt at converting me before I left the dream altogether. But all I could think about were the questions on the mountain, so many trivial issues that the Vissarionites were still seeking personal guidance from the Messiah over. Judging by what I had seen, they had hardly learned anything. In fact they were less confident in their moral decision-making than the vast majority of unbelievers.

Suddenly the bus crashed to a halt. We climbed out and saw that a wheel had flown off the UAZ. The driver, the same man who had stolen from me earlier, wandered about in the darkness looking for missing bolts in the snow. He couldn't find them, but that wasn't a problem: he removed some bolts from the other three wheels and re-attached the one that had gone flying. It was a classical display of the Russian ability to make do with limited means, to improvise a way out of an unpromising situation. After that, however, he drove more slowly. There weren't enough bolts to reattach the wheel a second time, and so if it came off we would be obliged to walk twenty kilometres through the taiga at night, up to our waists in snow.

Back in the van Adrian had given up on my soul. The rest of the journey passed in silence. At the end of it the driver ripped me off again.

5

Natasha was happy to see me, full of questions as she ladled *kasha* into a bowl, but then she asked one that was so startling in its simplicity that it caught me completely by surprise:

'Did you feel the Christ?'

I paused, momentarily deliberating whether I ought to say something polite to protect her feelings.

'No,' I said.

The light in her eyes dimmed a fraction.

6

Natasha didn't want to live on the mountain. In fact, she had moved to Petropavlovka after initially being settled in another village, 120 kilometres away. It was too boring, too far from the centre of things, so she had given her house to someone else and moved in with Tatiana. 'I don't think I could live without a shop. It's not the cold, or the hunger, but . . .'

A man entered the kitchen, planting himself at the table. He had a bony face and a ponytail and moved rapidly and decisively, grabbing his bowl and spoon as if it were a declaration. Natasha was excited by this guest. He was somebody I had to know about.

'Daniel! Do you remember the sculpture on the mountain?'

'The one of the angels?'

'Yes.'

'This man is the artist responsible!'

He was staring at me, waiting for praise. But I was leaving soon. 'Oh,' I said, and left it at that.

He bristled with hostility. And suddenly he had lots of questions, as if, since I clearly thought his art was shit, he was trying to catch me out in mine, trying to prove me false: 'Where are you from? What's your book about?'

I gave the usual answers.

'Do you know any other communities in Scotland, then?'

'I think there's a bunch of hippies on St Kilda or some island or other . . . I don't know.'

'Have you been there?' He stared at me wildly.

'Me? Oh, no.'

7

But it wasn't interesting to attack me if I wasn't going to play. He quickly grew bored and started talking about himself.

'I just got back from China. I was there for two months. I was sent to learn new artistic techniques. I tell you, all the time I was there I didn't stop drawing or taking pictures. But I didn't like Chinese girls . . . they have a very . . . particular figure.' He drew a straight line in the air with his finger. 'I tell you, it was nice to get back to Russia and see Russian girls. My eyes popped out, my tongue hung out my head –'

Natasha interrupted him. 'Are you going back to the mountain?'

'Do you think they'd take me back?'

'Will you start getting violent again?'

'Probably.' He laughed. Then: 'I tell you, when I first came here I was quiet and shy. But you can't spend ten years here and stay calm. It's impossible to stay calm. All this non-aggression, all this stuff about loving each other. It's just . . . something must be done about it . . . something has to change.'

He didn't seem to care that I was there, listening in. They started talking about a Kazakh woman who had joined the community. She had travelled the world, studying different religions and esoteric traditions. Her husband was some kind of guru. However, when she had arrived at Petropavlovka she had declared it her spiritual home and had decided to stay.

'But she was crazy!' said Natasha, turning to address me. 'She had multiple personalities.'

'What do you mean?'

'When she first lived here, she was a four-year-old boy. Then she was a young Russian woman. And so on; she just kept changing. But she's a middle-aged Kazakh! But the Teacher, *he* said she was an example to us all, that she was his best student, that she was an example of a person with almost no ego.' Natasha shook her head. The Teacher was always right; but then he had said this, and it was nonsense. She just didn't understand. It reminded me of Sanya, bristling when I raised the topic of Vissarion's second wife: the Teacher was always right, yes, but this – this didn't make any sense. It was better not to think about it.

'But then she left, and spent some time in India. Life was peaceful without her. She got back a few months ago. And now *she* says that *we* all live in a madhouse!'

8

We left Petropavlovka before dawn, arriving in Abakan while it was still dark. The sun rose only to reveal that a thick veil of mist had fallen, obscuring most of the world beyond the airport windows. We were entombed behind glass in a white void. After eight hours of announcing postponements to our flight the airline finally moved us to a hotel 200 metres away, from which we were warned not to move. If the weather changed, the plane would leave immediately, with or without its passengers.

The room was rudimentary, but after days of shitting in buckets and eating straw it felt almost luxurious. I spent the evening lying in bed watching Russian MTV, breaking my vigil only to eat some meatballs in a Soviet-style canteen. It was relaxing, like being in an airlock, or quarantine chamber, where I could acclimatise to new conditions before entering my own reality again . . .

That happened almost as soon as I set foot on the aeroplane. It was there that I found myself reacting with violence to so much of what I had seen and listened to, purging myself of Vissarion's dream reality by ridiculing the bad aesthetics, the second wife, the mediocrity of Vissarion's thought, the flagrant ego-stroking of his personality cult, the obsessive-compulsive mania of the *Last Testament*, the naïve notion that human nature can be conquered by an act of will, and especially the totalitarian system which had led to the infantilisation of his followers, who were so insecure in their moral judgements that even the most dedicated of them had to climb a mountain once a week to ask permission from their master to do the simplest things. That, clearly, was dangerous.

I ranted to Semyon like this for a good two hours. And yet once I was finished, I did not doubt that Vissarion believed he was who he said he was; nor could I deny that his followers, many of them good people, children of a totalitarian system they had rejected only to freely submit to another one, were nevertheless engaged in a colossal act of self-sacrifice and creation that enabled them to transcend themselves and achieve great things, and that Vissarion's derivative mishmash of ideas nabbed from communism, religion and science fiction nevertheless filled their lives with meaning. They seemed almost heroic to me.

And as for Sergei Torop, the unaccomplished traffic cop who, lost in his own dream of the end of days, had set out to build a new world in Siberia that would be an ark for a future human race of which he would be the God-anointed supreme leader, adored father, and infallible Teacher to an elite tribe of intellectuals and artists, well . . . he really had pulled it off.

'Doesn't matter,' said Semyon. 'He's still going to hell.'

THE TOWER AT THE TOP OF THE WORLD

I

Chance

1

Chance is a scary thing to rely upon when you're engaged on an epic metaphysical-existential-cosmic quest, but that's what I had been guided by up to this point, and so far surrendering to fate had proven a successful strategy. An article in the back of a magazine had sparked off a memory of a strange story I had heard years earlier. Pursuing that had led to a bizarre encounter in a dirty kitchen. The consequences of that meeting had ultimately caused me to remember a throwaway comment once made to me by an editor as he rejected an article I had written – and so on, and so on. Yet out of these chance encounters a theme had emerged, seemingly of its own accord, or perhaps, and more likely, I had been pursuing it for a long time without fully realising what I was doing myself. Certainly it was a theme that fascinated me: the struggles of radical dreamers to make their improbable visions solid in a landscape that seemed to invite reinvention, and yet which was at best indifferent if not outright hostile to their goals.

After Vissarion, however, I was at a loss. I couldn't see any way to bring my investigations forward. The journey from the Digger, via Edward to Vissarion was a smooth arc, from near-total solipsism, to reaching out, to bringing into physical being a new reality that was spreading and colonising the world, rather like Borges' story *Tlön, Uqbar, Orbis Tertius*, in which over the centuries a secret society elaborates on an imaginary planet (Tlön) until it eventually comes to supplant the real one. Where else was there to go now but sideways? The trajectory, surely, was complete.

And yet my journey didn't feel finished. Vissarion's triumph was not, could not be the end: I knew it. There was another story to tell, there was some element of this phenomenon I had not yet explored. Unfortunately, I had no idea what it was.

2 Phantom worlds

I

Ghost narratives run parallel to the ones I have written in this book: the unrecorded stories of the other possible worlds I investigated at the same time as I was crawling through sewers and chasing demons.

For example: I spent half a year attending communist rallies and sitting in kitchens with neo-Bolshevik radicals, conducting interviews and collating notes. I was intrigued by the transformation of socialism from a myth that looked forward to a future paradise to one that looked back towards a lost Eden. This imaginary kingdom was even larger and more complex than Vissarion's, and contrary to most reporting in the Western media, it did not appeal exclusively to old people nostalgic for a more ordered world either – there were several youth groups espousing fairly hardcore communist ideology. I was especially interested in the teenagers, unborn when the USSR dissolved, who insisted it was their homeland. They described a magical world where there was no want and no injustice, where all races had lived together in brotherhood and harmony. They were aliens, exiles from a perfect planet they had never actually known, and they seemed to believe that if they sang and chanted loud enough it would manifest itself and they would at last be able to return home.

Now that Vissarion had left me stranded, I looked back to these investigations, hoping I might find there the story I was looking for. But communism was a collective myth with multiple authors, and so it didn't fit alongside the much more personal worlds authored by Vadim, Edward and Vissarion. It was too diffuse. The closest I came to their kind of reality was on October Revolution Day 2005, when I marched alongside a lonely woman who had fused Orthodoxy with Bolshevism, and who told me that Lenin, killer of priests and transformer of monasteries into prison camps, was the greatest friend the Church had ever had. There was an elaborately contrived logic for these statements, of course, but she knew how preposterous it all sounded, and almost winced as she gingerly trotted out her gibberish. She didn't live boldly and unapologetically in her world the way Vadim, Edward and Vissarion did. Walking in a column with atheists who found her ideas comical was the best she could do, but it was a gesture towards action, a shadow play, and nothing more. She knew she had lost before she'd even started. The way forward did not lie here, either for her or for me.

II

But if politics was a dead end, then there was always my Soviet movie-star neighbour, Vasily Lanovoi to consider. I thought he might have a place in this book precisely because he so obviously didn't – his life story negated absolutely the theme of my travels. Everyone else I had encountered was a marginal figure in society and, having rejected or been rejected by the world, was struggling to create some alternative cosmos in which they, or their ideas, governed. Even Vissarion's success was predicated to a large degree on his distance from the centre of power in the country. If his community had been located on prime real estate outside Moscow, it would never have lasted so long.

But that negation was what attracted me to Lanovoi. While the others struggled, life seemed to slip onto him as comfortably as a pair of silk pyjamas. He had risen almost effortlessly to the top of his profession in the 1950s and 1960s, once even playing Felix Dzerzhinsky, the founder of the Soviet secret police and a gleeful practitioner of torture and summary execution. A grateful KGB awarded Lanovoi a medal for his portrayal. Once the Soviet Union collapsed, however, he became a Russian nationalist and patriot, who happily lent his sonorous voice to celebrations of dead tsars on Red Square during national holidays. I was intrigued by this ability to shift with the times and always be on the right side of events: happy the man who is always able to believe the right thing at the right time, and not be aware that that is what he is doing.

But after Vissarion, Lanovoi's achievements seemed underwhelming. What was he really? A representation of Soviet dreams, yes, but once again, he was a collective creation. As an actor, he stepped through illusions, but they were always other people's illusions, and he was always uttering other people's words. It shouldn't have been surprising then that he could shift so smoothly from communist to nationalist. Vadim, Edward and Vissarion were much more creative, much more driven, much greater men. Lanovoi was tiny in comparison to them.

III

I wasn't getting anywhere. Vissarion was still towering triumphant over me, chuckling away, amused that I was still somehow trapped in his accomplishment, unable to find a way to get beyond what he had done. I investigated some skinheads who had developed their own mythology, a Mongolian mystic who had worked for Leonid Brezhnev, and even, in a moment of desperation, considered a return to the family in Uglich who had filled their living room with *papier mâché* effigies of historical figures demonstrating the centrality of their little town in the Divine Order. None of them offered a path forward. They were all smaller, less complete, failures in comparison to the Son of God.

But then I stumbled upon some stories in the Russian press about a faith healer called Grigory Grabovoi. Grabovoi was a slick-looking character with a penchant for sharp suits and fraternising with post-Soviet government authorities: allegedly he had used his powers to aid the Russian and Uzbek ministries of defence, using his superhuman ESP abilities to scan aeroplanes for 'faults'. He could also cure diseases with his mind and planned to stand for president in 2008. If elected, his first act would be to abolish death – because, like Vissarion, Grabovoi was Christ reborn. Not bad for a boy born in a village near Shymkent, Kazakhstan.

Grabovoi wasn't president yet, however, and consequently he still had some time on his hands. So he was offering to use his remarkable powers to bring joy to the bereaved mothers of Beslan, by effecting the reincarnation of their children. For a fee, of course: the living Christ could not be expected to work for nothing.

Apparently he had offered the same service to the victims of *Nord Ost*, and nobody had complained. But this time he had gone too far. Grabovoi was denounced in the media as a charlatan and impostor, engaged in the cruellest exploitation. Demands were made for the authorities to conduct an investigation. The abolitionist of death had reaped the wind, and now he was sowing the whirlwind.

IV

And now I remembered how, a year earlier, Dmitri the photographer had corrected himself when he called the Digger 'crazy'. Yes, Vadim had strange ideas, but under no circumstances could he be considered crazy. On the contrary, he was very rational: he never went near the

Kremlin or did anything that would jeopardise his ability to keep doing the things that enabled him to breathe. He knew where his reality ended and the other one, with police and punishments, began. However inspired or visionary or deluded he seemed, *he knew his limits.*

Edward was the same. He had spoken about making two films: a conservative version for the Orthodox and another 'more speculative' one for general consumption. In the world of non-believers he was absolutely free, and would express the wildest ideas when he proselytised, but he would do or say nothing that would risk his access to the exorcists, who were the key to his remaining inside the world he loved.

But nowhere was awareness of this 'line between realities' more evident than it was in the actions of Vissarion. He gave no clear date for the end of the world and claimed no miracles; he could never be proven a fraud. He didn't like coming to Moscow, and I knew why. Nobody took him seriously in the capital. Here he was just another freak show among many, and he had to compete with transvestite pop stars and debutantes and all the rest of the city's overdriven cultural life for attention. It was only in the provinces, where nobody came, nobody went and life, in general, was terrible that he had power, and that his appearances struck people as impressive. There, he drew not derision, but crowds.

But even on his home turf, where his power was strongest, Vissarion cooperated at every level with the Krasnoyarsk regional authorities. He knew that he had a powerful enemy in the Orthodox Church and a capricious overlord in the Russian state. He needed to be exceedingly careful and well organised if everything he had built was to avoid destruction.

V

Each of the three unique creators I had encountered so far, no matter how committed to his personal vision of the world, nevertheless displayed by his actions *at all times* an acute awareness of the brutal and uncompromising reality outside of it. Consciously or unconsciously, they all knew *precisely* when to transgress and when to step in line. They could never surrender fully to their vision, because to do so would mean to bring about its demise.

Grabovoi, however, was different. Whether he truly believed what he said, half-believed it, or didn't believe it at all, canvassing for money from the bereaved of Beslan had been a colossal misjudgement, a monumental loss of perspective. He had crossed the line the others danced around with such verve, and he was about to pay the penalty.

I had been right all along: Vissarion's community was not the logical conclusion of my investigations. Sergei Torop was only half-lost, and it was Grigory Grabovoi who was pointing the way forward for me. I needed to talk to someone who, intoxicated by his reality, hubristic about its power, had passed to the 'other side', someone who couldn't tell where the world he wanted to exist ended and the other one began. What happened to the dreamer when he lost control, when he went too far?

Grabovoi wasn't going to be much help, however. He charged hundreds of dollars for group consultations and well over a thousand for a one-to-one meeting. I had no desire to line his pockets further, and besides, he was only just beginning his journey to the 'other side'. Certainly I fully anticipated that the Russian state would eventually crush this Christ like a gnat between forefinger and thumb, transforming him into a greasy smear of ex-Messiah. But at the moment he was free and brazen and still making his claims.*

But if not Grabovoi, then who?

3

I *The Tower*

A looming Gothic nightmare transported from dreams into reality, unfinished because impossible to finish, made entirely of pieces of tree and by far the tallest such building I had ever seen, clustered with hidden rooms, attics, trapdoors, dead ends, blind walls and staircases leading to nowhere; ramshackle construction reaching up, up into the sky, culminating in two crooked tin peaks, the highest of which contains THE ROOM with the glazed aperture through which the unseen inhabitant of this monstrous edifice may look down, down, down on the world he did not create . . .

Wait. Breathe in, breathe out: reorient yourself, change position.

---

* As I write this, in May 2007, he is sitting in a jail cell awaiting the results of a trial for fraud, after he took money from an undercover journalist to reincarnate someone who had never actually existed. Oops. Grabovoi has complained that the government is trying to demoralise him by keeping him in isolation. He claims Putin and co. are afraid he will convert all the other prisoners in the jail to a belief in him.

View it in profile. Is it still so astonishing? Yes. What is this alien structure imposed on an unwilling landscape, eruption of unrestrained fantasy into a dead world, product of vision and energy devoted to an idea no one else understands? Who is responsible for this monstrous aberration?

I stare and stare, and I know: this tower was built by a brother to Vadim, to Edward, to Vissarion, to all the others who, toiling in obscurity, are not included in this book but certainly exist. He too is a member of this undeclared society of pointless visionaries and futile rebels, these 'conquistadors of the useless'. I know nothing about him but I can say this: 'architect' does not do justice to whoever raised this monster out of the mud. That word suggests planning, rationalism, a consciousness of limitations. But this tower is an assault on reality, a triumph over it. It proudly makes no sense at all to those who behold it, and is all the more beautiful for it. It is organic and whole and wild as the unconscious. 'Builder' shall hardly suffice either, so in that case let us call him

II *The Constructor*

A certain Nikolai Sutyagin, native to Arkhangelsk, born and raised among descendants of prisoners exiled by tsars and general secretaries to this city located just south of the Arctic Circle, at an unspecified point in the early 1990s acquired the rights to some land in the industrial zone of Solombola, and then started building a house. He was unaware at the time of the epic nature of his undertaking. In the early stages, in fact, he planned simply to build one floor, and then another; nothing extraordinary, simply an *izba*, a structure to inhabit, with toilets for shitting in and furniture for sitting in, much like any other. But then *something shifted inside his head* and once the second floor was complete he knew that in fact he had not finished, and that there was more work to be done. And from that point he continued working, reaching up, up towards the cold, grey northern sky. By the time his work was interrupted the tower was thirteen storeys high, the tallest wooden building in the world. But do not look in the *Guinness Book of Records*, for the tower is not there. After all, how could it sit there, as a mere *photograph* and a *short descriptive entry* alongside big marrows, very fast tap dancers and Men Who Can Hold Their Breath for a Very Long Time? The tower wanted no part of that banal world. It represented an obsession of a very different order.

III *In the shadow of impossible towers*

And what was it for? The structure itself gave no clues: it was impossible to read. There were rumours, of course: that Sutyagin had built a wooden spacecraft, intended for interstellar travel, or that he planned it as an ark for all the Slav peoples – Czechs, Poles, Russians, Ukrainians, Serbs, Slovenes, Bulgarians and all the others scattered across Europe and Asia – and that he would gather them together and lead them safely into the future, protected inside his wooden tower. Now *that* was a reason to build a tower. I loved the wildness, the impossibility of it. It echoed Vissarion's plan to build an ark in Siberia where righteous men and women would survive the apocalypse in the wilderness, but also brought me back to Sergei's original claim (later denied) that the Diggers were a tribe of civilised intellectuals who had chosen to live underground permanently, rejecting the wicked ways of an evil world. And although Edward was not constructing an ark, he was fighting a deluge . . .

But that was not all. For Sutyagin's structure immediately brought other impossible towers to mind, all of them Soviet, as if he were continuing a tradition of grandiose dreaming into this new age. One of the most famous was Tatlin's 'Monument to the Third International', a leaning iron spiral 400 metres tall, containing a rotating glass cylinder, a rotating glass cone, a rotating glass cube and a device for projecting messages onto clouds, and this was to have been built in the aftermath of a Civil War by a ravaged and impoverished society; and then, of course, there was the legendary Palace of Soviets with which Stalin had intended to out-skyscraper New York, and which would also have served as a podium for a monstrously engorged statue of Lenin, a handy platform in the clouds from which the Father of the World Proletariat would eternally wag a scolding finger at a God who was supposed to be dead.

Even in their unrealised state, existing nowhere except in the imagination, these towers cast a shadow over history. They were more written about, more beloved and more hated than the vast majority of structures that had actually been built in Russia. People still admired them, still lamented them, still dreamt of them – and that was why Sutyagin's 'impossible tower', for all that it reminded me of these two precursors, was as much their inversion as a continuation. Because although his structure existed it cast a shadow over nothing; hardly anyone knew it was there, and those who did had no idea what it was intended to glorify or represent. But that didn't make it any the less attractive to me; on the contrary, it only increased its mystery, its allure.

Two impossible towers: 1) Vladimir Tatlin's 'Monument to the Third International', and 2) Boris Iofan's sketch of the Palace of Soviets, complete with outsize Lenin

But that was not the real reason I had to go, no. That was much simpler.

IV *The line*

The line, the line – I wanted someone who had crossed 'the line'. I mentioned that Sutyagin's work on the tower was 'interrupted'. For there was a legend that read like something from the *Count of Monte Cristo*, Alexandre Dumas' monumental novel of fortresses, subterranean chambers, drug abuse, torture and labyrinthine revenge – except for one significant detail. In the novel, it is Edmond Dantès, the future 'count' himself, who is imprisoned in a desolate fortress and later seeks revenge. In the Legend of the Tower, Sutyagin is both avenging Count and villain, punishing someone who transgressed against him by locking him in the basement of his citadel.

I couldn't find any details as to what the crime was, or whether Sutyagin's prisoner had survived the ordeal, but it was clear that the constructor had crossed the line that Vadim, Edward and Vissarion knew instinctively to avoid. He had believed himself above the law, that in his fortress other rules applied and he was invincible. But the police found out, Sutyagin went to prison, and thus ended the dream of an ark for the Slavs.

Sutyagin was out of jail now, but no one had seen him in years. The rumour was that he lived with his mother in a flat in Arkhangelsk. Whatever money he had had was now lost; no work had been done on the tower since he was imprisoned. And so for years it had stood, simultaneously a memorial to the dream he had lost control of and also as a rotting wooden carcass awaiting the day of its collapse, when it would release the souls of the neighbouring villagers from their meat-prisons and itself cross over into the realm of ghost-buildings. But that day had not yet come, and until then Sutyagin, invisible or not, was going to protect his creation: massive Caucasian shepherd dogs prowled the territory at night, scaring away those who would burn it down or otherwise inflict damage, howling at the indifferent moon a lament for the impossible tower.

4

And where did I learn about all this? In the back of a free magazine, of course, on the page opposite an incisive pictorial feature on our planet's 'Top Ten Greatest Pairs of Knockers', under the stunningly inventive headline *Russian Tower of Babel*. I'd seen this particular magazine in the rack of the internet café a thousand times but had never picked it up. The cover, starting with the gruesome typeface, was always ugly, and the cover stories never seemed to be about anything at all. So why I picked it up now I can't say. It was just an impulse, a few neurons firing randomly in some dark place in my skull. And adding to the arbitrariness, I was only there in the first place because my printer had broken down.

So it was Chance, fickle goddess of the ancient Greeks, who delivered the story unto me, rewarding my faith. This only strengthened my certainty that Sutyagin's Tower was the answer, that I would find the end to my quest there. I had three weeks left in Russia before my visa ran out, three weeks in which I now had to find this Sutyagin who had first disappeared into his dream, then disappeared into jail, before disappearing entirely.

I had no idea how to do it. But I had to at least try.

II

A Test of Faith

1

Pavel was waiting at the exit from the airport, though I wasn't sure if he wanted to see me or not. There was a look in the eyes squinting behind those round spectacles that suggested he was contemplating running away. The son of the friend of a mother of a friend, we had spoken only once and then very briefly, trading descriptions of ourselves on the phone the night before. 'I am a big man with a red beard,' he had said. His hushed and mellifluous tones had given no indication how big, however. From a distance he resembled a shy, lumbering, ginger bear. Walking alongside him, however, I felt as though I was in the shadow of a living mountain.

Pavel ushered me onto a blue minibus that was waiting in the airport car park. It was clean and modern and entirely at our disposal (he had commandeered it from work). Defying every known law of the physical universe, the living mountain squeezed into the front seat. The driver started the engine, Pavel gave him some instructions, and soon we were travelling on the road leading to Arkhangelsk. Pavel explained that we were going to a hotel in the centre of town where he had booked a room for me.

Everything was progressing smoothly.

2

Pavel talked about the history of Arkhangelsk, giving me the date of its founding (1584, as the fortified monastery of Archangel Michael) and then relaying the sort of Important Facts you might find in an encyclopaedia – that there were two Arkhangelsks, the city and the surrounding *oblast* (which was more than twice the size of the UK); that in 1693 Peter the Great ordered the construction of a shipyard; that it was the first Russian port to trade with England; that its population was 480,000; that it was situated fifty kilometres from the White Sea and that it was much longer than it was broad, running for twenty kilometres along the River Dvina. From time to time I nodded, but said no more than I needed to reassure him I was listening. It had been an early morning flight and the channels for issuing instructions from my brain to my tongue were still blocked. I was grateful to him for filling the space around us with noise.

But still, as the external world passed by and he continued listing events, names, dates and objects I started to wonder if he actually knew why I was in Arkhangelsk in the first place. Had my friend told his mother to tell her friend to tell her son that I was in search of Nikolai Sutyagin, constructor of the great wooden tower of the Arctic Circle (or close enough)? I was starting to doubt it. But then suddenly Pavel broke off his narrative:

' . . . and if you look out the window on your right you will see Sutyagin's Tower . . .'

And there it was, rising out of the harsh northern icescape, looming heavy and dark in the distance over a frozen world that extended from here to the tip of the earth.

' . . . but we shall talk about that later. It is too muddy to go today: the structure is located on a sort of island, and there are no roads there.'

The bus sped onward, leaving the tower behind, stuck in the swamp. A friend who had visited Arkhangelsk several times and yet never seen it nor even heard of it had suggested that perhaps it was located somewhere in the *oblast*, amid woods or tundra. I was relieved he was wrong.

3

Pavel installed me in the Hotel Dvina in the centre of town. It was pleasant and comfortable and priced reasonably. 'Is it satisfactory?' he asked. 'There is another, more luxurious hotel on the banks of the river . . .'

'It's fine,' I said. We stared at each other in silence for a moment, not sure what to do next. Pavel was the first to come up with an idea: 'Shall we have lunch?'

But it wasn't yet noon, and so it was too early to eat – or it was for me, at least. However, as I stood there in the hotel room I now realised that I had no plans for Arkhangelsk other than to find Sutyagin and talk to him about his tower, to find out exactly why he had built it, and what had happened to him after he had been imprisoned; but Pavel had ruled that out back on the bus – as far as today was concerned, at least.

'Maybe we can walk around the centre,' I said. 'So I can orient myself.'

Outside the mist was thickening rapidly. Like explorers probing a frozen lake, we trod warily forward, cars, buildings, trees and people appearing and then disappearing in the shimmering polar haze. Even the normal noises of the city seemed dampened by the annihilating mist, and the extreme cold caused it to freeze on contact with the trees, coating each individual branch and twig with a crystalline shadow of itself. Immediately I was struck by a powerful sense of déjà vu: there had been identical weather conditions in Abakan the day we left. I remembered breaking off my MTV vigil in the hotel to go outside and pay tribute to the eerie beauty of the frostbitten trees, positioned like alien sentries around the concrete world of the airport.

And suddenly that silent, frozen planet was bleeding into this one, and the intervening time I had spent in Moscow seemed to vanish, as if I was waking from a dream to find that I had never left Abakan, and that Vissarion's landscape and Sutyagin's landscape were somehow one and the same and always had been. The three time zones and the thousands of miles that lay in between were irrelevant. This was the same place; I was on the same quest. Vissarion felt very close to me, as if his mountain were just on the outskirts of town, and he was still keeping vigil from his eyrie, and could still see everything – including me.

4 The higher criticism, part 1

Pavel was showing me the half-collapsed wooden house of a pre-revolutionary merchant. He didn't have much to say about it: just that 'some rich guy' had lived there a hundred or so years earlier. Apparently in the early 1900s Arkhangelsk had consisted entirely of wooden buildings, and was the largest city of its kind in the world.

Wars and Sovietisation had seen most of the old town destroyed and replaced with concrete high rises.

There was, however, a recently built street of replicas in the centre, restrained and tasteful little houses in the old style that I knew I was supposed to approve of. But there were no signs of business or habitation, and they seemed as dead and awkward as a glass eye in a human face. Pavel didn't want to linger: for him too, there was something not quite right about this theme-park reconstruction. The exuberantly grotesque tower of Sutyagin, that half-completed, half-rotted enigma, was far more vibrant, far more alluring.

And yet, as we walked away towards the central shopping street, I realised that this street of rubbishy pink and yellow Wendy houses shared something with Sutyagin's structure – both were a response to Arkhangelsk's lost history as a wooden metropolis, both had emerged from the same context. And now Sutyagin's Tower no longer stood completely apart in my imagination as a bizarre, Arctic echo of earlier impossible buildings designed by utopian architects in the metropolis, but rather I saw that it had its roots in the life and soil of *this* region, that it was an extension and mutation of the traditional buildings of this part of northern Russia, something common filtered through an uncommon mind. It was becoming more real, more solid: not understood yet, but easier to understand.

I wasn't sure if I liked that. Fortunately Pavel was feeding me with other data, and so I was able to think about other things. He had become an encyclopaedia again, reciting facts and details learned in school. He was trying hard, straining to think of things that might be interesting for an alien, but it was difficult for him, a local, to 'see' the city that he passed through every day. He showed me:

- The KGB HQ (conveniently located next door to a children's play park).
- Residential Stalin-era buildings (in one of which he lived).
- The house (wooden, of course) where Arkady Gaidar, author of the Soviet children's classic *Timur and His Team* had lived and worked.
- A tank sitting on the pavement outside a supermarket (which had some rare specifications I didn't quite catch).
- The Lutheran church, which housed the second largest pipe organ in Russia (the largest was in Krasnoyarsk).

- The surviving eighth of Arkhangelsk's Gostiny Dvor, the seventeenth-century covered market area where for hundreds of years foreign merchants had stayed on their visits to the city. Even that eighth was in bad shape, however, a semi-ruin of crumbling brick, decayed plaster and old wood that sat rotting on the chilly banks of the Dvina: 'It used to be a museum, but it went through some hard times in the nineties,' said Pavel.
- The river Dvina itself. I stared at the surface of the frozen river, rock hard and yet somehow dissolving into the white, white sky with the mist, obscuring the boundary between the elements. I wondered about the fate of the fish trapped under the ice. Was it too cold for them?

Pavel checked his watch. An hour had passed since we left the hotel. 'Daniel,' he said.
'Yes?'
'Shall we have lunch?'

5 The higher criticism, part 2

The Gross Vagon was a German beer cellar, according to Pavel the best of its kind in Arkhangelsk. He reassured me that the quality of the food was 'not worse than' in similar establishments in St Petersburg or Moscow. The cold had sapped the warmth right out of my blood, however, and so I sat, gazing dully at a programme on Peter Jackson's tedious remake of *King Kong*, trying to heat myself up. The images of the big cartoon monkey on the screen irritated me: *Why?* I wondered. *Why is he doing this to such a great film?* The new *Kong* wasn't out yet but I knew it was going to be bloated, pompous and pointless, an absolutely monumental waste of time, money and celluloid. At the same time I also knew that I was still going to watch it, the same way I had watched those fucking awful *Lord of the Rings* movies and the *Star Wars* prequels . . .

But then my food arrived and I stopped caring. Once I had swallowed a few mouthfuls of charred animal flesh I even started to remember who I was and what I was doing in Arkhangelsk. It was time to raise the topic Pavel was so assiduously avoiding.

'About Sutyagin . . .?' I said.
'Ah yes. My mother and I have spoken to some journalists . . .'
'And?'

'They have nothing to tell you.'

'*Nothing?* What do you mean?'

'They don't know where he is. Nobody does. It would be a waste of time to visit their offices.'

That wasn't good: I had expected that somehow the local newspapermen would have 'ways and means' of finding him. Whenever there's a particularly good murder, or if a child is abducted, journalists are always able to find everyone involved in the story within twenty-four hours – except for the missing children and the actual killers, of course. So Pavel's assertion that the journalists didn't know anything didn't sound right. Something was amiss.

'But . . . maybe they can tell me something about the origins of the tower, or some of the stories surrounding it. I mean, is it true that he went to jail?'

'Yes, but after that he disappeared. They don't know what happened to him. Nobody knows.'

From Pavel's tone I got the impression that it wasn't that nobody *knew* where he was; it was that nobody *cared*. It wasn't the first time I had encountered such indifference. A few days before I had left Moscow, the friend through whom I had ultimately made contact with Pavel had sent me a letter from his mother, who felt compelled to inform me that my quest was a waste of time: 'Tell Dan this tower will probably be crap. This is the sort of story that's interesting to foreigners, but not Russians, who are too busy trying to stay alive. Sutyagin is probably just a vulgar *nouveau riche*, building himself a very big *dacha*, the sort of thing you see in the surrounding suburbs.'

The letter irritated me. It had been written by a successful Russian émigré who had lived in the US for over twenty years and had never seen or even heard of Sutyagin's Tower, even though she had passed through Arkhangelsk several times in the 1990s. In spite of her obvious detachment from her roots and her failure to notice something colossal on the skyline of the city, however, she had automatically made assumptions about both the tower and me that were extremely condescending. I had dismissed the contents of the letter out of hand as a tedious example of the snobbery you sometimes encountered among those more self-satisfied members of the Russian intelligentsia, who make such a fetish out of their education and reading, and look upon the thoughts and ideas of anyone who is not a member of their own subculture as so much shit on their shoe. But now, here I was in the place where it stood, and I started to get the impression that the locals might not see it all that differently . . .

'But did they have any information, about the story of why he went to jail? I heard he locked someone in the basement of the tower . . .'

'I can tell you about that,' Pavel chuckled. 'It was a business dispute.'

'Business?'

'Yes. He made a lot of money in timber in the early nineties. Somebody crossed him, maybe one of his workers or business associates. I remember reading about it in the papers . . .'

'Wait,' I said. 'Sutyagin was a businessman?'

'Of course,' said Pavel. 'He was one of our New Russians. Lots of people worked for him. Timber is big money in Arkhangelsk. The hotel you are staying in, for example is owned by Krupchak, our local timber magnate. He owns the supermarket next door and many other businesses. Arkhangelsk has a satellite town called Novodvinsk, and Krupchak is "person number one" over there. You know, it's not all that shocking that Sutyagin did what he did. It was the 1990s, the period of "wild capitalism" in Russia. Sutyagin was part of that wave . . .'

Suddenly I saw an image of Sutyagin as a flathead in a shell-suit, jangling the gold keys to his Mercedes 600. It made him into a tawdry figure, his alleged violence banal rather than mysterious. I felt cold, damp doubt seeping into my soul: *Am I just wasting my time here?*

6 A sign

But then I remembered why the tower had been built – as an ark for the Slavs. And that was obviously a visionary idea, an attempt to bring something truly impossible into the world on a par with Vissarion's colony of righteous men and women. It proved that Sutyagin could not be defined strictly by the cliché 'New Russian' term, that even if he was some kind of entrepreneur, it was only one aspect of his personality. He clearly saw the world in his own, unique way. Yes, there had to be more to Sutyagin than I was getting from Pavel . . .

But then I looked over at the living mountain, and as he polished off the last remnants of his *schnitzel* I knew there was no room for an ark for the Slavs in his world. It would be embarrassing to ask; inviting another ironic smile like the one my friend Sergei had given me when I repeated the legend of the Diggers he had told me in the first place, the smile that had said: *you think there's a tribe of intellectuals living under the city? How naïve of you.*

And now I doubted again, but it was much worse than before, as if the ground were opening up under me, and when I looked down I saw the jaws of drab reality, waiting for me to fall, to lock shut around my neck and trap me in a world where there was nothing more to life than paper mills, 'business disputes' and colourless reconstructions of wooden houses in heritage districts.

No: I knew that there was more to the tower than just this. I had seen it, and it was extraordinary, much more than a 'big house'. It was an eruption of the unconscious, the world of dream made real. All the same, I knew that it was important to visit it as quickly as possible. Pavel's *it's impossible today* was the same *it's futile any day* I had read in my friend's mother's note, and I knew that his scepticism, his outright disbelief, might become corrosive if I didn't act quickly. I needed to see it, to touch it to bolster my belief. I needed Sutyagin to give me a sign.

'Pavel,' I said. 'I really want to see the tower now . . . Is it *absolutely* impossible to go there?'

'Yes.'

'But –'

'In this weather, we couldn't reach it. It's not possible.'

And that was that. Pavel wasn't going to move. It was clear, in fact, that he didn't want to go to the tower now, or ever. It was nothing to him; absolutely nothing.

'Well, do you at least know if it's still occupied? Do I stand a chance of meeting him if I go out there?'

Pavel nodded. 'A friend of my mother's lives near the tower. We phoned her. A few nights ago, she heard the dogs barking. There are four, maybe five dogs, and they are proof of his existence. If there was no Sutyagin there would be no one to feed them.'

7 Prison

It was only three o'clock and already the darkness was setting in. Arkhangelsk in December only saw a couple of hours of sunlight a day. Pavel wanted to go home; I needed to be alone too, but there was one thing he wanted to show me before he left me.

'There are many prisons in Arkhangelsk,' he said, leading me away from the river. 'In fact, our whole region was initially settled as a prison. Ivan the Terrible exiled his enemies here, and the first gulag was opened in the monastery at Solovki on the White Sea. Actually, I am incorrect: this area was first settled by monks who established religious retreats here, around which a few villages later grew up. But the same conditions that made this region suited to monasteries made it suitable for penal colonies. As a result, our population is mixed: we have Tatars, Russians, Ukrainians, Jews . . . though most of our Jews have left now, and gone to Israel . . .'

We came to a set of high walls. Pavel stopped.

'This is our local prison,' he said. 'A friend of mine lives right above it, in that building there.' He indicated a block of flats. 'In the morning, as she drinks her first cup of tea, she looks down and watches the prisoners exercising in the yard.'

'Did Sutyagin serve his sentence here?' I asked.

'Oh no. Sutyagin was sent to one of the prisons far from the city.'

'Which is worse.'

'Of course.'

I tried to imagine him stuck in some remote penal colony in the Arctic Circle, but I still had no idea what he looked like, or even how old he was; and though I had read about life in Russian prisons, that experience was too far removed from my own. Never mind the ability – did I have the right to even *speculate* about that world of misery and isolation?

And so my imagination, reaching out to construct a Sutyagin, encountered only impenetrable darkness. I could see the tower but beyond it, nothing.

8 What would Edward do?

By the time I got back to the hotel in the late afternoon it was as dark as midnight. There was nothing to do, nothing to be discovered, and although I wanted to go to bed, it was far too early to sleep. The first day's searching, meanwhile, had uncovered two things only:

(1) Sutyagin had been a businessman as well as a visionary.
(2) Everyone seemed to hate him.

I was going to have an even harder time finding him than I had anticipated. The help from the locals I thought would make the search easier I now realised might actually sabotage my plans instead. Their negative attitudes and total incomprehension of why I actually gave a shit were things I would have to fight against. The city had rejected him, it denied him – I was going to have to *force* Arkhangelsk to bend to my will and acknowledge that Sutyagin had a face and that he was real. And once I had done that, I was going to have to force the city to give him up to me.

But how?

Fortunately for me, a few months earlier I had been travelling in Ukraine with a man who often found himself in an analogous position, and when he did, rather than give up, he forced the world to give him what he wanted. And now I knew I had to be aggressive like him, tenacious like him, obsessed like him. More than anything, I needed to *believe* like him. *Yes,* I thought. *What would Edward do?*

9

Almost immediately I had an idea. I could get Pavel to work his way methodically through all the Sutyagins in the phone book, calling them until we found the one we wanted. Then, when Sutyagin answered I would persuade him to let me into his tower and there he would reveal the secret of why he built it, exactly how and why he crossed the line and what happened after he disappeared. Then I would go home and live happily ever after. Yes, it was brilliant!

And if Sutyagin didn't want to talk, well, I'd find some way to persuade him. Edward always found some way to loosen tongues and Edward was now my master. I texted Pavel with my ingenious plan, and waited for him to reply.

And waited.

And waited.

And then, after an hour had passed, texted him again.

Well, maybe he's busy, I thought. But more time passed and sitting in the hotel room, enclosed by the darkness and cold outside, made me nervous. I thought about doing it myself, but I didn't think my language skills were adequate to the task. I would have to call up strangers and make a strange request sound very reasonable in a matter of seconds; but I knew that I expressed myself too directly in Russian, and had been told that I could make a request for a cabbage pie sound threatening. So it had to be Pavel. I thought about phoning him to propose the idea directly, but he was very shy, and I knew that if I put too much pressure on him he would probably back off completely. He barely knew me, and he had nothing invested in the success of my mission. There was absolutely no obligation for him to help, especially if it put him in a position he found uncomfortable. He was like one of Edward's reluctant exorcists – I had to tread warily, carefully, and yet at the same time, refuse to take no for an answer . . .

I went out for a walk, resolving not to check my phone for messages until I was back at the hotel, in a couple of hours. That would give Pavel plenty of time to overcome his fear and agree to do my bidding.

10

Arkhangelsk was cold, eerie and abandoned, an excellent place for evil, especially down by the frozen seam of ancient space-ice that was the river. I followed its course to the Gostiny Dvor, trying to escape my thoughts, resisting the urge to check my mobile for messages, until I came to a single window in the wall that bled light into the vast night. Going closer I heard the faint sound of a female Russian folk-singing ensemble rehearsing a traditional song.

It was the only indication of life in a cold, cold cosmos. For a minute or two I stood under the light listening, but then a couple emerged from the darkness and, as they slowed down to stare at me, I suddenly felt very self-conscious. If I'd been Edward I would have greeted them heartily and said a few words about the beauty of the Russian north, of course. Instead I started to suspect myself, as if I had only just now remembered that I had come out to knife a stranger to death. And in fact, what exactly was I doing out there on my own in Arkhangelsk late at night in the middle of December? It was freezing.

Oh, that's right: I was giving Pavel time to chew over my proposal before deciding that it was a brilliant idea and that he'd start working on it straight away, sir! Well, I wasn't back at the hotel yet, but he'd had long enough to think about it by now. I pulled out my phone: no message. And there was still no message by the time I was back, thawing in my room, eating processed-cheese sandwiches and watching a rancid French 'comedy' about sex toys for the handicapped. Or hours later, when I finally switched it off and went to bed after having been awake in this city of mist, ice and darkness for far longer than was reasonable.

Pavel could ignore me all he wanted. I still believed.

III

Big Pile of Boxes 1 – Ancient Masterpieces 0

1

The next morning, in the hotel lobby, the fear of the unanswered texts was still visible in Pavel's eyes, mixed with the naked terror that I would make the same proposal again directly to his face. He immediately introduced me to his mother, Natalia, and then before I could open my mouth, he was gone, heading out the door to the office where he worked.

Natalia was a serious-looking woman in her late forties who bore about as much resemblance to her son as he did to a victim of the Ukrainian famine in the 1930s. Whereas he was physically huge but hesitant and shy, she was petite – and the two fierce pupils burning under her knotted brow suggested she was accustomed to slapping down much bigger men than I. 'Well?' she said. 'Shall we go?'

I followed her out onto the street. She skipped over the ice, nimbly avoiding the oncoming traffic until she was across the road, waiting for me at a bus stop positioned directly beneath a billboard which displayed the enormous image of a curvaceous beauty wearing nothing except a red bra and panties and a Santa hat. Flakes of snow whirled around exposed cleavage and naked thighs. She looked terribly cold to me, and just happened to be sensuously reclining next to a sign for a medical clinic that treated problems most of which included the prefix *urino-* or *vagino-*.

Suddenly a vision unfolded in my head, of the diseased Arkhangelogorodetzi lying together on hard mattresses in dark, freezing rooms, fucking out of boredom and a hunger for warmth, moving from bed to bed, spreading infection and a sense of dull, frustrated satiety.

'You look as though you're deep in thought, Dan,' said Natalia.

'It's just early for me,' I said. 'I'm still trying to wake up.'

The bus arrived: we climbed on. Natalia, faithful to the traditions of Russian hospitality, insisted on paying for my ticket.

2

Malye Karely is an open-air museum of wooden architecture located twenty-five kilometres south of Arkhangelsk. According to Natalia, it was an obligatory stop for any visitor to the area, one of the biggest 'reservations' of its kind in the whole of Russia, housing all kinds of wooden structures both sacred and profane, including huge forest-cathedrals built entirely without nails, the oldest of which dated back to the sixteenth century. I had been to a similar complex outside Novgorod some years earlier and the religious buildings, unlike anything I'd seen before, had blown the roof off my skull. I told Natalia this, hoping to impress her with my familiarity with and admiration for traditional wooden Russian architecture. In fact, she was disappointed. She had wanted this to be a completely new experience for me. 'The Novogorod museum is smaller and less diverse,' she said, a little sniffily. 'Malye Karely is better.'

Natalia continued talking and I realised I had misjudged her. She wasn't intimidating at all, but rather a highly cultured, witty woman with a sharp intelligence and an interest in life that kept her vital. If she didn't think much of Sutyagin's Tower herself, she at least understood that it was interesting to me, and indulged me a little.

'You know,' she said, 'it's so strange. I have lots of connections in our local media and I spoke to numerous journalists who are friends of mine, but no one remembers anything: neither how old Sutyagin is nor what he looks like . . .'

'But it wasn't all that long ago,' I said. 'Surely there are photographs, records . . .'

'You'd expect that, yes. And Sutyagin was famous, very famous at one time. But now – it's as if he's just been erased from history. They couldn't find anything – no phone numbers, no addresses, not one picture.'

'Do you remember anything yourself?'

'Oh yes. I was a journalist myself when it all happened, working for one of our newspapers. It was *very* controversial, what he did.

Everybody talked about it. Because he didn't have any architectural training whatsoever or even any permission to build, but still he started erecting the tower, and it just got higher and higher . . . And it was all completely illegal.'

'How did he get away with it?' But before the question was even halfway out of my mouth, I was embarrassed to have asked. I already knew the answer.

'It was the early nineties,' said Natalia. 'The old laws were not working; the new ones were not yet fixed in place. We were in a new time, everything was in chaos. He took advantage of this situation, and that was that. And then there was all that business with the prisoner in the basement!'

'Why did he do that? Pavel said it was a business dispute.'

Natalia laughed. 'Maybe. I don't know . . . It's like something out of a Gothic novel, not real at all!'

I thought of the ark for the Slavs, but once again decided not to mention it. I was starting to think it was a piece of apocrypha, a later addition to the legend, an accretion tacked on by a journalist to give his story some colour. I would wait until I met Sutyagin to find out if it was true: until then I'd be agnostic on the question of its truth or falsehood. Anyway, the tower retained its allure without it. If anything, it became more inexplicable – less ridiculous and more mysterious.

'Anyway,' said Natalia, 'I have organised for you to speak to Professor Barashkov. He is the chief architect of Arkhangelsk, a very clever man. He is an expert on wooden architecture and has written books on the subject. But he's not just a narrow specialist. He is very creative and energetic. He was a deputy in the Supreme Soviet – not our local soviet, but the national one! He is a man of taste, he knows quality . . . Actually I remember once, I met him in the street while I was on my way to work. It was very early, the morning after a terrible storm that had torn up trees and destroyed houses. He looked very sad, very distracted. "What's the matter, Professor Barashkov?" I asked. "Did the storm damage your property?"

'"No," he said. "But last night, as the wind and the rain raged, I was really hoping that Sutyagin's Tower would be blown over and we would finally be free of that repulsive scar on the face of our town! I could hardly sleep for the excitement. So this morning, the first thing I did when I woke up was take the tram out there to see if it was still standing. Trees were lying in the road, homes had been smashed in and there was devastation everywhere. But Sutyagin's eyesore – it's still standing!"

'He buried his face in his hands. He couldn't believe it, that the half-completed tower, built by a man with no architectural training, had not been destroyed. I understood him. After all, it is terrible, terrible. Just a set of boxes, placed one on top of the other, *bonk bonk bonk*, like a child working with toy bricks, without any taste or skill . . .'

She couldn't resist the dig. It was disappointing. Anger at a New Russian crook I could understand, but this was something different, reminiscent of the tone of the letter I had received from the all-knowing Russian émigré. But at the same time I wondered if there wasn't something else at play in the dismissive, scornful attitude the locals had towards the tower. Being British, I am of course intimately familiar with the sour mash of resentment and anger that rots in the bellies of individuals without great fortunes or glittering destinies, which can erupt and flow towards those who seek to set themselves apart, to rise above their station, who presume to 'give themselves airs and graces'. I was not immune to this dyspepsia myself, and thought I recognised its acrid tang on the bus . . .

I turned to look out of the window. Arkhangelsk slipped past, refracted by the mud and condensation smeared across the old glass into a metropolis of sludge.

3 Malye Karely

I

The bell tower in the Kargopol-Onezhsky section, transplanted to the reservation from the village of Kuliga-Drakovanovo, dated from the end of the fifteenth century – and thus this apparently fragile wooden construction which stood rather modestly in a clearing pre-dated the founding of St Petersburg by over a century; the American Declaration of Independence by two centuries; the Russian Revolution by over three centuries, and the child's swing across from it, on which the bloated, drooling, ape-like Boris Yeltsin had once performed a drunken caper, by almost four. All that history and yet for most of that time the tower had stood resolutely unwitness to any of it, obscure, lost in the forests of the Russian north among people so accustomed to the sight of it that it can barely have registered on their retinas. Now, however, it was an important relic, the oldest structure of its type in the country, and Natalia was appalled by the discoloration at the base that had occurred after Soviet restorers had treated it with the wrong substance, turning the wood green, and by the iron nails that so crudely pierced the wood, forcing into continued existence a structure that its unknown, 'primitive' builders had seamlessly slotted together with pegs and cunningly carved beams and logs.

Instinctively I agreed with her. But then I wasn't so sure, and thought that this might just be knee-jerk Soviet bashing, and that she was probably unjustified in her criticisms. After all, the whole complex was an initiative of the Soviet era, and without the efforts of those early restorers, the tower would simply have rotted away and collapsed, and all the history it hadn't witnessed would have rolled on without anyone ever knowing it had been there, and the work of all the unknown artisans, the men who were not architects and yet knew how to build a bell tower that could stand for four centuries, would have been lost for ever. The restorers had damaged it, yes, but everyone has to learn, and they did not repeat the same mistake with later additions to the complex.

Besides, the nails and the discoloured patches actually had a value of their own: as markers and indicators of a truth that preservationists usually seek to conceal – that this was not the same bell tower as it had been, and that by moving it, it had changed, in the same way a holy icon placed in a museum becomes mere paint on wood, or that an animal stuffed and placed in a zoological display cabinet is hardly an animal at all. These scars were the glass eyes, the comical grimace, the half-split seams holding together the belly of a sawdust mastodon . . .

II

A bridge linked Kargopol-Onezhsky to the other sections, 150 steps that seemed to stand unsupported in the sky. And so I strode across treetops to the main body of the reservation, where sample structures of three regions with the fine names of Mezensky, Pinezhsky and Dvinsky were preserved. The forest and severe climate had isolated the residents of the villages in each area so much that they had developed their own styles, and thus their buildings differed from each other to a far greater extent than a block of flats in Moscow and another in Vladivostok, seven time zones away, would.

There were giant cathedrals with domes that resembled enormous pine cones, *izbas*, chicken coops and little barns standing on squat legs to protect the contents from raids by rodents. These and the seven fantastical windmills that stood like sentinels around the territory looked like the natural habitat of flesh-eating witches, wish-granting goldfish and lazy peasants sleeping on magical clay ovens. Natalia, however, cursed with knowledge, insisted on explaining the distinctions to me, indicating how this horse-carving differed from that one, how the ornate window frames here were not the same as the ones over there, why this house had a pagan carving of the sun on it, and that one did not.

I took notes for a while, but then stopped. I didn't want to know all this stuff, about an anonymous life spent eating porridge, sleeping next to pigs and growing turnips. Too much context stripped the structures of their mystery. It was like melting the ice around a frozen mammoth with a hair dryer, cutting it up with a chainsaw, and putting the clumps of old flesh in jars in a lab.

That work is necessary, of course, but I prefer to see the whole beast, intact in its block, and work my way around it with my hands and eyes, letting my imagination do the rest . . .

III

But Natalia's narrative was not always so dry, and there were moments when she was able to breathe real life into these old husks. A small church stood close to a cluster of trees. She made me turn my back to the buildings that faced it and now, isolated on the edge of the forest, it looked as though it had been sitting there for centuries. Natalia led me onto the covered porch that ran all the way round it, breaking only at the staircase that led upwards to the front door.

'Look at this,' she said. 'Do you know why they added this porch to the church?'

The question was rhetorical. She continued:

'It's very simple. Not every village had a church, and so some peasants had to walk for miles and miles through the forest to attend a service. It would take hours; and so they added this covered section so that those who arrived early could rest and shelter from the elements as they waited for the priest to arrive.'

The piety of these long-dead residents of the north held Natalia breathless. And it was easy for me to picture them, the men bearded, the women in headscarves, standing where I now stood, waiting patiently to cross over to another, higher reality where their lives were rich with transcendent meaning. For a second these phantoms Natalia had conjured up breathed again, and it was hard to believe that if I stepped inside I wouldn't smell incense burning and see ancient icons gleaming in the half-light.

I tried the door: it was locked. And just like that, the phantoms vanished and the cathedral, flattened out, died once more. By the time we reached the end of the museum I was exhausted, and glad the buildings were uninhabited. I admired the builders who had reshaped the raw material of the forest into these cubes and domes and spires that had stood for centuries, but unlike Natalia, I felt no nostalgia for the world that had vanished.

IV

The Gregorievskaya cathedral, the climactic centrepiece of the complex, dated from 1672; it had many domes and it was so tall I could barely frame it in the lens of my camera. 'This one always reminds me of Sutyagin's Tower,' said Natalia.

This was the first time she had mentioned my whole reason for being in Arkhangelsk since the bus and, I now realised, it was the first time I had thought about it too. The museum had been too official, too serious, too representative of the 'real Russia' and the state-sanctioned, 'approved' past and I had automatically switched over to accepting it the way Natalia presented it to me, as representative of this style and that trend et cetera, et cetera. Sutyagin had no place here. Suddenly, however, it seemed obvious that I was wrong, that Sutyagin's Tower was not just a refraction of Arkhangelsk itself, the onetime timber metropolis of the world, but consciously or unconsciously, it was also a mutation of all these fragments of a dead world, his peculiar and unique sensibility producing a fantastical continuation of the work of his ancestors in the same way that Vissarion had single-handedly produced a theological-mythological-ethical-cosmological-philosophical fusion. In both cases, if the results seemed crude or bizarre, that was understandable. Normally this sort of thing was the product of many hands and minds.

'Maybe when Sutyagin was a schoolchild he came out here and was inspired by what he saw . . .' I said.

'Oh no,' Natalia replied almost immediately. 'Sutyagin is not so young. This complex was opened in the 1970s. He was already long out of school.'

'How old is he?'

'I don't know . . . But if he had come here as a child that would put him in his forties. And he is older than that . . . And besides, he is not that sort of man.'

'What do you mean?'

'He is not cultured enough to appreciate this.'

Those last words irritated me. My friend's mother; the journalists; Pavel; and now Natalia – everyone dismissed the tower and its builder. It was clearly the resentment of provincials for the dreamer in their midst, an anger at the man of vision, the one who could create, for making those who could not feel small – mixed together with generous helpings of the cultural conservatism that was typical of the Soviet-trained intelligentsia and the universal condescension of intellectuals towards the efforts of an unschooled outsider.

'Do you remember the storm I told you about?' said Natalia.

'Yes.'

'It damaged this cathedral.'

'Really?'

'Sutyagin's monstrosity wasn't touched, but this was.' She shook her head. 'Unbelievable.'

V

We left the complex and waited on the bus, inhaling the scent of porridge wafting across the road from the New Malye Karely resort complex that faced the entrance to the museum. It had been built by Krupchak, owner of my hotel and so much else, the master of Arkhangelsk. Natalia told me that the restaurant inside was excellent, though she had never eaten there. But although I was hungry, I didn't really want to eat. The cold had sunk through my meat and into my bones, sapping my jaws of the energy to chew and my stomach of the desire to be filled. If anything, I wanted to climb *into* that giant tureen of porridge myself, and be cooked on a low heat for several hours.

'So, have I finally cured you of your interest in Sutyagin?' asked Natalia flatly. I looked across at her, to see if I could detect any irony in her eyes, a smile curling at the edges of the mouth, perhaps; but no – she was serious. Deadly serious, in fact – the look I had noticed in the hotel lobby had returned. And so I knew now that the tour around the complex had been intended not simply to show me the 'treasures of Arkhangelsk' but rather to re-educate me, to remove the cataracts from my eyes and make me see the tower for the tottering mound of dried-up dog shit all the locals knew it to be.

Alas for Natalia, I was still blind. However well constructed the chicken coops were, they were still for keeping chickens in, and all the other buildings, whether blandly functional or grandiose and sacred, all belonged in this world, and resembled thousands of other buildings, and did not deviate from the collective norms of their times. They were, at the end of the day, familiar and easy to understand.

The tower, however, was different. It was impolite, gargantuan, grotesque; it served no apparent purpose other than as an expression of a man following his own idea to the end, regardless of whether it made 'sense' or not. Soon it would collapse, and no modern restorer would try to preserve or rebuild it, while the timeless masterpieces of the unknown builders of Kargopol and elsewhere would live on and be admired by generations to come. But Sutyagin had done something none of those old masters had managed – he had built something that had never existed before. His was the only wooden skyscraper in the world, and he had erected it in the face of almost universal opposition.

Natalia was waiting for me to answer. I did.

'No.'

She was disappointed.

4

I spent the rest of the afternoon in Natalia's flat, listening to her talk about the history of Arkhangelsk. She was fascinated by the Englishmen and Germans who had settled in the city prior to the revolution, some of whose descendants she knew personally, men with startling names like Igor Stewart and Vladimir Sherwood. Before I returned to the hotel she agreed to take me out to visit the tower the next day. Although it was enormous and visible from miles away, she still thought that it was probably too difficult for me to find on my own – the area surrounding it was a maze of unpaved streets lined with wooden houses. And besides, I was a foreigner, a stranger to Arkhangelsk, and she had promised her friend she would look after me, and that was something she took seriously.

That night, I stayed in my hotel room, writing and thinking. Whereas the night before I had been racked with doubt, I now felt confident and excited. I was on the verge of making contact with the tower and its enigmatic constructor. I *would* see inside it, and learn its secret, and unravel the mystery of the prisoner in the basement. There was no guarantee that Sutyagin would be in, of course, but that didn't worry me. I would speak to a neighbour, to all his neighbours, knocking on their doors, irritating them until someone coughed up his whereabouts. Somebody out there had to know what had happened to him, where he was. Even if his image and the precise details of his story had vanished from the annals of the city's newspapers, the folk memory would persist, I had faith in that.

Sutyagin was still a mystery, but not for much longer. Soon I would know what happened *after* you crossed 'the line'. Let the locals pour scorn on him: locals rarely see their surroundings clearly. Once I stepped inside, I wouldn't be disappointed.

Or at least that was what I told myself.

IV

Hunting a Human

1 First assault

I

SOLOMBOLA – the enormous blue letters, each one taller than two men, planted on a dirt island in the centre of the road, screamed that I had arrived somewhere memorable. But when I stepped past them, the tone of the letters changed from stridency to sheepish embarrassment – *all right, so it's not really* **SOLOMBOLA***, maybe just* SOLOMBOLA *or even* SOLOMBOLA. *We were just having you on. Visitors don't usually get past the sign, anyway.*

In fact, to the naked eye, the only remarkable feature of Solombola was its radical juxtaposition of two customarily distinct traditions of shabbiness. On the left there was an unremarkable settlement of decaying concrete and brick buildings, on the right an unremarkable cluster of aging wooden villages that ran along the river. But for me, to whom the truth had been given, **SOLOMBOLA** was in fact home to something fantastical and I still trembled before those enormous blue letters as a portent of the awesome. For beyond them, concealed among the wooden huts and trees, somehow invisible from the entrance in spite of its enormous size, was the great wonder of Arkhangelsk, Sutyagin's Tower.

II

'Aren't you afraid he'll lock you in the basement?' asked Natalia.

III

The unpaved streets were treacherous, covered with ice and snow, but Natalia guided me nimbly through them, until suddenly I had to stop. The tower had reared into view: it loomed in the distance, as jarring and outrageous as if Godzilla had risen from the depths to take a dump in a Russian village. I could see the twin tin roofs, the uneven walls, the openings, the black holes where windows should have been. 'There it is,' said Natalia. 'But soon it will vanish again.'

And she was right: as we stepped forward, the tower somehow managed to duck behind chimneys and conceal itself. It didn't seem possible. There were no other tall structures, and yet the laws of perspective had somehow ordained that it disappear from view, leaving us alone in a perfectly ordinary village.

IV

'But it is so quiet!' said Natalia. 'You know, Dan, I don't think anyone lives here. Look – there's no smoke coming from the houses and there is no light in any of the windows either. Maybe these are just summer houses, where people come to work in their gardens when the weather is good. There is no running water out here. You have to get it in the street. The toilet is just a hole in the earth. Conditions are not good for winter living.'

We walked on, and it seemed that Natalia was right. Not one of the houses we passed even hinted towards habitation, and that was not good, because if they were empty then the tower was more likely to be empty, and if it was, then how would I locate Sutyagin? Who would there be to ask? I could feel my confidence of the night before ebbing away, and began to hope for a sign, for some evidence that the village was not *completely* deserted.

None came.

V

But then a small girl stepped out from behind a fence, startling both of us. She was about nine, blonde, and was visibly shocked by the appearance of intruders in her private world. She eyed us warily, keeping her distance. The tower stood behind her, minded its own business.

'Little girl,' said Natalia. 'Do people live here?'

'Of course,' she replied, and then ran off, like Alice chasing the white rabbit.

'She must be very poor,' said Natalia. 'The conditions here are awful in winter.'

We didn't see anyone else.

VI

And then, after walking for about half an hour, following streets that appeared to lead towards it but terminated instead in a fence or a small house, we stood before Sutyagin's Tower. And up close it was no less mysterious than it had been in the photographs or in my imagination. It was as alien as I had hoped it would be, and much more deadly, because now I could see clearly that almost all of the floors were unfinished, and that all the holes, absent walls, missing windows, doorways leading to nowhere and dead ends were signs not simply of a grotesque phantasmagoria, but also of an almost entirely uninhabitable death-trap, a weird skeleton resting on only two completed floors, that teetered and tottered upwards for eleven more storeys, without any signs of organisation or design, and which, with a single tap from God's pinkie, would collapse and crush the homes which huddled around its base, annihilating their inhabitants in the process, ending their poverty and enthusiasm for kitchen gardening once and for all.

'And this thing didn't fall down in the storm?' I said.

'No,' said Natalia. 'It was a miracle. A bad miracle.'

'Not if you're one of the people living next door.'

'Yes. We should hope that it collapses during the winter, when the village is empty, like now. Sutyagin's neighbours will lose their homes, their belongings, but at least they will keep their lives.'

'And the city just let him build this?' I said, incredulous. Now that I was there, the scope of what he had done was overwhelming. 'Without permission? They didn't even try to stop him?'

'Maybe they tried. But Sutyagin was rich, and powerful . . .'

'But they threw him in jail. Didn't they try to demolish it then?'

'Maybe he bribed the city council. Or maybe they were scared of his dogs. Or maybe they were too lazy. Who knows?'

She shrugged. I was being terribly British. Terribly Western. I didn't understand. But even by the standards of the chaotic and corrupt 1990s, it seemed a half-done, utterly cynical, botched job. What was the point of tossing Sutyagin in jail if you weren't going to demolish his tower? It was like giving up on a burial halfway through, leaving the plot open, the corpse on view, rotting away inside, flies buzzing about its mouth, worms chewing on its eyes, the air filled with stench.

VII

A fence, about three metres high, had been built around it. I peered through a crack and saw a set of steps leading up to a very ordinary door. They had been swept clean, so I knew Sutyagin or at the very least a caretaker had visited recently; but other than that there were no signs of habitation. The tower was mute. It was painful to be so close, and yet not close at all.

'Look at this,' said Natalia. She indicated tyre tracks in the snow that led away from a set of padlocked double doors located to the right of the entrance. It was a garage. 'They're fresh,' she said. 'Nobody has stepped in them. Someone has been here recently.'

We stood around, thinking of what to do next. I noticed too that Natalia's attitude had changed. Gone was the scepticism and blasé indifference. She was enjoying playing detective.

'Let's talk to the neighbours,' she said. 'There must be someone living here apart from that little girl . . .'

VIII

So we walked around the perimeter of the tower, knocking on the doors of houses that were obviously abandoned, each time waiting a minute or two for confirmation of what we already knew: that nobody would answer. The village was even deader than Malye Karely, which at least had the excuse of being a museum piece.

But then, a couple of streets away from the tower, I saw a car. The boot was open. We rushed forward and saw that the front door of the house was ajar, leading into a small living room. Natalia knocked, and called for the occupant.

'Leave the box on the step,' said a gruff voice.

'That's not what we're here for,' said Natalia.

A head appeared in the doorway, shaved on top and bristling around the mouth. Its expression was *very* hostile.

'Who are you?'

'We're looking for Mr Sutyagin. Does he live here?'

A pause. Pale eyes scrutinised us both. Then: 'Yes.'

'Still?'

'Yes.'

'Has he been at home recently?'

'Why do you want to know?'

'This young man is a journalist. He would like to talk to Mr Sutyagin.'

'He comes, he goes.'

'Do you know if he'll be back tonight?'

'No.'

He stared at us, steadily, with no abatement in hostility. I remembered Semyon's astonishment in Petropavlovka: *In my mother's village, they wouldn't just let strangers walk around like this. Someone would kick the shit out of us.*

We thanked him and turned away from his step. He didn't say goodbye.

'He is protecting him,' said Natalia. 'He knows, but he's not talking . . . So what now?'

'Maybe Sutyagin will return tonight. Shall we try again later?'

Natalia's attitude had changed completely from the day before. When she walked alongside me, the tower was transformed, and she saw it through my eyes. It was interesting now, to stalk Sutyagin, to try and gain access to his tower, his mysteries. More than that: it was strangely meaningful. But I knew that as soon as I vanished, it would become an ugly nothing once again. Without me there would be no transforming spell, no glamour. I knew what had happened.

Natalia had entered my reality.

INTERLUDE

A graveyard: the empty plots of Tommies who, war-exhausted, had not been demobbed at the end of the Great War but rather sent by Churchill to fight Bolsheviks in 1919, and who had died in the swamps and forests of the Russian north. There was a monument on the river to the Soviet victims of the 'imperialist intervention'. These boys had played the part of villainous invaders in that narrative: the remains of some of them were now home, but others still grinned lipless beneath cold, alien soil. Futile deaths, dismal to contemplate: 'Your Prince Charles came here'.

An art gallery: icons displaying the cross of St Andrew, patron saint of Scotland, although in this context he watches over sailors, not my homeland. Apparently he endorses the actions of the Russian navy too.

A coffee bar: the cool kids of Arkhangelsk, pale and detached in the crossfire of neon against stainless steel, every now and then glancing over to study the old woman sitting with the much younger man near the bar. She is obviously not his mother, so who are they?

The street: across from the enormous swimming pool, men and women in thick coats, queuing to collect water from a truck. The cold has burst the pipes in their buildings. The same cold will freeze the contents of their tin buckets before they get home.

And so on: killing time with history and art, stripping Arkhangelsk bare until it was night, and we were back in Solombola, wandering once more through unlit smokeless streets towards the tower, which finally came into view, a jagged outline illuminated by the moon, everything inside it negative, a rip in space.

2 Second assault

I

Except –

. On the second floor, there was a light: a naked bulb behind glass, illuminating equally naked white walls.

Natalia was shocked. So was I. The hours we had spent wandering about in the freezing darkness had bred only scepticism and doubt. The emptiness of the village and the attitude of Sutyagin's neighbour had seemed a part with the unconcealed scorn that had surrounded the whole expedition from the start. Nobody knew anything, nobody gave a shit. Sutyagin was nowhere to be found, his tower was rubbish. You're wasting your time. Go home.

And now, finally: a sign. I could hardly believe it. But was it an indication of life, of habitation, or just a trick, something left on for security to stop Sutyagin's enemies from trying to break in?

The light seemed cold to me. It was not the light of life but rather that of an illuminated storage space.

II

I walked up to the door set in the tall fence. There was no bell, no buzzer. It was impossible to make contact with the inhabitants of the tower. Whoever was in there did not want to receive unexpected visitors. Undaunted, I started pounding on the wood, but the window was too far away and my glove muffled the impact of my fist. The sound wasn't travelling far enough.

'Maybe we should go,' said Natalia, who had suddenly lost her newfound enthusiasm for Sutyagin's masterpiece. 'It doesn't look as though anyone's home.'

'Nahh . . .' I said. 'I'm not giving up yet. Maybe I should throw a stone at the window.'

I had seen it done in movies. A handful of gravel tossed upwards, and then a talking face – it was always that easy. But Sutyagin's window was far away and located high above me. I would have to lob a rock at it to get the momentum I required. It would sail right through the glass, and that would just be embarrassing.

Suddenly I heard the sound of shuffling, of someone getting to his feet and walking across creaking floorboards. Had Sutyagin heard my violent knocking? But the sound was coming from the unfinished third floor of the tower which, without walls or windows, was entirely exposed to the elements. What was Sutyagin doing there? Was he insane?

I looked up. And suddenly I knew that the tower had all along been nothing but a smokescreen, a cover for Sutyagin-Moreau's real project: the man-wolf, the fruit of his sinister experiments in fusing human and animal DNA. The uncanny beast stood upright on the edge of the third floor, staring down at me, fury in its yellow eyes, viscous slobber swinging from its jaws, which were snapping and snarling, hungry for flesh.

It was too late to flee: the beast leapt from its position above me, sailing through the air, swallowing my head whole, ripping it off and then landing on its feet, all in one movement. My body staggered on its feet, spurted a few hot jets of blood in the air before sinking heavily into a crumpled heap in the snow, like a puppet abruptly dropped by its master.

III

That's all bollocks, obviously. In fact, it was just a big dog. I had forgotten the legend of Sutyagin's five canines from the Caucasus, the savage creatures that had guarded over his creation while he rotted in a penal colony in the remote north. After a minute of intense barking, the hound calmed down; but it didn't return to its resting place in the depths of the tower. It stayed up there, watching me, waiting to see what I was going to try next. I thought about all those nights spent alone in the darkness, whipped by Arctic winds. No wonder the pooch was angry.

'Dan!' Natalia whispered. '*Let's get out of here!*'

I looked around. She had vanished. Peering into the darkness I eventually made out the lines of a human figure.

'*Come on!*'

The beast heard her, and responded with a renewed outburst of barking. Then, more heavy footsteps, and another monster from the depths, hitherto too lazy to get involved, appeared. It stood at the side of the other one, lunging forwards, looking for something to kill.

'*Really Dan, I'm scared . . .* '

But now I was certain Sutyagin was in there, crouched under the harsh phosphoric glare of the light bulb, straining not to move, not to cast a shadow, holding his breath, listening, waiting for the beasts to attack or for me to leave, whichever happened first. He was behind that square of light, in his secret lair, a sinister count plotting revenge on the world that had wronged him . . .

IV

'SUTYAGIN!' I yelled. 'COME OUT! I WANT TO TALK TO YOU!'

I waited, waited . . . but there was no movement at the window, no new lights came on in the tower, and the village was still sleeping.

'SUTYAGIN! COME OUT! I MEAN YOU NO HARM!'

Only the dogs responded. They were growing more enraged by the second. I cupped my hands to my mouth again:

'SUTYAGIN! I WANT TO TALK ABOUT YOUR TOWER!'

Still no response. The dogs lunged as far forward as they could, snapping at the night, at the stars, at the cold and, of course, at the intruder below. I couldn't tell if they were chained up or not. They looked free enough to me.

I yelled a few more times, and then stopped. Suddenly I saw myself, and who was I? Some guy, standing in the street at night, yelling at the window of a man who didn't know him. Wasn't there a word for what I was doing? Yes, there was: harassment.

It wasn't that I was worried about the legality of what I was doing, or the police. But I knew that if someone had come to my tower in the Arctic and started shouting outside my window I would have reached for the nearest bucket of wet shit – or, if there was any to hand, boiling oil.

Then I remembered why the tower was unfinished. Sutyagin had gone too far, he had crashed through the invisible boundaries that restrain us all, and splattered against the hard rock of the world. He had been sent to prison. He had suffered. He had lost everything. The *game* of tracking him down had concealed the solidity of all that from me. Of course he didn't want to talk. And even if I could have somehow forced him to, it would have been wrong to do so. If he wanted to die, to cease to exist, to withdraw completely, then that was his right. It was up to him.

I was, in short, acting like a right arsehole. Natalia thought so too. She had already gone. It was just me and the dogs now, and over there, Sutyagin, hiding.

I had followed the trail as far as I could, and it had just petered out. *I did my best and that's all anyone can do; you can't win 'em all –* and all that jazz. But I had to face the facts: there was nothing left to do. Almost. I wrote a note, leaving him my mobile number, and put it inside a box on the fence. But I didn't have any hope that he'd call.

I turned away from the tower and started walking back through the village towards Arkhangelsk. I wasn't exactly leaping with happiness that it had ended this way, but at the same time I didn't feel all that disappointed. The journey that had begun when I found the Digger's phone number in the back of *Residential Property Shit* had finally resolved itself. And knowing that, I felt something close to relief.

But I was so close . . .

3 A monument to the great liberation

Natalia and I rode back into town on the bus. She was exhausted, freezing and wanted to go home. As for me, I was ready to return to the hotel. But I wanted to thank her, so I offered to buy her dinner in the Gross Vagon. She accepted.

Once we had thawed out a little she started asking about the book I was writing and the other places I had visited on my 'research trips' . It was the first time we had talked about it. Until now, I had always been the guest, listening to facts about Arkhangelsk, receiving an education in what others deemed important. Perhaps if I'd been more explicit about my goals from the start my interest in Sutyagin would have made more sense to her, but I wasn't as bold as Vadim, Edward or Vissarion and, aware that mine was an 'unusual' perspective, I had advanced under cover of vagueness. But now I talked about my excursion through the sewers of Moscow, the exorcisms in Ukraine and my encounter with the Son of God, elaborating upon the theme of 'personal realities' and my theory of the 'line' which everyone I had met was aware of but which only Sutyagin had crossed. She was very interested. And then suddenly I found myself continuing my thought in a new direction, which had been growing in me ever since my return from Siberia but which I had never fully articulated before. And it was almost as if the words were speaking *me*, and were forming in the air of their own volition, and all I could do was sit there and listen.

'You know,' I said, 'a few years ago I read an article by an English critic, dismissing the entire literary output of post-Soviet Russia. His argument was that, as no new Dostoevsky or Tolstoy had emerged to capture the 'spirit of the age' since 1991, the contemporary Russian novel was a failure. I thought this was an outrageously pompous thing to say, of course. First, the critic wasn't a Russian speaker, and as few contemporary Russian authors have been translated into English he could hardly have known what he was talking about. Secondly, it's not a fair comparison. No other country has produced a Dostoevsky or a Tolstoy either, not in the last *hundred* years, never mind fifteen.

'Recently, though, I remembered that article and started thinking about it again. And now I'm starting to wonder if he wasn't looking in the wrong place anyway. Of course, he was a literary critic so it was natural that he would greatly overestimate the significance of novels. But why should we expect the creative energies of a period in history to find their greatest fulfilment in the novel, or any art form for that matter? They could just as easily be expressed in other, stranger directions. My feeling now is that the collapse of Soviet reality, for all of the chaos and suffering it brought about, also led to a great liberation of personality and of dreaming, but that this has gone unnoticed because these manifestations of creativity rarely take the form of "objects" such as books or paintings, or if they do, those are secondary products. As a result, they're much harder to quantify or pin down, or even to find as, for the most part, they exist entirely in people's heads.

'I'm not saying that the people I've spoken to are on a par with Dostoevsky in the genius stakes, of course. But they have produced remarkable work that is strange and fascinating and meaningful if you look at it properly and don't just dismiss it with labels like "crazy" or "insane" or "eccentric".

'And now I think I finally understand why I've been so interested in these people. When I write my book it will be as a testament to what happened at a unique moment in history – when several remarkable individuals stepped from the ruins of the Soviet Union into a brand-new, chaotic world and the roofs of their skulls flew off and these visions of possible realities forced themselves out into the world . . . I will be a cartographer of the impossible, drawing maps of these creations so they don't just disappear into oblivion. I can't record all of them, of course – that would take years, and most of them would be impossible to locate anyway. These are just four of the most interesting ones that I found – or that found me.'

Natalia had let me speak without interrupting. I had grown quite impassioned as I went on, and now I wasn't sure if she had the faintest idea what I was talking about or whether she had just been humouring me. But then she started nodding. She had been listening very closely.

'And do you think this is a phenomenon unique to Russia?' she asked. 'Or are there people like this abroad?'

'No,' I said. 'Everyone "creates his own reality" to some extent. But in Britain, for example, where the government will supply you with money and a place to live if you don't work, there's much less risk involved. You can live in a dream world your whole life, eating pies and smoking dope, and though you'll be poor, you'll never starve to death. But here, perhaps because conditions are more . . .' I paused, choosing my words carefully, '. . . *severe*, and there are so many talented people dissatisfied with the environment in which they live, but unable to do anything about it, well, perhaps the manifestations are more extreme . . .'

'Yes,' she said. 'Russia is a perfect place for creating realities. And it is in our history: a tsar wills a European city to appear where a swamp exists, and it happens. It doesn't matter that it's impossible, or that there are other, far more habitable, fertile areas in the south. It must be done, and it is done. Other cities appear in Siberia, the flow of a river is reversed, deserts are forced to bear fruit . . .'

And now, for the first time since I had arrived, I wasn't being treated like a naïve foreigner. On the contrary, I had made her see her own world with new eyes, I had rendered the familiar strange, and I could see that she was thinking.

4

Back at the hotel, though, the 'relief' I had felt when I decided to walk away from the tower left me. I couldn't hide from the fact that I had failed. I still didn't really know why Sutyagin had built it; in fact I still hadn't found out what Sutyagin even looked like.

It was disappointing. More than that, it was a waste. The tower was too rich in symbolic possibilities. There had to be some way round this. After all, if I was writing a book about people who challenged the facts of the world that surrounded them, who worked so hard to create more satisfying alternatives, then why couldn't I follow suit?

Why should I be imprisoned by my 'events' and 'facts'? Why not walk right up to Sutyagin's door, have him answer, and welcome me in, as if he had been expecting me all along, and then reveal that the tower had been built as a sanctuary, and that here I would find Vadim, Edward, Vissarion and many others, working on their worlds. Then he would lead me up, up towards the highest point, to the room that looked out over the river, and he would open the door, saying, *Come and see, Daniel, come and see*, and we would step inside, and there I would find . . .

But no: it wouldn't work, and there was a very simple reason why. I would know I had invented the ending. If I was going to deny the facts of what had actually happened and accept some other, alternative reality as true, then I needed that denial to bubble up from deep within me and sweep me away in a flood. And that just wasn't going to happen.

I switched on the TV and flicked through the channels until, to my surprise, I saw someone I knew personally on the screen. It wasn't some fat guy struggling to fulfil his adolescent fantasies of becoming a movie star in a Russian *Die Hard* clone, however – rather it was someone much more powerful, a woman with a lot of influence in her world. She was the owner of a construction company in Moscow who had been accused of taking money for apartments in towers that had never been built. Poor people had placed their faith in her and been left with nothing.

She denied everything.

V

The Apotheosis of Nikolai Sutyagin

1

The chief architect of Arkhangelsk lived in a brutalist concrete structure in the city centre. The few trees in front were still encased in frost.
Pavel opened the door and we stepped inside: unlit steps led upwards
to the lift. The artificial wood-panelled doors closed, a pulley creaked
and the damp steel box reeking of piss lifted us upwards, shuddering
to a halt on the fifth floor. We stepped out: a black metal door faced
us. Pavel rang the bell.

A few seconds, and then the door swung open. Light flooded out
into the corridor, and Professor Yuri Anatolievich Barashkov – former
deputy of the Supreme Soviet of the USSR (1989–1991), acquaintance
of the celebrated dissident Andrei Sakharov, specialist in Russian
wooden architecture and author of many books – appeared in front of
us.

He was not what I had expected. He was in his sixties, but so youthful and energetic that I, at least thirty years younger than he was, suddenly felt old and decrepit in comparison. The silver hair cropped
close to his skull stood to attention as if charged by the electricity that
fizzed and crackled in his scalp. A clean and open face shone with a
frank enthusiasm for life. He thrust out a hand: his grip was very firm.

'Yura!' he said, beaming from ear to ear. '*How-do-you-do!*'

2

I followed him into an open living area, sitting down in the sleek, comfortable chair he offered me. The room was full of flowers ('It's my
wife's birthday,' he said, grinning), but they were not the source of its

beauty, which so completely belied the dismal exterior of the building – that lay in the careful arrangement of space. The apartment was open but not cavernous, orderly but not obsessive, form always reflected function and there was nothing on display that was not beautiful or useful.

I was particularly impressed by the slim, sleek bookshelves, each one of which was lined with attractive volumes on art. There was no thematic repetition – one volume for the Bauhaus, one for constructivism, one for baroque, one for the Renaissance and so on – and so I knew that he had thought long and hard before authoritatively selecting the precise tome he required. I had been in lots of rooms containing glossy coffee-table art books, but this was probably the first time I thought the owner actually referred to his reference books, and genuinely understood exactly what each one contained.

I wanted to kick him out and move in. But I knew I would just fill all the nice clean space with bizarre junk, random scraps of paper, books, CDs and dried-up tea bags. It wasn't a good idea.

3 Pissing from a great height

At first Yura spoke in English, but his thoughts quickly became too complex for a second language and he switched to Russian, Pavel interpreting for us. I hardly needed to ask questions: as soon as I mentioned the name Sutyagin, the details started flooding out of him, and immediately I learned that everything Natalia had told me about the professor and Sutyagin in Malye Karely was false. Yura did not hate the tower. He loved it. Not only was he chief architect but he had been elected to the local administration, where he described himself as 'Sutyagin's only defender'. 'Others want to tear it down,' he said. 'I am trying to protect it.'

I asked about the tower's origin.

'How did it start? Well, basically Sutyagin had made a lot of money in business, and he wanted to build a house for himself. At first he came to me and asked me to design it. I did as he asked and produced a plan for a traditional wooden two-storey house, but the final result – well, that's entirely his fantasy!'

'So he didn't have a plan for a tower from the start, then?'

'Not at all. He built the first two storeys according to the professional drawings. But then he decided that it wasn't tall enough. So he designed another storey and had his workers add it. After this third level was completed, he thought it was still too low. So he added another. By this point he was working entirely alone. Even though he had no architectural training whatsoever, it was now entirely his project. Then he decided that the nine-storey buildings in front of his house prevented him from seeing the main shipping channel, and so he decided to continue building to get a view of the river. That was when he first faced seriously the problems of architectural design: because he could not carry on constructing it in the same chaotic, improvisational way as before. So he made a cardboard model of what he wanted and told his men to build that, without even knowing what it was for in the end.'

'He really had no idea?'

'None,' said Yura, his face glowing, as if this fact pleased him more than any other. 'And this, this is a manifestation of Russian character! He had the money; and he had to express himself in some way, and so he did, and he let nothing stop him! Not even the fact that he didn't know what the tower was for. Only the top floor, which was originally designed as a room about the size of the one we're sitting in, well, that was the only thing he knew he wanted from the very beginning. He decided that he would put sofas around this room, a table in the middle and that he would sit there smoking, tapping his finger on the cigarette and dropping the ash on the ground. He didn't even bother to think about what the floors below it were for. He wanted to feel that everyone was below him. You know, like going to the toilet on an aeroplane – so he could feel like a big man by pissing on all the people and houses underneath him.'

The professor laughed, but there was no hostility in his tone.

'What amazed me was that . . . well, I like architectural drawings. I have a collection of them. And at the start of the twentieth century there was an architect called Suslov, a professor in St Petersburg. He published an album of his drawings – fantasies on the theme of Russian architecture. They were impossible buildings, dream buildings, ideas that he knew would never be realised. And of course, Kolya Sutyagin knew nothing about this. I repeat: he has no architectural education whatsoever. I don't even see any influence from our local wooden houses and churches. But as the tower rose, I couldn't believe my eyes. It looks as though he had taken one of the impossible designs of Suslov and actually *built* it.'

Yura leapt up and ran over to the shelves, neatly lined with exquisite art books. Selecting one he came over and showed me a line drawing of a fantastical cathedral-skyscraper with multiple angles and domes.

'So you see – how did Sutyagin do this? Where did it come from? It must be in the genes: his tower is a manifestation of the Russian soul in architecture . . .'

4 Tower of the Russian soul

The professor froze momentarily, transfixed, a smile on his lips. He was lost in blissful contemplation of the *russkaya dusha*, that wild, free, most ineffably mysterious of God's creations, which had erupted into reality so extravagantly and in such an unexpected form in the streets of Solombola. The tower was not just Sutyagin's – it was *his* tower, it was the long-dead Academician Suslov's tower, it was Pavel and Natalia's tower . . . it was all Russia's tower.

Which left me out, of course: because my soul, which was not Russian, could never truly understand the vast, enigmatic forces that had brought it into being. I could only stand back and admire it from a distance. And indeed, as the professor immersed himself deeper and deeper in the vast lagoon of his nation's collective essence, I could feel my own thoughts moving in a Germanic-Protestant-rationalist direction.

'But did he ever get planning permission?' I asked.

'Only for the first two storeys,' said Yura, suddenly returning to earth. 'As for the rest of the house, well, in building it he violated all existing constructional norms. The city authorities were aggressive towards him and wanted to tear it down. There was a war between the administration and Sutyagin; the tall fence and five Caucasian shepherds are a result of this confrontation. Not knowing how to stop him, the authorities invented a case to put him in jail for two years. This was not a difficult thing to do, because all New Russians started off as criminals. Just take a look at their dealings and you'll find something.

'He did do it, though – I mean, he did keep one of his colleagues locked up in the basement of the house, but beyond that I know nothing. Maybe the man stole money, or was in debt to Sutyagin. We are close acquaintances, but I never talk about it with him. It's a very delicate subject. He was originally sentenced to a longer term, but he was released after two years for good behaviour. That was five or six years ago. While he was in prison he lost his business and that dried up the material resources for his ideas. Now he doesn't have the money to finish it. That's why the building is now in such a state, and it is quite probable that it will just collapse. Everyone in construction knows that such a building cannot stand unattended for so long. It should be protected from the environment. But in the tower, all the structures are exposed . . .

'What do his neighbours think about it?'

'The population of the village is also quite aggressive. Mostly they dislike him. They're all afraid that the house will catch fire, or fall on top of them. One of his neighbours said to me, "I have already bought a grenade launcher, and I'm just waiting until he reaches the top, then I'll burn it down."' Yura laughed. 'This is a good example of Russian psychology. If an American farmer sees his neighbour is doing better than him, he just buys a new tractor and starts working harder. But a Russian, well he decides to burn down the church and destroy the work of his rival.'

Yura now took flight, and I could feel him guiding me to his conclusion.

'In fact, I am probably the only member of our administration and the only professional in the field of architecture protecting Sutyagin and the tower. Why do I do it? To me, the answer is simple: because this is something unique that does not exist anywhere else in the world. It could be entered in the *Guinness Book of Records*, because in Russia and around the world you only find wooden buildings that are two storeys high. In Finland I once saw an experimental three-floor building, but in fact it was about fifty per cent reinforced concrete mixed with some pieces of wood. So Sutyagin's Tower is not just taller, but much taller than every other wooden building in the world.

'But that's not all. It is also a monument to the times when such a building could be constructed, to this period of wild capitalism in the 1990s. Some people laugh at it, others fear it. But if you look around the village, all the other houses have one floor and three windows – they are all identical. In Russian popular architecture, terror of the environment was very strong. A young man starts building a house, and he wants to do something different, but then some older man comes along and says, "You should do the same as this other building – look, see, it's still standing. Yours will fall." But people like Sutyagin, who ignore this terror – well, they make progress for architecture, even if it manifests itself in such strange ways, and in wild forms . . .

'I'm working on a book about the history of world architecture for my students and the people of Arkhangelsk. There will only be one thousand copies. In it I have placed a chapter called the "Towers of Babel in the Twentieth Century". And there I write that the skyscraper was invented by Americans. But the wooden skyscraper was invented by Sutyagin. So I will sing a hymn for Sutyagin because his house will be placed in the same chapter as the World Trade Center and the Empire State Building and other famous buildings in Shanghai and Kuala Lumpur!'

5

The professor had finished his disquisition on the significance of Sutyagin's Tower. Theoretically the interview was over, but he was obviously a creative thinker, and so I sat there in silence, staring at him, waiting to see how he would fill the void. He was far too polite to tell me to piss off, and I was sure he would produce something interesting.

He paused for a few seconds, sitting on the edge of the sofa with mild panic in his eyes, wondering why I wasn't getting up to thank him and shake his hand. Then, when he realised it was because I had no intention of leaving, he suddenly flew off on a long and inspired riff on the history of Arkhangelsk and how his own personal history was interwoven with it, before segueing into his own theories on the origins of world architecture, Russia's (unjustly neglected) place in it and his fascination for labyrinths, and in particular the numerous ancient labyrinths that were dotted around the Russian north.

'Architecture,' he said, 'is the art of arranging space. We tear off a little piece of the cosmos and organise it around ourselves . . .' But Yura did more than arrange physical space – as he looked around himself he was constantly arranging all aspects of the world, drawing it in, studying it, and then producing his own original interpretations and reinterpretations. Some of these were serious, others playful and provocative; but they were never frivolous. Finally, he returned to the tower: 'You know, in the past I redirected all people curious about it to Sutyagin himself . . . I have his telephone number. You should call. He never rejects people who are interested in him.'

'I'm not so sure,' I said. 'I've tried journalists and his neighbours. Nobody could tell me where he was or how to get in touch with him.

Nobody can even remember what he looks like. He's disappeared completely!' I didn't mention that I had spent ten minutes yelling at his window.

Yura shrugged. 'Maybe he's changed since prison. I'd call him for you, but . . . well, he's a strange kind of man. I know him, I like him, but I don't call him. I don't want to reopen the connection. He's from a different world. He's an *absolutely pure* New Russian. One time, probably back in 1991 or 1992, I brought some Norwegian journalists round to see him. They had coffee. One of the journalists asked for a little cognac. Sutyagin moved his foot under the table. There was a whole box of very expensive, high-quality cognac down there. Just a heap of bottles. And Sutyagin just shifted the box towards the Norwegian with his foot. The Norwegian was shocked.'

'How old is he?'

'I'm not sure. He's a lot younger than me. I'm sixty-seven; he's somewhere in his forties. Maybe forty-two. He has a wife, a young daughter.'

'Do you have a picture of him?'

'No . . . I used to, but not now. I don't even have a photograph of the tower now. What he's doing these days I don't know, and to be honest . . . I don't want to. His world is a complicated place. There were a lot of dark rumours about him . . . He is a very strong man, naturally strong. Once, in his house I saw a videotape of a dogfight. It was *disgusting*. It's illegal, of course, but this is the kind of thing that interests him. I mean, we have a good relationship. I even like him, but . . . I just don't want to renew our contact.'

The professor looked sideways for a second, as another thought came to him.

'Sutyagin wanted to go into politics. He asked me to "consult", but I really didn't see a politician in him. I am a Soviet man, a product of socialist reality, and in some respects I remain "Soviet" in my attitude to money. And people of this type – like Sutyagin, or Krupchak, our big local millionaire, all these New Russians . . . Well, at first I had a completely negative attitude towards them. Most people still do: they are attacked on all sides in Arkhangelsk. But I've changed. I realise that they are leaders. In any tragic situation, like the events in Russia at the start of the nineties, they are the ones who will find a way out, and who will help the nation to rise again. Of course they will commit crimes in doing so – but they have so much energy that they cannot stay within the boundaries of existing law, and the law meanwhile cannot keep up with them. Our society should support them by rejecting the excessive legal requirements for these people . . . in any crisis it will be enough to let them exercise their reasonable initiative and the situation will be improved.'

At last I got up to leave, and shook the professor's hand. He handed me a piece of paper. 'Here's Sutyagin's number,' he said. 'Call him. Tell him I vouch for you. He won't turn you away.'

There was just one problem. My flight back to Moscow was scheduled to depart in three hours' time.

6

Pavel switched off the mobile. 'It rang out.'

'Try again,' I said. 'Sutyagin might be hiding behind the sofa, waiting for the phone to stop ringing.'

He hesitated, but then punched in the numbers again. 'Still no answer. Looks like you're out of luck . . .'

'Try again,' I said. Pavel winced in pain: this was all too aggressive and alien to his peaceful nature.

'Now the phone's been switched off. Well, never mind, you'll be in Arkhangelsk again, won't you?'

'Probably not,' I said. 'I have to see him now.'

'Shall we have lunch . . .?'

'No. I might need to go to the airport and cancel my ticket.'

'Perhaps a meal would help you relax and to think clearly. We could call the airport from the Gross Vagon.'

I couldn't think of a better idea. We had just turned in that direction when the phone rang: I listened to Pavel explaining who he was, who I was, and that we had just come from a meeting with Professor Barashkov. The conversation didn't last long.

'That was a woman. I think she's Sutyagin's wife. She says he's out, but she'll have him call us when he gets back.'

'How long will that be?'

'She didn't say. But they already know who you are.'

I pictured myself, standing in the dark, deserted streets of Solombola, yelling at the illuminated window. I still wasn't sure if it had been a good idea. Pavel could tell what I was thinking about, and smiled.

'Yes. My mother told me about last night's . . . adventure.'

7

The Gross Vagon was too far from the centre of town; I needed instant access to a taxi. We turned back to the hotel. We were on the steps of Krupchak's supermarket when the mobile rang. It was Sutyagin. The call was extremely brief.

'He wants to know where you got this number. He's going to check with Yura.'

I thought about the professor, so keen to avoid contact with his old acquaintance, Kolya Sutyagin, lest it open up a portal into that other world, of which he now covertly approved but nevertheless sought to know nothing about. I had just brought an abrupt end to that dream.

The mobile rang again.

'He says you can come – if you're not afraid of a big, unfinished house, that is.'

There was a row of taxis parked in front of the hotel. Pavel picked the one closest to us, a dirty cream-coloured Lada.

'Where to?' asked the driver.

'Sutyagin's house,' Pavel replied.

No more explanation was necessary.

8 The Secret Architect of the Post-Communist World

I

The driver took us through the darkening maze of streets, turning into dead ends and alleys that promised to lead to the tower but which terminated instead in little huts and kitchen gardens, until at last he reached the tall fence that surrounded it. The light bulb on the second floor was shining as it had the night before, as though it had been left on, to guide me home.

Pavel called.

'He's going to call off the dogs.'

We waited a few minutes, and then from behind the fence I heard the sound of a door being unbolted, two feet stepping forward in the night, a scrabbling on wooden floorboards, dogs rising to greet their master. There was a pause, then silence, then I heard the steps renewed, moving by some unknown route towards us. Snow was crunched underfoot and then the door in the fence opened and Nikolai Sutyagin stood before us in a shiny ski jacket and a woolly hat with a label on it, announcing its non-Russian origins. The twilight was thick around us, so it was difficult to make out his features: all I could establish was that he was of average height and neither fat nor thin. His eyes, however, glinting in the moonlight, darted rapidly back and forth between Pavel and myself, and I knew that he was shrewdly and sharply assessing these arrivals on his doorstep.

'Which is which?' he said.

'Excuse me?'

'Which one of you is Russian and which one's the foreigner?'

'I'm the Russian,' said Pavel.

'I'm the foreigner,' I added.

'Nice to meet you. Now follow me.'

II

Sutyagin darted ahead of us, flying up stairs and over piles of planks and logs and miscellaneous junk that lay around in big, dark, unfinished rooms until he came to a door which was pushed firmly shut, zealously guarding the warmth and light inside. He paused, and turned to us. 'You do know that it's not finished, yes, that there are piles of logs and dirt everywhere . . .?'

'I know.'

'Then come in.'

We stepped through the hall and into a very spare kitchen, furnished with simple wooden items. Sutyagin's wife, a thin, tired woman in a puffy blue tracksuit, smiled briefly, weakly at us. Her hair, dark at the roots, stained blonde at the ends, was dry and brittle, ravaged by the cheap dye of the Russian provinces. We didn't stop. Sutyagin, in a blizzard of movement, hurled us into the living room and then demanded to know what we wanted to drink.

'A little vodka, perhaps?'

'Tea's fine,' I said.

Sutyagin raised his eyebrows. He didn't approve. 'Suit yourself. And you?'

'Tea,' said Pavel.

Sutyagin turned to his wife. 'Make them some tea,' he commanded. Then he opened a cupboard, pulled out a torch and turned back to us. 'She'll bring you drinks and give you a video to watch. I'll just step out for a minute.'

He disappeared back through the door that led into the tower. But as the Vissarionites had taught me, sound travels in wooden houses, and I could hear him stamping about, up and down steps, going in and out of rooms, switching on lights, preparing the tower for its visitors.

III

I felt like Howard Carter stumbling into Tutankhamun's tomb – except that instead of marvelling at the treasures buried with an Egyptian boy-king to make his voyage to the afterlife smoother, I was gazing in wonder at the trinkets the equally extinct genus *Homo novy-russky* had amassed to smooth his passage through this world.

Every single object dated from the glory days of bandit capitalism in the mid 1990s, and was preserved intact, perfectly displaying the ostentatious vulgarity that had defined the tastes of the now vanished elite. The weird, shiny blue wallpaper and the luxurious sofas wrapped around the room were appropriately gaudy, and although I had no doubt they were expensive the overall impression was one of cheapness. The enormous black Hi-Fi system glittering in the corner (CDs and tapes only; it pre-dated the MP3 revolution), the colossal 'Goldstar' TV (cathode-ray tube, not flat screen. Goldstar was later renamed LG) and the VHS player under it (there was no DVD player) were all exactly the same age, and although they were once no doubt objects of great desire in Arkhangelsk, they were now museum pieces, with the same sad, bulky, useless look as all dated technology.

Pavel was especially impressed by the Hi-Fi system. He made the 'devil horns' sign of the Russian gangster. 'A friend of mine had that stereo system,' he said. 'He was so proud . . . as if by owning it he had become a New Russian himself.'

O Sutyagin, what did they do to you? The tower, incomplete on the outside, was incomplete within too – time was frozen, destiny jammed, Sutyagin unable to move on. The room was a mausoleum; Sutyagin slept in it like Lenin, soft and pickled in a glass tank. And how quickly the New Russian, once the subject of countless asinine newspaper features, crap documentaries and Hollywood schlock, had slipped from the stage of history! He was as obsolete as the rock 'n' roll records Soviet teenagers had once pressed on X-ray scans; as embarrassing as a futurologist in 1993 explaining that virtual-reality headsets were the technology of the future. Under Yeltsin's debauched, anarchic misrule it may have paid to dress in a tracksuit and overtly advertise your propensity for violence. Now, however, it was necessary to wear an expensive suit and at least affect the language and pose of business. Those who could not play by the new rules were either dead, in prison or had somehow been frozen out, and were probably working as security guards in bazaars. The proud beast that had roamed the vast spaces of Russia stealing and pillaging was now a comical footnote – and no one had even noticed its passing.

The strangest thing, however, was that I realised Sutyagin had entered jail at exactly the moment when I had arrived in Russia. Time had stopped for him at precisely the point when it had begun for me. And so I felt as though I had somehow stepped back to my first arrival in the country, when I had been wandering around Smolensk on my own, knowing nothing more than what I had read in newspapers and books, unable to speak the language or read the alphabet. It was an unsettling feeling, especially as I was leaving the country in a matter of weeks, and for the first time in nine years I had not applied for a new visa, and did not know when I would be returning. There was a strange, unnatural sense of circularity, as if my presence here denied everything I had seen and experienced in all that time.

My reverie was broken when Sutyagin's wife came in, poured us some tea and fed a black cassette into the VHS player.

IV *Film 1*

Thumping, primitive techno music: the house appears, though at this point in time it is only half-built; the upper levels remain locked in Sutyagin's mind. Perhaps he has not even visualised them yet (except for that top-floor room; Yura said he always knew what the top-floor room would contain). The camera zooms in on a jagged wooden crater, already towering above the neighbouring houses.

Inside, Sutyagin is sitting on a sofa. This sofa, in fact, in this very room. His hair is dark and he is wearing a suit – the very image of a *biznesmen*. A voiceover explains that he works in the timber business. Sutyagin explains the tower thus: 'I like company. I am building this tower so I can have my friends around me.' He responds to accusations that he is a gangster with a chuckle: 'My reputation is such that I don't need to cheat.'

Somehow that doesn't sound so reassuring. There is something of waking up with a horse's head next to you in bed about the man in the suit, who is otherwise so effusive, so cheerful: *I'll make you an offer you can't refuse . . .*

V *Film 2*

A few years have passed, and yet the same bad techno is playing as the camera zooms in on the tower, now as complete as it will ever be, though Sutyagin doesn't know that yet. The room for pissing on the world has been built.

Sutyagin is still in this room, however, the one I am sitting in ten years later, surrounded by the same shiny blue wallpaper, sitting on the same sofa. On the screen, he is silver haired. The ten years that have elapsed since this piece of footage aired don't seem to have aged him. If anything, he looks younger today, in spite of prison. The Sutyagin currently roaming through the tower, flicking switches, is blond.

Sutyagin is surrounded by his family: his wife, an old woman (his mother?) and a child. He seems very pleased, the model patriarch. The camera cuts and he is walking up wooden steps, higher and higher, passing through empty granaries until he reaches the room at the top. It is bare; there is no table, no armchair, no ashtray. Sutyagin explains that he wanted to get a view of the whole peninsula, and so the building rose higher and higher to accommodate his desire. But the view is grim: overcast, muddy, the master of Solombola gazes out upon a vast, rotting post-industrial complex. I note that the narrator, so much weaker and poorer than the master of the tower, rebels in his own snivelling way, referring to Sutyagin as 'Kolya' throughout the narration, thus denying the master of the tower the elementary respect of name and patronymic. He never does this to his face, of course.

Cut to Professor Barashkov, ten years ago, still smiling, though his hair is darker than it was two hours earlier. He is standing in Solombola, the tower in the background, talking excitedly about its uniqueness: 'Like the Tower of Babel, it is a symbol of man's desire to reach the heavens. I respect Sutyagin because out here, in the depths of the Russian north, he has transcended provincial mediocrity and built something unique!'

And then the video stopped, dead. I knew what followed, however: disgrace, and jail. But there was no record of that, though it must have been reported on the local TV. And I remembered the words of Yura: 'I never talk about it with him. It is a very delicate subject.'

The screen filled with hissing interference and then the video switched itself off. The TV started barking at us. There were some explosions in London. It had already reached the end of the story, however, and swiftly cut to images of verdant nature in Kaliningrad.

Some old peasants were complaining that enormous houses were being built in a national park, on land that was supposed to be kept pristine, untouched. The camera showed us a settlement of huge lakeside 'cottages', a word which in Russian usually refers not to charming little abodes with thatched roofs but rather huge, candy-coloured brick atrocities bereft of charm or style. One St Petersburg businessman had allegedly paid a $300,000 bribe to build his; a leading police officer said that following an investigation it and the others might be torn down. I didn't believe him.

Pavel shook his head: '*Russia* . . .' he groaned, half in agony. The Kaliningrad fiasco was followed by a report on neo-Nazi groups beating up Tadjik *Gastarbeiters*. Pavel shook his head again.

'*Russia* . . .'

VI

Sutyagin returned and sat down in a chair on my left, leaning forward as if ready to clock me, should I irritate him. At some point between our arrival and his voyage through the tower he had located a pair of sunglasses and placed them on top of his head, though the sun was unlikely to emerge any moment soon. The tight white top he was wearing clung to a muscular physique. It was open at the neck, revealing a thin gold chain. Sutyagin was still a New Russian peacock, his years in jail notwithstanding.

Instantly he began negotiating – leaning yet further forward, gesturing rapidly with his hands, catching me off guard. Was I a writer or a journalist? He didn't like journalists. He didn't trust them. I said I was a writer. But this only made him mournful.

'It's a pity,' he said.

'Why?'

'Only foreign writers are interested in Russia! Russians don't give a shit. We don't read books any more, except for detective novels and shoot 'em ups . . .' He made two fingers into a gun: 'You know, *bang bang!*'

And then Sutyagin grilled me, really grilled me, about my aims, my goals, even the source of my financing. I knew that he was testing me, that he was probing for something: but I wasn't sure what, and that made me nervous. I remembered the Digger, with his ever shifting conditions. It had taken weeks to get him to agree to anything. But at least then I had had weeks to spend on negotiations. Right now, I had one hour, after which I had to leave for the airport. There was no time for meta-discussions. I had to get Sutyagin to trust me, and fast.

But Sutyagin was shrewd, and wily, and paranoid. We danced around like this for a long time. Every time I answered a question it led to another question, as if he didn't believe anything I said, as if it *a priori* couldn't be true, and he was trying to force some confession out of me. I tried to figure out what he wanted, what he was listening for, but it wasn't clear. And then it started to become unclear to me too. *What was I doing in the tower?* The 'ark for the Slavs' idea was obviously bullshit, long since lost to me. And as for 'crossing the line', well, there wasn't any great mystery to it. He had lost everything: he had been stripped of power, and was now chained and muzzled, pacing back and forth in his tower, trapped within the rotting edifice of his uncompleted dream. So aside from fact checking some of Yura's statements, such as the claim that Sutyagin had never known why he built it, all that remained really was my fascination with him as the architect. I just wanted to see him, to meet him, to sit in his tower, to hear him talk.

'What do you know about me?' he snapped.

Tired of providing explanations I tried the mystic angle. 'I saw a picture,' I said. 'I came.' Sutyagin sneered. He was a businessman; he didn't even dignify my statement with a response. Then I repeated, in truncated form, what I had said to Natalia the night before. That was better, yet still not good enough: 'But there's lots of information about me, about my life. There's a website. Have you seen it? It contains lots of stories. Most of them are completely false . . .'

'No I haven't,' I said. We were down to about forty-five minutes now before I had to leave. It was getting exasperating. I had to get him to say something, to reveal some truth before I left. 'Let's assume I know nothing, and that's why I'm here – to find out the truth from you.'

Sutyagin looked blank. 'I don't know if I'm interested in a book,' he said, shrugging and sitting back. Then suddenly he had a thought. 'Do you have any contacts with TV?'

I didn't understand. Maybe he thought a book wasn't important enough, that his life's work deserved more recognition, a wider audience. 'Would you rather be featured in a documentary?' I asked.

'Yes . . . No. I have a lot to say – about politics, about my experiences, about this house,' he paused. 'But it would be better if it were broadcast live.'

394

Now I was totally lost. Who did he think was waiting in the outside world to hear his words? Nobody had heard of him; nobody even knew his tower existed.

'Live?'

'Yeah, you know, by satellite link. Unedited.'

Kolya Sutyagin was clearly a man of rare significance, on a par with the Pope, or the president of the United States. 'Is he saying what I think he's saying?' I asked Pavel.

'Yes.'

'That's crazy.'

'I think he's very worried. His words have been twisted beyond recognition so many times before, he thinks it'll happen again.'

I tried to reassure Sutyagin, that I was interested only in his point of view, and that I wouldn't distort it. He continued trying to arm-wrestle me into submission, and I could feel the force of his personality, and started to understand what Yura had meant when he had described him as a man from 'another world'. Vissarion, the Son of God, had been easier than this: less opaque, less difficult. Sutyagin argued some more, frittering away another five minutes, until he finally told me about two 'French guys', filmmakers, who had visited him a few weeks earlier. He had rejected them. I nodded. 'I see,' I said.

And then suddenly, the urge to beat me into submission just evaporated into the air. He shrugged, and looked up.

'OK. So what do you want to know?'

I pulled out my dictaphone. 'Can I record this?'

'Sure . . . wait – will that be checked when you leave the country?'

'I'm sorry?'

'The tape – will it be checked when you leave?'

'I don't think so.'

'Because I might say some things, you know and I wouldn't want them to be intercepted . . .'

Not only was the Great Constructor, locked up in his tower, virtually a prisoner, a man on a par with the Pope, but when he spoke, he expected the world to quake.

Sutyagin took a deep breath, composing himself. I started recording.

VII

But before I could open my mouth, Sutyagin had already asked a bizarre question:

'How old do you think I am?'

It was such a strange thing to say I didn't know how to answer. Was he looking for flattery? 'I don't know,' I said. 'Forty-two, forty-three . . .'

'I'm sixty-two.'

I froze. 'What did he say?' I asked Pavel. I knew I had understood, but it seemed impossible.

'He says he's sixty-two.'

'Is he taking the piss?'

And then I wondered if this wasn't going to be a waste of time, if Sutyagin wasn't just playing mind games to set me on edge and establish his superiority. Perhaps it was an instinct of his. 'My reputation is such,' he had said on the television, 'that I don't need to cheat.' And then there were the dark rumours that Yura had hinted at: the dog-fights; the man locked in the basement. Yes, the man locked in the basement. It was easy to forget about him while Sutyagin's wife stood meekly in the kitchen preparing tea. This house was the scene of a crime. I didn't think Sutyagin was going to try any psychotropic violence on me, but I knew that there were many areas of life he was familiar with that I had only read about. This was a man who had forged a kind of order out of chaos; and it was better not to dwell too much on how he had done it.

'Sixty-two?' I said. He could hear the disbelief in my voice.

'Sixty-two,' he echoed. And then I looked more closely, and although Sutyagin was built like an ox, with a barrel chest, his skin did seem old and pasty, and it was wrinkled around the neck. I still wasn't sure if I believed him, though.

Sutyagin was pleased, and not only from a sense of satisfied vanity. He had subverted my faith not only in what he might say, but also in my own perceptions. He was in control now.

VIII

And then, and only then, did he start to talk. But not about the tower; or not much, at least. He had told that story too many times before, and the words fell lifeless around us, thudding to the floor like dead pigeons. The origin story was pretty much identical to what Yura had said, only with a few added details, some extra flourishes. At first he said he had started building it simply as a big house, so when businessmen came to visit they would not need to stay in a hotel, but would rather stay with him, where the hospitality would be much greater. But the house was too big, and when he added a roof, it looked like a giant mushroom. That was when it had started to grow upwards. At that point he seemed to be saying that he would gather all his friends together and everyone he knew would live in the tower with him, but it seemed like a rationalisation after the fact. The tower, as Yura had said, had simply happened, erupting out of the soil, and out of his mind. There was no plan, at least not in the early stages. After a while he had built a model of what he wanted. He still had it, lying around in a cupboard. It was a bit damaged now. He went to fetch it. It was indeed made out of cardboard boxes.

But really, he had more important things to talk about.

'Do you know what *perestroika* is?' he asked.

Another nonsense question: where was he taking me now?

'Of course.'

'When did it happen?'

'In the mid eighties,' I said.

'Right. And who invented it?'

I looked over at Pavel. He shrugged. 'Er . . . Gorbachev?'

'Wrong. I did. Twenty years earlier. In 1966.'

And then Sutyagin revealed what had been building up inside of him, at least one of the truths he wanted to share with the planet. And although I cannot claim to have fully understood the process by which he had presaged the actions of the reformist leader of the Soviet Union by so many years, or the means by which he introduced his country to openness, freedom of the press and its first capitalist reforms from his position amid the penal colonies and barren towns of the frozen north, I can affirm that the story involved more than one stint in prison, and not only in the nineties, but much earlier, in the sixties and seventies, when he had been a much younger man. Yura had said jail was a sensitive subject for Sutyagin; he spoke about it to me openly, though his acts of violence had, of course, been committed in self-defence, and he had never served very long sentences. I can also affirm that *perestroika* involved timber, construction, and a complicated (and yet entirely legal) system of payment which he had discovered that had enabled him to reward his workers handsomely. He had made enemies among the communist establishment, of course, but by the time Gorbachev had caught up with the innovations he had set in place, Sutyagin had already become a rich man.

IX

And so when the nineties arrived, and everyone else was making money, Sutyagin's urge to acquire was already sated. This new reality, which was so exciting to others, was old to him. He had invented it, after all. Material goods, luxuries had lost their novelty. That was when he started to think about a tower.

But it was when he crossed into this new metaphysical realm, when he reached beyond the mere accumulation of wealth and power, and began to turn his attention towards the heavens, that events turned against him. The details were less clear now, but he had many enemies. One day he was shown a piece of paper with a list of names written on it, his among them. Today most of those names are chiselled on tombstones. His is not. He went to prison, he lost his business, his fortune, and all his friends deserted him – but Nikolai Sutyagin is still standing.

'I am hard to kill,' he said. From most people, of course, those words would have sounded like outrageous bombast. But when Sutyagin said them, he was merely stating a fact. It was less interesting to him than his condition for his age, or his invention of *perestroika*. It was like saying 'I eat meat' or 'I drink vodka'. These were words from another, more dangerous world, one of violence and paranoia and sudden death. It was a world I didn't know much about, the world that Yura Barashkov now believed held Russia's salvation, but which he feared.

And so it continued, right up until the last minute, when I had to dash for the aeroplane that I knew was already sitting on the frostbitten runway in pitch Arctic darkness. Even as I stood up to get my coat the words poured forth, as he exposed the truth about his central place in history: for if he had invented *perestroika* then was not the collapse of the Berlin Wall, the opening up of the East to capitalism, democracy and NATO membership also down to him? He did not say as much. Perhaps modesty restrained him. But certainly this was implied by his words. I had met the Secret Architect of the Post-Communist World. And it was to him therefore that I owed a debt of gratitude for my own years of free movement within Russia, years which had been so rich in experience and encounters, in beauty and ugliness, in frustration, friendship and astonishment. I was sitting not simply in the world's only wooden skyscraper, but at the nexus of epochal changes that had swept across the globe, transforming it and my own self for ever. And he, Nikolia Sutyagin, sat unheralded at the centre of all of this.

There was just one curious thing – for all the details he gave me about *perestroika*, he remained vague to the point of coyness about the man he had locked in the basement. When pressed directly, he chuckled, as if embarrassed. 'Well that's er . . . that's . . . well . . .' And then some kind of explanation followed, but it was rushed and mumbled. It probably wasn't important anyway. And besides, my time was up. I had an aeroplane to catch.

'But don't you want a tour of the tower?' he asked.

'I really don't have time,' I said.

It was true; I didn't. But there was more to my declining his offer than simply that. It just didn't seem important any more. I had already penetrated the mysterious structure, and had just spent an hour in the mausoleum of its still breathing constructor. For me, that was enough. The rest of the building was only a skeleton chilled to its desiccated marrow, a mess of steps leading nowhere in particular and floorboards frozen by polluted air, all of it haunted by some sad dogs. The real tower lay elsewhere, and I had already explored it in great detail. This rotting, physical thing was not even its reflection, but a mere shadow of a shadow cast upon the snow.

Sutyagin shrugged. He didn't care either.

9 Strange telescopes

The taxi was waiting for us outside, headlamps piercing the icy darkness. There was no time to waste, but still I hesitated. I would probably never breathe this air or see the tower again, and though I wasn't feeling particularly sentimental, I knew that this last fragment of another too-long night on the edge of the Arctic Circle, this moment after the climax, was somehow precious. I needed to feel the hopeless void burn my cheeks if I was to fix it in my memory. So I tilted my head towards the sky, and as it was a clear night I could see deep into our cosmos, which was empty except for a few rocks and the dismal, slow light that blinked on and off in memoriam of some old gas that had annihilated itself in fire millions of years earlier. That was enough: I was ready now. I opened the cab door and climbed inside. The driver started the engine. We pulled away from the tower.

Yes, it was definitely time to leave these other worlds behind. Perhaps, even, to create one of my own. As for Sutyagin, Vissarion, Edward and the Digger, well – I had never been anything more than a combination of vibrating air particles in their ears and light reflected on the back of their eyeballs, a fleeting distraction, an interruption in the midst of their important work. They had already forgotten me. And now they continued to gaze through their strange telescopes at marvellous stars so distant that no one else could see them. They are still gazing at them today, as you read these words, and will continue to do so, long after you have closed this book.

And they are not the only ones.

Postscript: From *The Last Testament*

The narrative from Vadim

Chapter 14
November 45 ED

(1) In November the Teacher painted a great deal. These were portraits of Latvian gypsies, of friends of the Accomplishment: Normunda, Lily, Roksana, Raimonda.

(2) On the 12th November, the Teacher gave an interview to Daniel, a Scottish writer, working on a book about spiritual Russia.

(3) For some time Daniel negotiated through his friend and translator from Moscow about an interview with Vissarion, and finally, after travelling a long way, arrived at his desire . . .

Moscow–Texas–Moscow
2005–2007

Acknowledgements

Thanks to:
The heroic constructors of the alternative realities explored in this book

Thanks also to:
Yevgeny Safronov
Leon Henderson
Annie Henderson
Auntie Lyuda
Uncle Yuri
Tatiana Denisova, Sr
Professor Yuri Barashkov
Vadim Redkin
Roy Humphries
Natalia Lapina
Pavel Smirnov
Glen Cox
Kate Hodges
Alex Godfrey
Jeff Pretes
Masha Minasyan
Camilla Hornby and all at Curtis Brown
Lee Brackstone and all at Faber

Extraordinary thanks to:
Semyon Stankevich
David Humphries
Nik White